Paul Matt's
Scale Airplane Drawings
Volume 1

Drawn by the late, great

Paul Matt

Published as part of the
"Aviation Heritage Library Series"
by

SunShine House, Inc.
P.O. Box 2065
Terre Haute, IN 47802
© Copyright Historical Aviation Album
SunShine House, Inc.

(812) 232-3076

Publishers: Alan Abel, Drina Welch Abel

First Printing, 1991
Second Printing, 1992
Printed in the United States of America
ISBN 0-943691-04-4

The Aviation Heritage Library Series is published to preserve the history of the men and women, and of their airplanes, during the era of the Golden Years of Aviation. The books in the series include:

First Edition
Printed in the United States of America

ISBN 0-943691-04-4

3-View Scale Drawings by Paul Matt

Volume 1 contains all airplanes listed from A through G. Volume 2 contains all airplanes listed from H through W. If you would like individual, large sheets of any of the below listed scale drawings, send request, catalog #, appropriate fee, and shipping charge of $2.50. If you want your drawing rolled in a tube – add $4.00. Clear, concise, uncluttered 3- and 4-view engineering presentations, in large (17" x 22"), easy to work with standard scales. Drawing is highly detailed and is an accurate working print with all dimensions, specifications, airfoils, cross sections, templates, and color scheme included. These drawings are part of the collection of the internationally acclaimed and highly honored *Historical Aviation Album*. All orders are folded unless a tube is ordered. Each has 2 to 6 large sheets. **Rolled in tube– add $4.00.**

DRAWING SCALE:
CODE: Last letter of catalog numer indicates scale of drawing.
A = 1:24 .... 1/2" = 1'
B = 1:16 .... 3/4" = 1'
C = 1:48 .... 1/4" = 1'
D = 1:32 .... 3/8" = 1'
E = 1:8 ... 1 1/2" = 1'
F = 1:6 .... 2" = 1'

Volume 1 contents:

_ Aeromarine 39B .... (#9-78A, 3 shts.) $9.50
_ Aeronca 7AC "Champion" .... (#AM-41A, 2 shts.) 8.00
_ Aeronca C-2 .... (#10-80A, 2 shts.) 8.00
_ Aeronca C-3 "Collegian" .... (#10-81A, 2 shts.) 8.00
_ Aeronca C-3 "Master" .... (#10-82A, 2 shts.) 8.00
_ Aeronca K .... (#15-103A, 2 shts.) 8.00
_ Aeronca LB "Low wing" .... (#AM-60A, 2 shts.) 8.00
_ Alcor C.6.1 Jr. Transport .... (#4-33D, 2 shts.) 8.00
_ Anderson-Greenwood AG-14 .... (#12-94A, 2 shts.) 8.00
_ Beechcraft D-18S Twin .... (#6-59A, 3 shts.) 9.50
_ Bell P-39Q "Airacobra" .... (#1-7A, 2 shts.) 8.00
_ Berckmans "Speed Scout" .... (#2-12B, 2 shts.) 8.00
_ Berliner-Joyce OJ-2 .... (#AM-48A, 2 shts.) 8.00
_ Berliner-Joyce XF3J-1 .... (#15-104A, 2 shts.) 8.00
_ Boeing 307 "Stratoliner" .... (#7-63C, 2 shts.) 8.00
_ Boeing F3B-1 .... (#AM-56A, 2 shts.) 8.00
_ Boeing XF7B-1 .... (#AM-38A, 2 shts.) 8.00
_ Brewster F2A-3 "Buffalo" .... (#5-47A, 2 shts.) 8.00
_ Cessna 120/140 .... (#1-9A, 2 shts.) 8.00
_ Cessna C-37 "Airmaster" .... (#6-50A, 2 shts.) 8.00
_ Cessna T-50 "Bobcat" .... (#17-115A, 2 shts.) 8.00
_ Consolidated P2Y-2 .... (#9-71C,3 shts.) 9.50
_ Consolidated PBY-5A "Catalina" ..... (#17-114C, 4shts.) 11.00
_ Curtiss "Carrier Pigeon I" .... (#2-15A, 2 shts.) 8.00
_ Curtiss 1st Milit. Tract. S.C. No. 21/22 1913.(#6-55A, 2 shts.) 8.00
_ Curtiss A-3B "Falcon" .... (#AM-39A, 2 shts.) 8.00
_ Curtiss AT-9 "Jeep" .... (#2-18A, 2 shts.) 8.00
_ Curtiss B-2 Condor Bomber .... (#18-116C, 2 shts.) 8.00
_ Curtiss B-20 Condor Transport ...... (#18-117C, 2 shts.) 8.00
_ Curtiss F Boat .... (#1-1A, 2 shts.) 8.00
_ Curtiss F92 "Sparrowhawk" .... (#18-118A, 2 shts.) 8.00
_ Curtiss MF-K-6 "Seagull" .... (#AM-37A, 2 shts.) 8.00
_ Curtiss P-36 "Hawk" .... (#7-62A, 2 shts.) 8.00
_ Curtiss P-6E "Hawk" .... (#5-42A, 2 shts.) 8.00
_ Curtiss PW-8 .... (#10-79A, 2 shts.) 8.00
_ Curtiss R-6 Racer .... (#HS-73A, 2 shts.) 8.00
_ Curtiss SC-1 "Seahawk" .... (#1-8A, 2 shts.) 8.00
_ Curtiss SNC-1 "Falcon" .... (#AA-65A, 2 shts) 8.00
_ Curtiss SO3C-1 "Seagull" .... (#AM-34A, 2 shts.) 8.00
_ Curtiss Twin JN .... (#3-21A, 2 shts.) 8.00
_ Curtiss-Cox "Texas Wildcat" .... (#2-14B, 2 shts.) 8.00
_ Curtiss-Wright "Condor II" .... (#1-6C, 2 shts) 8.00
_ Curtiss-Wright CW-1 "Jr." .... (#11-88A, 3 shts.) 9.50
_ Douglas 0-2 .... (#11-86A, 3 shts.) 9.50
_ Douglas 0-2H .... (#11-87A, 2 shts.) 8.00
_ Douglas 0-38 .... (#12-92A, 2 shts.) 8.00
_ Douglas 0-38E .... (#12-93A, 2 shts.) 8.00
_ Douglas M-2 .... (#14-68A, 2 shts.) 8.00
_ Douglas A-20G "Havoc" .... (#15-102D, 6 shts.) 13.00
_ Etrich 1913 Taube .... (#TB-105D, 3 shts.) 9.50
_ Fairchild FC-1 .... (#17-111A, 2 shts.) 8.00
_ Fairchild FC-2 .... (#17-112A, 2 shts.) 8.00
_ Fairchild FC-2W "Stars & Stripes" ... (#17-113A, 2 shts.) 8.00
_ Fairchild M-62, PT-19 "Cornell" ...... (#AA-69A, 2 shts.) 8.00
_ Fokker T.5 Netherlands Bomber ..... (#AA-61C, 2 shts.) 8.00
_ Gallaudet D-1 .... (#3-20A, 2 shts.) 8.00
_ General Aviation Clark GA-43 .... (#13-95A, 2 shts.) 8.00
_ Grumman F-11F-1 "Tiger" .... (#2-19D, 2 shts.) 8.00
_ Grumman FF-1 .... (#AA-77A, 2 shts.) 8.00
_ Grumman G-44 "Widgeon" .... (#AM5-30A, 2 shts.) ... 8.00
_ Grumman J2F-5 "Duck" .... (#6-53A, 3 shts.) 9.50

Volume 2 contents:

_ Heath LNB-4 Parasol .... (#4-35B, 2 shts.) $8.00
_ Howard DGA-15P .... (#AM-52A, 2 shts.) 8.00
_ Howard DGA-3 "Pete" .... (#12-89A, 2 shts.) 8.00
_ Howard DGA-4 "Mike" .... (#13-90A, 2 shts.) 8.00
_ Howard DGA-5 "Ike" .... (#13-91A, 2 shts.) 8.00
_ Howard DGA-6 "Mr. Mulligan" .... (#14-99A, 3 shts.) 9.50
_ Hughes 1B Longwing Racer .... (#16-108A, 3 shts.) 9.50
_ Hughes 1B Shortwing Racer .... (#16-107A, 3 shts.) 9.50
_ Laird LC-DW-300 "Solution" .... (#7-64A, 2 shts.) 8.00
_ Laird LC-DW-500 "Super Solution" ... (#8-74A, 2 shts.) 8.00
_ Laird-Turner LTR-14 .... (#10-83A, 2 shts.) 8.00
_ Lavochkin LA-7 .... (#AA-46A, 4 shts.) 11.00
_ Lockheed F-80 "Shooting Star" .... (#2-10A, 2 shts.) 8.00
_ Lockheed Model 9 "Orion" .... (#3-22A, 2 shts.) 8.00
_ Lockheed PV-1 "Ventura" .... (#E-101C, 3 shts.) 9.50
_ LWF Cato Model L "Butterfly" .... (#10-84A, 2 shts.) 8.00
_ LWF Model G-2 .... (#2-13A, 2 shts.) 8.00
_ LWF Model H "Owl" .... (#11-85C, 2 shts.) 8.00
_ Martin BM-1/2 .... (#1-5A, 2 shts.) 8.00
_ Martin T4M-1, Great Lakes TG-1 ..... (#4-29D, 2 shts.) 8.00
_ Martin TT, 1913 Trainer .... (#5-40A, 2 shts.) 8.00
_ Messerschmitt ME 109E-3 .... (#AA-75A, 2 shts.) 8.00
_ Morehouse 2 Cyl. Aero Engine .... (#3-27E, 1 sht.) 8.00
_ Navy-Wright NW-1 Mystery Racer .... (#4-31A, 2 shts.) 8.00
_ Navy-Wright NW-2 Mystery Racer .... (#4-32A, 2 shts.) 8.00
_ North American 0-47A .... (#13-98A, 3 shts.) 9.50
_ North American AT-6D .... (#16-106A, 3 shts.) 9.50
_ North American XB-70-1 "Valkyrie" ... (#7-66G, 3 shts.) 9.50
_ Packard-Lepere LUSAC-11 .... (#1-3A, 2 shts.) 8.00
_ Pfitzner 1910 Monoplane .... (#2-11A, 2 shts.) 8.00
_ Piper J-3 "Cub" .... (#18-121A, 2 shts.) 8.00
_ Piper J-4 "Cub Coupe" .... (#18-122A, 2 shts.) 8.00
_ Piper PA-12 "Super Cruiser" .... (#4-36A, 2 shts.) 8.00
_ Republic RC-3 Seabee .... (#16-109A, 3 shts.) 9.50
_ Rover Inverted Aero Engine .... (#5-45F, 1 sht.) 5.00
_ Ryan B-5 "Brougham" .... (#RB-96A, 2 shts.) 8.00
_ Ryan FR-1 "Fireball" .... (#3-26A, 2 shts.) 8.00
_ Ryan SCW Low Wing .... (#AM9-49A, 2 shts.) ... 8.00
_ Ryan ST-A .... (#9-76A, 2 shts.) 8.00
_ Seversky BT-8 .... (#3-23A, 2 shts.) 8.00
_ Seversky P-35 .... (#AA-57A, 2 shts.) 8.00
_ Sikorsky S-39B .... (#14-100A, 5 shts.) 10.50
_ Standard J-1 .... (#17-110A, 2 shts.) 8.00
_ Taylor E-2 "Cub" .... (#18-119A, 2 shts.) 8.00
_ Taylor J-2 "Cub" .... (#18-120A, 2 shts.) 8.00
_ Thomas-Boeing MB-3A
_ Thomas-Morse MB-3 .... (#4-28B, 2 shts.) 8.00
_ Timm TC-170 "Collegiate" .... (#8-72A, s shts.) 8.00
_ Verville R-3 Racer .... (#6-58A, 2 shts.) 8.00
_ Vought F4U-1 "Corsair" .... (#AA-51A, 3 shts.) 9.50
_ Vought SBU-1 .... (#3-24A, 2 shts.) 8.00
_ Vought XF5U .... (#8-70A, 3 shts.) 9.50
_ Vultee V-1A .... (#2-16A, 2 shts.) 8.00
_ Waco UMF/YMF-5 .... (#13-97A, 3 shts.) 9.50
_ Waco UPF-7 .... (#8-67A, 2 shts.) 8.00
_ Waco YKS-6 Cabin .... (#2-17A, 2 shts.) 8.00
_ Waterman "Arrowbile" .... (#3-25A, 2 shts.) 8.00
_ Waterman "Gosling" Racer .... (#1-4B, 2 shts.) 8.00
_ Wright F2W-1 Racer .... (#5-43A, 1 sht.) 4.50
_ Wright F2W-2 Racer .... (#5-44A, 2 shts.) 8.00
_ Wright Brothers 1903 Flyer .... (#0-123A, 2 shts.) 8.00
_ Wright-Martin V .... (#1-2A, 2 shts.) 8.00

send to: **Aviation Heritage**
P.O. Box 2065
Terre Haute, IN 47802

DEDICATION

Dedicated to the late
Paul R. Matt
and his wife, the late
Joan Woeste Matt
who both contributed greatly to the
recording of aviation history

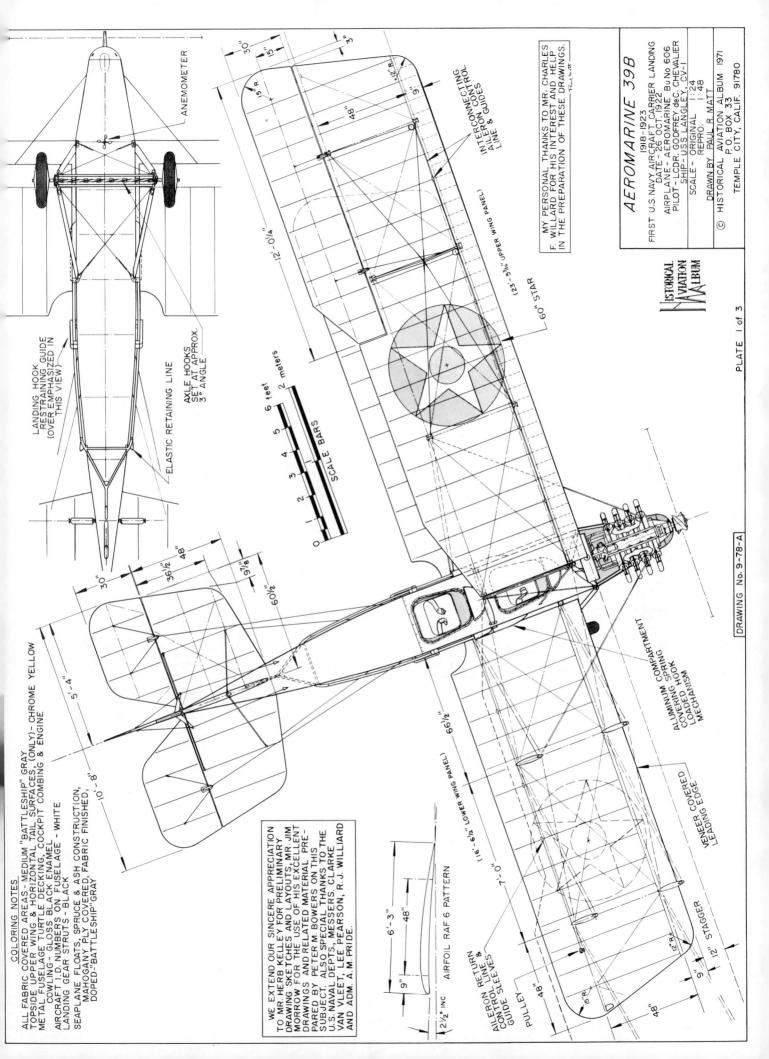

ANEMOMETER

LANDING HOOK
RESTRAINING GUIDE
(OVER EMPHASIZED IN
THIS VIEW)

ELASTIC RETAINING LINE

AXLE HOOKS
SET AT APPROX.
3° ANGLE.

INTERCONNECTING
AILERON CONTROL
LINE & GUIDES

12" R.

9"

48"

15" R.

5" R.

30"

15"

3"

(12'-0¼")

(23'-5¹⁵⁄₁₆" UPPER WING PANEL)

60" STAR

SCALE BARS

6 feet
5
4
3
2
0

2 meters

COLORING NOTES

ALL FABRIC COVERED AREAS — MEDIUM "BATTLESHIP" GRAY
TOPSIDE UPPER WING & HORIZONTAL TAIL SURFACES, (ONLY) — CHROME YELLOW
METAL FUSELAGE TURTLE DECKING, COCKPIT COMBING & ENGINE
COWLING — GLOSS BLACK ENAMEL
AIRCRAFT I.D. NUMBERS ON FUSELAGE — WHITE
LANDING GEAR STRUTS — BLACK

SEAPLANE FLOATS, SPRUCE & ASH CONSTRUCTION,
MAHOGANY PLY COVERED, FABRIC FINISHED,
DOPED "BATTLESHIP" GRAY

30"
36½"
48"
9⅞"
60½"
5'-4"
10'-8"

WE EXTEND OUR SINCERE APPRECIATION
TO MR. HERB KELLEY FOR PRELIMINARY
DRAWING SKETCHES AND LAYOUTS, MR. JIM
MORROW FOR THE USE OF HIS EXCELLENT
DRAWINGS AND RELATED MATERIAL PRE-
PARED BY PETER M. BOWERS ON THIS
SUBJECT. ALSO SPECIAL THANKS TO THE
U.S. NAVAL DEPTS., MESSERS. CLARKE
VAN VLEET, LEE PEARSON, R.J. WILLIARD
AND ADM. A.M. PRIDE.

2½" INC.   AIRFOIL RAF 6 PATTERN

6'-3"
9"
48"

AILERON RETURN
LINE & CONTROL
SLEEVES
GUIDE

PULLEY

48"

15" R.

(16'-6½" LOWER WING PANEL)

7'-0"

66½"

ALUMINUM COMPARTMENT
COVERING HOOK
LOADED SPRING
MECHANISM

VENEER COVERED
LEADING EDGE

12" STAGGER

12" R.

9"

48"

MY PERSONAL THANKS TO MR. CHARLES
F. WILLARD FOR HIS INTEREST AND HELP
IN THE PREPARATION OF THESE DRAWINGS.

Paul R. Matt

AEROMARINE 39B
1918–1923
FIRST U.S. NAVY AIRCRAFT CARRIER LANDING
DATE — 26 OCT. 1922
AIRPLANE — AEROMARINE BuNo 606
PILOT — LCDR. GODFREY deC. CHEVALIER
SHIP — USS LANGLEY, CV-1
SCALE — ORIGINAL   1:24
REPRO.   1:48
DRAWN BY PAUL R. MATT

© HISTORICAL AVIATION ALBUM 1971
P.O. BOX 33
TEMPLE CITY, CALIF. 91780

HISTORICAL
AVIATION
ALBUM

PLATE 1 of 3

DRAWING No. 9-78-A

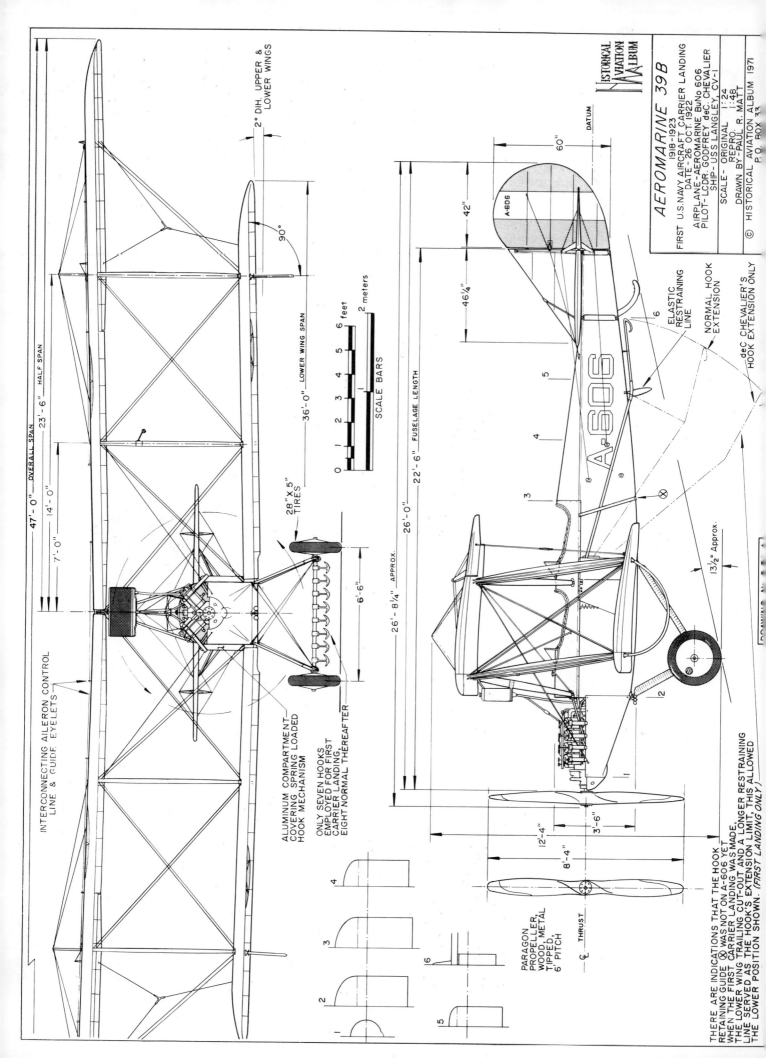

2° DIH. UPPER &
LOWER WINGS

90°

INTERCONNECTING AILERON CONTROL
LINE & GUIDE EYELETS

47'- 0" OVERALL SPAN

23'- 6" HALF SPAN

14'- 0"

7'- 0"

36'- 0" LOWER WING SPAN

28" x 5" TIRES

6'- 6"

ALUMINUM COMPARTMENT
COVERING SPRING LOADED
HOOK MECHANISM

ONLY SEVEN HOOKS
EMPLOYED FOR FIRST
CARRIER LANDING,
EIGHT NORMAL THEREAFTER

SCALE BARS

0 1 2 3 4 5 6 feet
         2 meters

ᴴistorical ᴬviation ᴬlbum

AEROMARINE 39B
1918-1923
FIRST U.S. NAVY AIRCRAFT CARRIER LANDING
DATE- 26 OCT. 1922
AIRPLANE- AEROMARINE BuNo 606
PILOT- LCDR. GODFREY deC. CHEVALIER
SHIP- USS LANGLEY, CV-I

SCALE- ORIGINAL   1:24
REPRO.   1:48
DRAWN BY- PAUL R. MATT

© HISTORICAL AVIATION ALBUM 1971
P.O. BOX 33

60"

42"

A-606

46¼"

22'- 6" FUSELAGE LENGTH

26'- 0"

26'- 8¼" APPROX.

DATUM

ELASTIC
RESTRAINING
LINE

NORMAL HOOK
EXTENSION

deC CHEVALIER'S
HOOK EXTENSION ONLY

6

5

4

3

A-606

13½ Approx.

2

1

12'- 4"

8'- 4"

3'- 6"

℄ THRUST

PARAGON
PROPELLER,
WOOD, METAL
TIPPED,
6' PITCH

4

3

6

2

5

THERE ARE INDICATIONS THAT THE HOOK
RETAINING GUIDE ⊗ WAS NOT ON A-606 YET
WHEN THE FIRST CARRIER LANDING WAS MADE.
THE LOWER WING TRAILING CUT-OUT AND A LONGER RESTRAINING
LINE SERVED AS THE HOOK'S EXTENSION LIMIT, THIS ALLOWED
THE LOWER POSITION SHOWN. (FIRST LANDING ONLY)

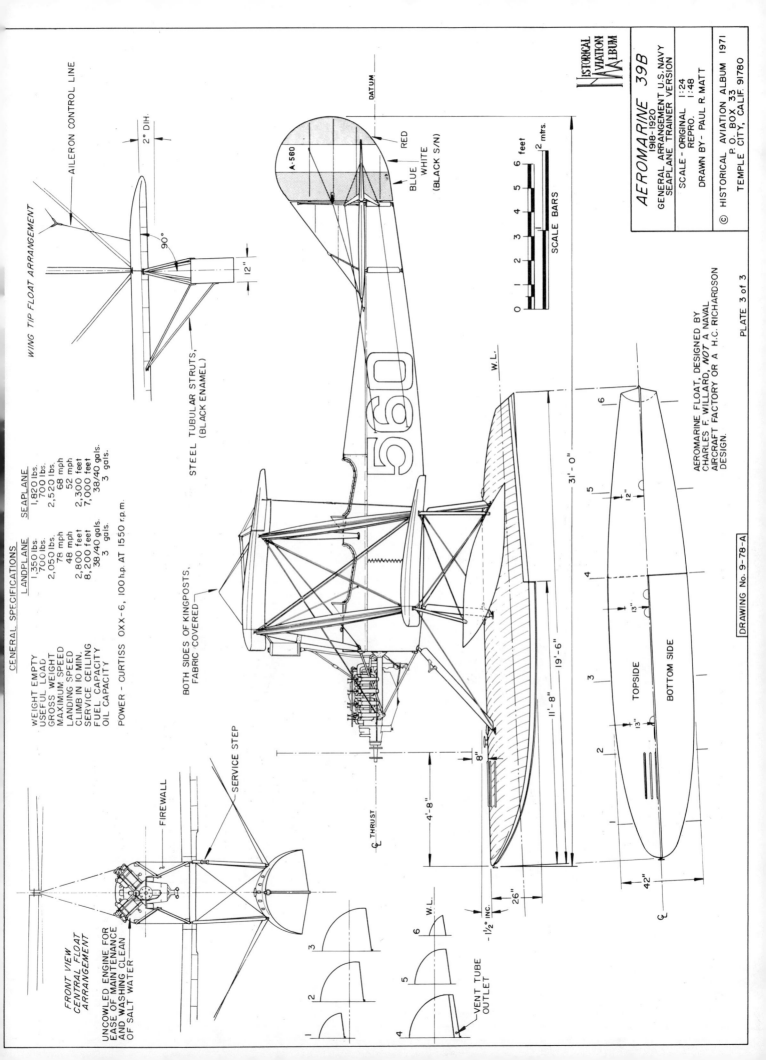

WING TIP FLOAT ARRANGEMENT

AILERON CONTROL LINE

2° DIH.

90°

12"

STEEL TUBULAR STRUTS, (BLACK ENAMEL)

BOTH SIDES OF KINGPOSTS, FABRIC COVERED

FRONT VIEW CENTRAL FLOAT ARRANGEMENT

FIREWALL

SERVICE STEP

UNCOWLED ENGINE FOR EASE OF MAINTENANCE AND WASHING CLEAN OF SALT WATER

VENT TUBE OUTLET

GENERAL SPECIFICATIONS

	LANDPLANE	SEAPLANE
WEIGHT EMPTY	1,350 lbs.	1,820 lbs.
USEFUL LOAD	700 lbs.	700 lbs.
GROSS WEIGHT	2,050 lbs.	2,520 lbs.
MAXIMUM SPEED	78 mph	68 mph
LANDING SPEED	48 mph	52 mph
CLIMB IN 10 MIN.	2,800 feet	2,300 feet
SERVICE CEILING	8,200 feet	7,000 feet
FUEL CAPACITY	38/40 gals.	38/40 gals.
OIL CAPACITY	3 gals.	3 gals.

POWER - CURTISS OXX-6, 100 h.p. AT 1550 r.p.m.

RED
BLUE
WHITE
(BLACK S/N)
A-560

DATUM

560

℄ THRUST

W.L.

8"

4'-8"

26"

-1½° INC.

11'-8"

19'-6"

31'-0"

W.L.

6
5
4
3
2
1

6
5
4
3
2
1

6

TOPSIDE

BOTTOM SIDE

12"
13"
13"
42"

AEROMARINE FLOAT, DESIGNED BY CHARLES F. WILLARD, *NOT* A NAVAL AIRCRAFT FACTORY OR A H.C. RICHARDSON DESIGN.

2 mtrs.

6 feet
5
4
3
2
1
0

SCALE BARS

AEROMARINE 39B
1918-1920
GENERAL ARRANGEMENT U.S. NAVY
SEAPLANE TRAINER VERSION

SCALE - ORIGINAL 1:24
REPRO. 1:48
DRAWN BY - PAUL R. MATT

© HISTORICAL AVIATION ALBUM 1971
P.O. BOX 33
TEMPLE CITY, CALIF. 91780

HISTORICAL AVIATION ALBUM

PLATE 3 of 3

DRAWING No. 9-78-A

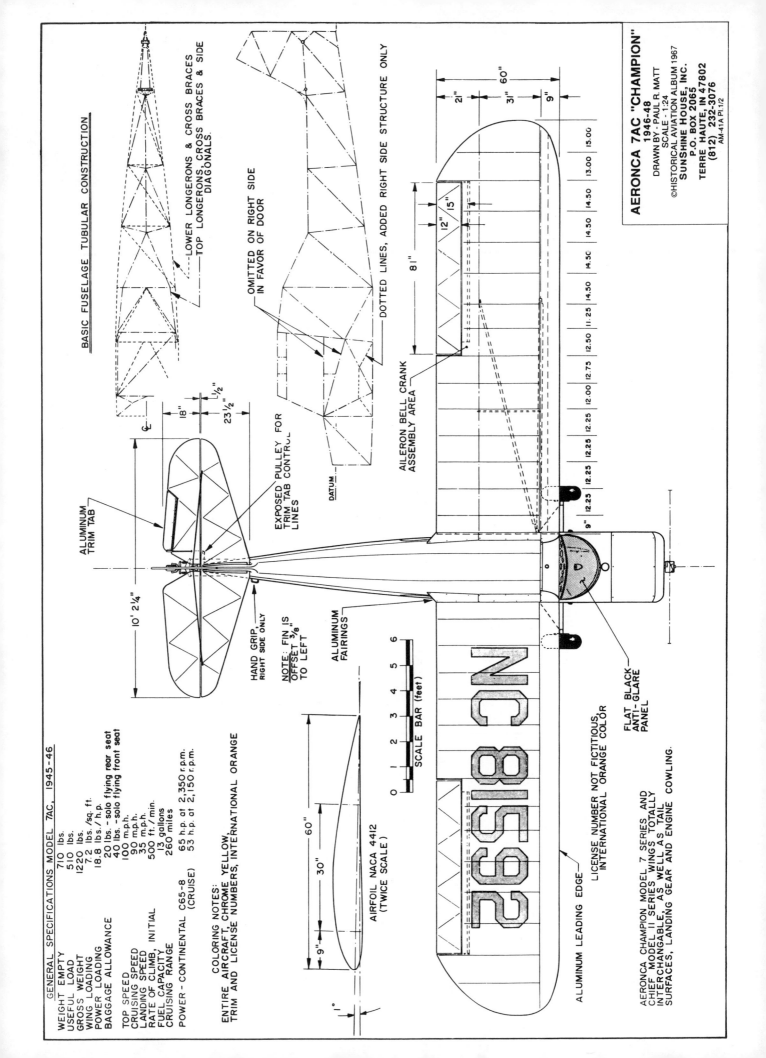

BASIC FUSELAGE TUBULAR CONSTRUCTION

LOWER LONGERONS & CROSS BRACES
TOP LONGERONS, CROSS BRACES & SIDE DIAGONALS.

OMITTED ON RIGHT SIDE IN FAVOR OF DOOR

DOTTED LINES, ADDED RIGHT SIDE STRUCTURE ONLY

EXPOSED PULLEY FOR TRIM TAB CONTROL LINES

DATUM

ALUMINUM TRIM TAB

HAND GRIP, RIGHT SIDE ONLY

NOTE: FIN IS OFFSET 3/8" TO LEFT

ALUMINUM FAIRINGS

AILERON BELL CRANK ASSEMBLY AREA

10' 2¼"

18"
½"
23½"

60"
21"
31"
9"

12"
15"
81"
9"

15.00
13.00
14.50
14.50
14.50
14.50
11.25
12.50
12.00
12.75
12.25
12.25
12.25
12.25
9"

AIRFOIL NACA 4412 (TWICE SCALE)

60"
30"
9"
1"

SCALE BAR (feet)
0 1 2 3 4 5 6

NC 81592

ALUMINUM LEADING EDGE

LICENSE NUMBER NOT FICTITIOUS, INTERNATIONAL ORANGE COLOR

FLAT BLACK ANTI-GLARE PANEL

GENERAL SPECIFICATIONS MODEL 7AC, 1945-46

WEIGHT EMPTY   710 lbs.
USEFUL LOAD   510 lbs.
GROSS WEIGHT   1220 lbs.
WING LOADING   7.2 lbs./sq. ft.
POWER LOADING   18.8 lbs./h.p.
BAGGAGE ALLOWANCE   20 lbs. - solo flying rear seat
                      40 lbs. - solo flying front seat

TOP SPEED   100 m.p.h.
CRUISING SPEED   90 m.p.h.
LANDING SPEED   35 m.p.h.
RATE OF CLIMB, INITIAL 500 ft./min.
FUEL CAPACITY   13 gallons
CRUISING RANGE   260 miles

POWER - CONTINENTAL C65-8   65 h.p. at 2,350 r.p.m.
        (CRUISE)   53 h.p. at 2,150 r.p.m.

COLORING NOTES:

ENTIRE AIRCRAFT, CHROME YELLOW,
TRIM AND LICENSE NUMBERS, INTERNATIONAL ORANGE

AERONCA CHAMPION MODEL 7 SERIES AND
CHIEF MODEL 11 SERIES WINGS TOTALLY
INTERCHANGABLE, AS WELL AS TAIL
SURFACES, LANDING GEAR AND ENGINE COWLING.

AERONCA 7AC "CHAMPION"
1946-48
DRAWN BY - PAUL R. MATT
SCALE - 1:24
©HISTORICAL AVIATION ALBUM 1967
SUNSHINE HOUSE, INC.
P.O. BOX 2065
TERRE HAUTE, IN 47802
(812) 232-3076
AM-41A Pl.1/2

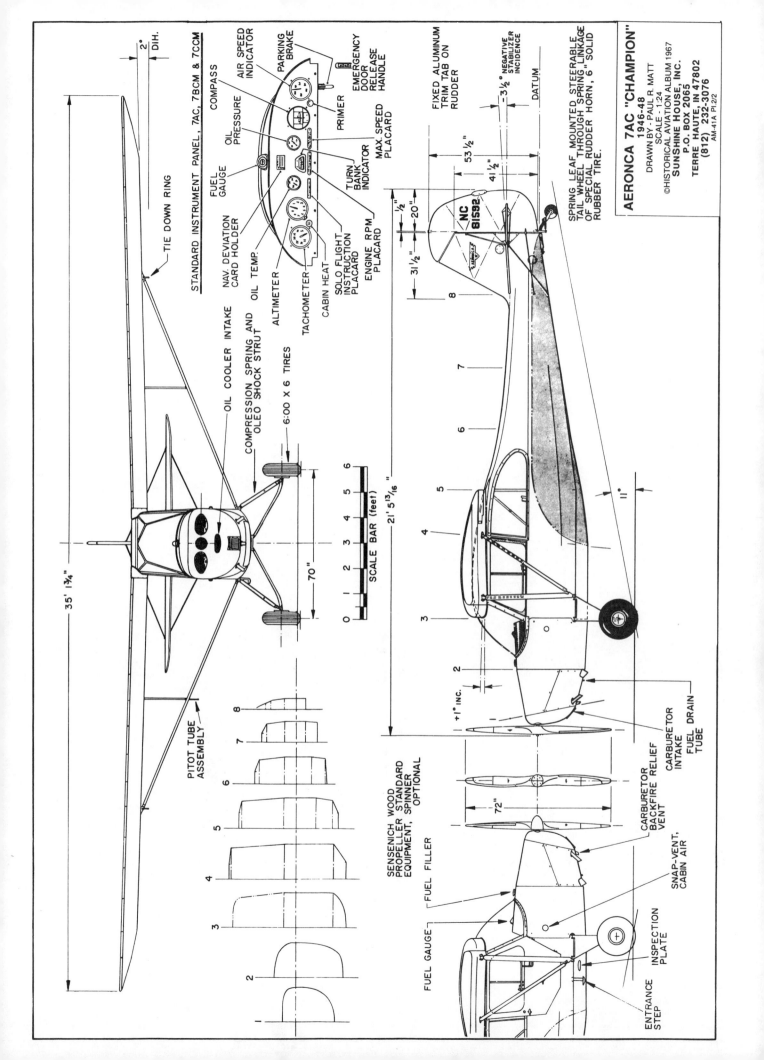

STANDARD INSTRUMENT PANEL, 7AC, 7BCM & 7CCM

PARKING BRAKE
AIR SPEED INDICATOR
COMPASS
PRIMER
EMERGENCY DOOR RELEASE HANDLE
OIL PRESSURE
FUEL GAUGE
NAV. DEVIATION CARD HOLDER
MAX. SPEED PLACARD
TURN BANK INDICATOR
OIL TEMP.
ALTIMETER
TACHOMETER
CABIN HEAT
SOLO FLIGHT INSTRUCTION PLACARD
ENGINE RPM PLACARD

2° DIH.

TIE DOWN RING

OIL COOLER INTAKE

COMPRESSION SPRING AND OLEO SHOCK STRUT

6:00 X 6 TIRES

PITOT TUBE ASSEMBLY

35' 1¾"

70"

8
7
6
5
4
3
2

6
5
4
3
2
1
0

SCALE BAR (feet)

21' 5¹³/₁₆"

FIXED ALUMINUM TRIM TAB ON RUDDER

3½° NEGATIVE STABILIZER INCIDENCE

DATUM

SPRING LEAF MOUNTED STEERABLE TAIL WHEEL THROUGH SPRING "LINKAGE OF SPECIAL RUDDER HORN, 6" SOLID RUBBER TIRE.

53½"
41½"
½"
20"
31½"

NC 81592

8
7
6
5
4
3
2

+1° INC.

−1°

72"

SENSENICH WOOD PROPELLER STANDARD EQUIPMENT, SPINNER OPTIONAL

FUEL FILLER

FUEL GAUGE

CARBURETOR BACKFIRE RELIEF VENT

CARBURETOR INTAKE

FUEL DRAIN TUBE

SNAP-VENT, CABIN AIR

ENTRANCE STEP

INSPECTION PLATE

AERONCA 7AC "CHAMPION"
1946-48
DRAWN BY - PAUL R. MATT
SCALE - 1:24
©HISTORICAL AVIATION ALBUM 1967
SUNSHINE HOUSE, INC.
P.O. BOX 2065
TERRE HAUTE, IN 47802
(812) 232-3076
AM-41A Pl.2/2

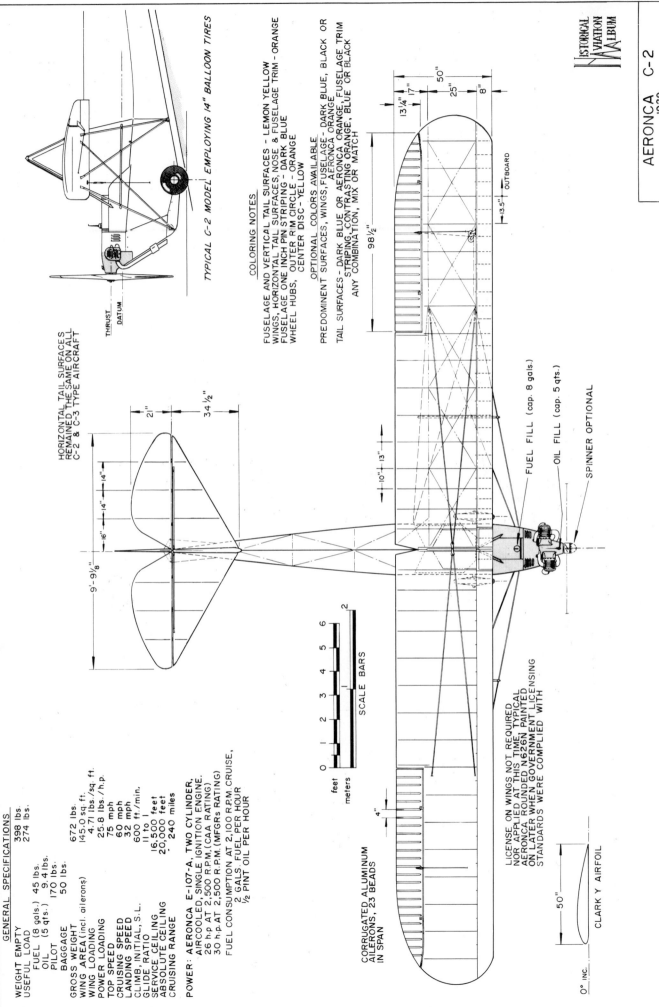

GENERAL SPECIFICATIONS

WEIGHT EMPTY		398 lbs.
USEFUL LOAD		274 lbs.
FUEL (8 gals.)	45 lbs.	
OIL (5 qts.)	9.4 lbs.	
PILOT	170 lbs.	
BAGGAGE	50 lbs.	
GROSS WEIGHT		672 lbs.
WING AREA (incl. ailerons)		145.0 sq. ft.
POWER LOADING		4.71 lbs./sq. ft.
		25.8 lbs./h.p.
TOP SPEED		75 mph
CRUISING SPEED		60 mph
LANDING SPEED		32 mph
CLIMB, INITIAL, S.L.		600 ft./min.
GLIDE RATIO		11 to 1
SERVICE CEILING		16,500 feet
ABSOLUTE CEILING		20,000 feet
CRUISING RANGE		240 miles

POWER: AERONCA E-107-A, TWO CYLINDER, AIRCOOLED, SINGLE IGNITION ENGINE. 26 h.p. AT 2,500 R.P.M. (CAA RATING) 30 h.p. AT 2,500 R.P.M. (MFGRs RATING)

FUEL CONSUMPTION AT 2,100 R.P.M. CRUISE, 2 GALS. FUEL PER HOUR ½ PINT OIL PER HOUR

HORIZONTAL TAIL SURFACES REMAINED THE SAME ON ALL C-2 & C-3 TYPE AIRCRAFT

TYPICAL C-2 MODEL EMPLOYING 14" BALLOON TIRES

COLORING NOTES

FUSELAGE AND VERTICAL TAIL SURFACES - LEMON YELLOW
WINGS, HORIZONTAL TAIL SURFACES, NOSE & FUSELAGE TRIM - ORANGE
FUSELAGE ONE INCH PIN STRIPING - DARK BLUE
WHEEL HUBS, OUTER RIM CIRCLE - ORANGE
CENTER DISC - YELLOW

OPTIONAL COLORS AVAILABLE

PREDOMINENT SURFACES, WINGS, FUSELAGE - DARK BLUE, BLACK OR AERONCA ORANGE

TAIL SURFACES - DARK BLUE OR AERONCA ORANGE, FUSELAGE TRIM STRIPING, CONTRASTING ORANGE, BLUE OR BLACK ANY COMBINATION, MIX OR MATCH

THRUST
DATUM

FUEL FILL (cap. 8 gals.)
OIL FILL (cap. 5 qts.)
SPINNER OPTIONAL

OUTBOARD

LICENSE ON WINGS NOT REQUIRED NOR APPLIED AT THIS TIME. TYPICAL AERONCA ROUNDED N626N PAINTED ON LATER WHEN GOVERNMENT LICENSING STANDARDS WERE COMPLIED WITH

SCALE BARS
feet
meters

CORRUGATED ALUMINUM AILERONS, 23 BEADS IN SPAN

CLARK Y AIRFOIL
0° INC.

OUR SINCERE APPRECIATION IS EXTENDED TO MR JOHN HOUSER, SERVICE ENGINEER, AERONCA, INC. FOR HIS UNTIRING HELP IN MAKING THESE DRAWINGS POSSIBLE.

HISTORICAL AVIATION ALBUM
AERONCA C-2
1929
FIRST PRODUCTION AIRCRAFT
SCALE: ORIGINAL 1:24
REPRO. 1:48
DRAWN BY: PAUL R. MATT
© HISTORICAL AVIATION ALBUM 1971
P.O. BOX 33
TEMPLE CITY, CALIF. 91780

PLATE 1 of 2

DRAWING No. 10-80-A

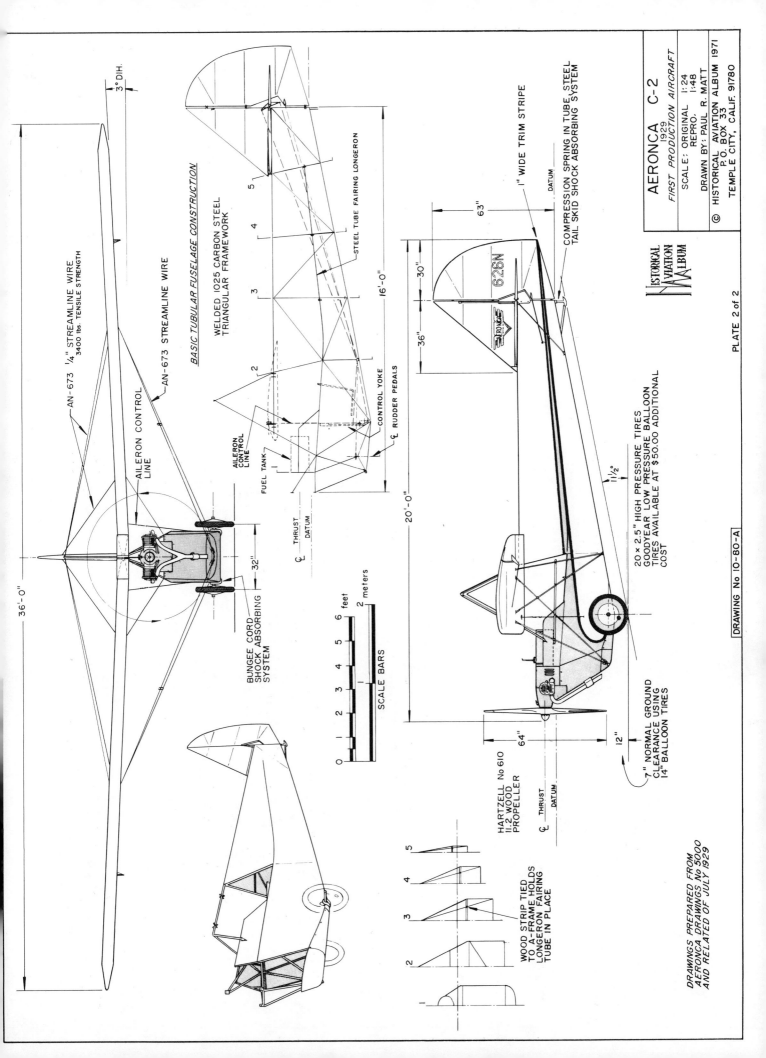

3° DIH.

AN-673 ¼" STREAMLINE WIRE 3400 lbs. TENSILE STRENGTH

AN-673 STREAMLINE WIRE

AILERON CONTROL LINE

36'-0"

32"

BUNGEE CORD SHOCK ABSORBING SYSTEM

BASIC TUBULAR FUSELAGE CONSTRUCTION

WELDED 1025 CARBON STEEL TRIANGULAR FRAMEWORK

STEEL TUBE FAIRING LONGERON

16'-0"

5
4
3
2

AILERON CONTROL LINE

FUEL TANK

CONTROL YOKE

Ⅽ RUDDER PEDALS

Ⅽ THRUST

DATUM

20'-0"

2 meters

6 feet
5
4
3
2
1
0

SCALE BARS

HARTZELL No 610 11.2 WOOD PROPELLER

Ⅽ THRUST

DATUM

64"

WOOD STRIP TIED TO A-FRAME HOLDS LONGERON FAIRING TUBE IN PLACE

5
4
3
2

1" WIDE TRIM STRIPE

COMPRESSION SPRING IN TUBE STEEL TAIL SKID SHOCK ABSORBING SYSTEM

63"

30"

36"

626N

AERONCA

DATUM

1½"

11½°

20 × 2.5" HIGH PRESSURE TIRES GOODYEAR LOW PRESSURE BALLOON TIRES AVAILABLE AT $50.00 ADDITIONAL COST

7" NORMAL GROUND CLEARANCE USING 14" BALLOON TIRES

12"

AERONCA C-2
1929
FIRST PRODUCTION AIRCRAFT

SCALE: ORIGINAL 1:24
REPRO. 1:48

DRAWN BY: PAUL R. MATT

© HISTORICAL AVIATION ALBUM 1971
P.O. BOX 33
TEMPLE CITY, CALIF. 91780

Historical Aviation Album

PLATE 2 of 2

DRAWING No 10-80-A

DRAWINGS PREPARED FROM
AERONCA DRAWINGS No 5000
AND RELATED OF JULY 1929

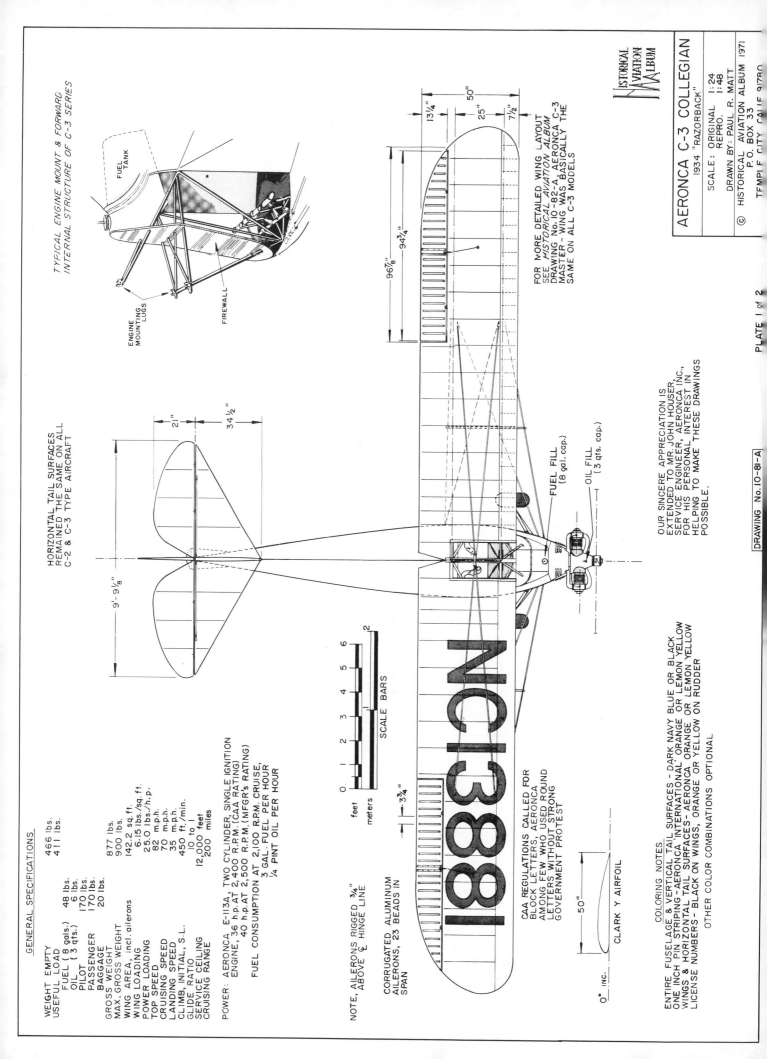

TYPICAL ENGINE MOUNT & FORWARD
INTERNAL STRUCTURE OF C-3 SERIES

FUEL TANK

ENGINE MOUNTING LUGS

FIREWALL

HORIZONTAL TAIL SURFACES
REMAINED THE SAME ON ALL
C-2 & C-3 TYPE AIRCRAFT

21"
34½"

9'-9⅛"

FOR MORE DETAILED WING LAYOUT
SEE HISTORICAL AVIATION ALBUM
DRAWING No.10-82-A, AERONCA C-3
MASTER-WING WAS BASICALLY THE
SAME ON ALL C-3 MODELS

13¼"
50"
25"
7½"

96⅞"
94¾"

FUEL FILL
(8 gal. cap.)

OIL FILL
(3 qts. cap.)

OUR SINCERE APPRECIATION IS
EXTENDED TO MR. JOHN HOUSER,
SERVICE ENGINEER, AERONCA INC.,
FOR HIS PERSONAL INTEREST IN
HELPING TO MAKE THESE DRAWINGS
POSSIBLE.

AERONCA C-3 COLLEGIAN
1934 "RAZORBACK"

SCALE: ORIGINAL 1:24
REPRO. 1:48
DRAWN BY: PAUL R. MATT

© HISTORICAL AVIATION ALBUM 1971
P.O. BOX 33
TEMPLE CITY, CALIF. 91780

PLATE 1 of 2

DRAWING No.10-81-A

GENERAL SPECIFICATIONS

WEIGHT EMPTY   466 lbs.
USEFUL LOAD   411 lbs.
    FUEL (8 gals.)   48 lbs.
    OIL (3 qts.)   6 lbs.
    PILOT   170 lbs.
    PASSENGER   170 lbs.
    BAGGAGE   20 lbs.
GROSS WEIGHT   877 lbs.
MAX. GROSS WEIGHT   900 lbs.
WING AREA, incl. ailerons   142.2 sq. ft.
WING LOADING   6.15 lbs./sq. ft.
POWER LOADING   25.0 lbs./h.p.
TOP SPEED   82 m.p.h.
CRUISING SPEED   70 m.p.h.
LANDING SPEED   35 m.p.h.
CLIMB, INITIAL, S.L.   450 ft./min.
GLIDE RATIO   10 to 1
SERVICE CEILING   12,000 feet
CRUISING RANGE   200 miles

POWER: AERONCA E-113A, TWO CYLINDER, SINGLE IGNITION
ENGINE, 36 h.p. AT 2,400 R.P.M. (CAA RATING)
40 h.p. AT 2,500 R.P.M. (MFGR's RATING)

FUEL CONSUMPTION AT 2,100 R.P.M. CRUISE,
3 GAL. FUEL PER HOUR
¼ PINT OIL PER HOUR

6
5
4
3
2
1
0   feet
                  meters
1
2

SCALE BARS

3¾"

NOTE, AILERONS RIGGED ¾"
ABOVE ₵ HINGE LINE

CORRUGATED ALUMINUM
AILERONS, 23 BEADS IN
SPAN

50"

0° INC.

CLARK Y AIRFOIL

COLORING NOTES
ENTIRE FUSELAGE & VERTICAL TAIL SURFACES - DARK NAVY BLUE OR BLACK
ONE INCH PIN STRIPING - AERONCA INTERNATIONAL ORANGE OR LEMON YELLOW
WINGS & HORIZONTAL TAIL SURFACES - AERONCA ORANGE OR LEMON YELLOW
LICENSE NUMBERS - BLACK ON WINGS, ORANGE OR YELLOW ON RUDDER

OTHER COLOR COMBINATIONS OPTIONAL

CAA REGULATIONS CALLED FOR
BLOCK LETTERS, AERONCA
AMONG FEW WHO USED ROUND
LETTERS WITHOUT STRONG
GOVERNMENT PROTEST

NC13881

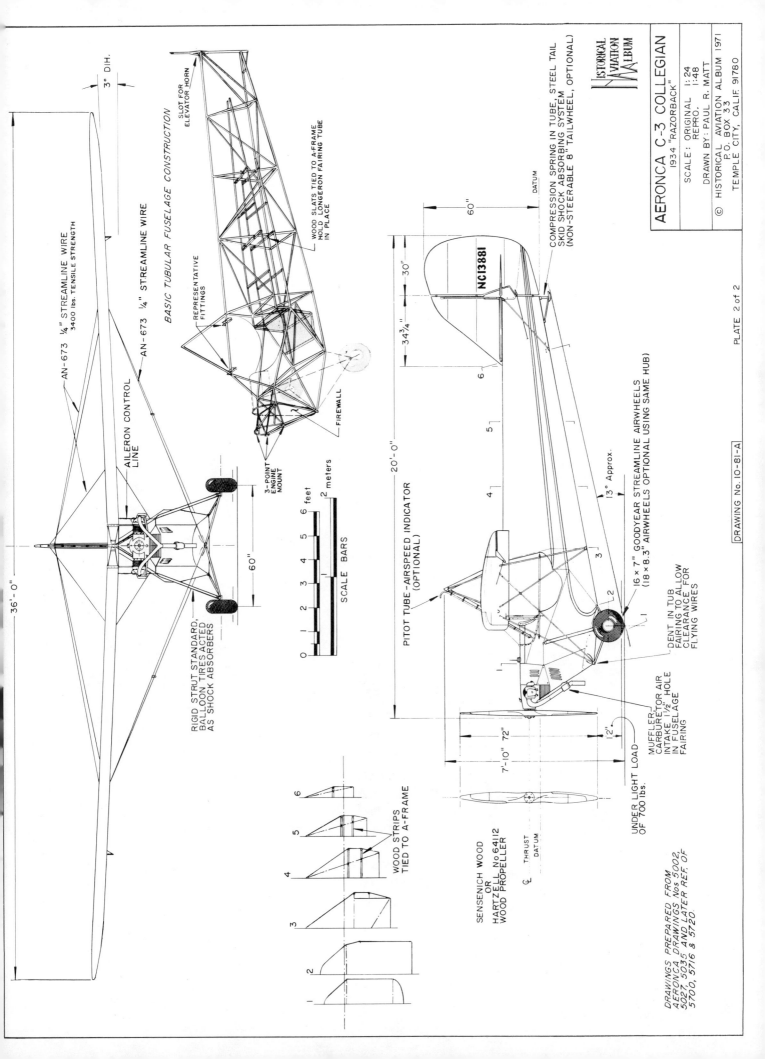

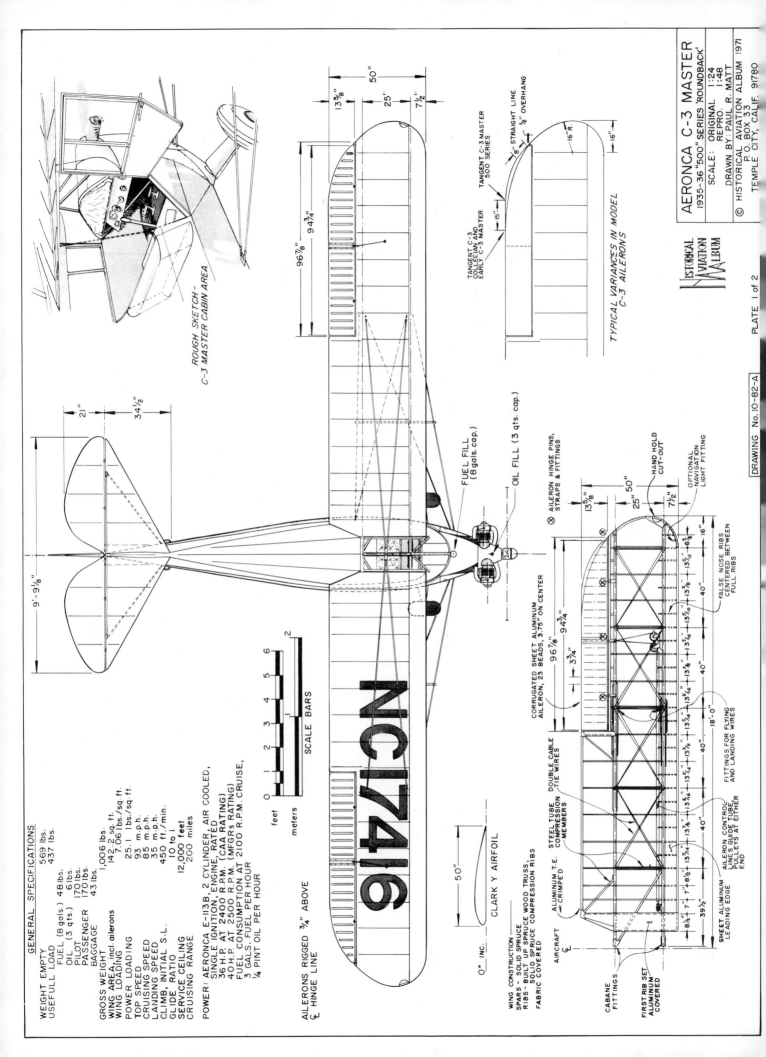

ROUGH SKETCH—
C-3 MASTER CABIN AREA

GENERAL SPECIFICATIONS

WEIGHT EMPTY .... 569 lbs.
USEFULL LOAD .... 437 lbs.
    FUEL (8 gals.) .... 48 lbs.
    OIL (3 qts.) .... 6 lbs.
    PILOT .... 170 lbs.
    PASSENGER .... 170 lbs.
    BAGGAGE .... 43 lbs.
GROSS WEIGHT .... 1,006 lbs.
WING AREA, incl. ailerons .... 142.2 sq. ft.
WING LOADING .... 7.06 lbs./sq. ft.
POWER LOADING .... 25.1 lbs./sq. ft.
TOP SPEED .... 93 m.p.h.
CRUISING SPEED .... 85 m.p.h.
LANDING SPEED .... 35 m.p.h.
CLIMB, INITIAL S.L. .... 450 ft./min.
GLIDE RATIO .... 10 to 1
SERVICE CEILING .... 12,000 feet
CRUISING RANGE .... 200 miles

POWER: AERONCA E-113B, 2 CYLINDER, AIR COOLED,
SINGLE IGNITION, ENGINE, RATED
36 H.P. AT 2400 R.P.M. (CAA RATING)
40 H.P. AT 2500 R.P.M. (MFGRs RATING)
FUEL CONSUMPTION AT 2100 R.P.M. CRUISE,
3 GALS. FUEL PER HOUR
¼ PINT OIL PER HOUR

WING CONSTRUCTION -
SPARS - SOLID SPRUCE
RIBS - BUILT UP SPRUCE WOOD TRUSS,
SPRUCE COMPRESSION RIBS
FABRIC COVERED

AIRCRAFT ₵

CABANE FITTINGS

FIRST RIB SET ALUMINUM COVERED

ALUMINUM T.E. CRIMPED

STEEL TUBE COMPRESSION MEMBERS

DOUBLE CABLE TIE WIRES

AILERON CONTROL LINES GUIDE TUBE, PULLEYS AT EITHER END

FITTINGS FOR FLYING AND LANDING WIRES

SHEET ALUMINUM LEADING EDGE

FALSE NOSE RIBS CENTERED BETWEEN FULL RIBS

HAND HOLD CUT-OUT

OPTIONAL NAVIGATION LIGHT FITTING

⊗ AILERON HINGE PINS, STRAPS & FITTINGS

CORRUGATED SHEET ALUMINUM AILERON, 23 BEADS, 3.75" ON CENTER

FUEL FILL (8 gals. cap.)

OIL FILL (3 qts. cap.)

0° INC.

CLARK Y AIRFOIL

AILERONS RIGGED ¾" ABOVE
₵ HINGE LINE

50"

SCALE BARS

feet
meters

NC17416

TANGENT C-3, COLEMAN AND EARLY C-3 MASTER

TANGENT C-3 MASTER 500 SERIES

⅛" STRAIGHT LINE
½" OVERHANG

16" R.

16"

15"

TYPICAL VARIANCES IN MODEL
C-3 AILERONS

AERONCA C-3 MASTER
1935-36 "500" SERIES 'ROUNDBACK'

SCALE: ORIGINAL 1:24
REPRO. 1:48
DRAWN BY: PAUL R. MATT

© HISTORICAL AVIATION ALBUM 1971
P.O. BOX 33
TEMPLE CITY, CALIF. 91780

PLATE 1 of 2

DRAWING No. IO-82-A

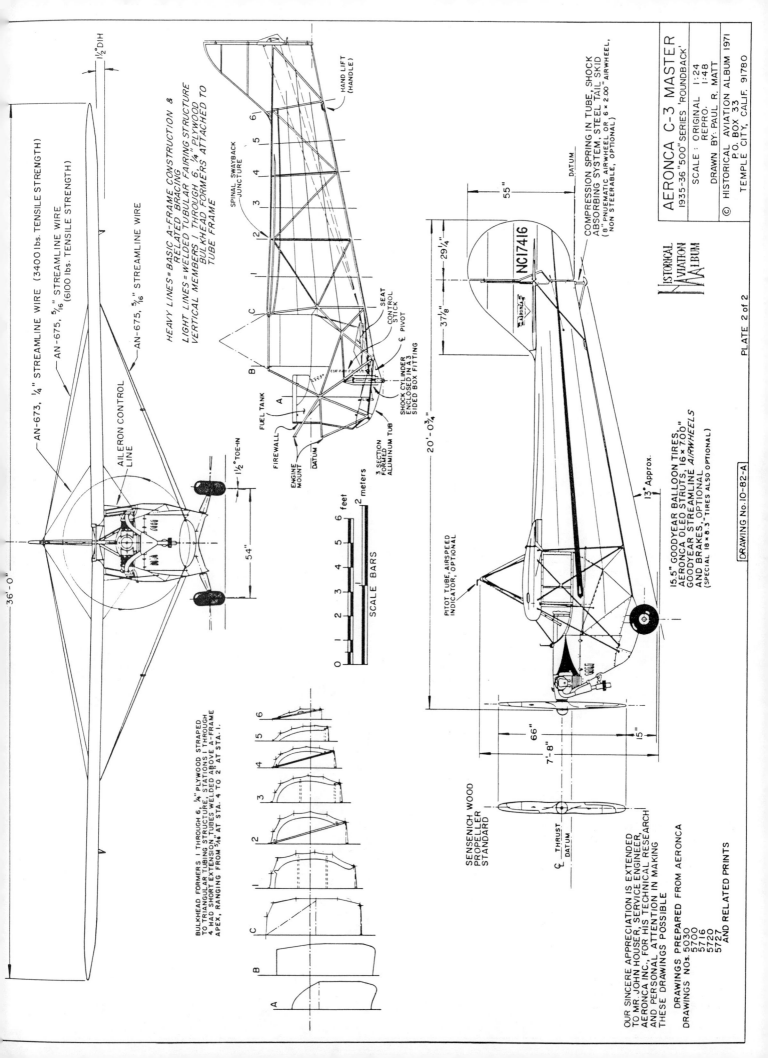

1½" DIH

AN-673, ¼" STREAMLINE WIRE (3400 lbs. TENSILE STRENGTH)

AN-675, ⁵/₁₆" STREAMLINE WIRE (6100 lbs. TENSILE STRENGTH)

AN-675, ⁵/₁₆" STREAMLINE WIRE

AILERON CONTROL LINE

36'-0"

1½° TOE-IN

54"

HEAVY LINES = BASIC A-FRAME CONSTRUCTION & RELATED BRACING

LIGHT LINES = WELDED TUBULAR FAIRING STRUCTURE. VERTICAL MEMBERS 1 THROUGH 6. ¼" PLYWOOD BULKHEAD FORMERS ATTACHED TO TUBE FRAME

HAND LIFT (HANDLE)

SPINAL SWAYBACK JUNCTURE

6
5
4
3
2
1

C
B
A

SEAT

CONTROL STICK

₵ PIVOT

SHOCK CYLINDER ENCLOSED IN A 3 SIDED BOX FITTING

FUEL TANK

FIREWALL

DATUM

ENGINE MOUNT

3 SECTION FORMED ALUMINUM TUB

BULKHEAD FORMERS 1 THROUGH 6, ¼" PLYWOOD STRAPED TO TRIANGULAR TUBING STRUCTURE, STATIONS 1 THROUGH 4 HAD SHORT EXTENSION TUBES WELDED ABOVE A-FRAME APEX, RANGING FROM ⁵/₁₆ AT STA. 4 TO 2 AT STA. 1.

0 1 2 3 4 5 6 feet
0   1   2 meters

SCALE BARS

OUR SINCERE APPRECIATION IS EXTENDED TO MR. JOHN HOUSER, SERVICE ENGINEER, AERONCA INC., FOR HIS TECHNICAL RESEARCH AND PERSONAL ATTENTION IN MAKING THESE DRAWINGS POSSIBLE

DRAWINGS PREPARED FROM AERONCA DRAWINGS NOS. 5030
5716
5700
5720
5727
AND RELATED PRINTS

6
5
4
3
2
1

C
B
A

COMPRESSION SPRING IN TUBE, SHOCK ABSORBING SYSTEM, STEEL TAIL SKID (8" PNEUMATIC AIRWHEEL OR 6 × 2.00" AIRWHEEL, NON STEERABLE, OPTIONAL)

DATUM

55"

29¼"

37⅞"

NC17416

20'-0¾"

13° Approx.

15.5" GOODYEAR BALLOON TIRES, AERONCA OLEO STRUTS, 16 × 7.00" GOODYEAR STREAMLINE AIRWHEELS AND BRAKES, OPTIONAL (SPECIAL 18 × 8.3" TIRES ALSO OPTIONAL)

PITOT TUBE, AIRSPEED INDICATOR, OPTIONAL

66"

7'-8"

15"

SENSENICH WOOD PROPELLER STANDARD

₵ THRUST
DATUM

AERONCA C-3 MASTER
1935-36 "500" SERIES 'ROUNDBACK'

SCALE : ORIGINAL 1:24
REPRO. 1:48
DRAWN BY: PAUL R. MATT

© HISTORICAL AVIATION ALBUM 1971
P.O. BOX 33
TEMPLE CITY, CALIF. 91780

HISTORICAL AVIATION ALBUM

PLATE 2 of 2

DRAWING No. IO-82-A

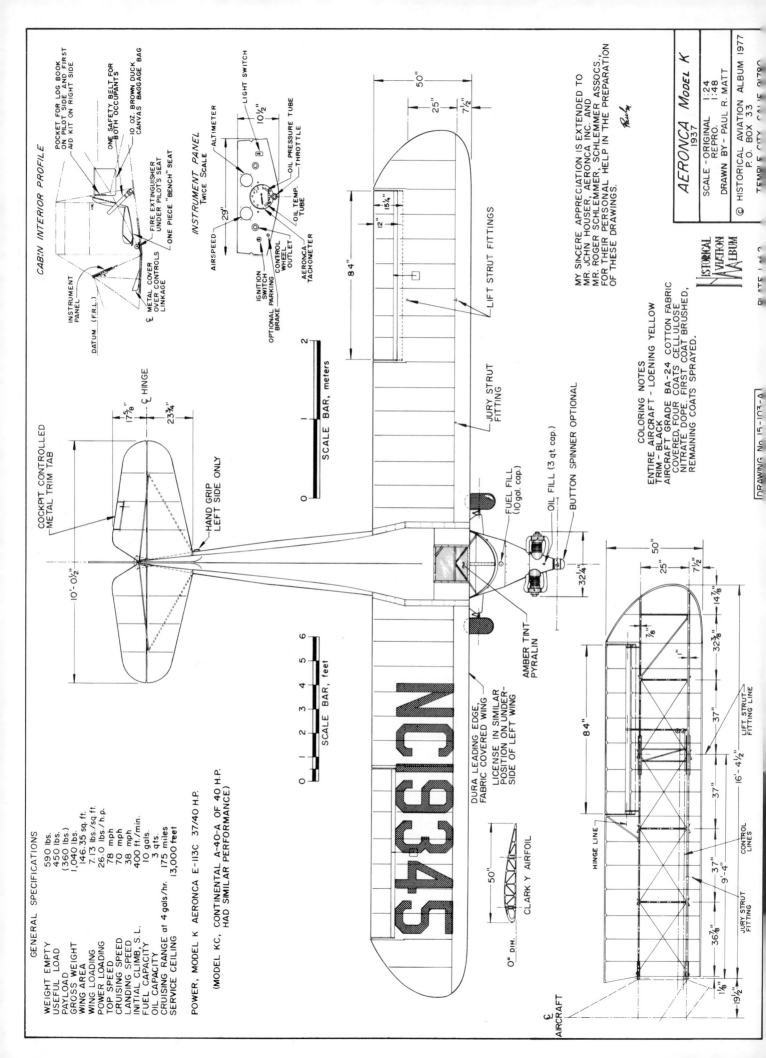

AERONCA MODEL K
1937

SCALE - ORIGINAL   1:24
REPRO.   1:48
DRAWN BY - PAUL R. MATT

© HISTORICAL AVIATION ALBUM 1977
P.O. BOX 33
TEMPLE CITY, CALIF. 91780

MY SINCERE APPRECIATION IS EXTENDED TO
MR. JOHN HOUSER, AERONCA INC. AND
MR. ROGER SCHLEMMER, SCHLEMMER ASSOCS.,
FOR THEIR PERSONAL HELP IN THE PREPARATION
OF THESE DRAWINGS.

HISTORICAL AVIATION ALBUM

DRAWING No. 15-103-A

CABIN INTERIOR PROFILE

POCKET FOR LOG BOOK
ON PILOT SIDE AND FIRST
AID KIT ON RIGHT SIDE

ONE SAFETY BELT FOR
BOTH OCCUPANTS

10 OZ. BROWN DUCK
CANVAS BAGGAGE BAG

FIRE EXTINGUISHER
UNDER PILOT'S SEAT

ONE PIECE "BENCH" SEAT

METAL COVER
OVER CONTROLS
LINKAGE

INSTRUMENT
PANEL

DATUM (F.R.L.)

INSTRUMENT PANEL
TWICE SCALE

LIGHT SWITCH
ALTIMETER
OIL PRESSURE TUBE
THROTTLE
OIL TEMP. TUBE
AERONCA TACHOMETER
CONTROL WHEEL OUTLET
PARKING
OPTIONAL BRAKE
IGNITION SWITCH
AIRSPEED

10½"
29"

GENERAL SPECIFICATIONS

WEIGHT EMPTY   590 lbs.
USEFUL LOAD   450 lbs.
PAYLOAD   (360 lbs.)
GROSS WEIGHT   1,040 lbs.
WING AREA   146.35 sq. ft.
WING LOADING   7.13 lbs./sq.ft.
POWER LOADING   26.0 lbs./h.p.
TOP SPEED   78 mph
CRUISING SPEED   70 mph
LANDING SPEED   38 mph
INITIAL CLIMB, S.L.   400 ft./min.
FUEL CAPACITY   10 gals.
OIL CAPACITY   3 qts.
CRUISING RANGE at 4 gals/hr. 175 miles
SERVICE CEILING   13,000 feet

POWER, MODEL K AERONCA E-113C 37/40 H.P.

(MODEL KC, CONTINENTAL A-40-A OF 40 H.P.
HAD SIMILAR PERFORMANCE)

COCKPIT CONTROLLED
METAL TRIM TAB

HAND GRIP
LEFT SIDE ONLY

HINGE

17⅝"
23¾"
10'-0½"

SCALE BAR, meters
0   1   2

SCALE BAR, feet
0 1 2 3 4 5 6

NC18345

DURA LEADING EDGE,
FABRIC COVERED WING

LICENSE IN SIMILAR
POSITION ON UNDER-
SIDE OF LEFT WING

AMBER TINT
PYRALIN

FUEL FILL
(10 gal. cap.)

OIL FILL (3 qt. cap.)

BUTTON SPINNER OPTIONAL

32¼"

50"

CLARK Y AIRFOIL

0° DIH.

COLORING NOTES
ENTIRE AIRCRAFT - LOENING YELLOW
TRIM - BLACK
AIRCRAFT GRADE BA-24 COTTON FABRIC
COVERED, FOUR COATS CELLULOSE
NITRATE DOPE. FIRST COAT BRUSHED,
REMAINING COATS SPRAYED.

LIFT STRUT FITTINGS
JURY STRUT FITTING

50"
25"
7½"
84"
12"   15¼"

HINGE LINE
CONTROL LINES
JURY STRUT FITTING
LIFT STRUT FITTING LINE

50"
25"
7½"
84"
14⅞"
37"
37"
37"
36⅞"
7⁄8"
1"
1⅛"
9'-4"
16'-4½"
19½"

AIRCRAFT

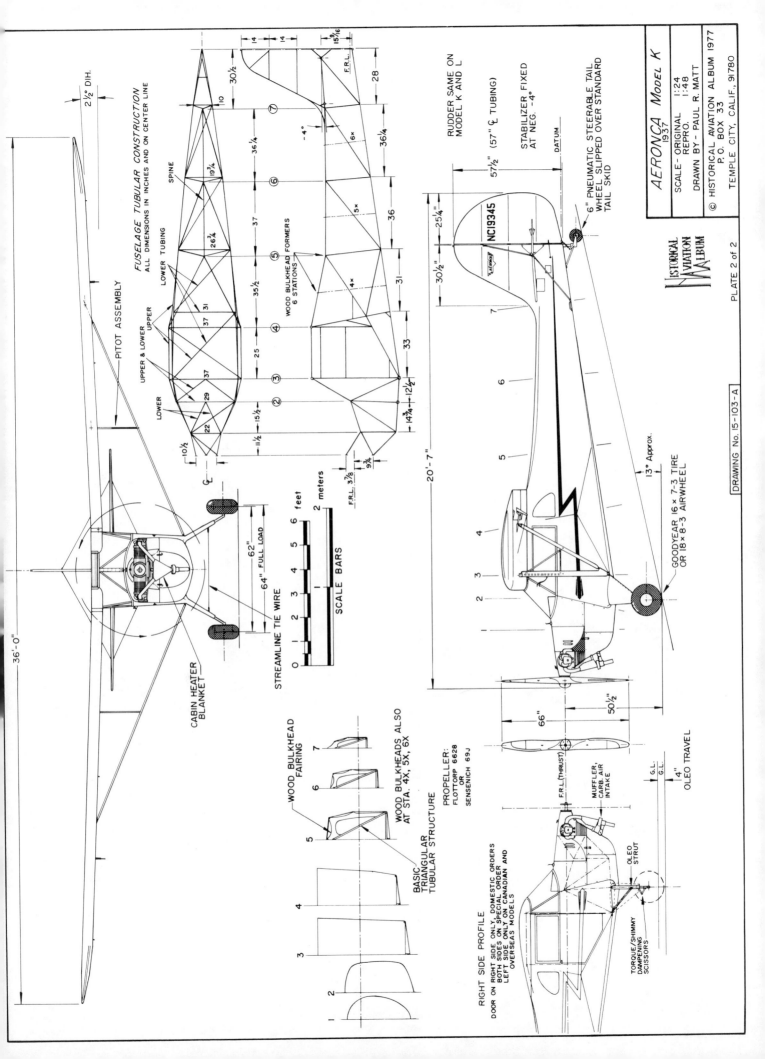

AERONCA MODEL K
1937

SCALE - ORIGINAL 1:24
REPRO. 1:48
DRAWN BY - PAUL R. MATT

© HISTORICAL AVIATION ALBUM 1977
P.O. BOX 33
TEMPLE CITY, CALIF., 91780

HISTORICAL AVIATION ALBUM

PLATE 2 of 2

DRAWING No. 15-103-A

RUDDER SAME ON
MODEL K AND L

STABILIZER FIXED
AT NEG. -4°

6" PNEUMATIC STEERABLE TAIL
WHEEL SLIPPED OVER STANDARD
TAIL SKID

NCI9345

GOODYEAR 16 x 7-3 TIRE
OR 18 x 8-3 AIRWHEEL

13° Approx.

FUSELAGE TUBULAR CONSTRUCTION
ALL DIMENSIONS IN INCHES AND ON CENTER LINE

SPINE

LOWER TUBING

UPPER

UPPER & LOWER

LOWER

WOOD BULKHEAD FORMERS
6 STATIONS

F.R.L.

2½ DIH.

PITOT ASSEMBLY

36'-0"

CABIN HEATER
BLANKET

STREAMLINE TIE WIRE

62"
64" FULL LOAD

SCALE BARS

6 feet
2 meters

RIGHT SIDE PROFILE

DOOR ON RIGHT SIDE ONLY, DOMESTIC ORDERS
BOTH SIDES ON SPECIAL ORDER
LEFT SIDE ONLY ON CANADIAN AND
OVERSEAS MODELS

PROPELLER:
FLOTTORP 6628
OR
SENSENICH 69J

WOOD BULKHEAD
FAIRING

WOOD BULKHEADS ALSO
AT STA. 4X, 5X, 6X

BASIC
TRIANGULAR
TUBULAR STRUCTURE

57½" (57" ℄ TUBING)

DATUM

20'-7"

F.R.L. 3⅜

66"

50½"

F.R.L. (THRUST)

MUFFLER,
CARB. AIR
INTAKE

OLEO
STRUT

TORQUE/SHIMMY
DAMPENING
SCISSORS

G.L.
G.L.

4" OLEO TRAVEL

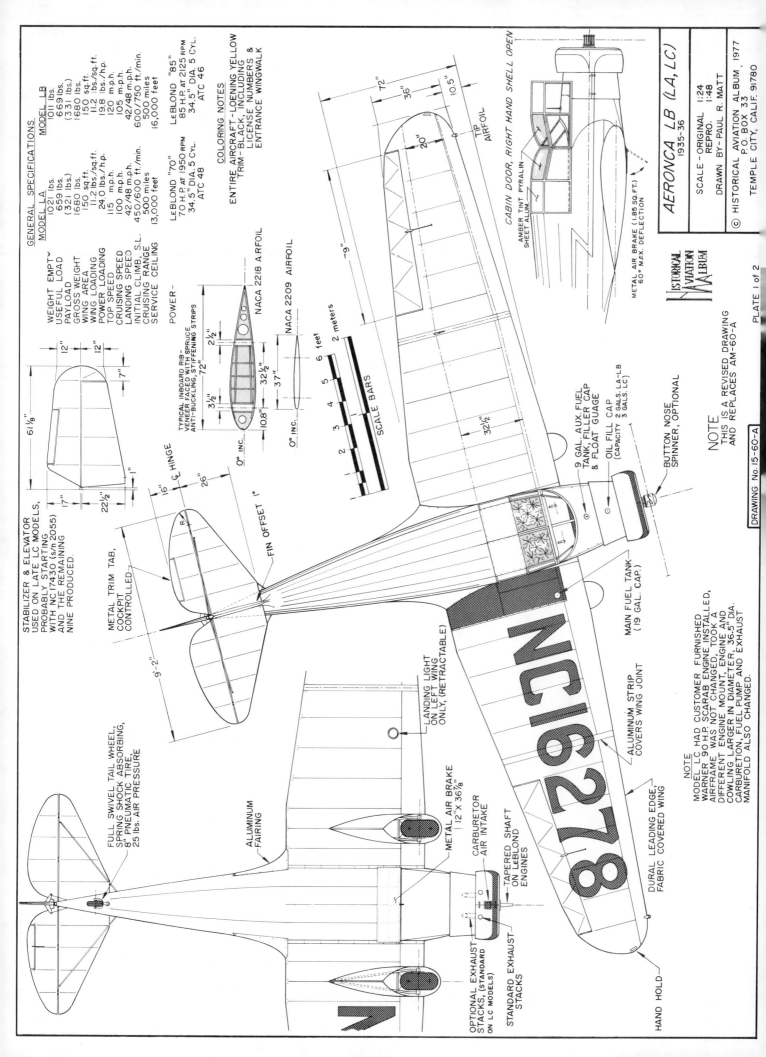

GENERAL SPECIFICATIONS

	MODEL LA	MODEL LB
WEIGHT EMPTY	1021 lbs.	1011 lbs.
USEFUL LOAD	659 lbs.	669 lbs.
PAYLOAD	(321 lbs.)	(331 lbs.)
GROSS WEIGHT	1680 lbs.	1680 lbs.
WING AREA	150 sq.ft.	150 sq.ft.
WING LOADING	11.2 lbs./sq.ft.	11.2 lbs./sq.ft.
POWER LOADING	24.0 lbs./h.p.	19.8 lbs./h.p.
TOP SPEED	115 m.p.h.	120 m.p.h.
CRUISING SPEED	100 m.p.h.	105 m.p.h.
LANDING SPEED	42/48 m.p.h.	42/48 m.p.h.
INITIAL CLIMB, S.L.	450/600 ft./min.	600/750 ft./min.
CRUISING RANGE	500 miles	500 miles
SERVICE CEILING	13,000 feet	16,000 feet

POWER -

LeBLOND "70"
70 H.P. AT 1950 RPM
34.5" DIA. 5 CYL.
ATC 48

LeBLOND "85"
85 H.P. AT 2125 RPM
34.5" DIA. 5 CYL.
ATC 46

COLORING NOTES

ENTIRE AIRCRAFT - LOENING YELLOW
TRIM - BLACK, INCLUDING
LICENSE NUMBERS &
ENTRANCE WINGWALK

NACA 2218 AIRFOIL

NACA 2209 AIRFOIL

TYPICAL INBOARD RIB -
VENEER FACED WITH SPRUCE
ANTI-BUCKLING, STIFFENING STRIPS

72"

2½"

3½"

32½"

10.8"

O° INC.

37"

O° INC.

SCALE BARS

feet 6 5 4 3 2

2 meters

STABILIZER & ELEVATOR
USED ON LATE LC MODELS,
PROBABLY STARTING
WITH NC17430 (s/n 2055)
AND THE REMAINING
NINE PRODUCED.

6⅛"

12"   12"

7"

17"

22½"   1"

Ç HINGE

16"   26"

R.

FIN OFFSET 1°

METAL TRIM TAB,
COCKPIT
CONTROLLED

9'-2"

FULL SWIVEL TAIL WHEEL,
SPRING SHOCK ABSORBING,
8" PNEUMATIC TIRE,
25 lbs. AIR PRESSURE

ALUMINUM
FAIRING

METAL AIR BRAKE
12" x 36⅞"

CARBURETOR
AIR INTAKE

TAPERED SHAFT
ON LEBLOND
ENGINES

OPTIONAL EXHAUST
STACKS, (STANDARD
ON LC MODELS)

STANDARD EXHAUST
STACKS

LANDING LIGHT
ON LEFT WING
ONLY, (RETRACTABLE)

ALUMINUM STRIP
COVERS WING JOINT

DURAL LEADING EDGE,
FABRIC COVERED WING

HAND HOLD

NC16278

MAIN FUEL TANK
(19 GAL. CAP.)

9 GAL. AUX. FUEL
TANK, FILLER CAP
& FLOAT GUAGE

OIL FILL CAP
(CAPACITY 2 GALS. LA-LB
3 GALS. LC)

BUTTON NOSE
SPINNER, OPTIONAL

72"

36"

10.5"

20"

TIP
AIRFOIL

32½"

9"

CABIN DOOR, RIGHT HAND SHELL OPEN

AMBER TINT PYRALIN
SHEET ALUM.

METAL AIR BRAKE (1.85 SQ.FT.)
60° MAX. DEFLECTION

AERONCA LB (LA, LC)
1935-36

SCALE - ORIGINAL 1:24
REPRO. 1:48
DRAWN BY - PAUL R. MATT

© HISTORICAL AVIATION ALBUM, 1977
P.O. BOX 33
TEMPLE CITY, CALIF. 91780

Historical Aviation Album

NOTE
THIS IS A REVISED DRAWING
AND REPLACES AM-60-A

PLATE 1 of 2

NOTE
MODEL LC HAD CUSTOMER FURNISHED
WARNER 90 H.P. SCARAB ENGINE INSTALLED,
AIRFRAME WAS NOT CHANGED, TOOK A
DIFFERENT ENGINE MOUNT, ENGINE AND
COWLING LARGER IN DIAMETER, 36.5" DIA.
CARBURETION, FUEL PUMP AND EXHAUST
MANIFOLD ALSO CHANGED.

DRAWING No. 15-60-A

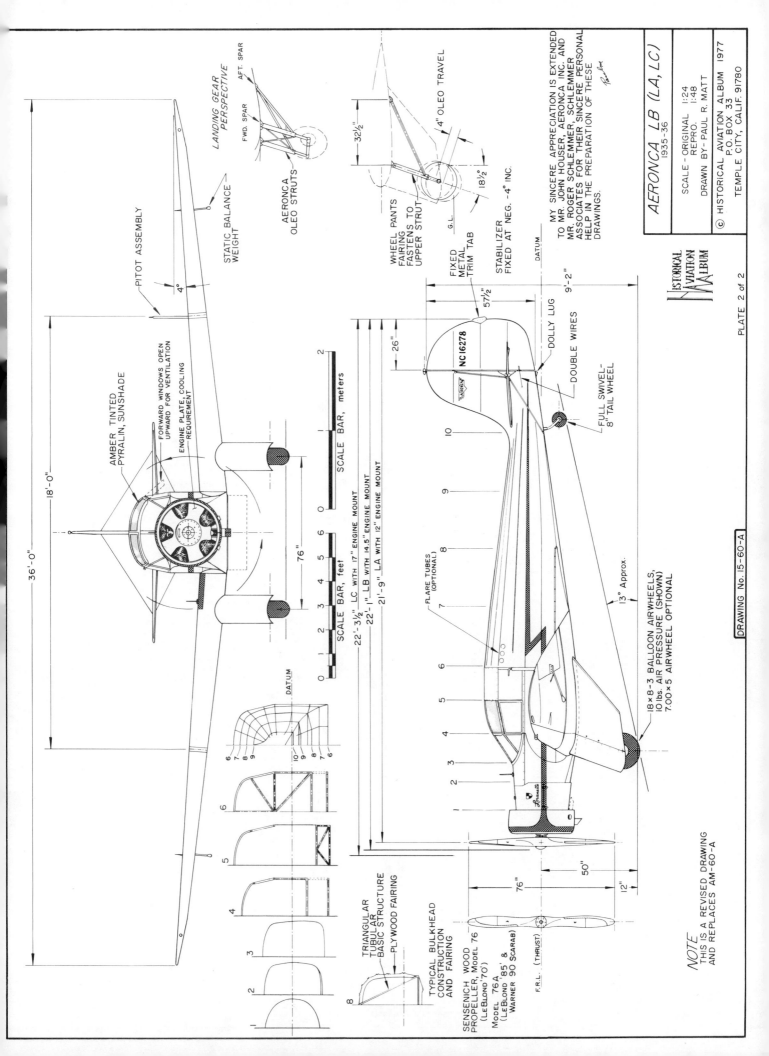

LANDING GEAR
PERSPECTIVE

AFT. SPAR

FWD. SPAR

AERONCA
OLEO STRUTS

STATIC BALANCE
WEIGHT

PITOT ASSEMBLY

4°

AMBER TINTED
PYRALIN, SUNSHADE

FORWARD WINDOWS OPEN
UPWARD FOR VENTILATION

ENGINE PLATE, COOLING
REQUIREMENT

18'-0"

36'-0"

76"

DATUM

SCALE BAR, meters

SCALE BAR, feet

6
7
8
9
10
8
7
6

6

5

4

3

2

8

TRIANGULAR
TUBULAR
BASIC STRUCTURE

PLYWOOD FAIRING

TYPICAL BULKHEAD
CONSTRUCTION
AND FAIRING

SENSENICH WOOD
PROPELLER, MODEL 76
(LeBLOND '70')

MODEL 76A
(LeBLOND '85' &
WARNER 90 SCARAB)

F.R.L. (THRUST)

76"

50"

12"

32½"

4" OLEO TRAVEL

G.L.

18½°

WHEEL PANTS
FAIRING
FASTENS TO
UPPER STRUT

FIXED
METAL
TRIM TAB

STABILIZER
FIXED AT NEG. -4° INC.

DATUM

57½"

26"

9'-2"

NC16278

DOLLY LUG

DOUBLE WIRES

FULL SWIVEL
8" TAIL WHEEL

10

9

8

7

6

5

4

3

2

FLARE TUBES
(OPTIONAL)

13° Approx.

18×8-3 BALLOON AIRWHEELS,
10 lbs. AIR PRESSURE (SHOWN)
7.00×5 AIRWHEEL OPTIONAL

22'-3½" LC WITH 17" ENGINE MOUNT
22'-1" LB WITH 14.5" ENGINE MOUNT
21'-9" LA WITH 12" ENGINE MOUNT

NOTE
THIS IS A REVISED DRAWING
AND REPLACES AM-60-A

AERONCA LB (LA, LC)
1935-36

SCALE - ORIGINAL 1:24
REPRO. 1:48
DRAWN BY- PAUL R. MATT

© HISTORICAL AVIATION ALBUM 1977
P.O. BOX 33
TEMPLE CITY, CALIF. 91780

HISTORICAL
AVIATION
ALBUM

PLATE 2 of 2

MY SINCERE APPRECIATION IS EXTENDED
TO MR. JOHN HOUSER, AERONCA INC. AND
MR. ROGER SCHLEMMER, SCHLEMMER
ASSOCIATES FOR THEIR SINCERE PERSONAL
HELP IN THE PREPARATION OF THESE
DRAWINGS.

DRAWING No. 15-60-A

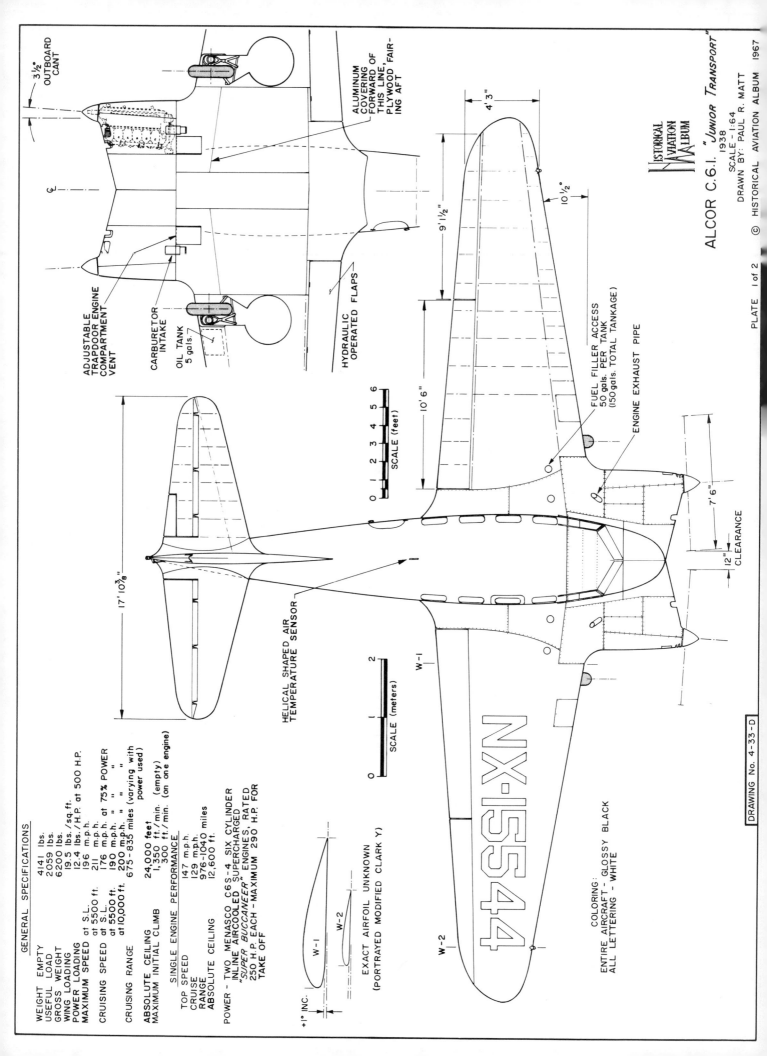

3½" OUTBOARD CANT

ALUMINUM COVERING FORWARD OF THIS LINE, PLYWOOD FAIRING AFT

ADJUSTABLE TRAPDOOR ENGINE COMPARTMENT VENT

CARBURETOR INTAKE

OIL TANK 5 gals.

HYDRAULIC OPERATED FLAPS

℄

4' 3"

10½°

9' 1½"

10' 6"

FUEL FILLER ACCESS 50 gals. PER TANK (150 gals. TOTAL TANKAGE)

ENGINE EXHAUST PIPE

7' 6"

12" CLEARANCE

SCALE (feet)
0 1 2 3 4 5 6

HELICAL SHAPED AIR TEMPERATURE SENSOR

17' 10⅜"

W-1

W-2

SCALE (meters)
0 1 2

NX-1554

W-1
W-2

+1° INC.

EXACT AIRFOIL UNKNOWN (PORTRAYED MODIFIED CLARK Y)

COLORING:
ENTIRE AIRCRAFT - GLOSSY BLACK
ALL LETTERING - WHITE

GENERAL SPECIFICATIONS

WEIGHT EMPTY	4141 lbs.
USEFUL LOAD	2059 lbs.
GROSS WEIGHT	6200 lbs.
WING LOADING	19.5 lbs./sq.ft.
POWER LOADING	12.4 lbs./H.P. at 500 H.P.
MAXIMUM SPEED	196 m.p.h.
CRUISING SPEED at S.L.	211 m.p.h.
at 5500 ft.	176 m.p.h. at 75% POWER
at S.L.	190 m.p.h. " "
at 5500 ft.	200 m.p.h. " "
CRUISING RANGE	675 - 835 miles (varying with power used)

ABSOLUTE CEILING   24,000 feet
MAXIMUM INITIAL CLIMB   1,350 ft./min. (empty)
                         300 ft./min. (on one engine)

SINGLE ENGINE PERFORMANCE

TOP SPEED   147 m.p.h.
CRUISE   129 m.p.h.
RANGE   976-1040 miles
ABSOLUTE CEILING 12,600 ft.

POWER - TWO MENASCO C6S-4 SIX CYLINDER INLINE AIRCOOLED SUPERCHARGED "SUPER BUCCANEER" ENGINES, RATED 250 H.P. EACH - MAXIMUM 290 H.P. FOR TAKE OFF

ALCOR C.6.I. "JUNIOR TRANSPORT"
1938
SCALE - 1:64
DRAWN BY: PAUL R. MATT

Historical Aviation Album

© HISTORICAL AVIATION ALBUM 1967

PLATE 1 of 2

DRAWING No. 4-33-D

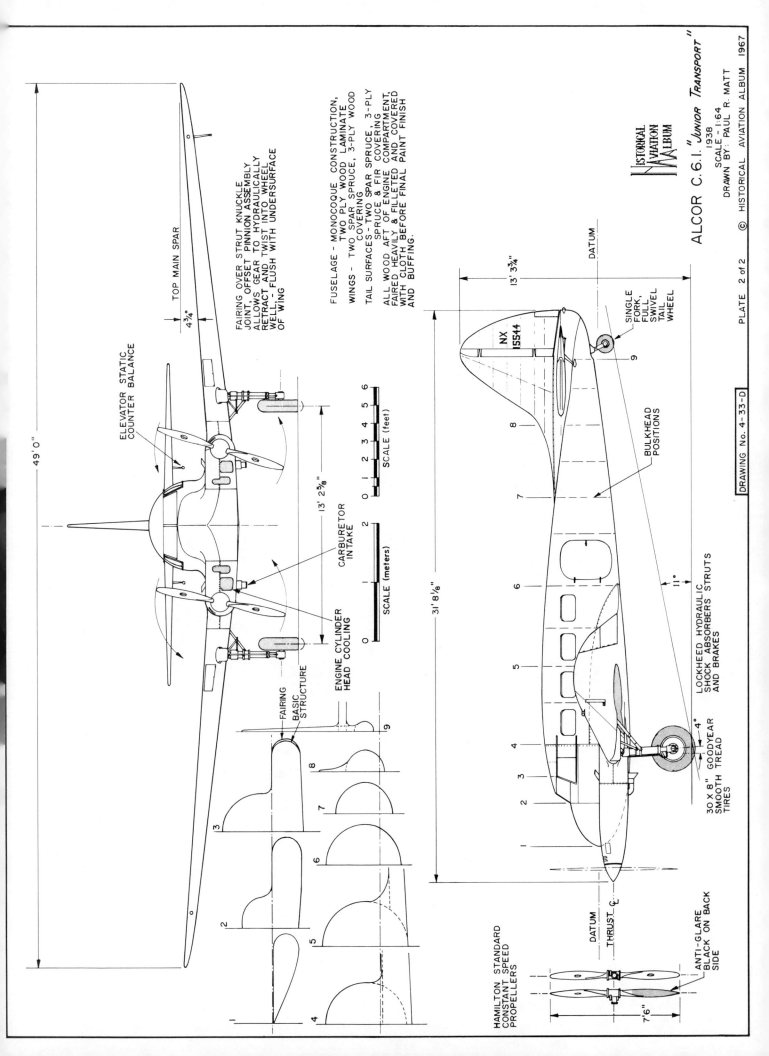

TOP MAIN SPAR

4¾°

FAIRING OVER STRUT KNUCKLE
JOINT, OFFSET PINNION ASSEMBLY
ALLOWS GEAR TO HYDRAULICALLY
RETRACT AND TWIST INTO WHEEL
WELL - FLUSH WITH UNDERSURFACE
OF WING

FUSELAGE - MONOCOQUE CONSTRUCTION,
TWO PLY WOOD LAMINATE
WINGS - TWO SPAR SPRUCE, 3-PLY WOOD
COVERING
TAIL SURFACES - TWO SPAR SPRUCE, 3-PLY
SPRUCE & FIR COVERING
ALL WOOD AFT OF ENGINE COMPARTMENT,
FAIRED HEAVILY & FILLETED AND COVERED
WITH CLOTH BEFORE FINAL PAINT FINISH
AND BUFFING.

49' 0"

ELEVATOR STATIC
COUNTER BALANCE

13' 2⅝"

SCALE (feet)
0 1 2 3 4 5 6

SCALE (meters)
0 1 2

CARBURETOR
INTAKE

ENGINE CYLINDER
HEAD COOLING

FAIRING

BASIC
STRUCTURE

ALCOR C.6.1. *Junior Transport*
1938
SCALE - 1:64
DRAWN BY: PAUL R. MATT

© HISTORICAL AVIATION ALBUM 1967

DATUM

NX 15544

SINGLE
FORK, FULL
SWIVEL TAIL
WHEEL

13' 3¾"

9

8

7

BULKHEAD
POSITIONS

6

5

4

3

2

1

11°

LOCKHEED HYDRAULIC
SHOCK ABSORBERS STRUTS
AND BRAKES

4°

30 x 8" GOODYEAR
SMOOTH TREAD
TIRES

31' 8⅛"

DATUM

THRUST ₵

ANTI-GLARE
BLACK ON BACK
SIDE

HAMILTON STANDARD
CONSTANT SPEED
PROPELLERS

7' 6"

DRAWING No. 4-33-D

PLATE 2 of 2

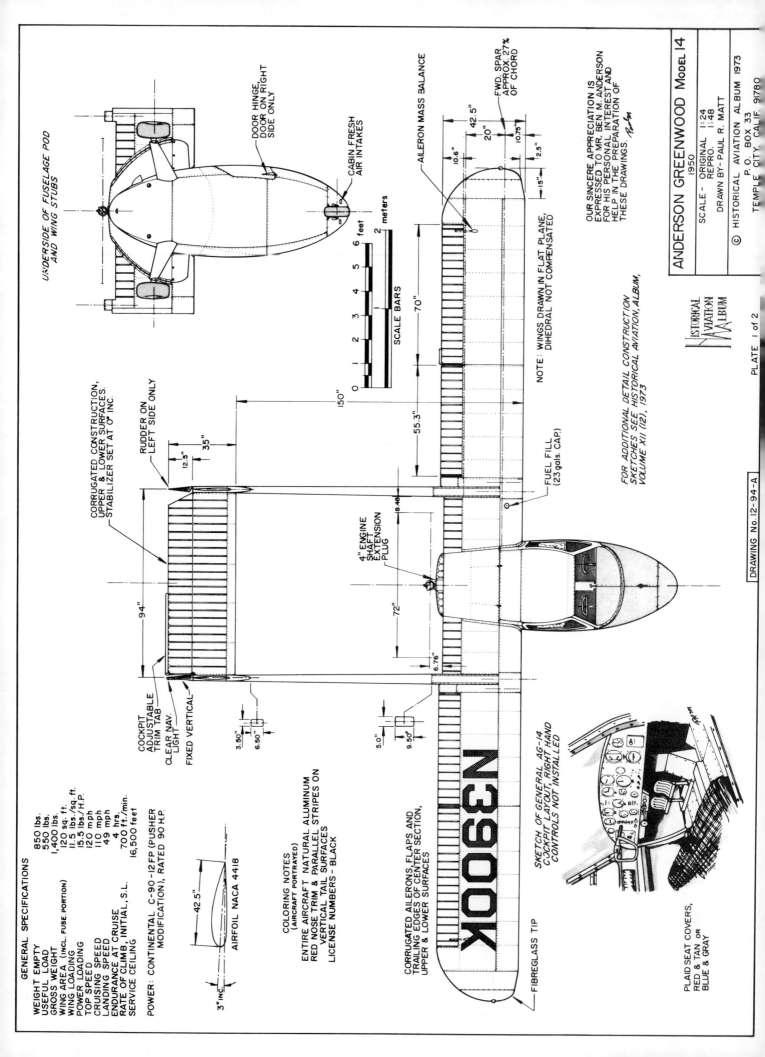

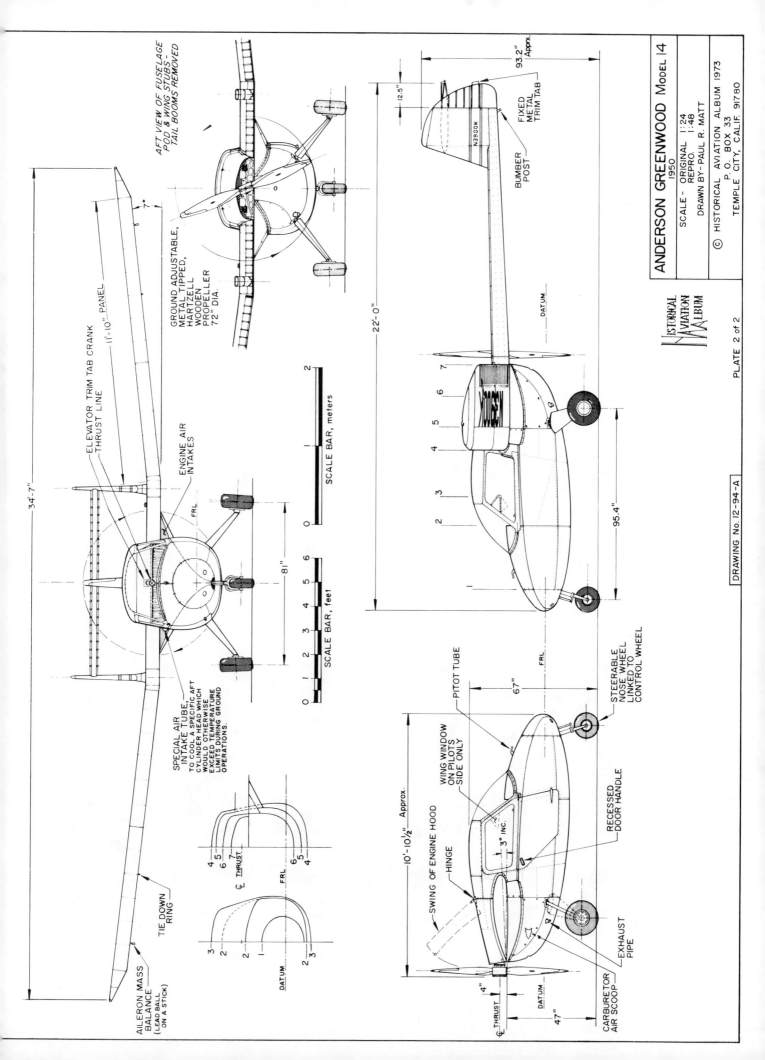

AFT VIEW OF FUSELAGE
POD & WING STUBS-
TAIL BOOMS REMOVED

ELEVATOR TRIM TAB CRANK
THRUST LINE
11'-10" PANEL

ENGINE AIR
INTAKES

GROUND ADJUSTABLE,
METAL TIPPED,
HARTZELL
WOODEN
PROPELLER
72" DIA.

SPECIAL AIR
INTAKE TUBE,
TO COOL A SPECIFIC AFT
CYLINDER HEAD WHICH
WOULD OTHERWISE
EXCEED TEMPERATURE
LIMITS DURING GROUND
OPERATIONS.

FRL

34'-7"

81"

7°

AILERON MASS
BALANCE
(LEAD BALL
ON A STICK)

TIE DOWN
RING

2 — SCALE BAR, meters — 0

6 5 4 3 2 1 0 — SCALE BAR, feet

4 5 6 ℄ THRUST FRL 6 5 4
3 2 2 1 2 2 3
DATUM

22'-0"

12.5"

93.2"
Approx.

N390K

FIXED
METAL
TRIM TAB

BUMBER
POST

DATUM

7 6 5 4 3 2

95.4"

FRL

N390K

STEERABLE
NOSE WHEEL
LINKED TO
CONTROL WHEEL

PITOT TUBE

67"

WING WINDOW
ON PILOTS
SIDE ONLY

SWING OF ENGINE HOOD

HINGE

3° INC.

RECESSED
DOOR HANDLE

10'-10½" Approx.

4"

47"

THRUST

DATUM

CARBURETOR
AIR SCOOP

EXHAUST
PIPE

ANDERSON GREENWOOD Model 14
1950

| SCALE - | ORIGINAL | 1:24 |
| | REPRO. | 1:48 |

DRAWN BY- PAUL R. MATT

© HISTORICAL AVIATION ALBUM 1973
P. O. BOX 33
TEMPLE CITY, CALIF. 91780

Historical Aviation Album

PLATE 2 of 2

DRAWING No. 12-94-A

Beechcraft Model 18

Beechcraft Model D 18S, an all metal twin engine 6 to 9 place monoplane.

Early Beechcraft Model 18 interior.

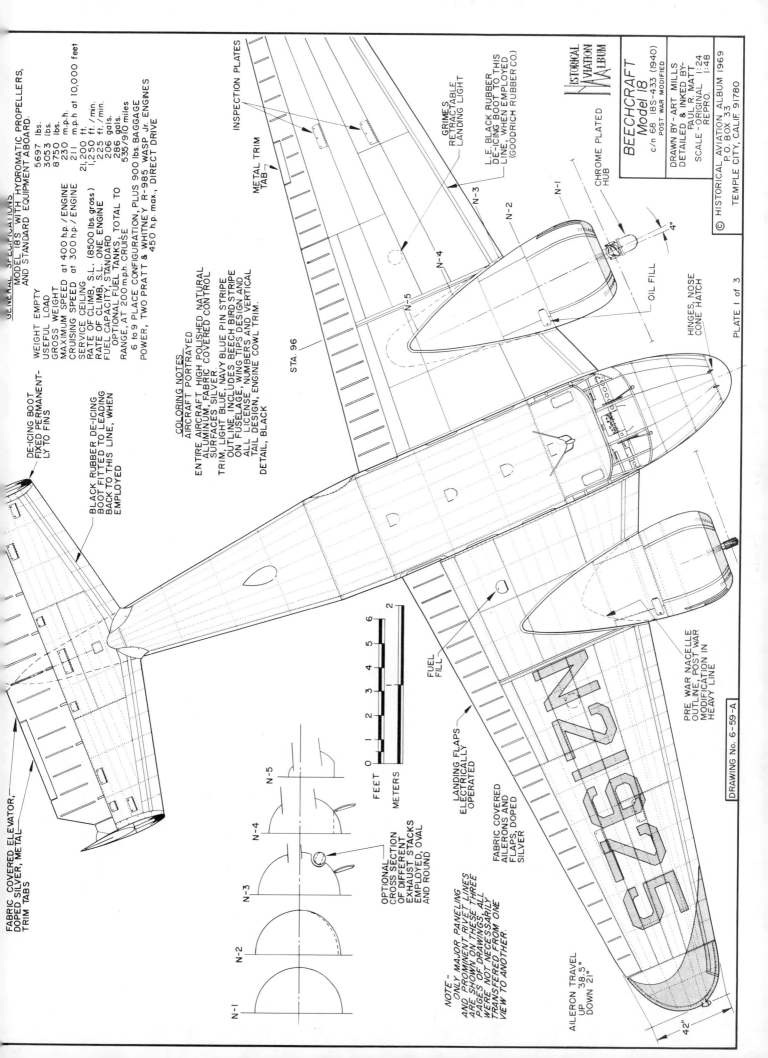

GENERAL SPECIFICATIONS

MODEL 18S WITH HYDROMATIC PROPELLERS,
AND STANDARD EQUIPMENT ABOARD.

WEIGHT EMPTY	5697	lbs.
USEFUL LOAD	3053	lbs.
GROSS WEIGHT	8750	lbs.
MAXIMUM SPEED at 400 h.p. / ENGINE	230	m.p.h.
CRUISING SPEED at 300 h.p. / ENGINE	211	m.p.h. at 10,000 feet
SERVICE CEILING	21,200	ft.
RATE OF CLIMB, S.L. (8500 lbs. gross)	1,250	ft. / min.
RATE OF CLIMB, S.L. ONE ENGINE	225	ft. / min.
FUEL CAPACITY, STANDARD	206	gals.
OPTIONAL FUEL TANKS, TOTAL TO	286	gals.
RANGE, AT 200 m.p.h. CRUISE	535/910	miles

6 to 9 PLACE CONFIGURATION, PLUS 900 lbs. BAGGAGE
POWER, TWO PRATT & WHITNEY R-985 WASP Jr. ENGINES
450 h.p. max., DIRECT DRIVE

COLORING NOTES
AIRCRAFT PORTRAYED

ENTIRE AIRCRAFT HIGH POLISHED NATURAL
ALUMINUM, FABRIC COVERED CONTROL
SURFACES SILVER.
TRIM, LIGHT BLUE, NAVY BLUE PIN STRIPE
OUTLINE. INCLUDES BEECH BIRD STRIPE
ON FUSELAGE, WING TIPS DESIGN AND
ALL LICENSE NUMBERS AND VERTICAL
TAIL DESIGN, ENGINE COWL TRIM.
DETAIL, BLACK

DE-ICING BOOT
FIXED PERMANENT-
LY TO FINS

BLACK RUBBER DE-ICING
BOOT FITTED TO LEADING
BACK TO THIS LINE, WHEN
EMPLOYED

FABRIC COVERED ELEVATOR,
DOPED SILVER, METAL
TRIM TABS

INSPECTION PLATES

METAL TRIM
TAB

STA. 96

GRIMES
RETRACTABLE
LANDING LIGHT

L.E. BLACK RUBBER
DE-ICING BOOT TO THIS
LINE, WHEN EMPLOYED
(GOODRICH RUBBER CO.)

N-3

N-4

N-5

N-1

CHROME PLATED
HUB

4°

OIL FILL

HINGES, NOSE
CONE HATCH

PLATE 1 of 3

BEECHCRAFT
Model 18
c/n 68 18S-433 (1940)
POST WAR MODIFIED

DRAWN BY - ART MILLS
DETAILED & INKED BY-
PAUL R. MATT
SCALE - ORIGINAL   1:24
REPRO.   1:48

HISTORICAL AVIATION ALBUM 1969
P.O. BOX 33
TEMPLE CITY, CALIF. 91780

© HISTORICAL AVIATION ALBUM 1969

FEET

METERS

0 1 2 3 4 5 6

FUEL
FILL

LANDING FLAPS
ELECTRICALLY
OPERATED

FABRIC COVERED
AILERONS AND
FLAPS, DOPED
SILVER

PRE WAR NACELLE
OUTLINE, POST WAR
MODIFICATION IN
HEAVY LINE

42"

NC21512

AILERON TRAVEL
UP 38.5°
DOWN 21°

N-2   N-1

N-3

N-4

N-5

OPTIONAL
CROSS SECTION
OF DIFFERENT
EXHAUST STACKS
EMPLOYED, OVAL
AND ROUND

NOTE-
ONLY MAJOR PANELING
AND PROMINENT RIVET LINES
ARE SHOWN ON THESE THREE
PAGES OF DRAWINGS, ALL
WERE NOT NECESSARILY
TRANSFERED FROM ONE
VIEW TO ANOTHER.

DRAWING No. 6-59-A

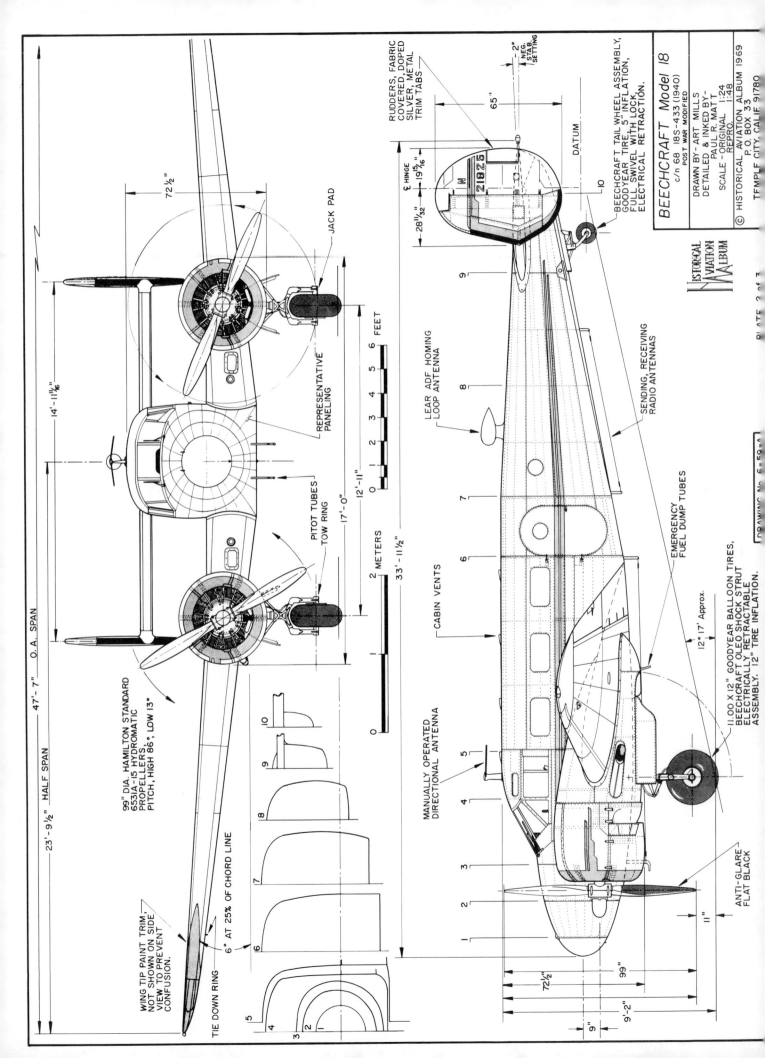

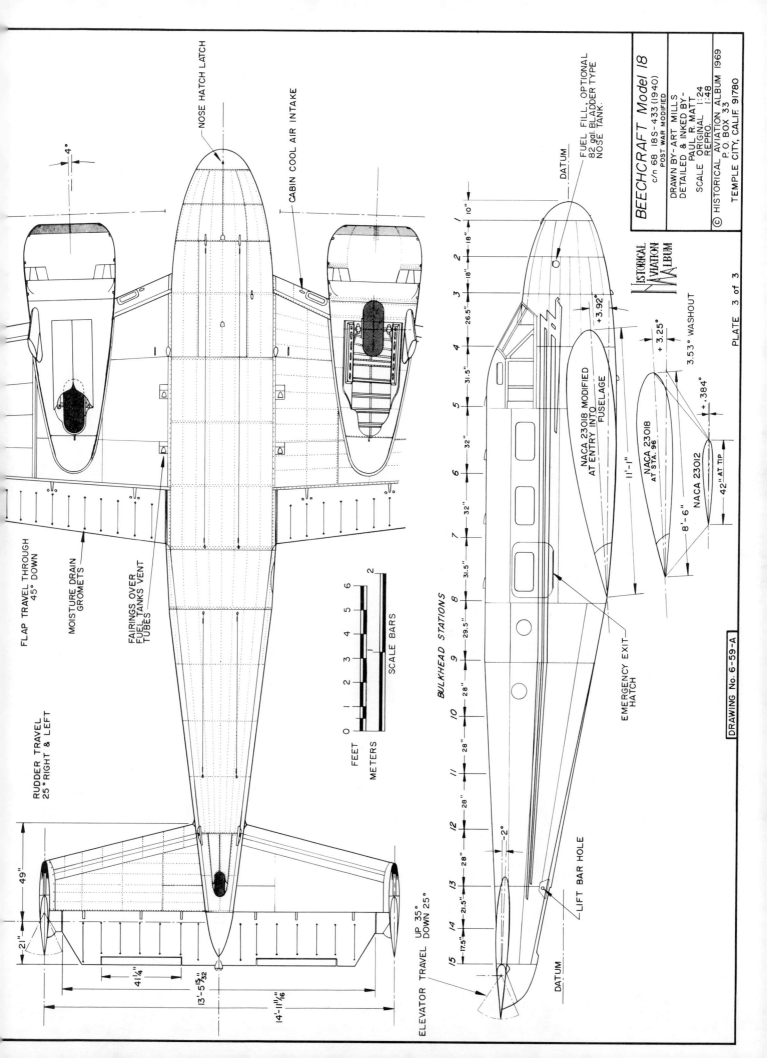

NOSE HATCH LATCH

CABIN COOL AIR INTAKE

4°

FLAP TRAVEL THROUGH
45° DOWN

MOISTURE DRAIN
GROMETS

FAIRINGS OVER
FUEL TANKS VENT
TUBES

RUDDER TRAVEL
25° RIGHT & LEFT

49"

21"

41¼"

13'-5⁵/₃₂"

14'-11¹¹/₁₆"

ELEVATOR TRAVEL
UP 35°
DOWN 25°

SCALE BARS

FEET
METERS

2 1 0 1 2 3 4 5 6

BULKHEAD STATIONS

1 10"
2 18"
3 18"
4 26.5"
5 31.5"
6 32"
7 32"
8 31.5"
9 29.5"
10 28"
11 28"
12 28"
13 28"
14 21.5"
15 17.5"

DATUM

FUEL FILL, OPTIONAL
82 gal. BLADDER TYPE
NOSE TANK.

NACA 23018 MODIFIED
AT ENTRY INTO
FUSELAGE

NACA 23018
AT STA. 96

NACA 23012

+3.92°

+3.25°

3.53° WASHOUT

+.384°

11'-1"

8'-6"

42" AT TIP

EMERGENCY EXIT
HATCH

−2°

LIFT BAR HOLE

DATUM

BEECHCRAFT Model 18
c/n 68 18S-433 (1940)
POST WAR MODIFIED

DRAWN BY-ART MILLS
DETAILED & INKED BY-
       PAUL R. MATT
SCALE ORIGINAL 1:24
       REPRO.   1:48

© HISTORICAL AVIATION ALBUM 1969
       P.O. BOX 33
       TEMPLE CITY, CALIF. 91780

HISTORICAL AVIATION ALBUM

PLATE 3 of 3

DRAWING No. 6-59-A

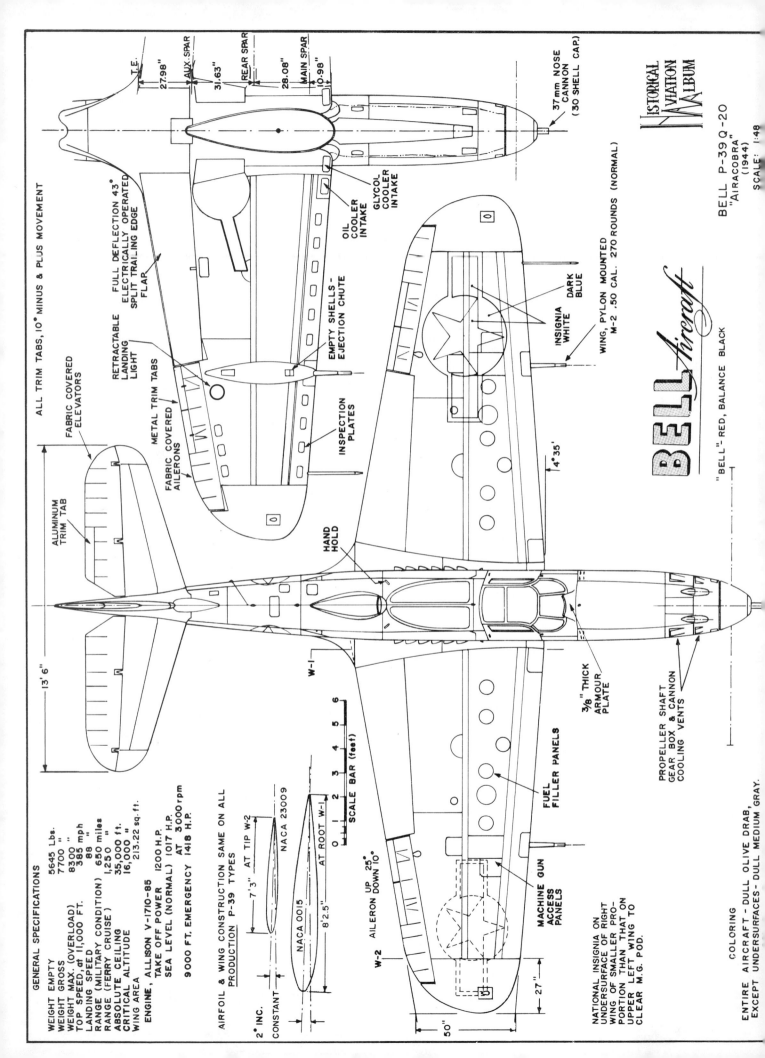

GENERAL SPECIFICATIONS

WEIGHT EMPTY   5645 Lbs.
WEIGHT GROSS   7700 "
WEIGHT MAX. (OVERLOAD) 8300 "
TOP SPEED, at 11,000 FT. 385 mph
LANDING SPEED   88 "
RANGE (MILITARY CONDITION) 650 miles
RANGE (FERRY CRUISE)   1,250 "
ABSOLUTE CEILING   35,000 ft.
CRITICAL ALTITUDE   16,000 "
WING AREA   213.22 sq. ft.

ENGINE, ALLISON V-1710-85
    TAKE OFF POWER 1200 H.P.
    SEA LEVEL (NORMAL) 1017 H.P.
                    AT 3000 rpm
    9000 FT. EMERGENCY 1418 H.P.

AIRFOIL & WING CONSTRUCTION SAME ON ALL
PRODUCTION P-39 TYPES

2° INC.

CONSTANT

NACA 23009

7'3" AT TIP W-2

NACA 0015

8'2.5" AT ROOT W-1

SCALE BAR (feet)
0 1 2 3 4 5 6

AILERON UP 25°
DOWN 10°

W-2

W-1

27"

50"

MACHINE GUN
ACCESS PANELS

FUEL
FILLER PANELS

3/8" THICK
ARMOUR PLATE

PROPELLER SHAFT
GEAR BOX & CANNON
COOLING VENTS

HAND
HOLD

13' 6"

ALUMINUM
TRIM TAB

FABRIC COVERED
ELEVATORS

METAL TRIM TABS

FABRIC COVERED
AILERONS

RETRACTABLE
LANDING LIGHT

FULL DEFLECTION 43°
ELECTRICALLY OPERATED
SPLIT TRAILING EDGE
FLAP

ALL TRIM TABS, 10° MINUS & PLUS MOVEMENT

27.98"
T.E.

AUX. SPAR
31.63"

REAR SPAR
28.08"

MAIN SPAR
10.98"

37mm NOSE CANNON
(30 SHELL CAP.)

OIL
COOLER
INTAKE

GLYCOL
COOLER
INTAKE

EMPTY SHELLS -
EJECTION CHUTE

INSPECTION
PLATES

DARK
BLUE

INSIGNIA WHITE

WING, PYLON MOUNTED
M-2 .50 CAL. 270 ROUNDS (NORMAL)

4° 35'

BELL Aircraft

BELL P-39 Q-20
"AIRACOBRA" (1944)
SCALE: 1:48

Historical Aviation Album

"BELL" RED, BALANCE BLACK

NATIONAL INSIGNIA ON
UNDERSURFACE OF RIGHT
WING OF SMALLER PRO-
PORTION THAN THAT ON
UPPER LEFT WING TO
CLEAR M.G. POD.

COLORING

ENTIRE AIRCRAFT - DULL OLIVE DRAB,
EXCEPT UNDERSURFACES - DULL MEDIUM GRAY.

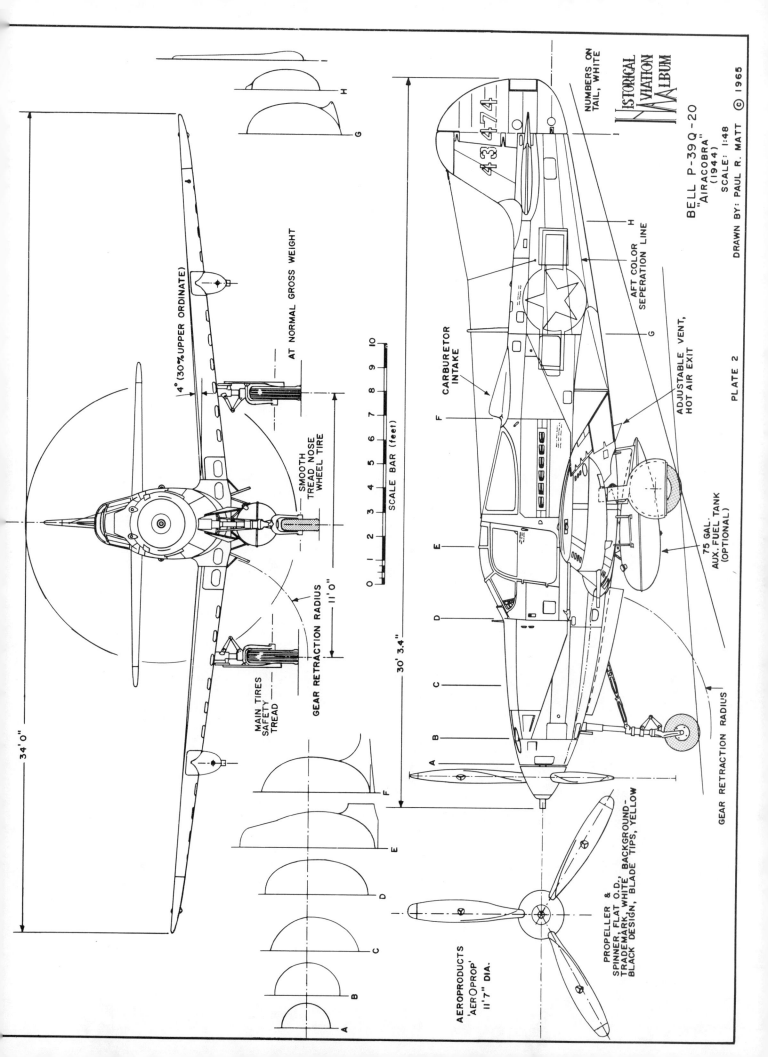

34' 0"

4° (30% UPPER ORDINATE)

AT NORMAL GROSS WEIGHT

SMOOTH TREAD NOSE WHEEL TIRE

MAIN TIRES SAFETY TREAD

GEAR RETRACTION RADIUS 11' 0"

SCALE BAR (feet)

0 1 2 3 4 5 6 7 8 9 10

H

G

CARBURETOR INTAKE

F

E

D

C

B

A

AFT COLOR SEPERATION LINE

H

G

ADJUSTABLE VENT, HOT AIR EXIT

75 GAL. AUX. FUEL TANK (OPTIONAL)

GEAR RETRACTION RADIUS

30' 3.4"

NUMBERS ON TAIL, WHITE

43474

AEROPRODUCTS 'AEROPROP' 11' 7" DIA.

PROPELLER & SPINNER, FLAT O.D. TRADEMARK, WHITE BACKGROUND- BLACK DESIGN, BLADE TIPS, YELLOW

HISTORICAL AVIATION ALBUM © 1965

BELL P-39Q-20 "AIRACOBRA" (1944)

SCALE: 1:48

DRAWN BY: PAUL R. MATT

PLATE 2

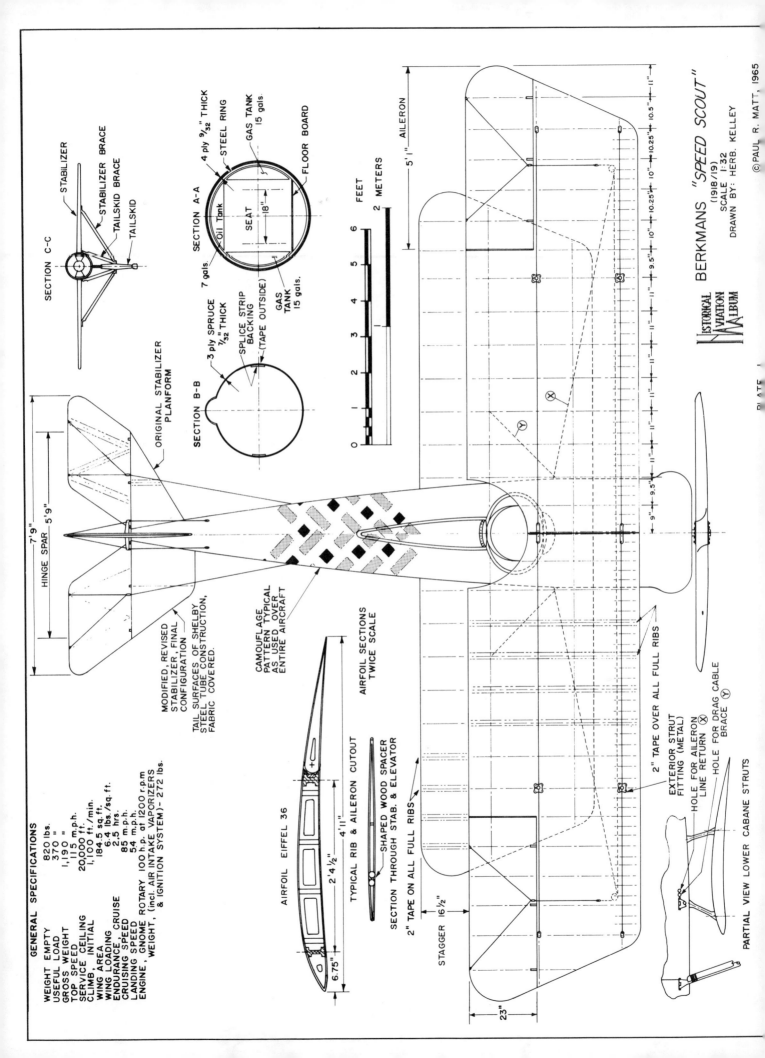

SECTION C-C

STABILIZER
STABILIZER BRACE
TAILSKID BRACE
TAILSKID
TAILSKID

ORIGINAL STABILIZER PLANFORM

SECTION A-A

4 ply 9/32" THICK
STEEL RING
GAS TANK 15 gals.
Oil Tank
SEAT
18"
FLOOR BOARD
7 gals.

SECTION B-B

3 ply SPRUCE 7/32" THICK
SPLICE STRIP BACKING
(TAPE OUTSIDE)
GAS TANK 15 gals.

FEET
METERS
0 1 2 3 4 5 6
2

BERKMANS "SPEED SCOUT"
(1918/19)
SCALE 1:32
DRAWN BY: HERB. KELLEY

Historical Aviation Album

© PAUL R. MATT, 1965

AILERON
5' 1"
AILERON

11" — 10.5" — 10.25" — 10" — 9.5" — 10" — 10.25" — 10.5" — 11"

9" — 9.5"
9" — 9.5"

X
Y

7' 9"
HINGE SPAR 5' 9"

MODIFIED, REVISED STABILIZER, FINAL CONFIGURATION.

TAIL SURFACES OF SHELBY STEEL TUBE CONSTRUCTION, FABRIC COVERED.

CAMOUFLAGE PATTERN TYPICAL AS USED OVER ENTIRE AIRCRAFT

AIRFOIL SECTIONS TWICE SCALE

AIRFOIL EIFFEL 36

6.75"
2' 4½"
4' 11"

TYPICAL RIB & AILERON CUTOUT

SHAPED WOOD SPACER
SECTION THROUGH STAB. & ELEVATOR

2" TAPE ON ALL FULL RIBS

STAGGER 16½"

2" TAPE OVER ALL FULL RIBS

EXTERIOR STRUT FITTING (METAL)
HOLE FOR AILERON LINE RETURN ⊗
HOLE FOR DRAG CABLE BRACE Ⓨ

PARTIAL VIEW LOWER CABANE STRUTS

23"

GENERAL SPECIFICATIONS

WEIGHT EMPTY   820 lbs.
USEFUL LOAD   370 "
GROSS WEIGHT   1,190 "
TOP SPEED   115 m.p.h.
SERVICE CEILING   20,000 ft.
CLIMB, INITIAL   1,100 ft./min.
WING AREA   184.5 sq. ft.
WING LOADING   6.4 lbs./sq. ft.
ENDURANCE, CRUISE   2.5 hrs.
CRUISING SPEED   85 m.p.h.
LANDING SPEED   54 m.p.h.
ENGINE, GNOME ROTARY 100 h.p. at 1200 r.p.m (incl. AIR INTAKE VAPORIZERS & IGNITION SYSTEM)- 272 lbs.

PLATE I

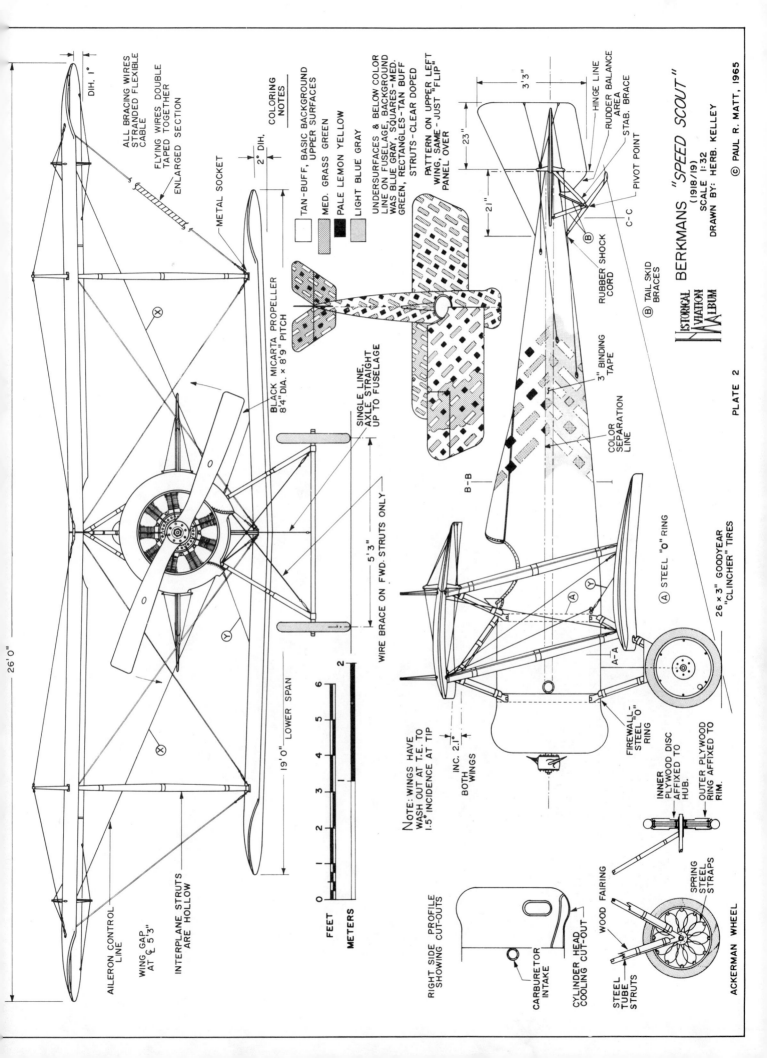

DIH. 1°

ALL BRACING WIRES
STRANDED FLEXIBLE
CABLE

FLYING WIRES DOUBLE
TAPED TOGETHER
ENLARGED SECTION

METAL SOCKET

2° DIH.

COLORING
NOTES

TAN-BUFF, BASIC BACKGROUND
UPPER SURFACES

MED. GRASS GREEN

PALE LEMON YELLOW

LIGHT BLUE GRAY

UNDERSURFACES & BELOW COLOR
LINE ON FUSELAGE, BACKGROUND
WAS BLUE GRAY, SQUARES–MED.
GREEN, RECTANGLES–TAN BUFF
STRUTS–CLEAR DOPED

PATTERN ON UPPER LEFT
WING, SAME – JUST "FLIP"
PANEL OVER

26' 0"

AILERON CONTROL
LINE

WING GAP
AT ₵ 5'3"

INTERPLANE STRUTS
ARE HOLLOW

BLACK MICARTA PROPELLER
8'4" DIA. × 8'9" PITCH

SINGLE LINE,
AXLE STRAIGHT
UP TO FUSELAGE

19' 0" LOWER SPAN

5'3"

WIRE BRACE ON FWD. STRUTS ONLY

NOTE: WINGS HAVE
WASH OUT AT T.E. TO
1.5° INCIDENCE AT TIP

FEET

METERS

RIGHT SIDE PROFILE
SHOWING CUT-OUTS

CARBURETOR
INTAKE

CYLINDER HEAD
COOLING CUT-OUT

23"

21"

3' 3"

HINGE LINE

RUDDER BALANCE
AREA

STAB. BRACE

PIVOT POINT

C–C

Ⓑ

RUBBER SHOCK
CORD

Ⓑ TAIL SKID
BRACES

3" BINDING
TAPE

COLOR
SEPARATION
LINE

B–B

STEEL "O" RING

A–A

Ⓐ

Ⓨ

INC. 2.1°
BOTH
WINGS

FIREWALL–
STEEL "O"
RING

26 × 3" GOODYEAR
"CLINCHER" TIRES

Ⓐ STEEL "O" RING

INNER
PLYWOOD DISC
AFFIXED TO
HUB.

OUTER PLYWOOD
RING AFFIXED TO
RIM.

WOOD FAIRING

SPRING
STEEL
STRAPS

STEEL
TUBE
STRUTS

ACKERMAN WHEEL

Ⓗ ISTORICAL
Ⓐ VIATION
Ⓐ LBUM

BERKMANS "SPEED SCOUT"
(1918/19)
SCALE 1:32
DRAWN BY: HERB. KELLEY

© PAUL R. MATT, 1965

PLATE 2

Berliner-Joyce OJ-2

This is the second of the two OJ-2s of VS-6B from the four-stack cruiser, USS Concord. Large letter "E" with the small "m" underneath was the symbol for Excellence in Machine Gunnery.

Going aboard for a check-up is this OJ-2. Operations of these aircraft were equally divided between land and seaplane versions. Wide, red stripe on main float is prop danger line.

Berliner-Joyce OJ-2 at Floyd Bennet Field, New York.

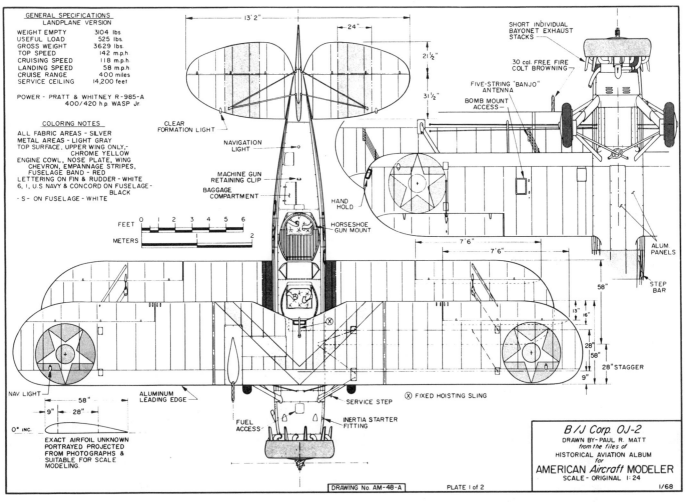

GENERAL SPECIFICATIONS
LANDPLANE VERSION

WEIGHT EMPTY	3104 lbs
USEFUL LOAD	525 lbs.
GROSS WEIGHT	3629 lbs.
TOP SPEED	142 m.p.h.
CRUISING SPEED	118 m.p.h.
LANDING SPEED	58 m.p.h.
CRUISE RANGE	400 miles
SERVICE CEILING	14,200 feet

POWER - PRATT & WHITNEY R-985-A
400/420 h.p. WASP Jr.

COLORING NOTES
ALL FABRIC AREAS - SILVER
METAL AREAS - LIGHT GRAY
TOP SURFACE, UPPER WING ONLY,-
CHROME YELLOW
ENGINE COWL, NOSE PLATE, WING
CHEVRON, EMPANNAGE STRIPES,
FUSELAGE BAND - RED
LETTERING ON FIN & RUDDER - WHITE
6, I, U.S. NAVY & CONCORD ON FUSELAGE-
BLACK
- S - ON FUSELAGE - WHITE

CLEAR FORMATION LIGHT
NAVIGATION LIGHT
MACHINE GUN RETAINING CLIP
BAGGAGE COMPARTMENT
HAND HOLD
HORSESHOE GUN MOUNT

SHORT INDIVIDUAL BAYONET EXHAUST STACKS
30 cal. FREE FIRE COLT BROWNING
FIVE-STRING "BANJO" ANTENNA
BOMB MOUNT ACCESS—
ALUM PANELS
STEP BAR

FEET
METERS

13' 2"
24"
21½"
31½"
7' 6"
7' 6"
58"
13"
16"
28"
58"
28" STAGGER
9"

NAV LIGHT
ALUMINUM LEADING EDGE
SERVICE STEP
Ⓧ FIXED HOISTING SLING
FUEL ACCESS
INERTIA STARTER FITTING

58"
9"
28"
0° INC.

EXACT AIRFOIL UNKNOWN
PORTRAYED PROJECTED
FROM PHOTOGRAPHS &
SUITABLE FOR SCALE
MODELING.

B/J Corp. OJ-2
DRAWN BY- PAUL R. MATT
from the files of
HISTORICAL AVIATION ALBUM
for
AMERICAN *Aircraft* MODELER
SCALE - ORIGINAL 1:24

DRAWING No. AM-48-A   PLATE 1 of 2   1/68

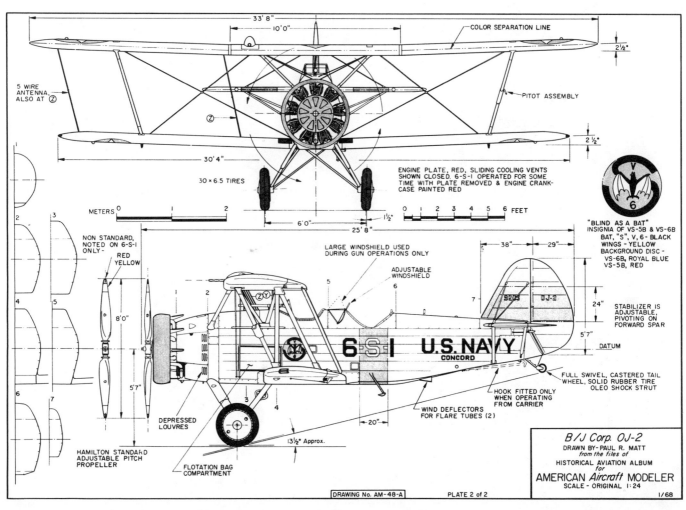

COLOR SEPARATION LINE
PITOT ASSEMBLY
5 WIRE ANTENNA, ALSO AT Ⓩ

33' 8"
10' 0"
2½°
2½°
30' 4"
30 × 6.5 TIRES

ENGINE PLATE, RED, SLIDING COOLING VENTS
SHOWN CLOSED, 6-S-I OPERATED FOR SOME
TIME WITH PLATE REMOVED & ENGINE CRANK-
CASE PAINTED RED

METERS
FEET
6' 0"
1½"
25' 8"

NON STANDARD,
NOTED ON 6-S-I
ONLY-
RED
YELLOW

LARGE WINDSHIELD USED
DURING GUN OPERATIONS ONLY
ADJUSTABLE WINDSHIELD

38"
29"
24"
5'7"
DATUM

"BLIND AS A BAT"
INSIGNIA OF VS-5B & VS-6B
BAT, "S", V, 6 - BLACK
WINGS - YELLOW
BACKGROUND DISC -
VS-6B, ROYAL BLUE
VS-5B, RED

STABILIZER IS
ADJUSTABLE,
PIVOTING ON
FORWARD SPAR

6-S-I U.S. NAVY
CONCORD

FULL SWIVEL, CASTERED TAIL
WHEEL, SOLID RUBBER TIRE
OLEO SHOCK STRUT

HOOK FITTED ONLY
WHEN OPERATING
FROM CARRIER

WIND DEFLECTORS
FOR FLARE TUBES (2)

20"
13½° Approx.
8' 0"
5'7"

HAMILTON STANDARD
ADJUSTABLE PITCH
PROPELLER

DEPRESSED
LOUVRES

FLOTATION BAG
COMPARTMENT

B/J Corp. OJ-2
DRAWN BY- PAUL R. MATT
from the files of
HISTORICAL AVIATION ALBUM
for
AMERICAN *Aircraft* MODELER
SCALE - ORIGINAL 1:24

DRAWING No. AM-48-A   PLATE 2 of 2   1/68

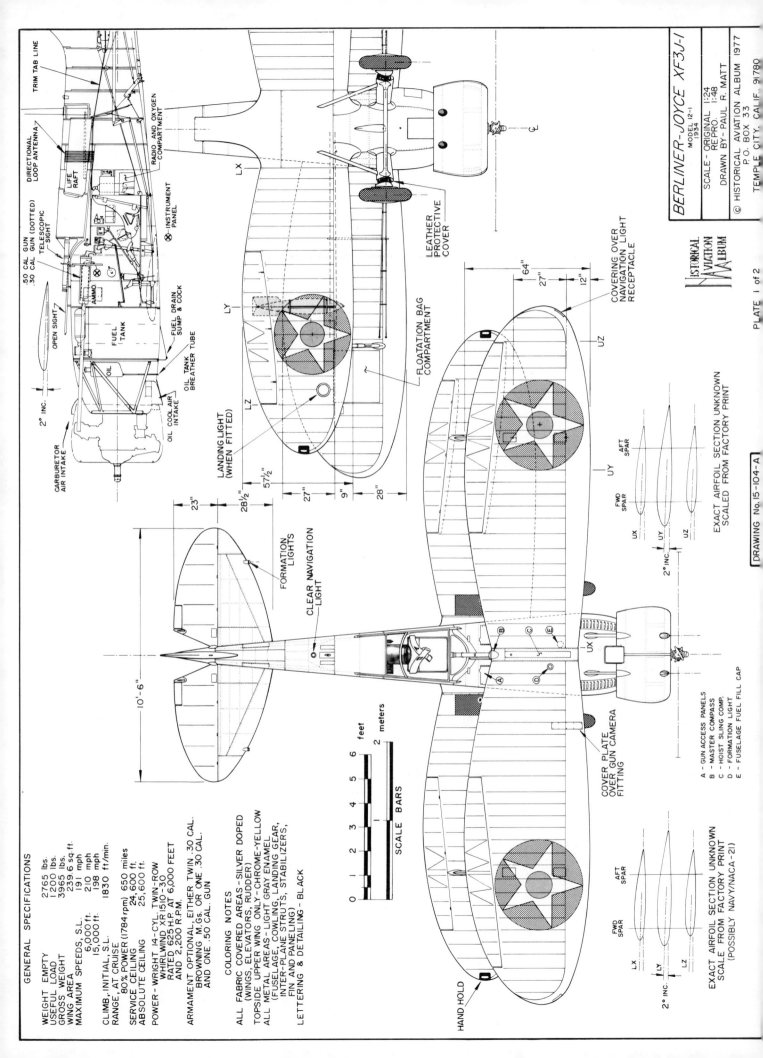

BERLINER-JOYCE XF3J-1

MODEL 12-1
1934

SCALE- ORIGINAL 1:24
REPRO. 1:48
DRAWN BY- PAUL R. MATT

© HISTORICAL AVIATION ALBUM 1977
P.O. BOX 33
TEMPLE CITY, CALIF. 91780

PLATE 1 of 2

DRAWING No. 15-104-A

GENERAL SPECIFICATIONS

WEIGHT EMPTY   2765 lbs.
USEFUL LOAD   1200 lbs.
GROSS WEIGHT   3965 lbs.
WING AREA   239.6 sq.ft.
MAXIMUM SPEEDS, S.L.   191 mph

CLIMB, INITIAL, S.L.   210 mph
  6,000 ft.   198 mph
 15,000 ft.   1830 ft/min.
RANGE, AT CRUISE (1784 rpm) 650 miles
  80% POWER

SERVICE CEILING   24,600 ft.
ABSOLUTE CEILING   25,600 ft.

POWER- WRIGHT 14-CYL. TWIN-ROW
  WHIRLWIND XR-1510-30
  RATED 625 H.P. AT 6,000 FEET
  AND 2,200 R.P.M.

ARMAMENT OPTIONAL, EITHER TWIN .30 CAL.
  BROWNING M.Gs. OR ONE .30 CAL.
  AND ONE .50 CAL. GUN

COLORING NOTES

ALL FABRIC COVERED AREAS- SILVER DOPED
  (WINGS, ELEVATORS, RUDDER)
TOPSIDE UPPER WING ONLY- CHROME-YELLOW
ALL METAL AREAS- LIGHT GRAY ENAMEL
  (FUSELAGE, COWLING, LANDING GEAR,
  INTER-PLANE STRUTS, STABILIZERS,
  FIN AND PANELING)
LETTERING & DETAILING- BLACK

SCALE BARS

EXACT AIRFOIL SECTION UNKNOWN
SCALE FROM FACTORY PRINT
(POSSIBLY NAVY/NACA-21)

EXACT AIRFOIL SECTION UNKNOWN
SCALED FROM FACTORY PRINT

A - GUN ACCESS PANELS
B - MASTER COMPASS
C - HOIST SLING COMP.
D - FORMATION LIGHT
E - FUSELAGE FUEL FILL CAP

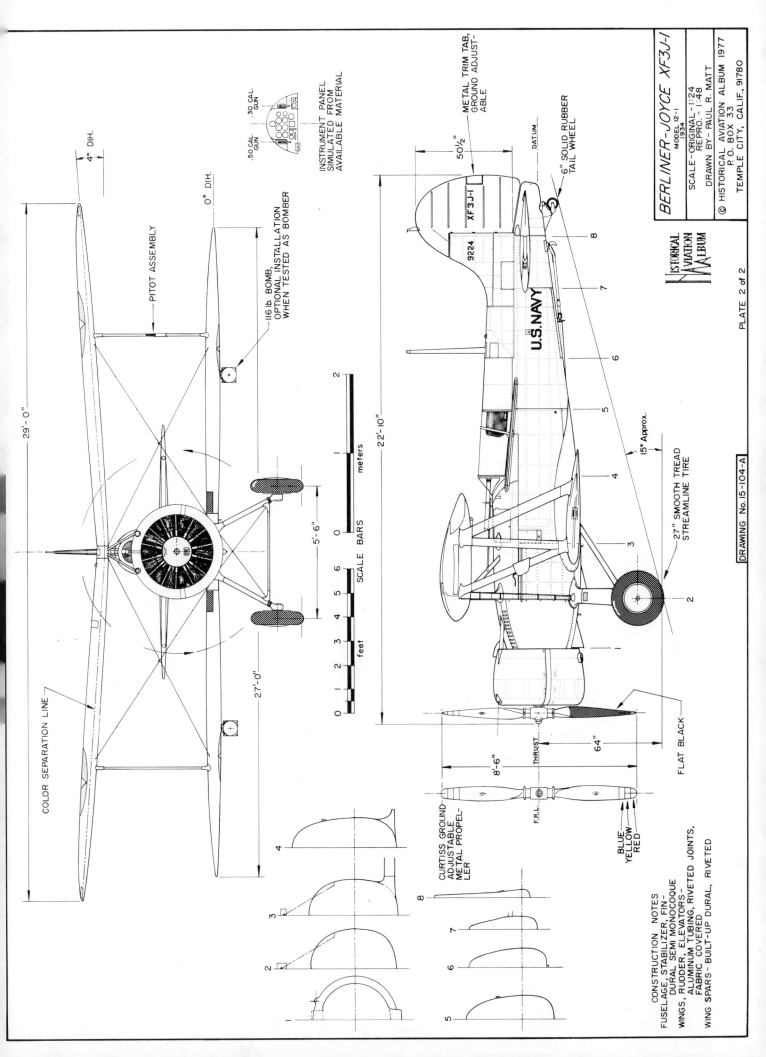

4° DIH.

0° DIH.

29'-0"

PITOT ASSEMBLY

COLOR SEPARATION LINE

116 lb. BOMB, OPTIONAL INSTALLATION WHEN TESTED AS BOMBER

INSTRUMENT PANEL SIMULATED FROM AVAILABLE MATERIAL

.30 CAL. GUN

.50 CAL. GUN

5'-6"

27'-0"

meters

SCALE BARS

feet

2

22'-10"

METAL TRIM TAB, GROUND ADJUST-ABLE

50½"

XF3J-1

9224

6" SOLID RUBBER TAIL WHEEL

DATUM

U.S.NAVY

15° Approx.

27" SMOOTH TREAD STREAMLINE TIRE

CURTISS GROUND ADJUSTABLE METAL PROPEL-LER

8'-6"

THRUST

64"

F.R.L.

BLUE
YELLOW
RED

FLAT BLACK

CONSTRUCTION NOTES
FUSELAGE, STABILIZER, FIN-
DURAL SEMI MONOCOQUE
WINGS, RUDDER, ELEVATORS-
ALUMINUM TUBING, RIVETED JOINTS,
FABRIC COVERED
WING SPARS- BUILT-UP DURAL, RIVETED

2   3   4   5   6   7   8

BERLINER-JOYCE XF3J-1
MODEL 12-1
1934
SCALE-ORIGINAL-1:24
REPRO.- 1:48
DRAWN BY-PAUL R. MATT

© HISTORICAL AVIATION ALBUM 1977
P.O. BOX 33
TEMPLE CITY, CALIF., 91780

Historical Aviation Album

PLATE 2 of 2

DRAWING No. 15-104-A

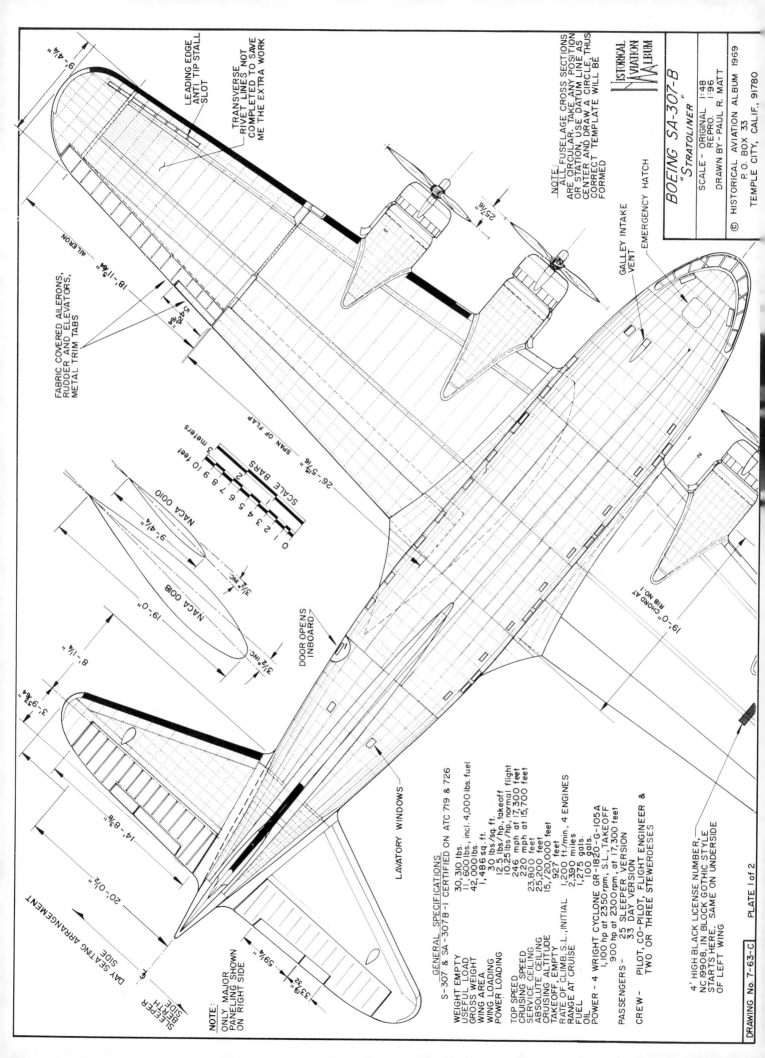

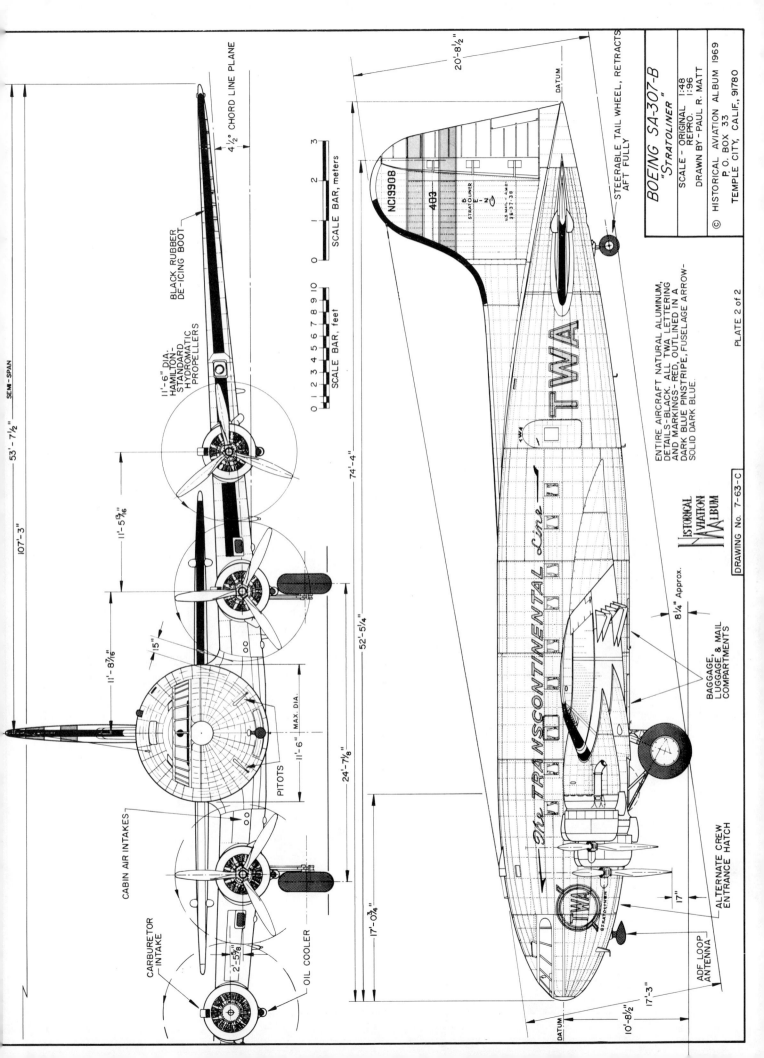

CHORD LINE PLANE

4½

BLACK RUBBER
DE-ICING BOOT

11'-6" DIA.
HAMILTON-
STANDARD
HYDROMATIC
PROPELLERS

SCALE BAR, meters

0 1 2 3

SCALE BAR, feet

0 1 2 3 4 5 6 7 8 9 10

53' - 7½" SEM-SPAN

107'-3"

11'-5¹³⁄₁₆"

11'- 8⁷⁄₁₆"

15"

PITOTS

CABIN AIR INTAKES

11'-6" MAX. DIA.

24'-7⅛"

CARBURETOR
INTAKE

2'-5⅝"

OIL COOLER

20'-8½"

STEERABLE TAIL WHEEL, RETRACTS
AFT FULLY

NC19908

403

B.
STRATOLINER

U.S MAIL- AMZ-
36-37-38

TWA

The TRANSCONTINENTAL Line

TWA

STRATOLINER

74'-4"

52'-5¼"

8¼" Approx.

BAGGAGE,
LUGGAGE & MAIL
COMPARTMENTS

17"

ALTERNATE CREW
ENTRANCE HATCH

ADF LOOP
ANTENNA

17'-0¾"

17'-3"

10'-8½"

DATUM

DATUM

BOEING SA-307-B
"STRATOLINER"

SCALE - ORIGINAL 1:48
REPRO. 1:96
DRAWN BY - PAUL R. MATT

© HISTORICAL AVIATION ALBUM 1969
P. O. BOX 33
TEMPLE CITY, CALIF, 91780

ENTIRE AIRCRAFT NATURAL ALUMINUM,
DETAILS-BLACK. ALL TWA LETTERING
AND MARKINGS- RED, OUTLINED IN A
DARK BLUE PINSTRIPE, FUSELAGE ARROW-
SOLID DARK BLUE.

HISTORICAL
AVIATION
ALBUM

PLATE 2 of 2

DRAWING No. 7-63-C

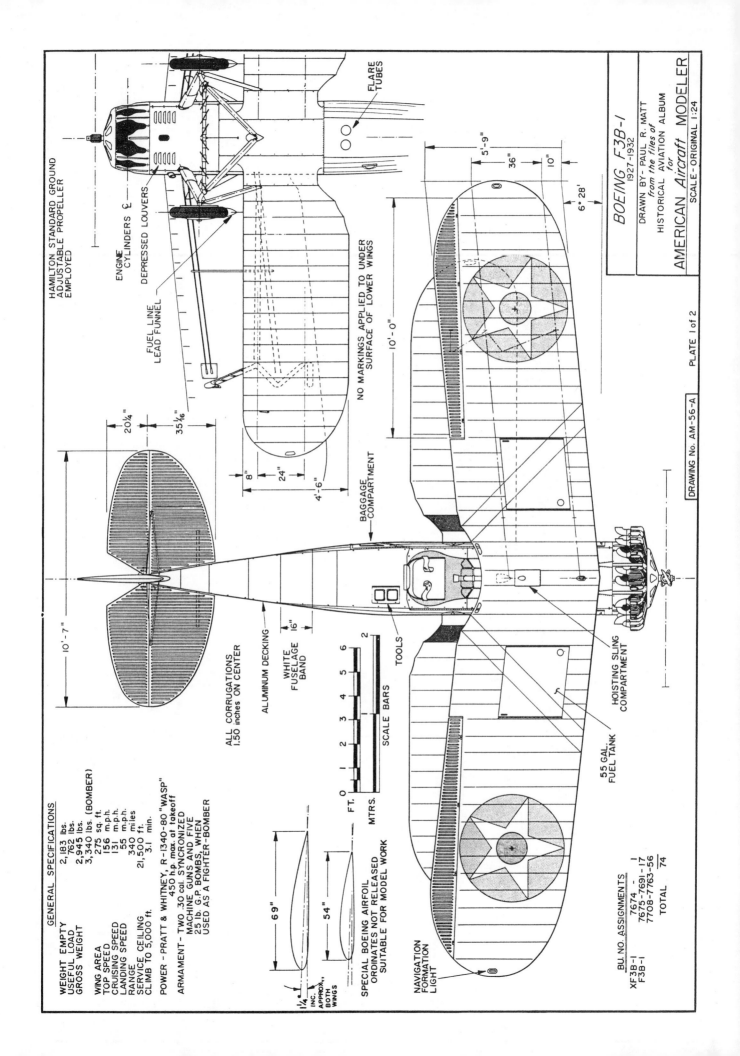

HAMILTON STANDARD GROUND
ADJUSTABLE PROPELLER
EMPLOYED

ENGINE
CYLINDERS &
DEPRESSED LOUVERS

FUEL LINE
LEAD FUNNEL

FLARE
TUBES

NO MARKINGS APPLIED TO UNDER
SURFACE OF LOWER WINGS

BAGGAGE
COMPARTMENT

ALL CORRUGATIONS
1.50 inches ON CENTER

ALUMINUM DECKING

WHITE
FUSELAGE
BAND

TOOLS

SCALE BARS

FT.
MTRS.

SPECIAL BOEING AIRFOIL
ORDINATES NOT RELEASED
SUITABLE FOR MODEL WORK

INC.
APPROX.,
BOTH
WINGS

69"

54"

1/4

HOISTING SLING
COMPARTMENT

55 GAL.
FUEL TANK

NAVIGATION
FORMATION
LIGHT

5'-9"
36"
10"
6° 28'

10'-0"

4'-6"
20¼"
35⅟₁₆
8"
24"
16"

10'-7"

GENERAL SPECIFICATIONS

WEIGHT EMPTY   2,183 lbs.
USEFUL LOAD   762 lbs.
GROSS WEIGHT   2,945 lbs.
                     3,340 lbs. (BOMBER)

WING AREA   275 sq. ft.
TOP SPEED   156 m.p.h.
CRUISING SPEED   131 m.p.h.
LANDING SPEED   55 m.p.h.
RANGE   340 miles
SERVICE CEILING   21,500 ft.
CLIMB TO 5,000 ft.   3.1 min.

POWER - PRATT & WHITNEY, R-1340-80 "WASP"
         450 h.p. max. at takeoff

ARMAMENT - TWO .30 cal. SYNCRONIZED
  MACHINE GUNS AND FIVE
  25 lb. G.P. BOMBS, WHEN
  USED AS A FIGHTER-BOMBER

BU. NO. ASSIGNMENTS
XF3B-1   7674 -   I
F3B-1   7675-7691-17
           7708-7763-56
           TOTAL   74

BOEING F3B-1
1927-1932
DRAWN BY - PAUL R. MATT
from the files of
HISTORICAL AVIATION ALBUM
for
AMERICAN Aircraft MODELER
SCALE - ORIGINAL 1:24

DRAWING No. AM-56-A   PLATE 1 of 2

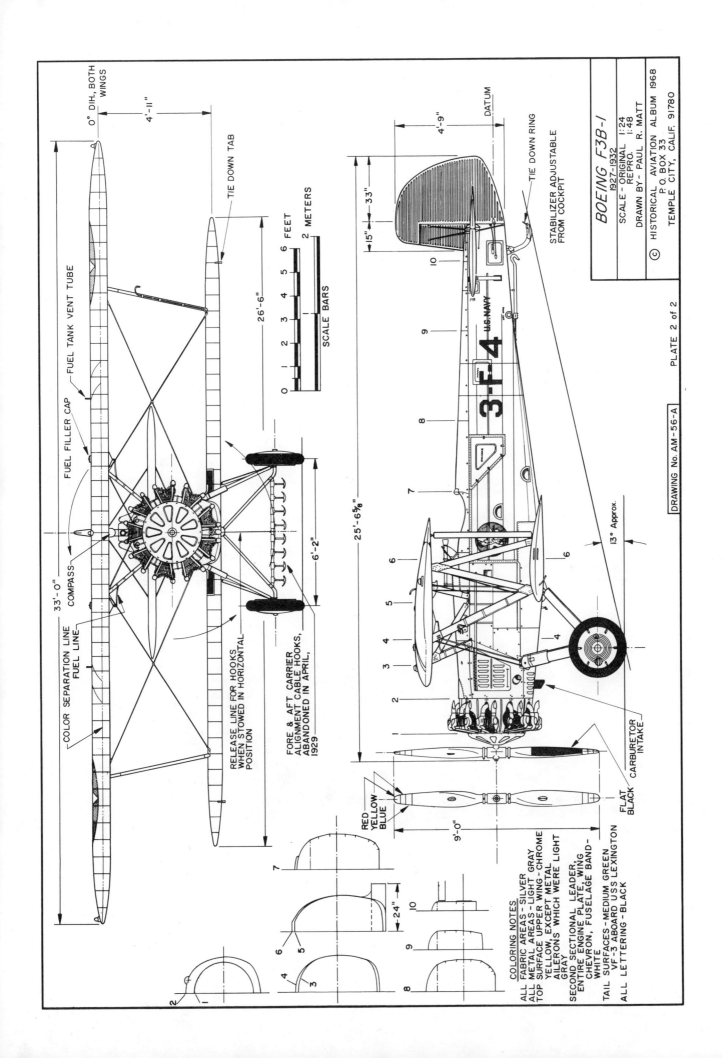

BOEING F3B-1
1927-1932
SCALE - ORIGINAL 1:24
REPRO. 1:48
DRAWN BY - PAUL R. MATT

© HISTORICAL AVIATION ALBUM 1968
P.O. BOX 33
TEMPLE CITY, CALIF. 91780

DRAWING No. AM-56-A   PLATE 2 of 2

0° DIH., BOTH WINGS

4'-11"

TIE DOWN TAB

FUEL TANK VENT TUBE

FUEL FILLER CAP

COMPASS

33'-0"

COLOR SEPARATION LINE
FUEL LINE

26'-6"

6'-2"

RELEASE LINE FOR HOOKS WHEN STOWED IN HORIZONTAL POSITION

FORE & AFT CARRIER ALIGNMENT CABLE HOOKS, ABANDONED IN APRIL, 1929

6 FEET
2 METERS
SCALE BARS

0 1 2 3 4 5 6

DATUM

4'-9"

33"

15"

10

STABILIZER ADJUSTABLE FROM COCKPIT

TIE DOWN RING

9

8

3-F-4

U.S.NAVY

7

6

6

5

4

4

3

2

13° Approx.

25'-6⅝"

CARBURETOR INTAKE

FLAT BLACK

RED
YELLOW
BLUE

9'-0"

24"

10

7

6
5

4
3

9

8

2
1

COLORING NOTES
ALL FABRIC AREAS - SILVER GRAY
ALL METAL AREAS - LIGHT GRAY
TOP SURFACE UPPER WING - CHROME YELLOW, EXCEPT METAL AILERONS WHICH WERE LIGHT GRAY

SECOND SECTIONAL LEADER, ENTIRE ENGINE PLATE, WING CHEVRON, FUSELAGE BAND - WHITE

TAIL SURFACES - MEDIUM GREEN VF-3 ABOARD USS LEXINGTON
ALL LETTERING - BLACK

Boeing XF7B-1

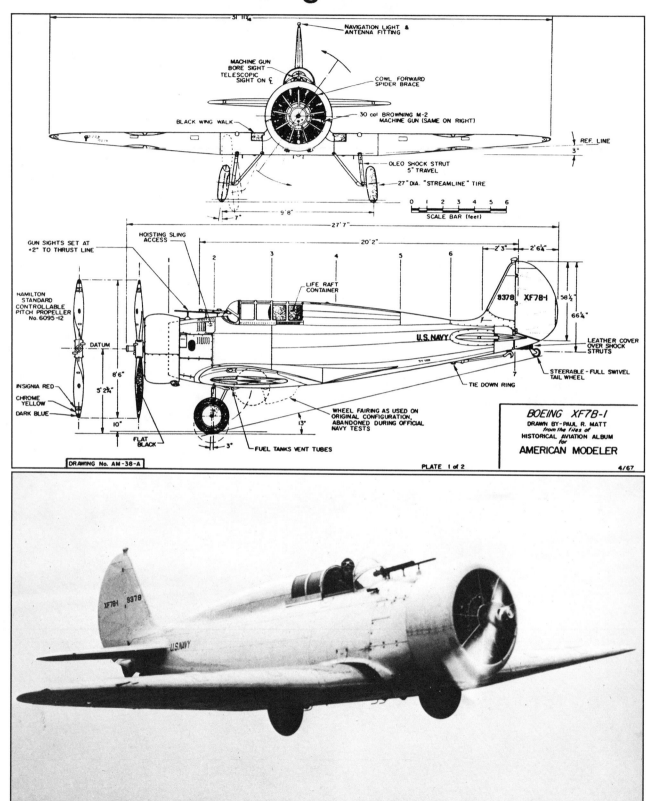

NAVIGATION LIGHT & ANTENNA FITTING

MACHINE GUN BORE SIGHT TELESCOPIC SIGHT ON ℄

COWL FORWARD SPIDER BRACE

BLACK WING WALK

30 cal BROWNING M-2 MACHINE GUN (SAME ON RIGHT)

REF. LINE
3"

OLEO SHOCK STRUT 5" TRAVEL

27" DIA. "STREAMLINE" TIRE

31' 11⅞"

9' 8"

7"

0 1 2 3 4 5 6
SCALE BAR (feet)

GUN SIGHTS SET AT +2° TO THRUST LINE

HOISTING SLING ACCESS

LIFE RAFT CONTAINER

HAMILTON STANDARD CONTROLLABLE PITCH PROPELLER No. 6095-12

DATUM

2   3   4   5   6

2' 3"   2' 6¼"

8378 XF7B-1

U.S.NAVY

58½"

66¼"

LEATHER COVER OVER SHOCK STRUTS

STEERABLE - FULL SWIVEL TAIL WHEEL

TIE DOWN RING

INSIGNIA RED

CHROME YELLOW

DARK BLUE

8' 6"

5' 2¾"

10"

FLAT BLACK

3"

FUEL TANKS VENT TUBES

13"

WHEEL FAIRING AS USED ON ORIGINAL CONFIGURATION, ABANDONED DURING OFFICIAL NAVY TESTS

27' 7"

20' 2"

BOEING XF7B-1
DRAWN BY-PAUL R. MATT
from the files of
HISTORICAL AVIATION ALBUM
for
AMERICAN MODELER

DRAWING No. AM-38-A

PLATE 1 of 2

4/67

XF7B-1 8378

U.S.NAVY

Boeing XF7B-1. Flight test at Anacostia in a revised configuration (January 9, 1934).

Boeing XF7B-1

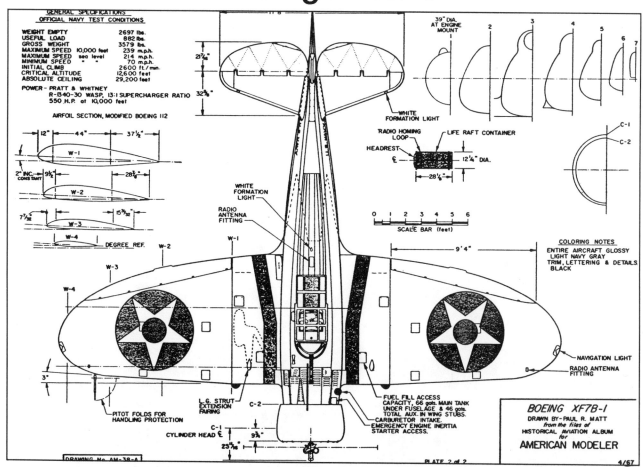

BOEING XF7B-1
DRAWN BY PAUL R. MATT
from the files of
HISTORICAL AVIATION ALBUM
for
AMERICAN MODELER

GENERAL SPECIFICATIONS
OFFICIAL NAVY TEST CONDITIONS

WEIGHT EMPTY	2697 lbs.
USEFUL LOAD	882 lbs.
GROSS WEIGHT	3579 lbs.
MAXIMUM SPEED 10,000 feet	239 m.p.h.
MAXIMUM SPEED sea level	214 m.p.h.
MINIMUM SPEED	70 m.p.h.
INITIAL CLIMB	2600 ft./min.
CRITICAL ALTITUDE	12,600 feet
ABSOLUTE CEILING	29,200 feet

POWER - PRATT & WHITNEY
R-1340-30 WASP, 13:1 SUPERCHARGER RATIO
550 H.P. at 10,000 feet

AIRFOIL SECTION, MODIFIED BOEING 112

WHITE FORMATION LIGHT

RADIO HOMING LOOP
HEADREST
LIFE RAFT CONTAINER
12¼" DIA.
28⅛"

WHITE FORMATION LIGHT
RADIO ANTENNA FITTING

39" DIA. AT ENGINE MOUNT

SCALE BAR (feet)

9'4"

COLORING NOTES
ENTIRE AIRCRAFT GLOSSY
LIGHT NAVY GRAY
TRIM, LETTERING & DETAILS
BLACK

NAVIGATION LIGHT
RADIO ANTENNA FITTING

DEGREE REF.

PITOT FOLDS FOR HANDLING PROTECTION

L.G. STRUT EXTENSION FAIRING
C-2

CYLINDER HEAD ₵
23¹³⁄₁₆"
9¾"
C-1

FUEL FILL ACCESS
CAPACITY, 66 gals. MAIN TANK
UNDER FUSELAGE & 46 gals.
TOTAL AUX. IN WING STUBS.
CARBURETOR INTAKE.
EMERGENCY ENGINE INERTIA
STARTER ACCESS.

DRAWING No. AM-38-A

PLATE 2 of 2

4/67

Original configuraton of a Boeing XF7B-1 on September 14, 1933.

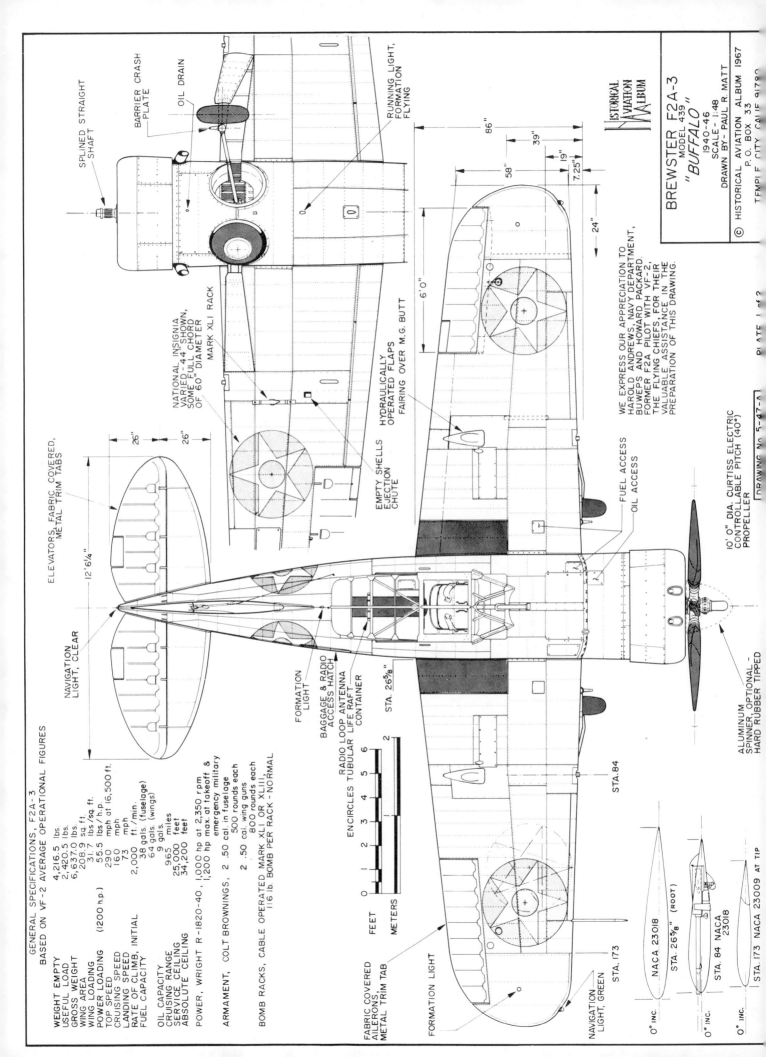

GENERAL SPECIFICATIONS, F2A-3
BASED ON VF-2 AVERAGE OPERATIONAL FIGURES

WEIGHT EMPTY   4,216.5 lbs.
USEFUL LOAD   2,420.5 lbs.
GROSS WEIGHT   6,637.0 lbs.
WING AREA   208.9 sq. ft.
WING LOADING   31.7 lbs./sq. ft.
POWER LOADING (1200 h.p.) 55.5 lbs./h.p.
TOP SPEED   290 mph at 16,500 ft.
CRUISING SPEED   160 mph
LANDING SPEED   73 mph
RATE OF CLIMB, INITIAL   2,000 ft./min.
FUEL CAPACITY   38 gals. (fuselage)
                            64 gals. (wings)
OIL CAPACITY   9 gals.
CRUISING RANGE   965 miles
SERVICE CEILING   25,000 feet
ABSOLUTE CEILING   34,200 feet

POWER, WRIGHT R-1820-40, 1,000 hp at 2,350 rpm
                         1,200 hp max. at takeoff &
                         emergency military

ARMAMENT, COLT BROWNINGS, 2 .50 cal. in fuselage
                            500 rounds each
                          2 .50 cal. wing guns
                            800 rounds each

BOMB RACKS, CABLE OPERATED MARK XLI OR XLIII,
            116 lb. BOMB PER RACK - NORMAL

ELEVATORS, FABRIC COVERED,
METAL TRIM TABS

NAVIGATION
LIGHT, CLEAR

SPLINED STRAIGHT
SHAFT

BARRIER CRASH
PLATE

OIL DRAIN

RUNNING LIGHT,
FORMATION
FLYING

NATIONAL INSIGNIA
VARIED - 44 SHOWN,
SOME FULL CHORD
OF 60" DIAMETER

MARK XLI RACK

HYDRAULICALLY
OPERATED FLAPS
FAIRING OVER M.G. BUTT

EMPTY SHELLS
EJECTION
CHUTE

FUEL ACCESS
OIL ACCESS

FORMATION
LIGHT

BAGGAGE & RADIO
ACCESS HATCH

RADIO LOOP ANTENNA
ENCIRCLES TUBULAR LIFE RAFT
CONTAINER

STA. 26 5/8"

STA.84

FABRIC COVERED
AILERONS,
METAL TRIM TAB

FORMATION LIGHT

NAVIGATION
LIGHT, GREEN

STA.173

26"   26"

12' 6 1/4"

86"

39"

19"

7.25"

58"

24"

6' 0"

FEET   0 1 2 3 4 5 6
METERS 0   1   2

10' 0" DIA. CURTISS ELECTRIC
CONTROLLABLE PITCH (40°)
PROPELLER

ALUMINUM
SPINNER OPTIONAL -
HARD RUBBER TIPPED

O° INC.   NACA 23018
STA. 26 5/8" (ROOT)

O° INC.   STA. 84 NACA
           23018

O° INC.   STA.173 NACA 23009 AT TIP

WE EXPRESS OUR APPRECIATION TO
HAROLD ANDREWS, NAVY DEPARTMENT,
BUWEPS AND HOWARD PACKARD,
FORMER F2A PILOT WITH VF-2,
THE FLYING CHIEFS, FOR THEIR
VALUABLE ASSISTANCE IN THE
PREPARATION OF THIS DRAWING.

BREWSTER F2A-3
MODEL 439
"BUFFALO"
1940-46
SCALE - 1:48
DRAWN BY - PAUL R. MATT

HISTORICAL AVIATION ALBUM 1967
P.O. BOX 33
TEMPLE CITY, CALIF. 91780

© HISTORICAL AVIATION ALBUM 1967

PLATE 1 of 2

DRAWING No. 5-47-A

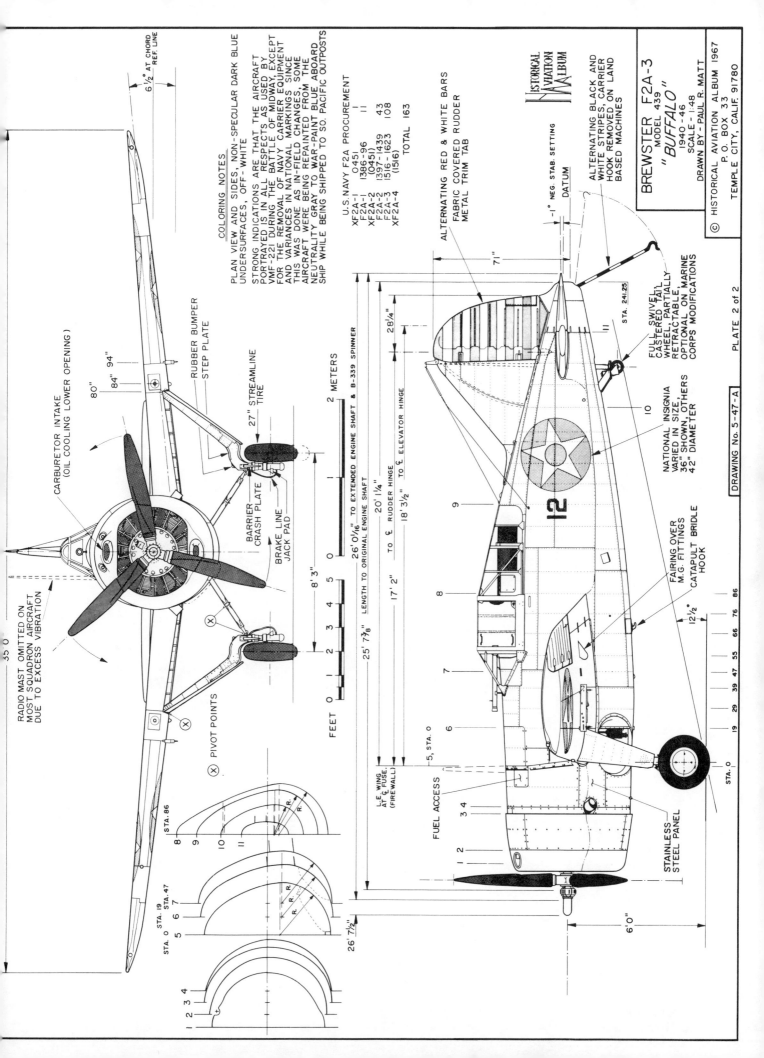

COLORING NOTES

PLAN VIEW AND SIDES, NON-SPECULAR DARK BLUE
UNDERSURFACES, OFF-WHITE

STRONG INDICATIONS ARE THAT THE AIRCRAFT
PORTRAYED IS IN ALL RESPECTS AS USED BY
VMF-221 DURING THE BATTLE OF MIDWAY, EXCEPT
FOR THE REMOVAL OF NAVY CARRIER EQUIPMENT
AND VARIANCES IN NATIONAL MARKINGS SINCE
THIS WAS DONE AS IN-FIELD CHANGES, SOME
AIRCRAFT WERE BEING REPAINTED FROM THE
NEUTRALITY GRAY TO WAR-PAINT BLUE ABOARD
SHIP WHILE BEING SHIPPED TO SO. PACIFIC OUTPOSTS

U.S. NAVY F2A PROCUREMENT

XF2A-1	0451	1
F2A-1	1386-96	11
XF2A-2	(0451)	
F2A-2	1397-1439	43
F2A-3	1516-1623	108
XF2A-4	(1516)	
	TOTAL	163

ALTERNATING RED & WHITE BARS

FABRIC COVERED RUDDER
METAL TRIM TAB

-1° NEG. STAB. SETTING

DATUM

ALTERNATING BLACK AND
WHITE STRIPES, CARRIER
HOOK REMOVED ON LAND
BASED MACHINES

FULL SWIVEL
CASTERED TAIL
WHEEL, PARTIALLY
RETRACTABLE,
OPTIONAL ON MARINE
CORPS MODIFICATIONS

STA. 241.25

NATIONAL INSIGNIA
VARIED IN SIZE,
36" SHOWN, OTHERS
42" DIAMETER

FAIRING OVER
M.G. FITTINGS

CATAPULT BRIDLE
HOOK

STAINLESS
STEEL PANEL

FUEL ACCESS

12½°

71"

28¼"

STA. 0

19 29 39 47 55 66 76 86

6'0"

BREWSTER F2A-3
MODEL 439
"BUFFALO"
1940-46
SCALE - 1:48
DRAWN BY - PAUL R. MATT

PLATE 2 of 2

DRAWING No. 5-47-A

CARBURETOR INTAKE
(OIL COOLING LOWER OPENING)

RADIO MAST OMITTED ON
MOST SQUADRON AIRCRAFT
DUE TO EXCESS VIBRATION

RUBBER BUMPER
STEP PLATE

80"

84" 94"

27" STREAMLINE
TIRE

BARRIER
CRASH PLATE

BRAKE LINE
JACK PAD

6½° AT CHORD
REF. LINE

35° 0'

⊗ PIVOT POINTS

26' 0⁵⁄₁₆" TO EXTENDED ENGINE SHAFT & B-339 SPINNER

25' 7⅞" LENGTH TO ORIGINAL ENGINE SHAFT

20' 1¼" TO ₵ RUDDER HINGE

17' 2" TO ₵ ELEVATOR HINGE

18' 3½"

8' 3"

26' 7½"

METERS

2

1

0

FEET

0 1 2 3 4 5

L.E. WING
AT ₵ FUSE.
(FIREWALL)

5, STA. 0

STA. 0   STA. 19   STA. 47   STA. 86

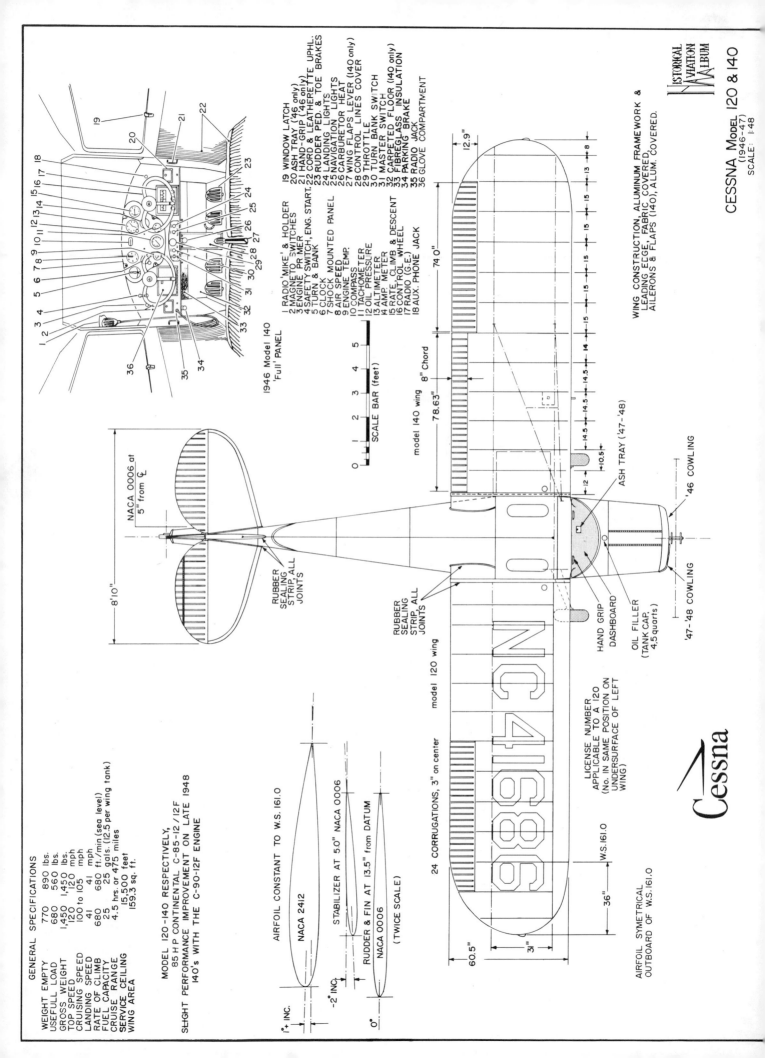

GENERAL SPECIFICATIONS

WEIGHT EMPTY	770	890 lbs.
USEFULL LOAD	680	560 lbs.
GROSS WEIGHT	1,450	1,450 lbs.
TOP SPEED	120	120 mph
CRUISING SPEED	100 to 105	mph
LANDING SPEED	41	41 mph
RATE OF CLIMB	680	680 ft./min (sea level)
FUEL CAPACITY	25	25 gals. (12.5 per wing tank)
CRUISE RANGE	4.5 hrs. or 475 miles	
SERVICE CEILING	15,500 feet	
WING AREA	159.3 sq. ft.	

MODEL 120-140 RESPECTIVELY,
85 H P CONTINENTAL C-85-12/12F

SLIGHT PERFORMANCE IMPROVEMENT ON LATE 1948
140's WITH THE C-90-12F ENGINE

AIRFOIL CONSTANT TO W.S. 161.0

NACA 2412

STABILIZER AT 5.0" NACA 0006

RUDDER & FIN AT 13.5" from DATUM

NACA 0006

(TWICE SCALE)

1° + INC.

-2° INC.

0°

NACA 0006 at
5" from ℄

8'10"

RUBBER SEALING STRIP ALL JOINTS

RUBBER SEALING STRIP ALL JOINTS

1946 Model 140
"Full" PANEL

1 RADIO 'MIKE' & HOLDER
2 MAGNETO SWITCHES
3 ENGINE PRIMER
4 SAFETY SWITCH, ENG. START.
5 TURN & BANK
6 CLOCK
7 SHOCK MOUNTED PANEL
8 AIR SPEED
9 ENGINE TEMP.
10 COMPASS
11 TACHOMETER
12 OIL PRESSURE
13 ALTIMETER
14 AMP. METER
15 RATE, CLIMB & DESCENT
16 CONTROL WHEEL
17 RADIO (G.E.)
18 AUX. PHONE JACK
19 WINDOW LATCH
20 ASH TRAY ('46 only)
21 HAND-GRIP ('46 only)
22 CORD & LEATHERETTE UPHL.
23 RUDDER PED. & TOE BRAKES
24 LANDING LIGHTS
25 NAVIGATION LIGHTS
26 CARBURETOR HEAT
27 WING FLAPS LEVER (140 only)
28 CONTROL LINES COVER
29 THROTTLE
30 TURN BANK SWITCH
31 MASTER SWITCH
32 CARPETED FLOOR (140 only)
33 FIBREGLASS INSULATION
34 PARKING BRAKE
35 RADIO JACK
36 GLOVE COMPARTMENT

SCALE BAR (feet)
0 1 2 3 4 5

WING CONSTRUCTION, ALUMINUM FRAMEWORK & LEADING EDGE, FABRIC COVERED, AILERONS & FLAPS (140), ALUM. COVERED.

12.9"

8
13
15
15
15
15
14
14.5
14.5
14.5

74.0"

8" Chord

model 140 wing

78.63"

+10.5"

12

ASH TRAY ('47-'48)

'46 COWLING

'47-'48 COWLING

HAND GRIP
DASHBOARD

OIL FILLER
(TANK CAP, 4.5 quarts)

RADIO JACK

PARKING BRAKE

NC 41689

24 CORRUGATIONS, 3" on center

model 120 wing

3" on center

LICENSE NUMBER
APPLICABLE TO A 120
(No. IN SAME POSITION ON
UNDERSURFACE OF LEFT
WING)

W.S. 161.0

36"

60.5"

3"

AIRFOIL SYMETRICAL
OUTBOARD OF W.S. 161.0

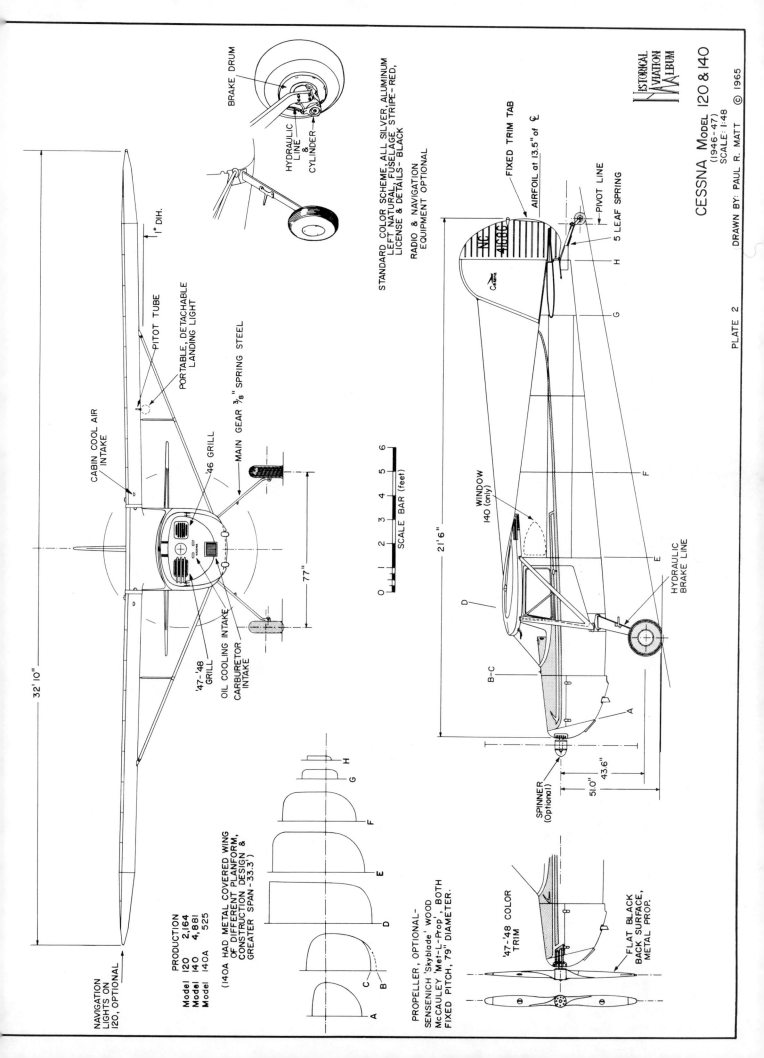

BRAKE DRUM

HYDRAULIC LINE & CYLINDER

STANDARD COLOR SCHEME, ALL SILVER, ALUMINUM LEFT NATURAL, FUSELAGE STRIPE- RED, LICENSE & DETAILS- BLACK

RADIO & NAVIGATION EQUIPMENT OPTIONAL

FIXED TRIM TAB

AIRFOIL at 13.5" of ℄

PIVOT LINE

5 LEAF SPRING

NC 41086

Cessna

1° DIH.

32' 10"

NAVIGATION LIGHTS ON 120, OPTIONAL

PITOT TUBE

CABIN COOL AIR INTAKE

PORTABLE, DETACHABLE LANDING LIGHT

46 GRILL

MAIN GEAR ⅜" SPRING STEEL

77"

'47-'48 GRILL

OIL COOLING INTAKE

CARBURETOR INTAKE

SCALE BAR (feet)
0 1 2 3 4 5 6

PRODUCTION

Model 120	2,164
Model 140	4,881
Model 140A	525

(140A HAD METAL COVERED WING OF DIFFERENT PLANFORM, CONSTRUCTION DESIGN & GREATER SPAN - 33.3')

PROPELLER, OPTIONAL-
SENSENICH 'Skyblade' WOOD
McCAULEY Met-L-Prop', BOTH
FIXED PITCH, 79" DIAMETER.

H G F E D C B A

WINDOW 140 (only)

21' 6"

D

B-C

A

F

E

H

G

HYDRAULIC BRAKE LINE

SPINNER (Optional)

51.0"

43.6"

'47-'48 COLOR TRIM

FLAT BLACK BACK SURFACE, METAL PROP.

CESSNA MODEL 120 & 140
(1946-47)
SCALE: 1:48

DRAWN BY: PAUL R. MATT   © 1965

Historical Aviation Album

PLATE 2

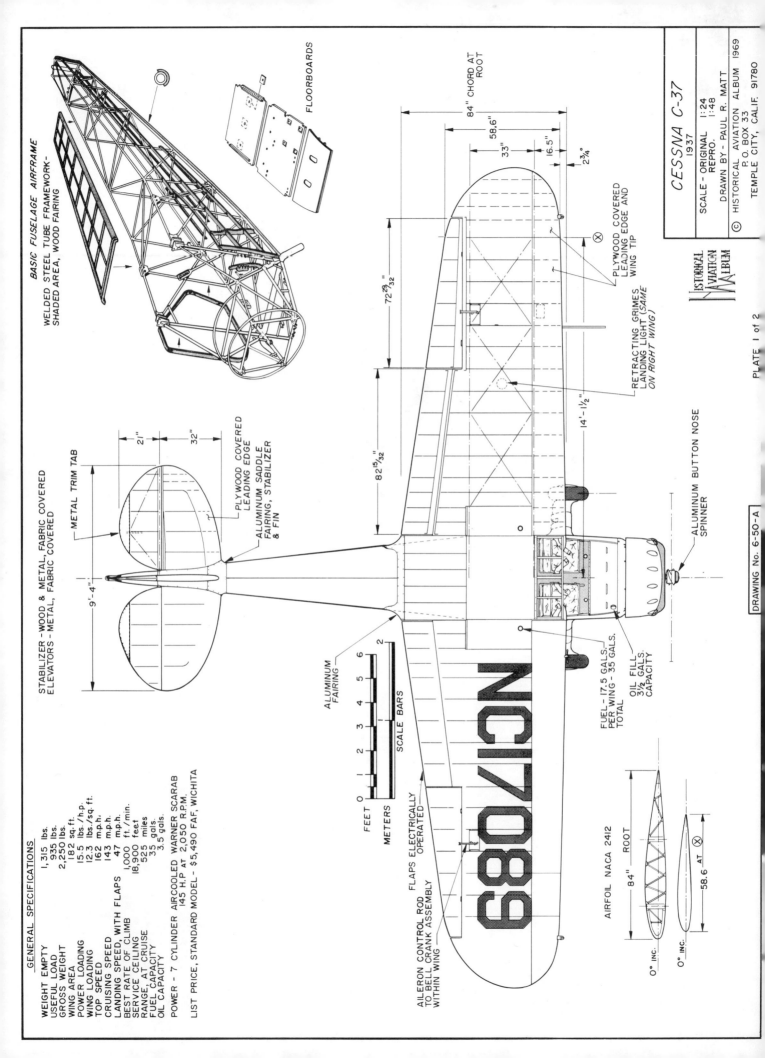

CESSNA C-37
1937

SCALE - ORIGINAL   1:24
REPRO.   1:48
DRAWN BY - PAUL R. MATT

© HISTORICAL AVIATION ALBUM 1969
P.O. BOX 33
TEMPLE CITY, CALIF. 91780

PLATE 1 of 2

DRAWING No. 6-50-A

BASIC FUSELAGE AIRFRAME

WELDED STEEL TUBE FRAMEWORK-
SHADED AREA, WOOD FAIRING

FLOORBOARDS

84" CHORD AT ROOT
58.6"
33"
16.5"
2 3/4°

PLYWOOD COVERED LEADING EDGE AND WING TIP

72 29/32"

RETRACTING GRIMES LANDING LIGHT (SAME ON RIGHT WING)

82 15/32"

14' - 1 1/2"

ALUMINUM BUTTON NOSE

ALUMINUM SPINNER

STABILIZER - WOOD & METAL, FABRIC COVERED
ELEVATORS - METAL, FABRIC COVERED

METAL TRIM TAB

21"
32"

PLYWOOD COVERED LEADING EDGE

ALUMINUM SADDLE FAIRING, STABILIZER & FIN

9' - 4"

ALUMINUM FAIRING

FUEL - 17.5 GALS. PER WING - 35 GALS. TOTAL

OIL FILL 3 1/2 GALS. CAPACITY

NC17089

GENERAL SPECIFICATIONS

WEIGHT EMPTY	1,315	lbs.
USEFUL LOAD	935	lbs.
GROSS WEIGHT	2,250	lbs.
WING AREA	182	sq.ft.
POWER LOADING	15.5	lbs./h.p.
WING LOADING	12.3	lbs./sq.ft.
TOP SPEED	162	m.p.h.
CRUISING SPEED	143	m.p.h.
LANDING SPEED, WITH FLAPS	47	m.p.h.
BEST RATE OF CLIMB	1,000	ft./min.
SERVICE CEILING	18,900	feet
RANGE, AT CRUISE	525	miles
FUEL CAPACITY	35	gals.
OIL CAPACITY	3.5	gals.

POWER - 7 CYLINDER AIRCOOLED WARNER SCARAB
145 H.P. AT 2,050 R.P.M.

LIST PRICE, STANDARD MODEL - $5,490 FAF, WICHITA

SCALE BARS

FEET 0 1 2 3 4 5 6
METERS 0 1 2

FLAPS ELECTRICALLY OPERATED

AILERON CONTROL ROD TO BELL CRANK ASSEMBLY WITHIN WING

AIRFOIL NACA 2412

84" ROOT
0° INC.

58.6
AT
0° INC.

HISTORICAL AVIATION ALBUM

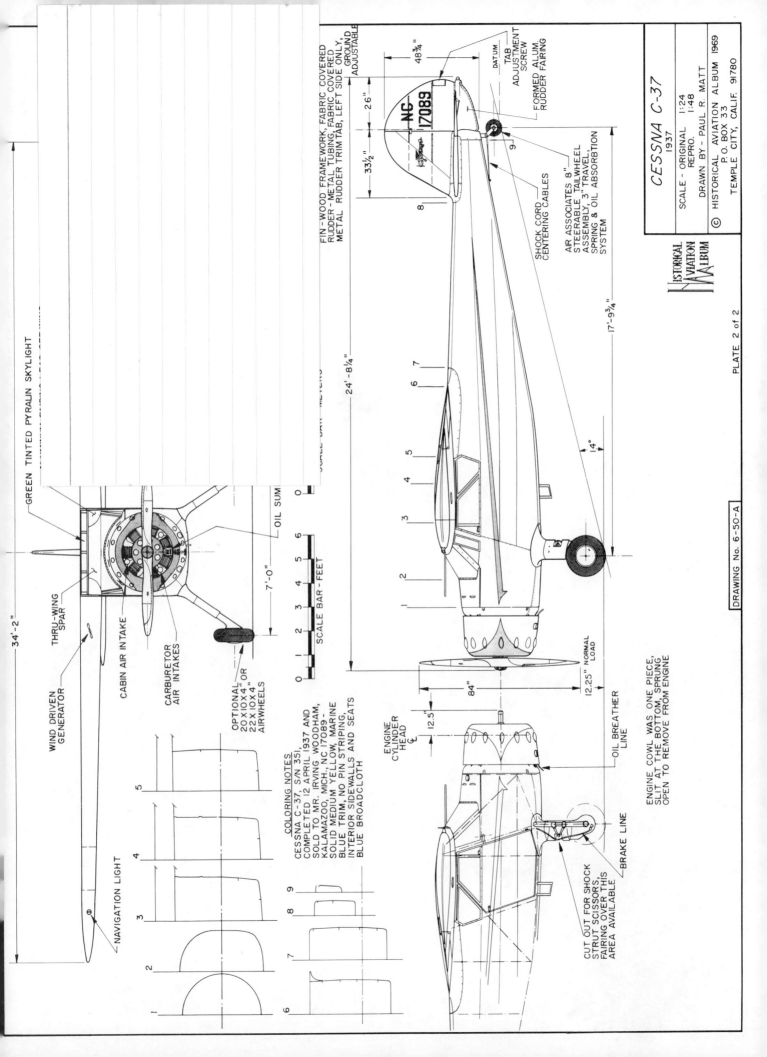

GREEN TINTED PYRALIN SKYLIGHT

THRU-WING SPAR

WIND DRIVEN GENERATOR

CABIN AIR INTAKE

CARBURETOR AIR INTAKES

NAVIGATION LIGHT

OPTIONAL 20 x 10 x 4" OR 22 x 10 x 4" AIRWHEELS

OIL SUMP

SCALE BAR - FEET

7'-0"

34'-2"

FIN - WOOD FRAMEWORK, FABRIC COVERED
RUDDER - METAL TUBING, FABRIC COVERED
METAL RUDDER TRIM TAB, LEFT SIDE ONLY,
GROUND ADJUSTABLE

48¾"

26"

33½"

NC 17089

DATUM

TAB ADJUSTMENT SCREW

FORMED ALUM. RUDDER FAIRING

SHOCK CORD CENTERING CABLES

AIR ASSOCIATES 8" STEERABLE TAILWHEEL ASSEMBLY, 3" TRAVEL, SPRING & OIL ABSORBTION SYSTEM

24'-8¼"

17'-9¾"

14°

84"

12.25" NORMAL LOAD

ENGINE CYLINDER HEAD

12.5"

OIL BREATHER LINE

BRAKE LINE

CUT OUT FOR SHOCK STRUT SCISSORS, FAIRING OVER THIS AREA AVAILABLE

ENGINE COWL WAS ONE PIECE, SLIT AT THE BOTTOM, SPRUNG OPEN TO REMOVE FROM ENGINE

COLORING NOTES

CESSNA C-37, S/N 351, COMPLETED 12 APRIL 1937 AND SOLD TO MR. IRVING WOODHAM, KALAMAZOO, MICH., NC 17089 - SOLID MEDIUM YELLOW, MARINE BLUE TRIM, NO PIN STRIPING, INTERIOR SIDEWALLS AND SEATS BLUE BROADCLOTH

CESSNA C-37
1937

SCALE - ORIGINAL 1:24
REPRO. 1:48

DRAWN BY - PAUL R. MATT

© HISTORICAL AVIATION ALBUM 1969
P.O. BOX 33
TEMPLE CITY, CALIF. 91780

HISTORICAL AVIATION ALBUM

PLATE 2 of 2

DRAWING No. 6-50-A

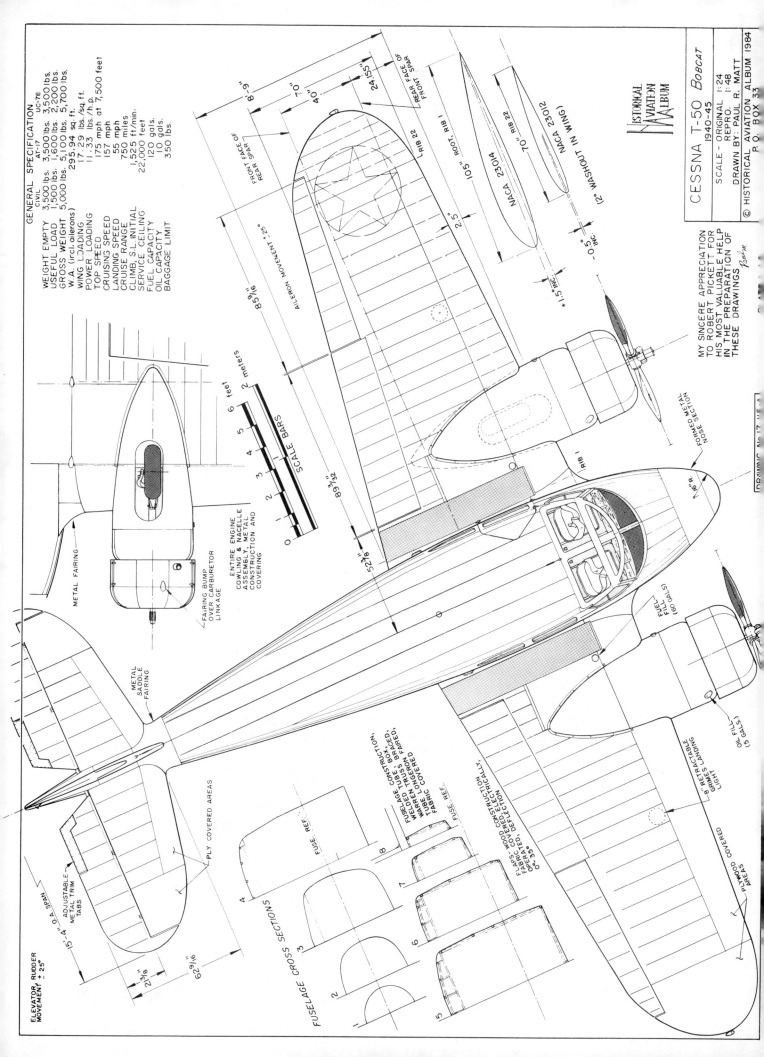

GENERAL SPECIFICATION

	CIVIL	AT-17	UC-78
WEIGHT EMPTY	3,500 lbs.		3,500 lbs.
USEFUL LOAD	1,500 lbs.		1,600 lbs.
GROSS WEIGHT	5,000 lbs.	5,100 lbs.	5,700 lbs.
W.A. (incl. ailerons)	295.94 sq. ft.		
WING LOADING	17.29 lbs./sq. ft.		
POWER LOADING	11.33 lbs./h.p.		
TOP SPEED	175 mph at 7,500 feet		
CRUISING SPEED	157 mph		
LANDING SPEED	55 mph		
CRUISE RANGE	750 miles		
CLIMB, S.L. INITIAL	1,525 ft/min.		
SERVICE CEILING	22,000 feet		
FUEL CAPACITY	120 gals.		
OIL CAPACITY	10 gals.		
BAGGAGE LIMIT	350 lbs.		

CESSNA T-50 *BOBCAT*
1940-45

SCALE - ORIGINAL 1:24
REPRO. 1:48
DRAWN BY: PAUL R. MATT

© HISTORICAL AVIATION ALBUM 1984
P.O. BOX 33

MY SINCERE APPRECIATION
TO ROBERT PICKETT FOR
HIS MOST VALUABLE HELP
IN THE PREPARATION OF
THESE DRAWINGS

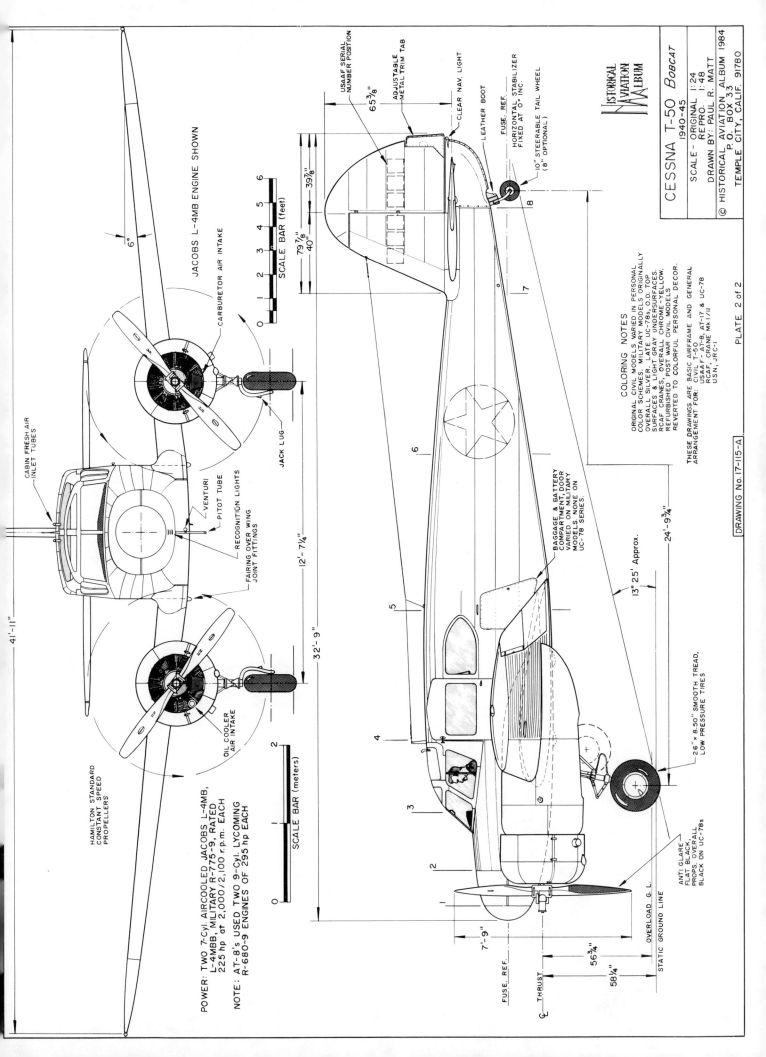

POWER: TWO 7-CYL. AIRCOOLED JACOBS L-4MB, L-4MBB, MILITARY R-775-9, RATED 225 hp at 2,000/2,100 r.p.m. EACH

NOTE: AT-8's USED TWO 9-CYL. LYCOMING R-680-9 ENGINES OF 295 hp EACH

JACOBS L-4MB ENGINE SHOWN

HAMILTON STANDARD CONSTANT SPEED PROPELLERS

CABIN FRESH AIR INLET TUBES

VENTURI
PITOT TUBE
RECOGNITION LIGHTS
FAIRING OVER WING JOINT FITTINGS

CARBURETOR AIR INTAKE
JACK LUG
OIL COOLER AIR INTAKE

6°

SCALE BAR (feet)

SCALE BAR (meters)

41'-11"

12'-7 1/4"

32'-9"

USAAF SERIAL NUMBER POSITION
ADJUSTABLE METAL TRIM TAB
CLEAR NAV. LIGHT
LEATHER BOOT
FUSE. REF.
HORIZONTAL STABILIZER FIXED AT 0° INC.
10" STEERABLE TAIL WHEEL (8" OPTIONAL)

65 3/8"
79 7/8"
39 7/8"
40"

13° 25' Approx.

24'-9 3/4"

BAGGAGE & BATTERY COMPARTMENT, DOOR VARIED ON MILITARY MODELS. NONE ON UC-78 SERIES.

26" x 8.50" SMOOTH TREAD, LOW PRESSURE TIRES

ANTI GLARE FLAT BLACK, PROPS, OVERALL BLACK ON UC-78s

OVERLOAD G.L.
STATIC GROUND LINE

FUSE. REF.
THRUST
7'-9"
56 1/4"
58 1/4"

CESSNA T-50 *Bobcat*
1940-45
SCALE - ORIGINAL 1:24
REPRO. 1:48
DRAWN BY: PAUL R. MATT
© HISTORICAL AVIATION ALBUM 1984
P.O. BOX 33
TEMPLE CITY, CALIF. 91780

COLORING NOTES

ORIGINAL CIVIL MODELS VARIED IN PERSONAL COLOR SCHEMES. MILITARY MODELS ORIGINALLY OVERALL SILVER. LATE UC-78s, O.D. TOP SURFACES & LIGHT GRAY UNDERSURFACES. RCAF CRANES, OVERALL CHROME-YELLOW. REFURBISHED POST WAR CIVIL MODELS REVERTED TO COLORFUL PERSONAL DECOR.

THESE DRAWINGS ARE BASIC AIRFRAME AND GENERAL ARRANGEMENT FOR: CIVIL T-50
USAAF - AT-8, AT-17 & UC-78
RCAF, CRANE MK I/II
USN, JRC-1

DRAWING No. 17-115-A

PLATE 2 of 2

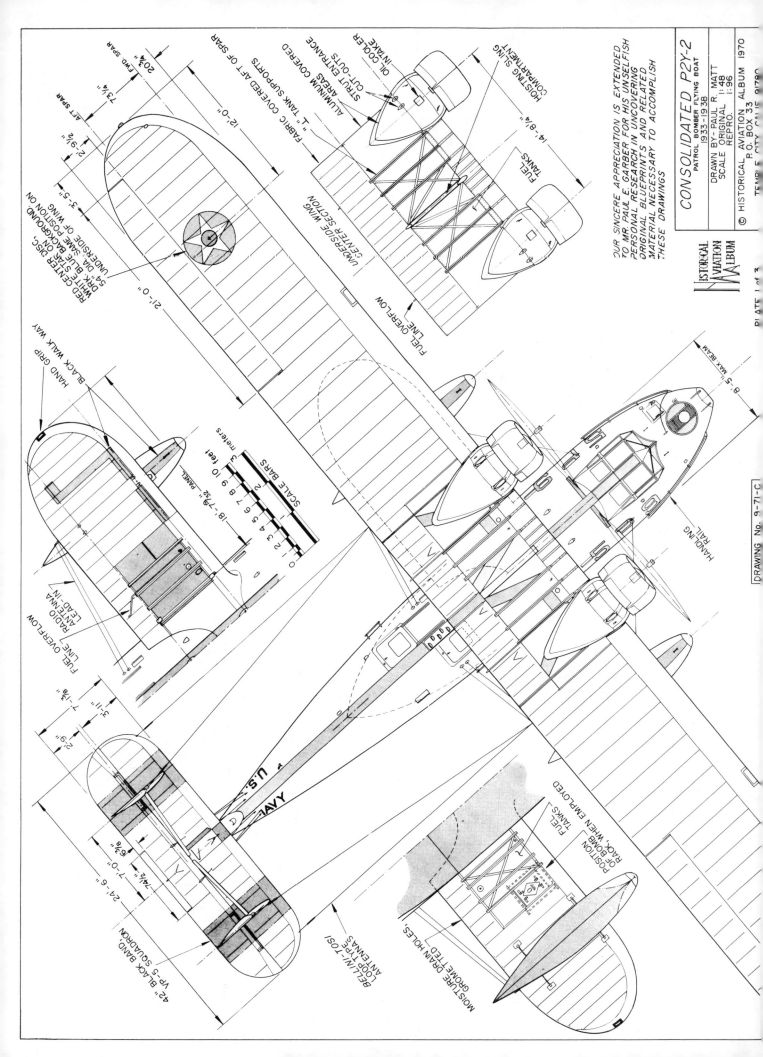

CONSOLIDATED P2Y-2
PATROL BOMBER FLYING BOAT
1933-1938

DRAWN BY- PAUL R. MATT
SCALE ORIGINAL 1:48
REPRO.   1:96

© HISTORICAL AVIATION ALBUM 1970

TEMPLE CITY, CALIF. 91780

OUR SINCERE APPRECIATION IS EXTENDED
TO MR. PAUL E. GARBER FOR HIS UNSELFISH
PERSONAL RESEARCH IN UNCOVERING
ORIGINAL BLUEPRINTS AND RELATED
MATERIAL NECESSARY TO ACCOMPLISH
THESE DRAWINGS

Historical Aviation Album

PLATE 1 of 3

DRAWING No. 9-71-C

SCALE BARS

0 1 2 3 4 5 6 7 8 9 10 feet
0 1 2 3 meters

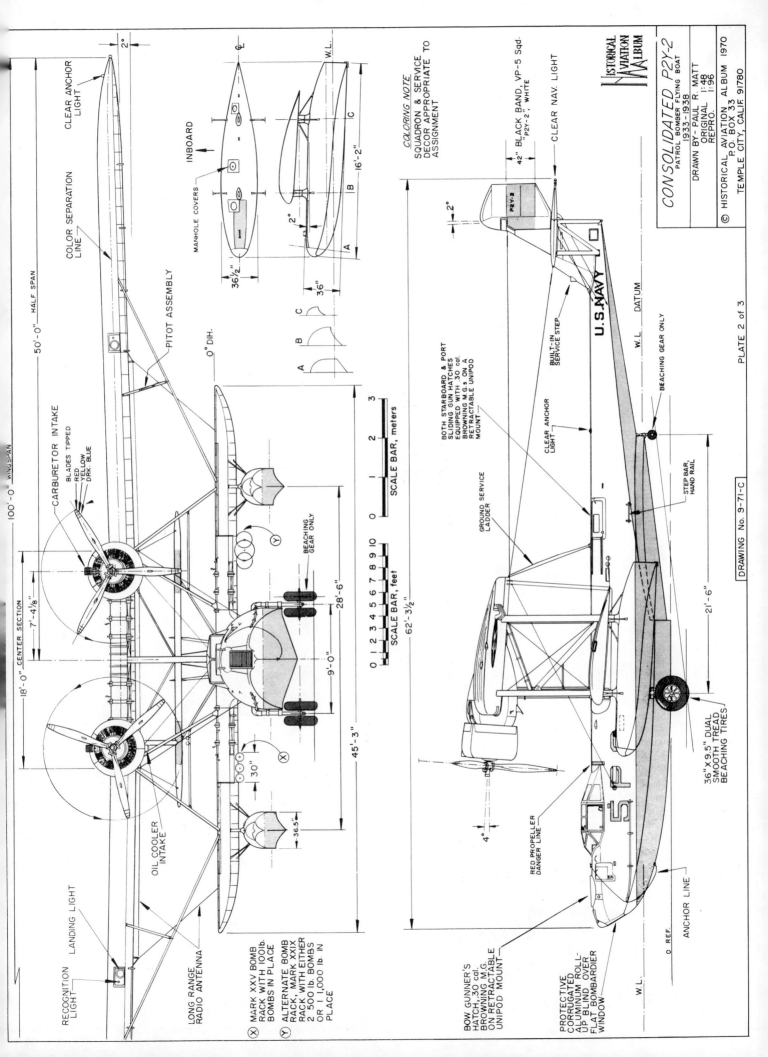

CONSOLIDATED P2Y-2
PATROL BOMBER FLYING BOAT
1933-1938
DRAWN BY- PAUL R. MATT
ORIGINAL 1:48
REPRO. 1:96

© HISTORICAL AVIATION ALBUM 1970
P.O. BOX 33
TEMPLE CITY, CALIF. 91780

PLATE 2 of 3

DRAWING No. 9-71-C

COLORING NOTE
SQUADRON & SERVICE
DECOR APPROPRIATE TO
ASSIGNMENT

CLEAR ANCHOR LIGHT

COLOR SEPARATION LINE

INBOARD

MANHOLE COVERS

PITOT ASSEMBLY

0° DIH.

CARBURETOR INTAKE

BLADES TIPPED
RED
YELLOW
DRK. BLUE

100'-0" WINGSPAN

50'-0" HALF SPAN

18'-0" CENTER SECTION

7'-4⅛"

OIL COOLER INTAKE

LANDING LIGHT

RECOGNITION LIGHT

LONG RANGE RADIO ANTENNA

X MARK XXV BOMB
RACK WITH 100 lb.
BOMBS IN PLACE

Y ALTERNATE BOMB
RACK, MARK XXIX
RACK WITH EITHER
2 500 lb. BOMBS
OR 1,000 lb. IN
PLACE

SCALE BAR, meters
0 1 2 3

SCALE BAR, feet
0 1 2 3 4 5 6 7 8 9 10

BEACHING GEAR ONLY

28'-6"

9'-0"

45'-3"

62'-3½"

30"

36.5"

A B C

36½"

2°

36"

16'-2"

W.L.

A B C

2°

2°

U.S. NAVY

P2Y-2

BUILT-IN SERVICE STEP

CLEAR ANCHOR LIGHT

CLEAR NAV. LIGHT

42" BLACK BAND, VP-5 Sqd.
P2Y-2, WHITE

W.L. DATUM

BEACHING GEAR ONLY

BOTH STARBOARD & PORT
SLIDING GUN HATCHES
EQUIPPED WITH .30 cal.
BROWNING M.G.s ON A
RETRACTABLE UNIPOD
MOUNT

GROUND SERVICE
LADDER

STEP BAR,
HAND RAIL

21'-6"

36"X 9.5" DUAL
SMOOTH TREAD
BEACHING TIRES

5 P

4°

RED PROPELLER
DANGER LINE

BOW GUNNER'S
HATCH, .30 cal.
BROWNING M.G.
ON RETRACTABLE
UNIPOD MOUNT

PROTECTIVE
CORRUGATED
ALUMINUM ROLL-
UP BLIND OVER
FLAT BOMBARDIER
WINDOW

ANCHOR LINE

0 REF.

W.L.

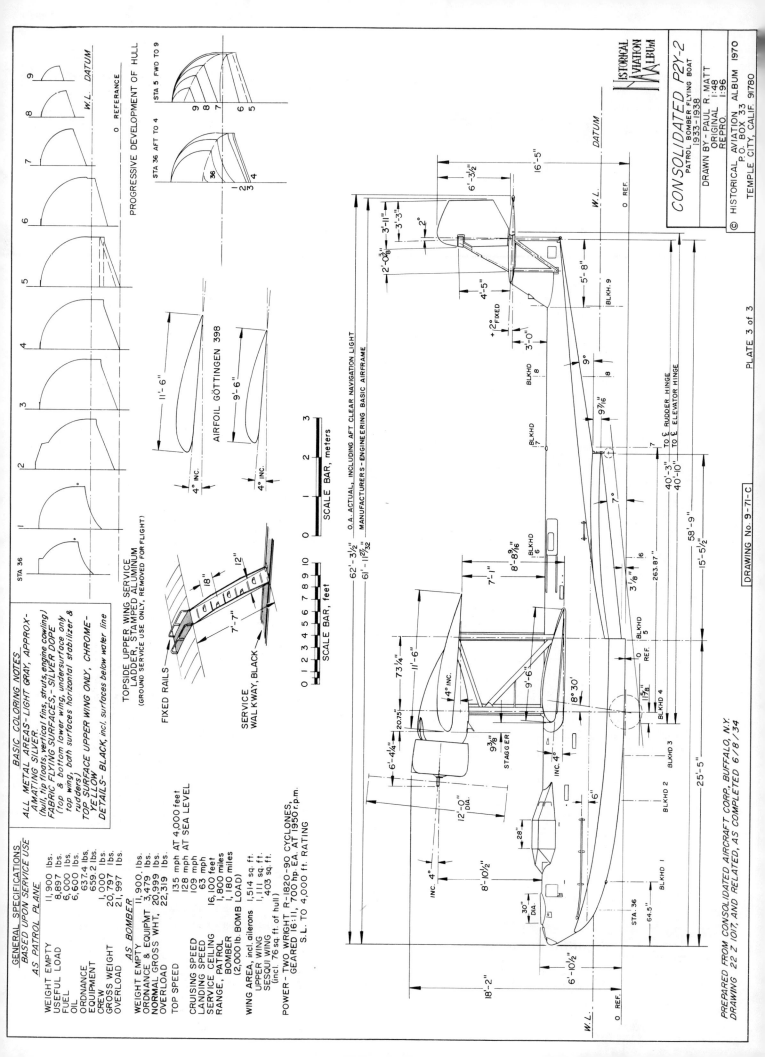

CONSOLIDATED P2Y-2
PATROL BOMBER FLYING BOAT
1933-1938

DRAWN BY - PAUL R. MATT
ORIGINAL 1:48
REPRO. 1:96

© HISTORICAL AVIATION ALBUM 1970
P.O. BOX 33
TEMPLE CITY, CALIF. 91780

PLATE 3 of 3

DRAWING No. 9-71-C

PREPARED FROM CONSOLIDATED AIRCRAFT CORP., BUFFALO, N.Y.
DRAWING 22 Z 1017, AND RELATED, AS COMPLETED 6/8/34

GENERAL SPECIFICATIONS
BASED UPON SERVICE USE

AS PATROL PLANE

WEIGHT EMPTY	11,900 lbs.
USEFUL LOAD	8,897 lbs.
FUEL	6,000 lbs.
OIL	6,600 lbs.
ORDNANCE	637.4 lbs.
EQUIPMENT	659.2 lbs.
CREW	1,000 lbs.
GROSS WEIGHT	20,797 lbs.
OVERLOAD	21,997 lbs.

AS BOMBER

WEIGHT EMPTY	11,900 lbs.
ORDNANCE & EQUIPMT	3,479 lbs.
NORMAL GROSS WHT,	20,999 lbs.
OVERLOAD	22,319 lbs.

TOP SPEED	135 mph AT 4,000 feet
	128 mph AT SEA LEVEL
CRUISING SPEED	109 mph
LANDING SPEED	63 mph
SERVICE CEILING	16,100 feet
RANGE, PATROL	1,800 miles
BOMBER	1,180 miles
(2,000 lb. BOMB LOAD)	

WING AREA, incl. ailerons 1,514 sq. ft.
UPPER WING 1,111 sq. ft.
SESQUI WING 403 sq. ft.
(incl. 76 sq. ft. of hull)

POWER - TWO WRIGHT R-1820-90 CYCLONES,
GEARED 16:11, 700 hp. EA. AT 1950 r.p.m.
S.L. TO 4,000 ft. RATING

BASIC COLORING NOTES

ALL METAL AREAS - LIGHT GRAY, APPROX-
AMATING SILVER.
(hull, tip floats, vertical fins, struts, engine cowling)
FABRIC FLYING SURFACES, - SILVER DOPE
(top & bottom lower wing, undersurface only
top wing, both surfaces horizontal stabilizer &
rudders)
TOP SURFACE UPPER WING ONLY, CHROME -
YELLOW
DETAILS - BLACK, incl. surfaces below water line

TOPSIDE UPPER WING SERVICE
LADDER, STAMPED ALUMINUM
(GROUND SERVICE USE ONLY, REMOVED FOR FLIGHT)

FIXED RAILS

SERVICE
WALKWAY, BLACK

AIRFOIL GÖTTINGEN 398

PROGRESSIVE DEVELOPMENT OF HULL

Consolidated PBY-5

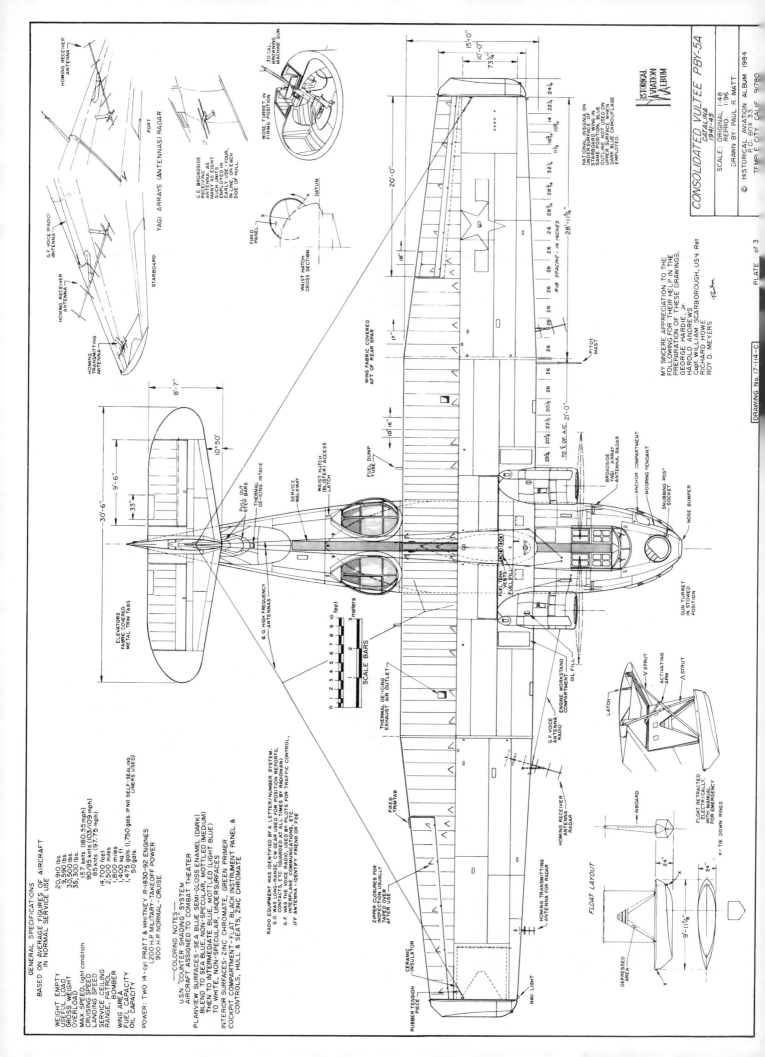

CONSOLIDATED VULTEE PBY-5A
CATALINA
1941-45

SCALE: ORIGINAL 1:48
REPRO. 1:96

DRAWN BY: PAUL R. MATT

© HISTORICAL AVIATION ALBUM 1984
P.O. BOX 33
TEMPLE CITY CALIF. 91780

PLATE 1 of 3

DRAWING No. 17-1114-C

MY SINCERE APPRECIATION TO THE FOLLOWING FOR THEIR HELP IN THE PREPARATION OF THESE DRAWINGS.
GEORGE HARDIE, Jr.
HAROLD ANDREWS
Capt. WILLIAM SCARBOROUGH, USN Ret.
RICHARD HOWE
ROY D. MEYERS

GENERAL SPECIFICATIONS
BASED ON AVERAGE FIGURES OF AIRCRAFT IN NORMAL SERVICE USE

WEIGHT EMPTY . . . . 20,910 lbs.
USEFUL LOAD . . . . 9,590 lbs.
GROSS WEIGHT . . . . 30,500 lbs.
OVERLOAD . . . . 35,300 lbs.
MAX. SPEED, light condition . . 157 knts (180.55mph)
CRUISING SPEED . . . 90/95 knts (103/109 mph)
LANDING SPEED . . . . . 85 knts (97.75 mph)
SERVICE CEILING . . . . 14,700 feet
RANGE, PATROL . . . . 2,500 miles
BOMBER . . . . 1,800 miles
WING AREA . . . . 1,400 sq.ft.
FUEL CAPACITY . . 1,475 gals.(1,750 gals. IF NO SELF-SEALING LINERS USED)
OIL CAPACITY . . . . 50 gals.

POWER: TWO 14-cyl. PRATT & WHITNEY R-1830-92 ENGINES
1,200 H.P. MILITARY-TAKEOFF POWER
900 H.P. NORMAL-CRUISE

—— COLORING NOTES——

U.S.N. "COUNTER SHADING" SYSTEM
AIRCRAFT ASSIGNED TO COMBAT THEATER

PLANVIEW SURFACES'S SEA BLUE SEMI-GLOSS ENAMEL (DARK) BLEND TO SEA BLUE, NON-SPECULAR, MOTTLED (MEDIUM) THEN TO INTERMEDIATE BLUE, MOTTLED (LIGHT BLUE) TO WHITE, NON-SPECULAR, UNDERSURFACES

INTERIOR SURFACES-ZINC CHROMATE, GREEN PRIMER COCKPIT COMPARTMENT-FLAT BLACK INSTRUMENT PANEL & CONTROLS, HULL & SEATS, ZINC CHROMATE

RADIO EQUIPMENT WAS IDENTIFIED BY A LETTER/NUMBER SYSTEM.
G.O. WAS LONG-RANGE, CW GEAR USED FOR POSITION REPORTS, G.O. CONTACTS, ETC. GUARDED AT ALL TIMES BY RADIOMAN.
G.F. WAS THE VOICE RADIO, USED BY PILOTS FOR TRAFFIC CONTROL, INTERPLANE COMMUNICATIONS, ETC.
IFF ANTENNA—IDENTIFY FRIEND OR FOE

HOMING RECEIVER ANTENNA

PORT

G.F. VOICE (RADIO) ANTENNA

STARBOARD

HOMING RECEIVER ANTENNA

HOMING TRANSMITTING ANTENNA

YAGI ARRAYS (ANTENNAS) RADAR

30 CAL. BROWNING MACHINE GUN

NOSE TURRET IN FIRING POSITION

G.E. BROADSIDE RECEIVING ANTENNA. AS MANY AS EIGHT SUCH UNITS EMPLOYED IN EARLY USE—FOUR, IN LINE, ON EACH SIDE OF HULL.

FIXED PANEL

DATUM

WAIST HATCH CROSS SECTION

NATIONAL INSIGNIA ON UNDER SURFACE OF STARBOARD WING IN SAME POSITION, BLUE OUTLINE NOT USED ON UPPER SURFACE WHEN DARK BLUE CAMOUFLAGE EMPLOYED.

15'-0"
10'-0"
73¾"
24½
22½
22½
14
16⅞¼
10¾
11⅛
32½
28⅝
28⅝
28½
26
RIB SPACING - IN INCHES
28'-11¾"
26
26
26
17"
26
26
26
PITOT MAST
20'-0"

WING, FABRIC COVERED AFT OF REAR SPAR

18"
10" 16"
23½
20½
22½
20½
TO ℄ OF A/C 21'-0"

BROADSIDE YAGI ARRAY ANTENNA, RADAR
ANCHOR COMPARTMENT
MOORING PENDANT
SNUBBING POST SOCKET
NOSE BUMPER
GUN TURRET IN STOWED POSITION

8'-7"

10° 50'

9'-6"

33"

30'-6"

ELEVATORS FABRIC COVERED METAL TRIM TABS

PULL OUT STEP BARS
THERMAL DE-ICING INTAKE
SERVICE WALKWAY
WAIST HATCH (BLISTER) ACCESS LATCH
FUEL DUMP TUBE

G.O. HIGH FREQUENCY ANTENNAS

BOMB (1,000#)
FUEL TANK VENTS FUEL FILL
ENGINE WORKSTAND COMPARTMENT
OIL FILL

0 1 2 3 4 5 6 7 8 9 10 feet
0 1 2 3 meters
SCALE BARS

THERMAL DE-ICING EXHAUST AIR OUTLET

FIXED TRIMTAB

G.F. VOICE ANTENNA RADIO

HOMING RECEIVER ANTENNA RADAR

HOMING TRANSMITTING ANTENNA FOR RADAR

ZIPPER CLOSURES FOR INSPECTION USUALLY TAPED AFTER USE

CERAMIC INSULATOR

RUBBER TENSION PIECE

NAV. LIGHT

FLOAT LAYOUT

LATCH
V STRUT
ACTIVATING ARM
A STRUT

FLOAT RETRACTED ELECTRICALLY, WITH MANUAL FOR EMERGENCY

INBOARD

24"
24"
9'-11⅞"

DEPRESSED AREA

X= TIE DOWN RINGS

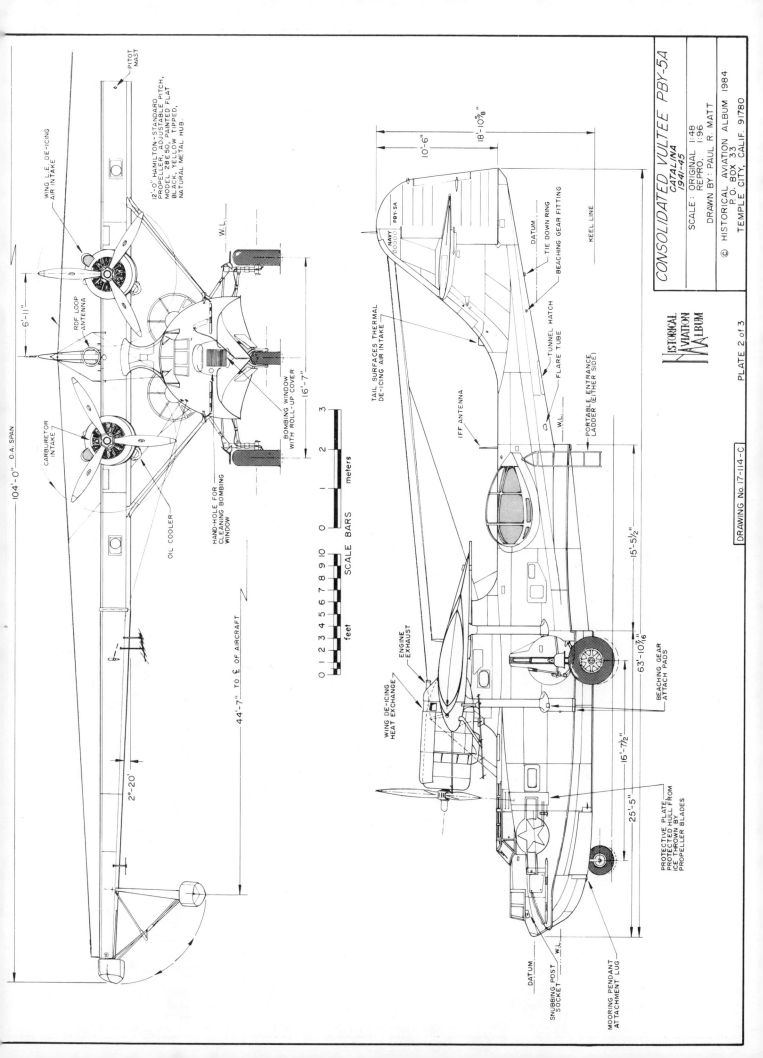

PITOT MAST

WING L.E. DE-ICING AIR INTAKE

12'-0" HAMILTON-STANDARD PROPELLER, ADJUSTABLE PITCH, MODEL 28E50, PAINTED FLAT BLACK, YELLOW TIPPED, NATURAL METAL HUB.

RDF LOOP ANTENNA

CARBURETOR INTAKE

OIL COOLER

BOMBING WINDOW WITH ROLL-UP COVER

HAND-HOLE FOR CLEANING BOMBING WINDOW

6'-11"

16'-7"

104'-0" O.A. SPAN

44'-7" TO ₵ OF AIRCRAFT

2°-20'

W.L.

0 1 2 3 meters
SCALE BARS
0 1 2 3 4 5 6 7 8 9 10 feet

TAIL SURFACES THERMAL DE-ICING AIR INTAKE

18'-10⅝"

10'-6"

PBY-5A

NAVY
000000

DATUM

TIE DOWN RING

BEACHING GEAR FITTING

KEEL LINE

TUNNEL HATCH

FLARE TUBE

W.L.

PORTABLE ENTRANCE LADDER (EITHER SIDE)

IFF ANTENNA

ENGINE EXHAUST

WING DE-ICING HEAT EXCHANGE

PROTECTIVE PLATE, PROTECTED HULL FROM ICE THROWN BY PROPELLER BLADES

DATUM

SNUBBING POST SOCKET

MOORING PENDANT ATTACHMENT LUG

W.L.

25'-5"

16'-7½"

63'-10⁷⁄₁₆"

BEACHING GEAR ATTACH PADS

15'-5½"

CONSOLIDATED VULTEE PBY-5A
CATALINA
1941-45

SCALE: ORIGINAL 1:48
REPRO. 1:96
DRAWN BY: PAUL R. MATT

© HISTORICAL AVIATION ALBUM 1984
P.O. BOX 33
TEMPLE CITY, CALIF. 91780

HISTORICAL AVIATION ALBUM

PLATE 2 of 3

DRAWING No. 17-1114-C

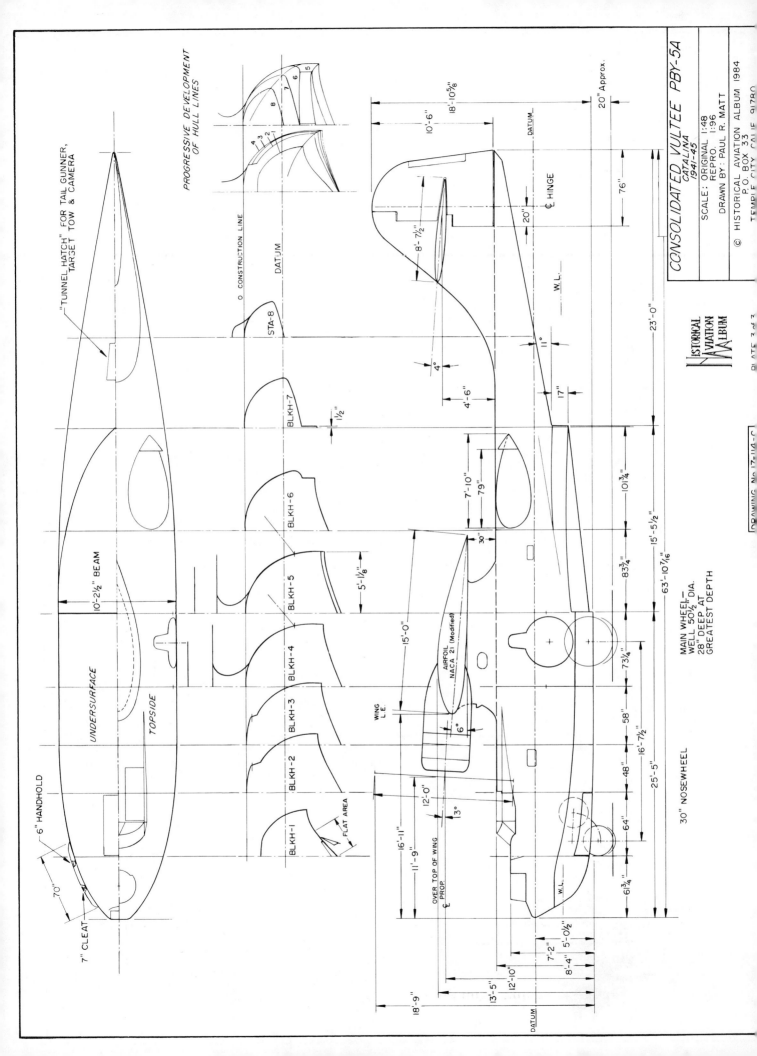

PROGRESSIVE DEVELOPMENT
OF HULL LINES

CONSOLIDATED VULTEE PBY-5A
CATALINA
1941-45

SCALE: ORIGINAL 1:48
REPRO. 1:96
DRAWN BY: PAUL R. MATT

© HISTORICAL AVIATION ALBUM 1984
P.O. BOX 33
TEMPLE CITY, CALIF. 91780

"TUNNEL HATCH" FOR TAIL GUNNER,
TARGET TOW & CAMERA

6" HANDHOLD

7" CLEAT

70"

UNDERSURFACE

TOPSIDE

10'-2½" BEAM

O CONSTRUCTION LINE

DATUM

STA-8

BLKH-7

BLKH-6

BLKH-5

BLKH-4

BLKH-3

BLKH-2

BLKH-1

FLAT AREA

1½"

5'-1⅛"

WING
L.E.

AIRFOIL
NACA 21 (Modified)

15'-0"

MAIN WHEEL—
WELL 50½" DIA.
28" DEEP AT
GREATEST DEPTH

30" NOSEWHEEL

18'-9"

16'-11"

11'-9"

12'-0"

OVER TOP OF WING
₵ PROP.

3°

6°

13'-5"

12'-10"

8'-4"

7'-2"

5'-0½"

DATUM

W.L.

6¾"

64"

48"

58"

16'-7½"

25'-5"

73¾"

83¾"

101¾"

15'-5½"

63'-10⁷⁄₁₆"

11°

17"

4°

4'-6"

7'-10"

79"

30"

8'-7½"

₵ HINGE

W.L.

DATUM

20"

76"

20" Approx.

10'-6"

18'-10⅝"

HISTORICAL AVIATION ALBUM

PLATE 3 of 3

DRAWING No. 17-114-C

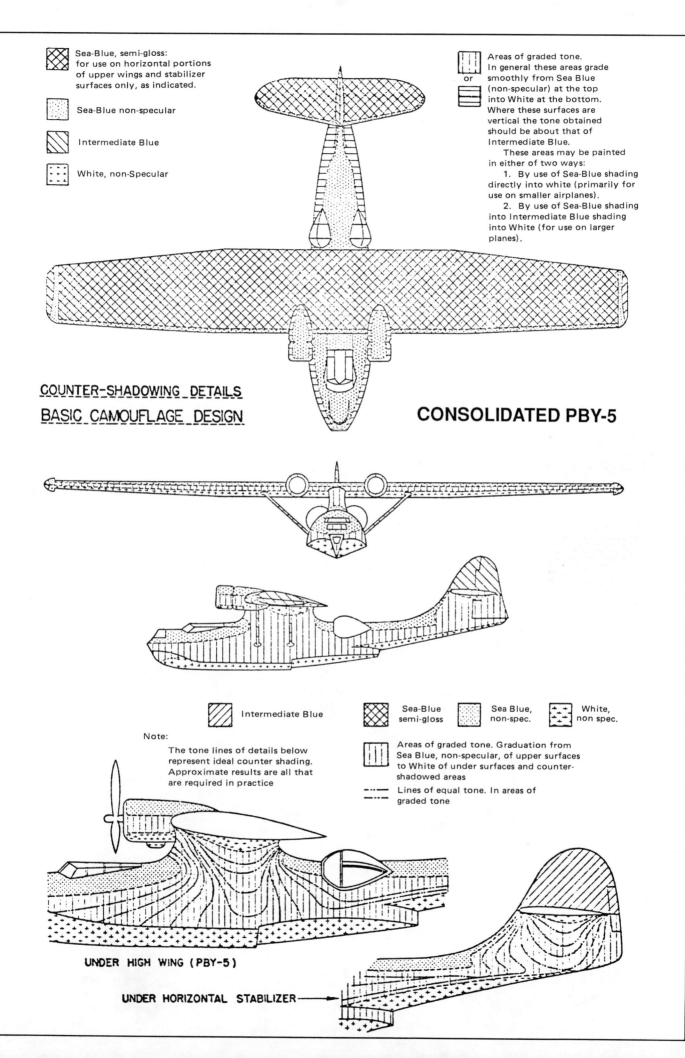

Sea-Blue, semi-gloss: for use on horizontal portions of upper wings and stabilizer surfaces only, as indicated.

Sea-Blue non-specular

Intermediate Blue

White, non-Specular

Areas of graded tone. In general these areas grade smoothly from Sea Blue (non-specular) at the top into White at the bottom. Where these surfaces are vertical the tone obtained should be about that of Intermediate Blue.

These areas may be painted in either of two ways:

1. By use of Sea-Blue shading directly into white (primarily for use on smaller airplanes).

2. By use of Sea-Blue shading into Intermediate Blue shading into White (for use on larger planes).

COUNTER-SHADOWING DETAILS
BASIC CAMOUFLAGE DESIGN

CONSOLIDATED PBY-5

Intermediate Blue

Note:
The tone lines of details below represent ideal counter shading. Approximate results are all that are required in practice

Sea-Blue semi-gloss

Sea Blue, non-spec.

White, non spec.

Areas of graded tone. Graduation from Sea Blue, non-specular, of upper surfaces to White of under surfaces and counter-shadowed areas

Lines of equal tone. In areas of graded tone

UNDER HIGH WING (PBY-5)

UNDER HORIZONTAL STABILIZER

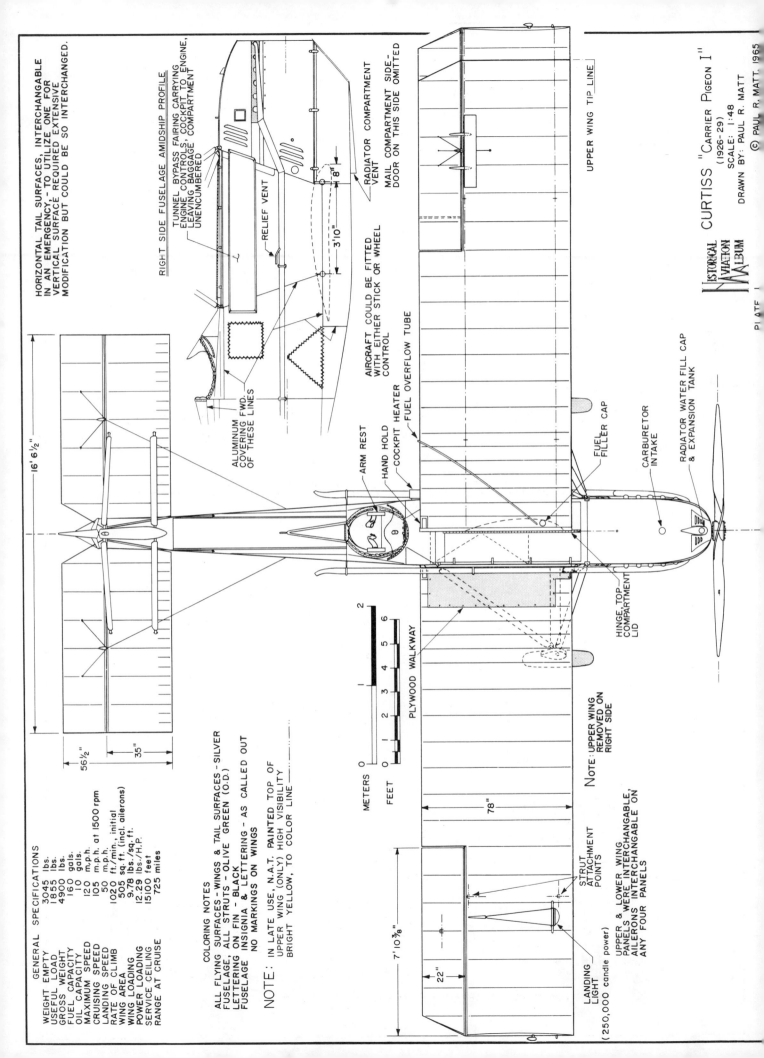

HORIZONTAL TAIL SURFACES, INTERCHANGABLE
IN AN EMERGENCY - TO UTILIZE ONE FOR
VERTICAL SURFACE REQUIRED EXTENSIVE
MODIFICATION BUT COULD BE SO INTERCHANGED.

RIGHT SIDE FUSELAGE AMIDSHIP PROFILE

TUNNEL BYPASS FAIRING CARRYING
ENGINE CONTROLS, COCKPIT TO ENGINE,
LEAVING BAGGAGE COMPARTMENT
UNENCUMBERED

RADIATOR COMPARTMENT
VENT

MAIL COMPARTMENT SIDE-
DOOR ON THIS SIDE OMITTED

UPPER WING TIP LINE

RELIEF VENT

8"

3'10"

AIRCRAFT COULD BE FITTED
WITH EITHER STICK OR WHEEL
CONTROL

ALUMINUM
COVERING FWD.
OF THESE LINES

FUEL OVERFLOW TUBE

COCKPIT HEATER

HAND HOLD

ARM REST

FUEL
FILLER CAP

CARBURETOR
INTAKE

RADIATOR WATER FILL CAP
& EXPANSION TANK

HINGE, TOP
COMPARTMENT
LID

16' 6½"

56½"

35"

METERS

FEET

0 1 2 3 4 5 6

0 1 2

PLYWOOD WALKWAY

78"

Note: UPPER WING
REMOVED ON
RIGHT SIDE

STRUT
ATTACHMENT
POINTS

7'10⅜"

22"

LANDING
LIGHT
(250,000 candle power)

GENERAL SPECIFICATIONS
WEIGHT EMPTY   3045 lbs.
USEFUL LOAD   1855 lbs.
GROSS WEIGHT   4900 lbs.
FUEL CAPACITY   160 gals.
OIL CAPACITY   10 gals.
MAXIMUM SPEED   120 m.p.h. at 1500 rpm
CRUISING SPEED   105 m.p.h.
LANDING SPEED   50 m.p.h.
RATE OF CLIMB   1020 ft./min., initial
WING AREA   505 sq. ft. (incl. ailerons)
WING LOADING   9.78 lbs./sq.ft.
POWER LOADING   12.29 lbs./H.P.
SERVICE CEILING   15100 feet
RANGE AT CRUISE   725 miles

COLORING NOTES
ALL FLYING SURFACES - WINGS & TAIL SURFACES - SILVER
FUSELAGE, ALL STRUTS - OLIVE GREEN (O.D.)
LETTERING ON FIN - BLACK
FUSELAGE INSIGNIA & LETTERING - AS CALLED OUT
NO MARKINGS ON WINGS

NOTE: IN LATE USE, N.A.T. PAINTED TOP OF
UPPER WING (ONLY) HIGH VISIBILITY
BRIGHT YELLOW, TO COLOR LINE

UPPER & LOWER WING
PANELS WERE INTERCHANGABLE,
AILERONS INTERCHANGABLE ON
ANY FOUR PANELS

HISTORICAL AVIATION ALBUM

CURTISS "CARRIER PIGEON I"
(1926-29)
SCALE: 1:48
DRAWN BY: PAUL R. MATT

© PAUL R. MATT, 1965

PLATE I

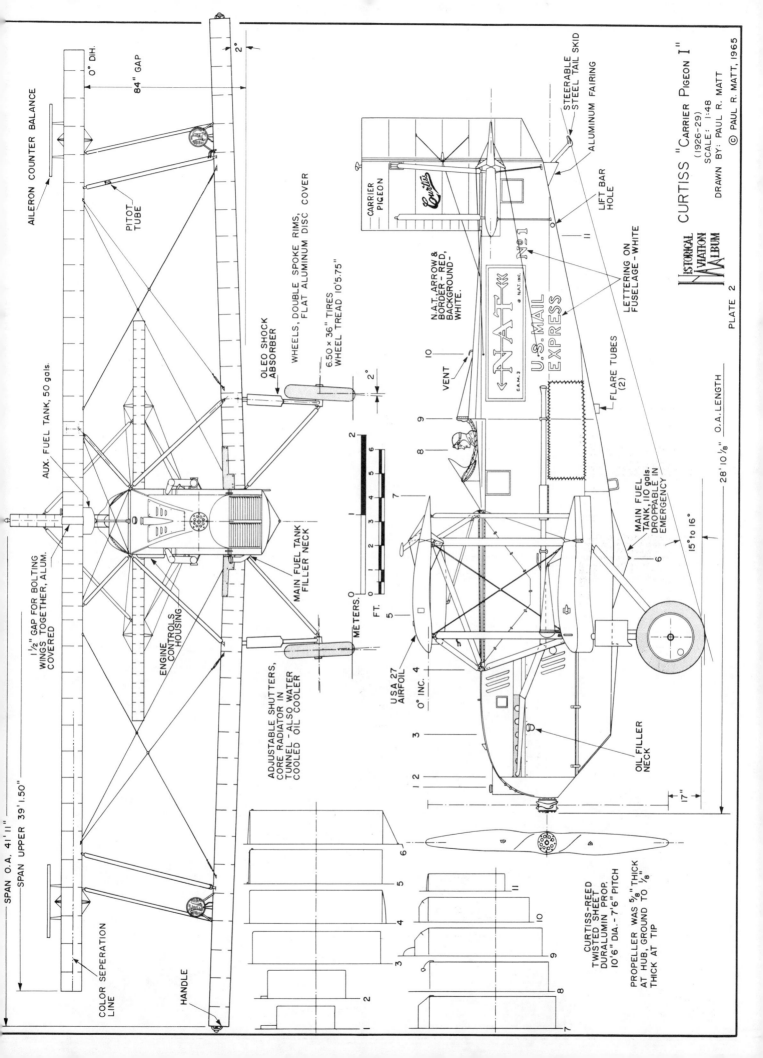

CURTISS "CARRIER PIGEON I"
(1926-29)
SCALE: 1:48
DRAWN BY: PAUL R. MATT
© PAUL R. MATT, 1965

ISTORICAL
AVIATION
ALBUM

PLATE 2

AILERON COUNTER BALANCE

0° DIH.

84" GAP

2°

PITOT TUBE

AUX. FUEL TANK, 50 gals.

SPAN O.A. 41'11"
SPAN UPPER 39'1.50"

1/2" GAP FOR BOLTING WINGS TOGETHER, ALUM. COVERED

COLOR SEPERATION LINE

HANDLE

ENGINE CONTROLS HOUSING

OLEO SHOCK ABSORBER

WHEELS, DOUBLE SPOKE RIMS, FLAT ALUMINUM DISC COVER

6.50 x 36" TIRES
WHEEL TREAD 10'5.75"

2°

MAIN FUEL TANK FILLER NECK

ADJUSTABLE SHUTTERS, CORE RADIATOR IN TUNNEL - ALSO WATER COOLED OIL COOLER

METERS.

FT.

CURTISS-REED TWISTED SHEET DURALUMIN PROP. 10'6" DIA.- 7'6" PITCH

PROPELLER WAS 5/8" THICK AT HUB, GROUND TO 1/8" THICK AT TIP

STEERABLE STEEL TAIL SKID

ALUMINUM FAIRING

LIFT BAR HOLE

LETTERING ON FUSELAGE - WHITE

CARRIER PIGEON

Curtiss

N°1

NAT
© N.A.T. INC.

U.S. MAIL EXPRESS

C.A.M. 3

N.A.T. ARROW & BORDER - RED, BACKGROUND - WHITE.

VENT

FLARE TUBES (2)

MAIN FUEL TANK, 110 gals. DROPPABLE IN EMERGENCY

28' 10 1/8" O.A. LENGTH

15° to 16°

USA 27 AIRFOIL

0° INC.

OIL FILLER NECK

17"

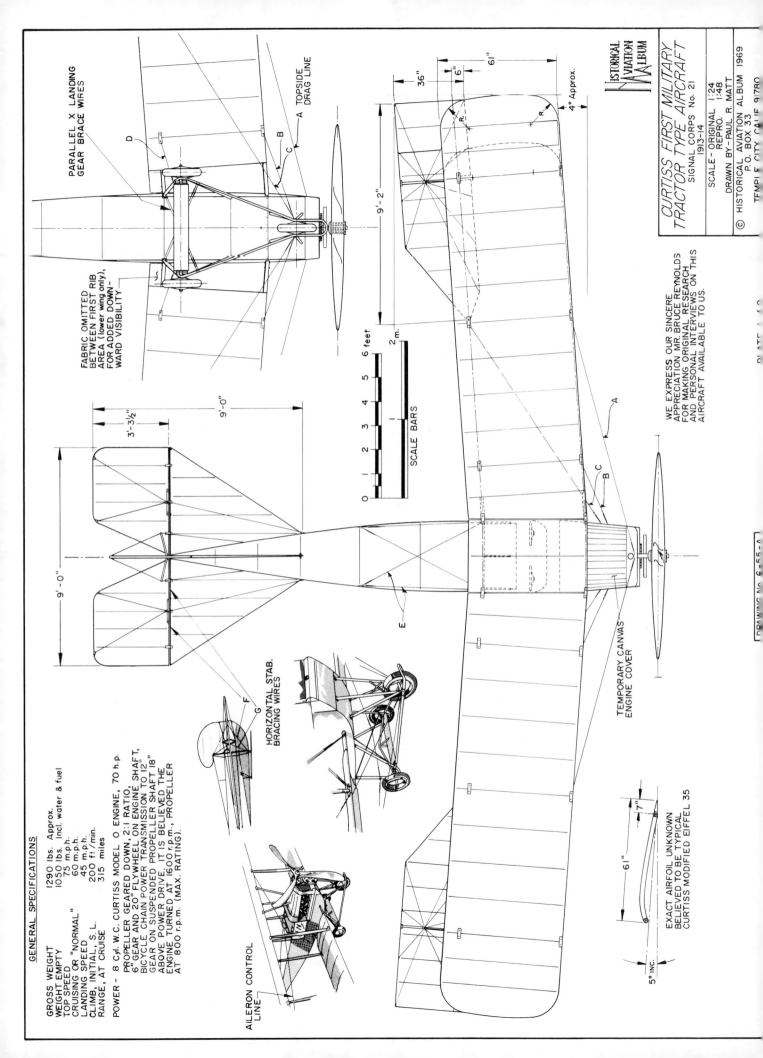

PARALLEL X LANDING GEAR BRACE WIRES

D

A TOPSIDE DRAG LINE

B

C

FABRIC OMITTED BETWEEN FIRST RIB AREA (lower wing only) FOR ADDED DOWN-WARD VISIBILITY

36"

6"

61"

4° Approx.

R

R

9' - 2"

2 m.

6 feet

SCALE BARS

5

4

3

2

1

0

3'- 3½"

9' - 0"

9' - 0"

A

C

B

TEMPORARY CANVAS ENGINE COVER

E

F

G

HORIZONTAL STAB. BRACING WIRES

AILERON CONTROL LINE

61"

7"

5° INC.

EXACT AIRFOIL UNKNOWN BELIEVED TO BE TYPICAL CURTISS MODIFIED EIFFEL 35

GENERAL SPECIFICATIONS

GROSS WEIGHT   1290 lbs. Approx.
WEIGHT EMPTY   1050 lbs. Incl. water & fuel
TOP SPEED   75 m.p.h.
CRUISING OR "NORMAL"   60 m.p.h.
LANDING SPEED   45 m.p.h.
CLIMB, INITIAL, S.L.   200 ft./min.
RANGE, AT CRUISE   315 miles

POWER - 8 Cyl. W.C. CURTISS MODEL O ENGINE, 70 h.p. PROPELLER GEARED DOWN, 2:1 RATIO, 6" GEAR AND 20" FLYWHEEL ON ENGINE SHAFT, BICYCLE CHAIN POWER TRANSMISSION TO 12" GEAR ON SUSPENDED PROPELLER SHAFT 18" ABOVE POWER DRIVE. IT IS BELIEVED THE ENGINE TURNED AT 1600 r.p.m., PROPELLER AT 800 r.p.m. (MAX. RATING).

WE EXPRESS OUR SINCERE APPRECIATION MR. BRUCE REYNOLDS FOR MAKING ORIGINAL RESEARCH AND PERSONAL INTERVIEWS ON THIS AIRCRAFT AVAILABLE TO US.

CURTISS FIRST MILITARY TRACTOR TYPE AIRCRAFT

SIGNAL CORPS No. 21
1913-14

SCALE - ORIGINAL   1:24
REPRO.   1:48

DRAWN BY - PAUL R. MATT

© HISTORICAL AVIATION ALBUM 1969
P.O. BOX 33
TEMPLE CITY, CALIF. 91780

DRAWING No. 6-55-A

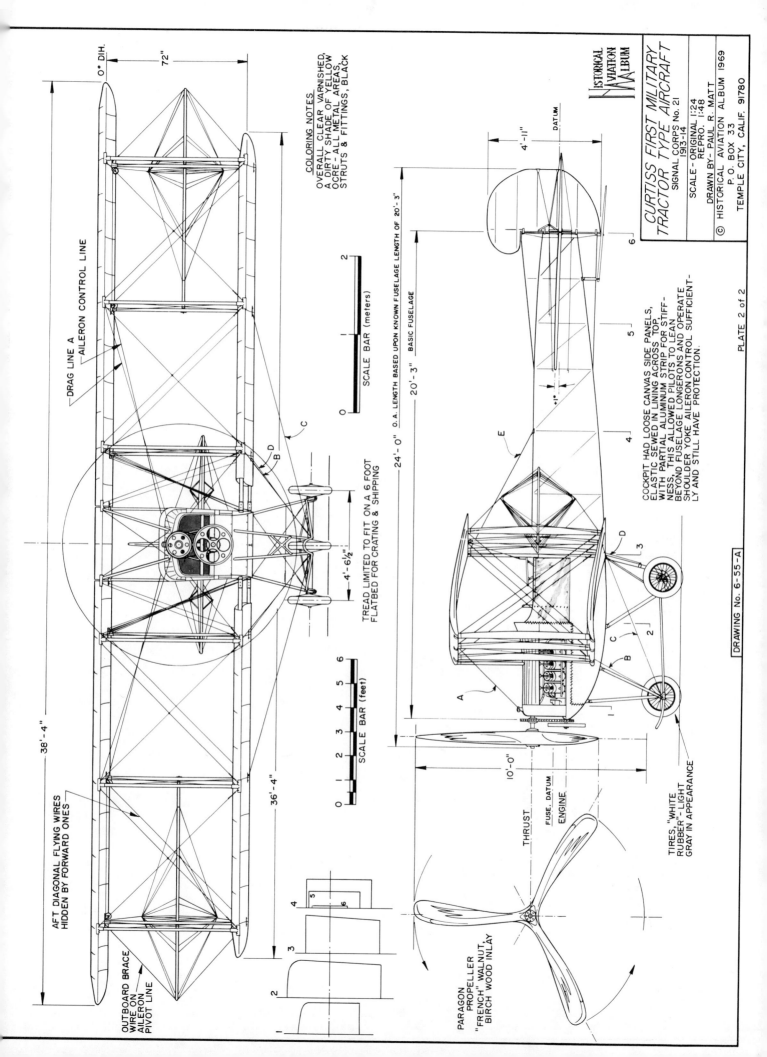

CURTISS FIRST MILITARY
TRACTOR TYPE AIRCRAFT
SIGNAL CORPS No. 21
1913-14

SCALE - ORIGINAL 1:24
REPRO. 1:48
DRAWN BY- PAUL R. MATT
© HISTORICAL AVIATION ALBUM 1969
P.O. BOX 33
TEMPLE CITY, CALIF. 91780

PLATE 2 of 2

DRAWING No. 6-55-A

COLORING NOTES
OVERALL CLEAR VARNISHED,
A DIRTY SHADE OF YELLOW
OCRE - ALL METAL AREAS,
STRUTS & FITTINGS, BLACK

SCALE BAR (meters)

SCALE BAR (feet)

0° DIH.

72"

DRAG LINE A
AILERON CONTROL LINE

38'- 4"

AFT DIAGONAL FLYING WIRES
HIDDEN BY FORWARD ONES

OUTBOARD BRACE
WIRE ON
AILERON
PIVOT LINE

36'- 4"

4'- 6½"

TREAD LIMITED TO FIT ON A 6 FOOT
FLATBED FOR CRATING & SHIPPING

24'- 0" O.A. LENGTH BASED UPON KNOWN FUSELAGE LENGTH OF 20'- 3"

20'- 3"
BASIC FUSELAGE

4'- 11"

DATUM

+1°

COCKPIT HAD LOOSE CANVAS SIDE PANELS,
ELASTIC SEWED IN LINING ACROSS TOP,
WITH PARTIAL ALUMINUM STRIP FOR STIFF-
NESS, THIS ALLOWED PILOTS TO LEAN
BEYOND FUSELAGE LONGERONS AND OPERATE
SHOULDER YOKE AILERON CONTROL SUFFICIENT-
LY AND STILL HAVE PROTECTION.

TIRES, "WHITE
RUBBER"- LIGHT
GRAY IN APPEARANCE

10'- 0"

THRUST

FUSE. DATUM

ENGINE

PARAGON
PROPELLER
"FRENCH" WALNUT,
BIRCH WOOD INLAY

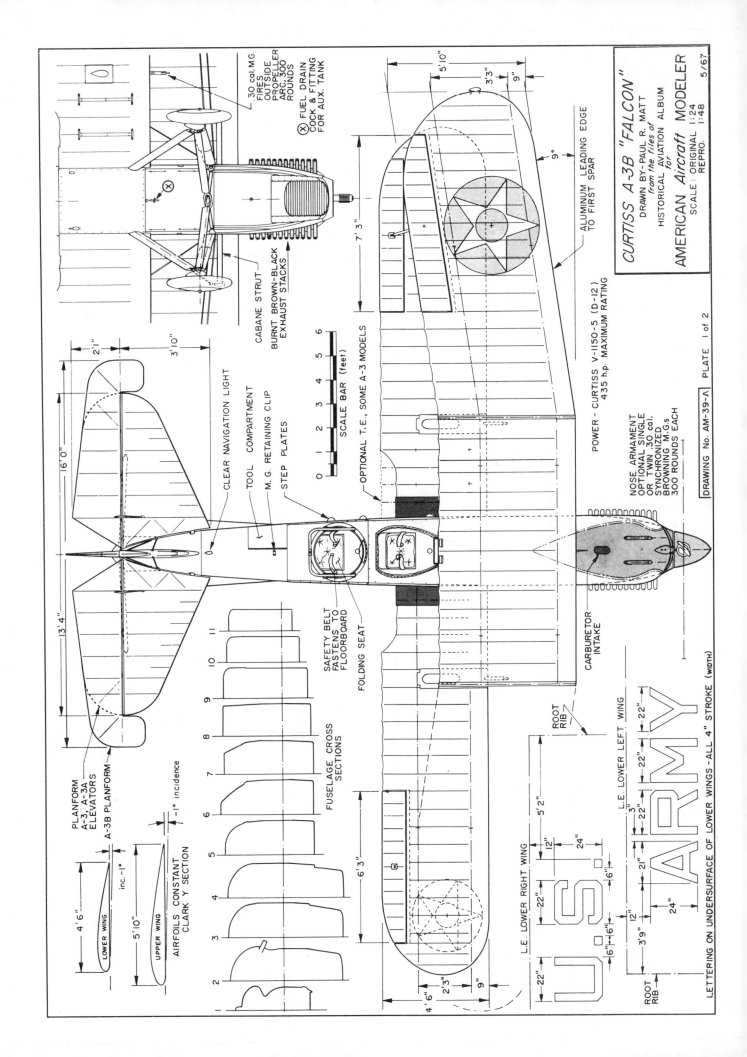

CURTISS A-3B "FALCON"
DRAWN BY-PAUL R. MATT
from the files of
HISTORICAL AVIATION ALBUM
for
AMERICAN *Aircraft* MODELER
SCALE: ORIGINAL 1:24
REPRO. 1:48
5/67

DRAWING No. AM-39-A | PLATE 1 of 2

.30 cal. M.G.
FIRES
OUTSIDE
PROPELLER
ARC. 300
ROUNDS

⊗ FUEL DRAIN
COCK & FITTING
FOR AUX. TANK

ALUMINUM LEADING EDGE
TO FIRST SPAR

POWER - CURTISS V-1150-5 (D-12)
435 h.p. MAXIMUM RATING

NOSE ARMAMENT
OPTIONAL SINGLE
OR TWIN .30 cal.
SYNCHRONIZED
BROWNING M.G.s
300 ROUNDS EACH

CABANE STRUT

BURNT BROWN-BLACK
EXHAUST STACKS

CLEAR NAVIGATION LIGHT

TOOL COMPARTMENT

M.G. RETAINING CLIP

STEP PLATES

SCALE BAR (feet)

OPTIONAL T.E., SOME A-3 MODELS

SAFETY BELT
FASTENS TO
FLOORBOARD

FOLDING SEAT

FUSELAGE CROSS
SECTIONS

PLANFORM
A-3, A-3A
ELEVATORS

A-3B PLANFORM

-1° incidence

AIRFOILS CONSTANT
CLARK Y SECTION

inc. -1°

LOWER WING

UPPER WING

CARBURETOR
INTAKE

ROOT
RIB

L.E. LOWER LEFT WING

L.E. LOWER RIGHT WING

ROOT RIB

U S ARMY

LETTERING ON UNDERSURFACE OF LOWER WINGS -ALL 4" STROKE (WIDTH)

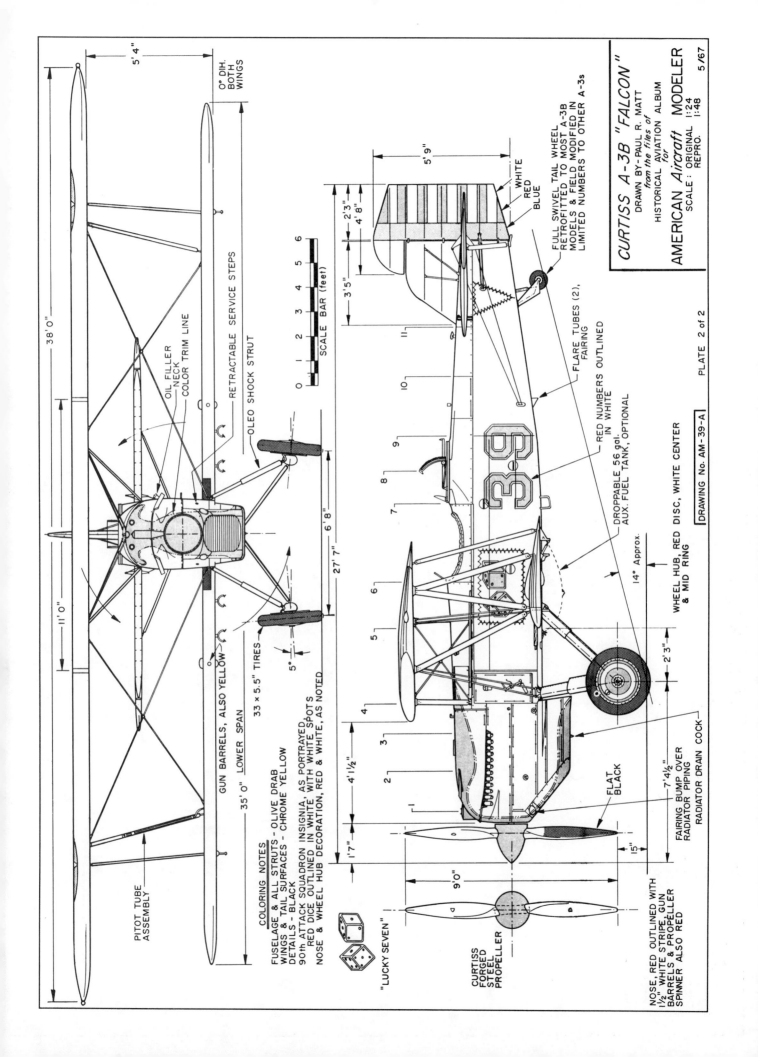

5' 4"

O° DIH.
BOTH
WINGS

38' 0"

11' 0"

PITOT TUBE
ASSEMBLY

OIL FILLER
NECK

COLOR TRIM LINE

RETRACTABLE SERVICE STEPS

OLEO SHOCK STRUT

GUN BARRELS, ALSO YELLOW

33 × 5.5" TIRES

35' 0" LOWER SPAN

6' 8"

27' 7"

5°

SCALE BAR (feet)
0 1 2 3 4 5 6

COLORING NOTES

FUSELAGE & ALL STRUTS - OLIVE DRAB
WINGS & TAIL SURFACES - CHROME YELLOW
DETAILS - BLACK
90th ATTACK SQUADRON INSIGNIA, AS PORTRAYED.
RED DICE OUTLINED IN WHITE, WITH WHITE SPOTS
NOSE & WHEEL HUB DECORATION, RED & WHITE, AS NOTED

"LUCKY SEVEN"

CURTISS
FORGED
STEEL
PROPELLER

NOSE, RED OUTLINED WITH
1½" WHITE STRIPE, GUN
BARRELS & PROPELLER
SPINNER ALSO RED

5' 9"

2' 3"
4' 8"
3' 5"

WHITE
RED
BLUE

FULL SWIVEL TAIL WHEEL
RETROFITTED TO MOST A-3B
MODELS & FIELD MODIFIED IN
LIMITED NUMBERS TO OTHER A-3s

FLARE TUBES (2),
FAIRING

RED NUMBERS OUTLINED
IN WHITE

DROPPABLE 56 gal.
AUX. FUEL TANK, OPTIONAL

14° Approx.

WHEEL HUB, RED DISC, WHITE CENTER
& MID RING

2' 3"

FLAT
BLACK

FAIRING BUMP OVER
RADIATOR PIPING

RADIATOR DRAIN COCK

7' 4½"

15"

9' 0"

1' 7"

4' 1½"

11

10

9

8

7

6

5

4

3

2

1

CURTISS A-3B "FALCON"

DRAWN BY- PAUL R. MATT
from the files of
HISTORICAL AVIATION ALBUM
for
AMERICAN *Aircraft* MODELER

5/67

SCALE: ORIGINAL   1:24
REPRO.   1:48

PLATE 2 of 2

DRAWING No. AM-39-A

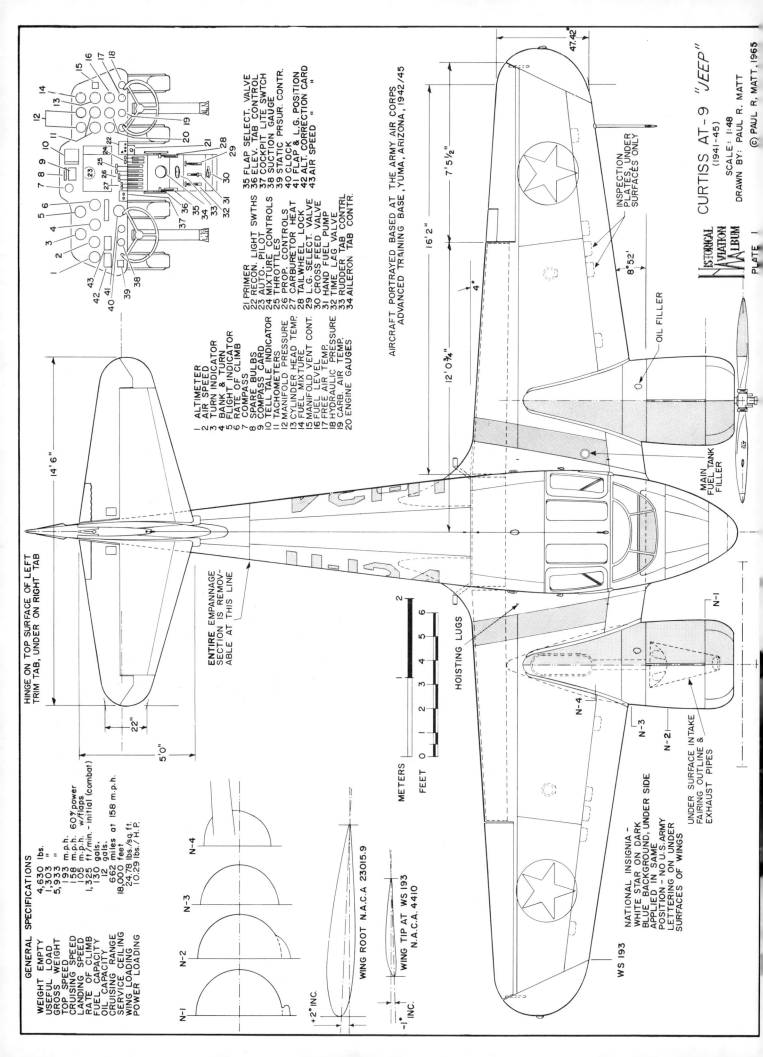

GENERAL SPECIFICATIONS

WEIGHT EMPTY .... 4,630 lbs.
USEFUL LOAD .... 1,303 "
GROSS WEIGHT .... 5,933 "
TOP SPEED .... 193 m.p.h. 60% power
CRUISING SPEED ...... 158 m.p.h. w/flaps
LANDING SPEED .... 105 m.p.h.
RATE OF CLIMB .... 1,325 ft/min.- initial (combat)
FUEL CAPACITY .... 130 gals.
OIL CAPACITY .... 12 gals.
CRUISING RANGE ...... 662 miles at 158 m.p.h.
SERVICE CEILING ..... 18,000 feet
WING LOADING .... 24.78 lbs./sq.ft.
POWER LOADING .... 10.29 lbs./H.P.

WING ROOT N.A.C.A. 23015.9

WING TIP AT WS 193
N.A.C.A. 4410

+2° INC.

-1° INC.

1 ALTIMETER
2 AIR SPEED
3 TURN INDICATOR
4 BANK & TURN
5 FLIGHT INDICATOR
6 RATE OF CLIMB
7 COMPASS
8 SPARE BULBS
9 COMPASS CARD
10 TELL TALE INDICATOR
11 TACHOMETERS
12 MANIFOLD PRESSURE
13 CYLINDER HEAD TEMP.
14 FUEL MIXTURE
15 MANIFOLD VENT CONT.
16 FUEL LEVEL
17 FREE AIR TEMP.
18 HYDRAULIC PRESSURE
19 CARB. AIR TEMP.
20 ENGINE GAUGES

21 PRIMER
22 RECON. LIGHT SWTHS
23 AUTO. PILOT
24 MIXTURE CONTROLS
25 THROTTLES
26 PROP. CONTROLS
27 CARBURETOR HEAT
28 TAILWHEEL LOCK
29 L.G. SELECT. VALVE
30 CROSS FEED VALVE
31 HAND FUEL PUMP
32 TIME LAG VALVE
33 RUDDER TAB CONTRL
34 AILERON TAB CONTR.

35 FLAP SELECT. VALVE
36 ELEV. TAB CONTROL
37 COCKPIT LITE SWTCH
38 SUCTION GAUGE
39 STATIC PRSUR. CONTR.
40 CLOCK
41 FLAP & L.G. POSITION
42 ALT. CORRECTION CARD
43 AIR SPEED " "

HINGE ON TOP SURFACE OF LEFT
TRIM TAB, UNDER ON RIGHT TAB

ENTIRE EMPANNAGE
SECTION IS REMOV-
ABLE AT THIS LINE

14' 6"

22"

5' 0"

AIRCRAFT PORTRAYED BASED AT THE ARMY AIR CORPS
ADVANCED TRAINING BASE, YUMA, ARIZONA, 1942/45

47.42

7' 5½"

16' 2"

12' 0¾"

4°

8°52'

INSPECTION
PLATES, UNDER
SURFACES ONLY

OIL FILLER

MAIN
FUEL TANK
FILLER

HOISTING LUGS

N-1

N-2

N-3

N-4

UNDER SURFACE INTAKE
FAIRING OUTLINE &
EXHAUST PIPES

WS 193

NATIONAL INSIGNIA -
WHITE STAR ON DARK
BLUE BACKGROUND, UNDER SIDE
APPLIED IN SAME
POSITION - NO U.S. ARMY
LETTERING ON UNDER
SURFACES OF WINGS

METERS

FEET

2

6 5 4 3 2 1 0

N-1

N-2

N-3

N-4

CURTISS AT-9 "JEEP"
(1941-45)

SCALE: 1:48
DRAWN BY: PAUL R. MATT

Historical Aviation Album

PLATE I

© PAUL R. MATT, 1965

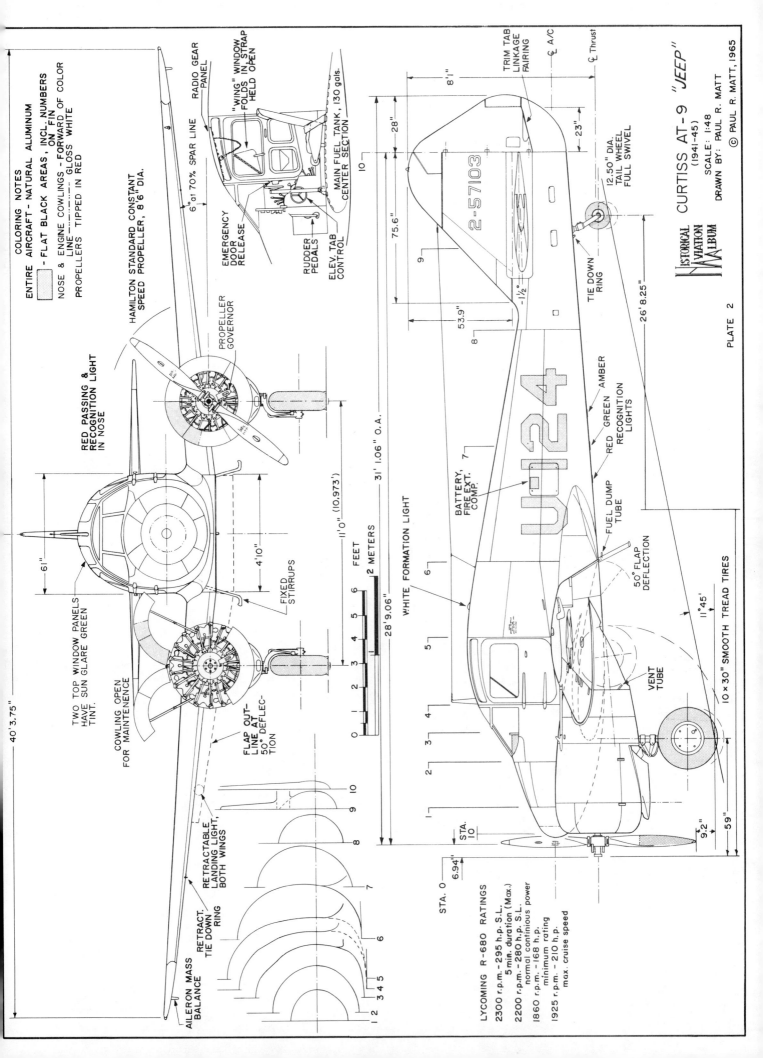

COLORING NOTES

ENTIRE AIRCRAFT - NATURAL ALUMINUM

■ - FLAT BLACK AREAS, INCL. NUMBERS ON FIN

NOSE & ENGINE COWLINGS - FORWARD OF COLOR LINE ⋯⋯⋯ GLOSS WHITE
PROPELLERS TIPPED IN RED

RADIO GEAR PANEL

"WING" WINDOW FOLDS IN STRAP HELD OPEN

6° at 70% SPAR LINE

HAMILTON STANDARD CONSTANT SPEED PROPELLER, 8'6" DIA.

PROPELLER GOVERNOR

EMERGENCY DOOR RELEASE

RUDDER PEDALS

ELEV. TAB CONTROL

MAIN FUEL TANK, 130 gals. CENTER SECTION

RED PASSING & RECOGNITION LIGHT IN NOSE

40' 3.75"

61"

TWO TOP WINDOW PANELS HAVE SUN GLARE GREEN TINT.

COWLING OPEN FOR MAINTENENCE

FIXED STIRRUPS

4'10"

11'0" (10.973')

31' 1.06" O.A.

FEET

2 METERS

FLAP OUT- LINE AT 50° DEFLEC- TION

28' 9.06"

AILERON MASS BALANCE

RETRACT. TIE DOWN RING

RETRACTABLE LANDING LIGHT, BOTH WINGS

LYCOMING R-680 RATINGS

2300 r.p.m. - 295 h.p. S.L.
5 min. duration (Max.)
2200 r.p.m. - 280 h.p. S.L.
normal continious power
1860 r.p.m. - 168 h.p.
minimum rating
1925 r.p.m. - 210 h.p.
max. cruise speed

STA. 0

6.94"

WHITE FORMATION LIGHT

BATTERY, FIRE EXT. COMP.

STA. 10

9.2"

59"

10 x 30" SMOOTH TREAD TIRES

VENT TUBE

11° 45'

50° FLAP DEFLECTION

FUEL DUMP TUBE

RED GREEN AMBER RECOGNITION LIGHTS

26' 8.25"

TIE DOWN RING

12.50" DIA. TAIL WHEEL FULL SWIVEL

23"

8'1"

28"

75.6"

53.9"

-1½°

TRIM TAB LINKAGE FAIRING

℄ A/C

℄ Thrust

2-57103

N124

HISTORICAL AVIATION ALBUM

CURTISS AT-9 "JEEP"

(1941-45)

SCALE: 1:48

DRAWN BY: PAUL R. MATT

© PAUL R. MATT, 1965

PLATE 2

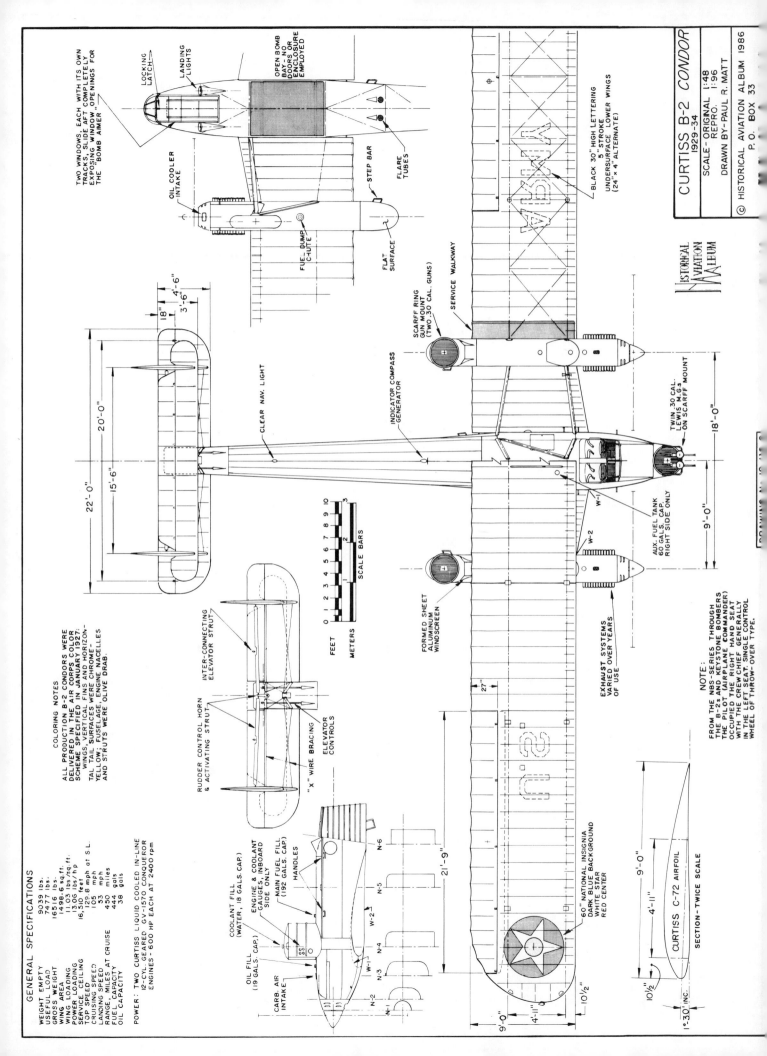

TWO WINDOWS, EACH WITH ITS OWN
TRACKS, SLIDE AFT COMPLETELY
EXPOSING WINDOW "OPENINGS FOR
THE "BOMB AIMER"

OPEN BOMB
BAY - NO
DOORS OR
ENCLOSURE
EMPLOYED

LOCKING
LATCH

LANDING
LIGHTS

OIL COOLER
INTAKE

STEP BAR

FLARE
TUBES

FUEL DUMP
CHUTE

FLAT
SURFACE

BLACK 30" HIGH LETTERING
5" STROKE
UNDERSURFACE LOWER WINGS
(24" x 4' ALTERNATE)

CURTISS B-2 CONDOR
1929-34
SCALE - ORIGINAL 1:48
REPRO. 1:96
DRAWN BY - PAUL R. MATT

© HISTORICAL AVIATION ALBUM 1986
P.O. BOX 33

SCARFF RING
GUN MOUNT
(TWO .30 CAL. GUNS)

SERVICE WALKWAY

INDICATOR COMPASS
GENERATOR

CLEAR NAV. LIGHT

TWIN .30 CAL.
LEWIS M.G.'S
ON SCARFF MOUNT

AUX. FUEL TANK
60 GALS. CAP.
RIGHT SIDE ONLY

W-1

W-2

18'-0"

9'-0"

4'-6"

3'-6"

18"

20'-0"

15'-6"

22'-0"

INTER-CONNECTING
ELEVATOR STRUT

RUDDER CONTROL HORN
& ACTIVATING STRUT

ELEVATOR
CONTROLS

"X" WIRE BRACING

FORMED SHEET
ALUMINUM
WINDSCREEN

EXHAUST SYSTEMS
VARIED OVER YEARS
OF USE

FEET
0 1 2 3 4 5 6 7 8 9 10

METERS
0 1 2 3

SCALE BARS

COOLANT FILL
(WATER, 18 GALS. CAP.)

ENGINE & COOLANT
GAUGES, INBOARD
SIDE ONLY

MAIN FUEL FILL
(192 GALS. CAP.)

HANDLES

OIL FILL
(19 GALS. CAP.)

CARB. AIR
INTAKE

N-6

N-5

N-4

N-3

N-2

N-1

W-2

W-1

21'-9"

27"

60" NATIONAL INSIGNIA
DARK BLUE BACKGROUND
WHITE STAR
RED CENTER

9'-0"

4'-11"

10 1/2"

CURTISS C-72 AIRFOIL

SECTION - TWICE SCALE

9'-0"

4'-11"

10 1/2"

1-30" INC.

GENERAL SPECIFICATIONS

WEIGHT EMPTY	9039 lbs.
USEFUL LOAD	7477 lbs.
GROSS WEIGHT	16516 lbs.
WING AREA	1498.6 sq.ft.
POWER LOADING	11.03 lbs/sq.ft.
WING LOADING	13.06 lbs/hp
SERVICE CEILING	16,510 feet
TOP SPEED	129.8 mph at S.L.
CRUISING SPEED	105 mph
LANDING SPEED	53 mph
RANGE, MILES AT CRUISE	450 miles
FUEL CAPACITY	444 gals
OIL CAPACITY	38 gals

POWER: TWO CURTISS LIQUID COOLED IN-LINE
12-CYL. GEARED GV-1570 CONQUEROR
ENGINES - 600 HP EACH AT 2400 rpm

COLORING NOTES

ALL PRODUCTION B-2 CONDORS WERE
DELIVERED IN THE AIR CORPS COLOR
SCHEME SPECIFIED IN JANUARY 1927:
WINGS, VERTICAL FINS AND HORIZON-
TAL TAIL SURFACES WERE CHROME-
YELLOW; FUSELAGE, ENGINE NACELLES
AND STRUTS WERE OLIVE DRAB.

NOTE:
FROM THE NBS-SERIES THROUGH
THE B-2s AND KEYSTONE BOMBERS
THE PILOT (AIRPLANE COMMANDER)
OCCUPIED THE RIGHT HAND SEAT
WITH THE CREW CHIEF GENERALLY
IN THE LEFT SEAT. SINGLE CONTROL
WHEEL OF THROW-OVER TYPE.

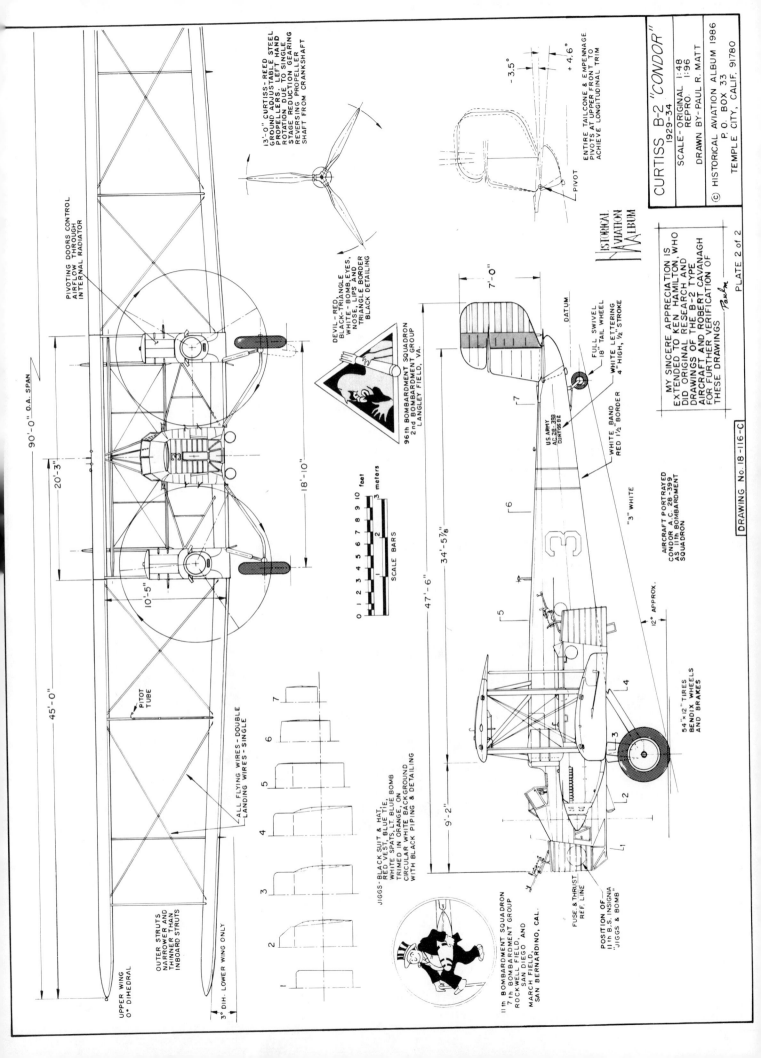

CURTISS B-2 *"CONDOR"*
1929-34

SCALE - ORIGINAL 1:48
REPRO. 1:96
DRAWN BY - PAUL R. MATT

© HISTORICAL AVIATION ALBUM 1986
P. O. BOX 33
TEMPLE CITY, CALIF. 91780

MY SINCERE APPRECIATION IS
EXTENDED TO KEN HAMILTON, WHO
DID ORIGINAL RESEARCH AND
DRAWINGS OF THE B-2 TYPE
AIRCRAFT AND ROBERT CAVANAGH
FOR FURTHER VERIFICATION OF
THESE DRAWINGS

PLATE 2 of 2

DRAWING No. 18-116-C

13'-0" CURTISS- REED STEEL
GROUND ADJUSTABLE
PROPELLERS. LEFT HAND
ROTATION DUE TO SINGLE
STAGE REDUCTION GEARING
REVERSING PROPELLER
SHAFT FROM CRANKSHAFT

ENTIRE TAILCONE & EMPENNAGE
PIVOTS AT UPPER FRONT TO
ACHIEVE LONGITUDINAL TRIM

- 3.5°

+ 4.6°

PIVOT

DEVIL - RED,
BLACK - TRIANGLE
WHITE - BOMB, EYES,
NOSE, LIPS AND
TRIANGLE BORDER
BLACK DETAILING

96th BOMBARDMENT SQUADRON
2nd BOMBARDMENT GROUP
LANGLEY FIELD, VA.

7'-0"

FULL SWIVEL
18" TAIL WHEEL

DATUM

WHITE LETTERING
4" HIGH, ½" STROKE

WHITE BAND
RED 1½" BORDER

US ARMY
A.C. 28-399
CURTISS B2

7

"3" WHITE

6

5

AIRCRAFT PORTRAYED
CONDOR A.C. 28-399
AS 11th BOMBARDMENT
SQUADRON

12" APPROX.

54"x12" TIRES
BENDIX WHEELS
AND BRAKES

4

3

2

1

FUSE & THRUST
REF. LINE

POSITION OF
11th B.S. INSIGNIA
"JIGGS & BOMB"

9'-2"

34'-5⅞"

47'-6"

PIVOTING DOORS CONTROL
AIRFLOW THROUGH
INTERNAL RADIATOR

90'-0" O.A. SPAN

45'-0"

20'-3"

18'-10"

10'-5"

PITOT
TUBE

ALL FLYING WIRES - DOUBLE
LANDING WIRES - SINGLE

OUTER STRUTS
NARROWER AND
THINNER THAN
INBOARD STRUTS

UPPER WING
0° DIHEDRAL

3° DIH. LOWER WING ONLY

SCALE BARS

0 1 2 3 4 5 6 7 8 9 10 feet

1 2 3 meters

2 3 4 5 6 7

JIGGS - BLACK SUIT & HAT,
RED VEST, BLUE TIE,
WHITE SPATS, LT. BLUE BOMB
TRIMED IN ORANGE, ON
CIRCULAR WHITE BACKGROUND
WITH BLACK PIPING & DETAILING

11th BOMBARDMENT SQUADRON
7th BOMBARDMENT GROUP
ROCKWELL FIELD,
SAN DIEGO AND
MARCH FIELD,
SAN BERNARDINO, CAL.

Curtiss B-2 Condor Bomber

Fuselage skeleton during engine run-up tests.

Engine nacelle and gunner's barrell.

No problem... a one ton bomb slung under a B-2 demonstrates the great lifting ability of the Condor, Fort Bill, VA. Oct. 23, 1930. This was one of a number of trials carried out by the 96th Bombardment Squadron at Langley Field.

Curtiss B-20 Condor Transport

Clarence Chamberlin barnstormed with the Condors taking sightseers up for $1.00 day or night excursions. He got a discount on the fuel bill by using and advertising American Oil Company (Amoco).

Cabin arrangements proposed by the Curtiss company for the B-20 Condor. All one class arrangement with lavatory aft. The B-20 was probably the first American airliner to have interchangeable passenger seating arragement. Interiors were featured for review by TAT airline officials using Condor G-1 as the model. Eastern Air settled on the all tourist 18-seat arrangement later on.

Split, "First Class" compartment aft and "Tourist Class" forward, with the lavatory between.

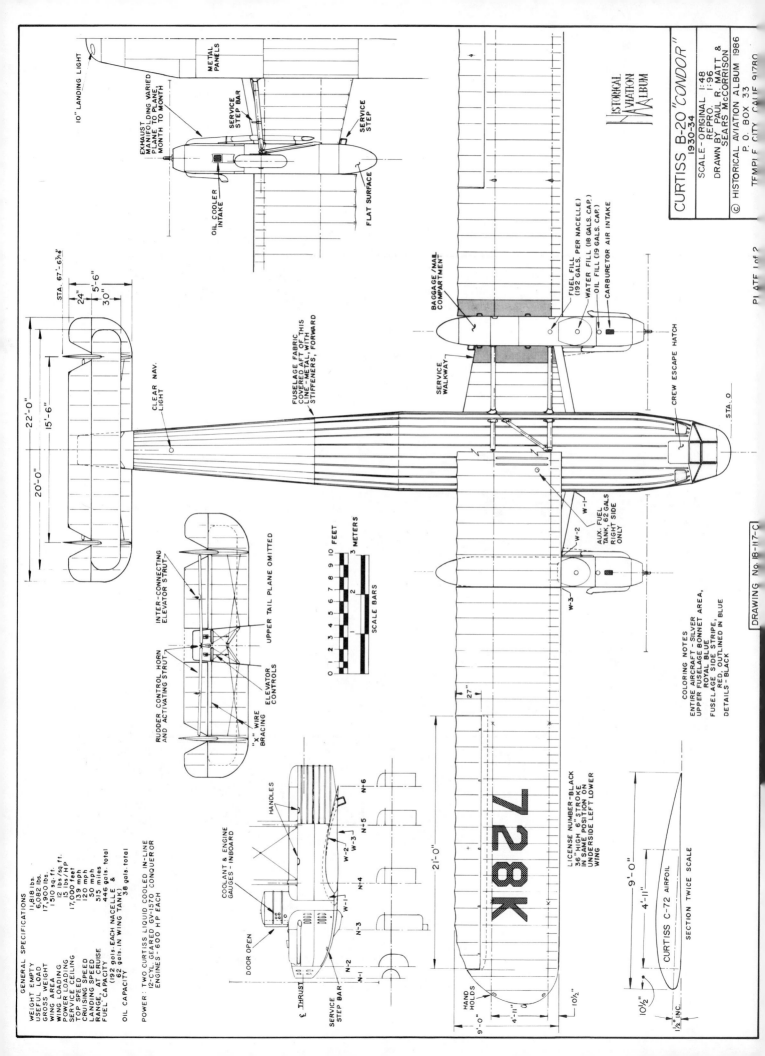

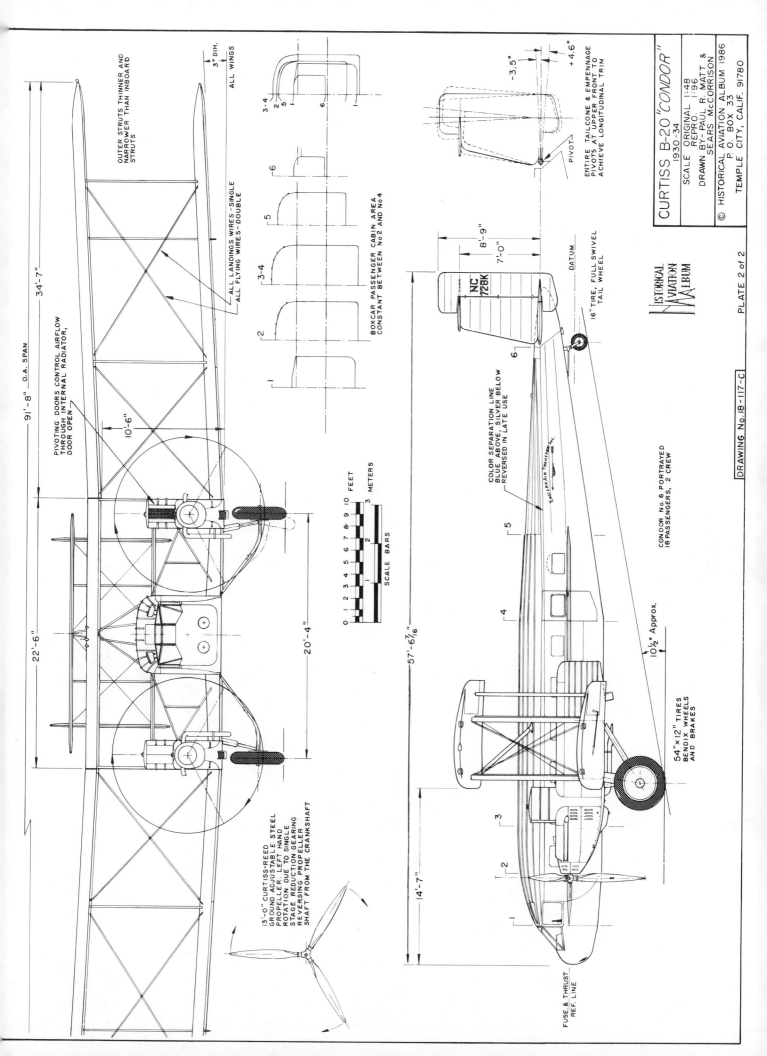

OUTER STRUTS THINNER AND
NARROWER THAN INBOARD
STRUTS

3° DIH.
ALL WINGS

3-4
2
5
1   6

ALL LANDINGS WIRES - SINGLE
ALL FLYING WIRES - DOUBLE

6

5

3-4

2

1

BOXCAR PASSENGER CABIN AREA
CONSTANT BETWEEN No 2 AND No 4

34'-7"

91'-8" O.A. SPAN

22'-6"

PIVOTING DOORS CONTROL AIRFLOW
THRO' OPEN INTERNAL RADIATOR,
DOOR OPEN

10'-6"

20'-4"

13'-0" CURTISS-REED
GROUND ADJUSTABLE STEEL
PROPELLER LEFT HAND
ROTATION DUE TO SINGLE
STAGE REDUCTION GEARING
REVERSING PROPELLER
SHAFT FROM THE CRANKSHAFT

0 1 2 3 4 5 6 7 8 9 10   FEET
                         METERS
1   2   3
SCALE BARS

-3.5°   +4.6°

PIVOT

ENTIRE TAILCONE & EMPENNAGE
PIVOTS AT UPPER FRONT TO
ACHIEVE LONGITUDINAL TRIM

CURTISS B-20 "CONDOR"
1930-34
SCALE ORIGINAL 1:48
REPRO.   1:96
DRAWN BY- PAUL R. MATT &
SEARS McCORRISON
© HISTORICAL AVIATION ALBUM 1986
P. O. BOX 33
TEMPLE CITY, CALIF. 91780

Historical
Aviation
Album

PLATE 2 of 2

DRAWING No. 18-117-C

8'-9"

7'-0"

NC
728K

16" TIRE, FULL SWIVEL
TAIL WHEEL

DATUM

6

COLOR SEPARATION LINE
BLUE ABOVE, SILVER BELOW
REVERSED IN LATE USE

Eastern Air Transport Inc.

5

4

CONDOR No. 6 PORTRAYED
18 PASSENGERS, 2 CREW

57'-6 7/16"

10½" Approx.

2
3

54"x12" TIRES
BENDIX WHEELS
AND BRAKES

14'-7"

2

1

FUSE & THRUST
REF. LINE

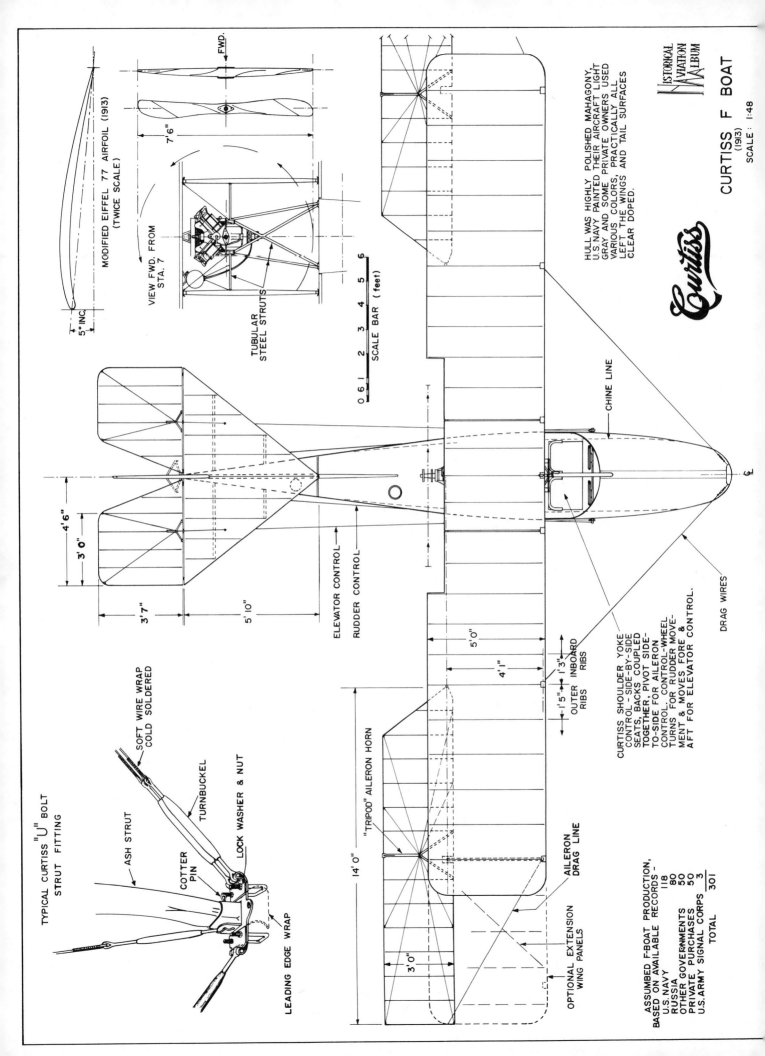

MODIFIED EIFFEL 77 AIRFOIL (1913)
(TWICE SCALE)

5° INC.

FWD.

7'6"

VIEW FWD. FROM STA. 7

TUBULAR STEEL STRUTS

SCALE BAR (feet)

0 6 1 2 3 4 5 6

HULL WAS HIGHLY POLISHED MAHOGANY.
U.S. NAVY PAINTED THEIR AIRCRAFT LIGHT
GRAY AND SOME PRIVATE OWNERS USED
VARIOUS COLORS, PRACTICALLY ALL
LEFT THE WINGS AND TAIL SURFACES
CLEAR DOPED.

Curtiss

CURTISS F BOAT

(1913)

SCALE : 1:48

CHINE LINE

4'6"

3'0"

3'7"

5'10"

ELEVATOR CONTROL

RUDDER CONTROL

DRAG WIRES

5'0"

4'1"

1'3"

1'5"

OUTER INBOARD
RIBS   RIBS

CURTISS SHOULDER-YOKE
CONTROL.-SIDE-BY-SIDE
SEATS, BACKS COUPLED
TOGETHER, PIVOT SIDE-
TO-SIDE FOR AILERON
CONTROL. CONTROL-WHEEL
TURNS FOR RUDDER MOVE-
MENT & MOVES FORE &
AFT FOR ELEVATOR CONTROL.

14'0"

"TRIPOD" AILERON HORN

3'0"

AILERON
DRAG LINE

OPTIONAL EXTENSION
WING PANELS

TYPICAL CURTISS "U" BOLT
STRUT FITTING

SOFT WIRE WRAP
COLD SOLDERED

ASH STRUT

TURNBUCKEL

COTTER
PIN

LOCK WASHER & NUT

LEADING EDGE WRAP

ASSUMBED F-BOAT PRODUCTION,
BASED ON AVAILABLE RECORDS –

U.S. NAVY   118
RUSSIA   80
OTHER GOVERNMENTS   50
PRIVATE PURCHASES   50
U.S. ARMY SIGNAL CORPS   3
TOTAL   301

Historical Aviation Album

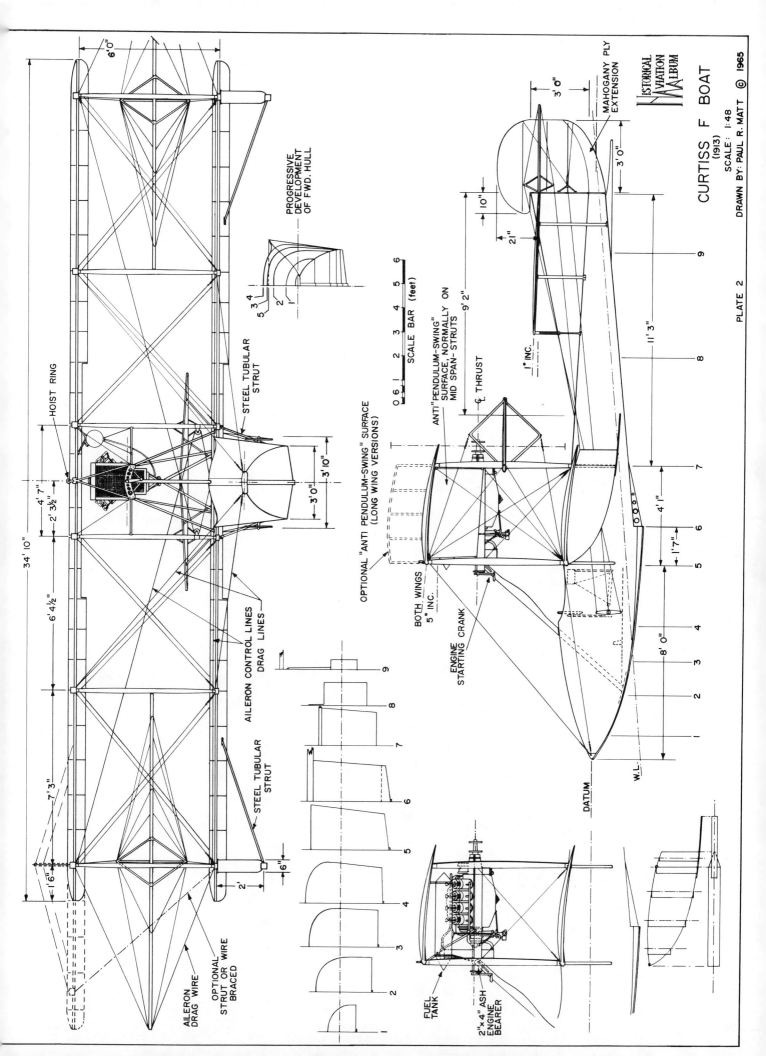

6' 0"

HOIST RING

STEEL TUBULAR STRUT

PROGRESSIVE DEVELOPMENT OF FWD. HULL

3' 10"

3' 0"

34' 10"

4' 7"

2' 3½"

6' 4½"

7' 3"

STEEL TUBULAR STRUT

AILERON CONTROL LINES

DRAG LINES

1' 6"

2'

6"

6"

AILERON DRAG WIRE

OPTIONAL STRUT OR WIRE BRACED

SCALE BAR (feet)
0 6 1 2 3 4 5 6

OPTIONAL "ANTI PENDULUM-SWING" SURFACE
(LONG WING VERSIONS)

ANTI "PENDULUM-SWING" SURFACE, NORMALLY ON MID SPAN-STRUTS

BOTH WINGS 5° INC.

ENGINE STARTING CRANK

FUEL TANK

2"x 4" ASH ENGINE BEARER

3' 0"

MAHOGANY PLY EXTENSION

3' 0"

10"

21"

1° INC.

9' 2"

Ɫ. THRUST

11' 3"

1' 7"

4' 1"

8' 0"

DATUM

W.L.

9

8

7

6

5

4

3

2

1

CURTISS F BOAT
(1913)

SCALE: 1:48

DRAWN BY: PAUL R. MATT © 1965

Historical Aviation Album

PLATE 2

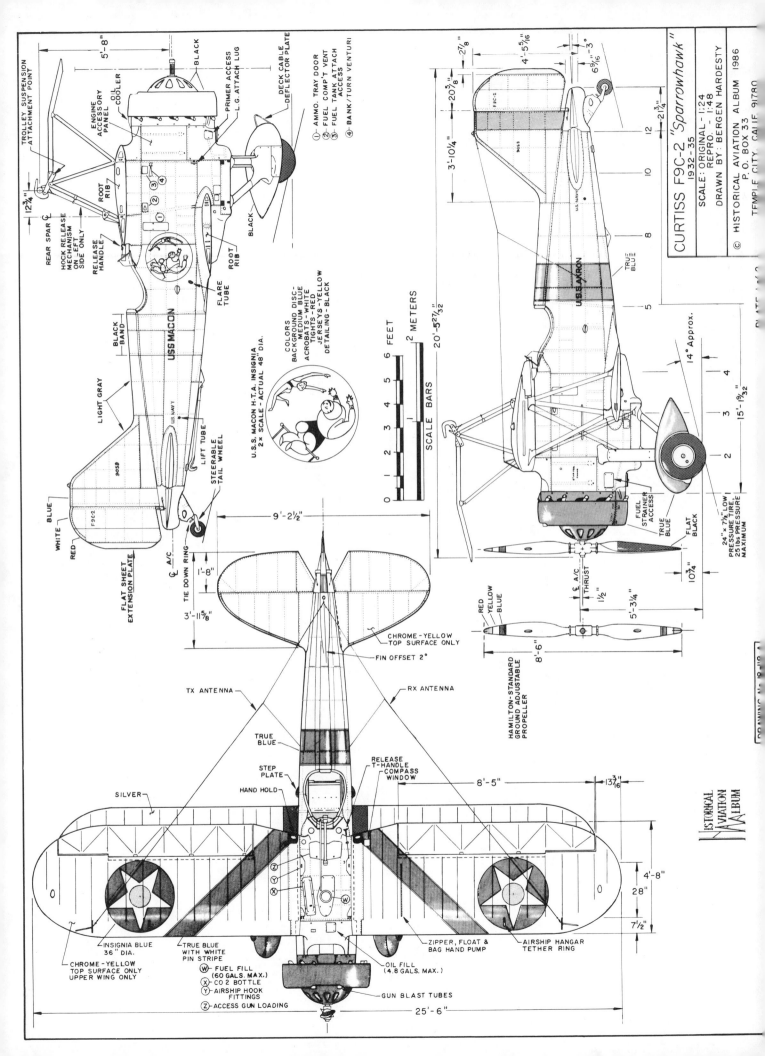

TROLLEY SUSPENSION ATTACHMENT POINT
5'-8"
BLACK
OIL COOLER
ENGINE ACCESSORY PANEL
PRIMER ACCESS
L.G. ATTACH LUG
DECK CABLE DEFLECTOR PLATE
REAR SPAR ℄
12¾"
HOOK RELEASE MECHANISM ON LEFT SIDE ONLY
ROOT RIB
RELEASE HANDLE
ROOT RIB
BLACK
FLARE TUBE
BLACK BAND
USS MACON
LIGHT GRAY
9059
US NAVY
LIFT TUBE
STEERABLE TAIL WHEEL
BLUE
WHITE
RED
F9C2
FLAT SHEET EXTENSION PLATE

① AMMO. TRAY DOOR
② FUEL COMP'T VENT
③ FUEL TANK ATTACH ACCESS
④ BANK/TURN VENTURI

U.S.S. MACON H.T.A. INSIGNIA
2 × SCALE - ACTUAL 48" DIA.

COLORS
BACKGROUND DISC - MEDIUM BLUE
ACROBATS - WHITE
TIGHTS - RED
JERSEYS - YELLOW
DETAILING - BLACK

6 FEET
5
4
3
2
1
0
2 METERS
SCALE BARS

CURTISS F9C-2 "Sparrowhawk"
1932-35
SCALE: ORIGINAL - 1:24
REPRO. - 1:48
DRAWN BY: BERGEN HARDESTY

© HISTORICAL AVIATION ALBUM 1986
P.O. BOX 33
TEMPLE CITY, CALIF. 91780

4'-5⁵⁄₁₆"
27⅛"
20⁵⁄₈"
6⁹⁄₁₆" -3°
2¼"
3'-10¼"
F9C-2
9C58
12
10
8
TRUE BLUE
U.S. NAVY
U.S.S. AKRON
5

14° Approx.
15'-1⁹⁄₃₂"
4
3
2
FUEL STRAINER ACCESS
TRUE BLUE
FLAT BLACK
24" × 7½" LOW PRESSURE TIRE, 25 lbs PRESSURE MAXIMUM
℄ A/C
THRUST
1½"
10¾"
5'-3¾"
8'-6"

9'-2½"
1'-8"
TIE DOWN RING
3'-11⁵⁄₈"
FIN OFFSET 2°
CHROME-YELLOW TOP SURFACE ONLY

RED
YELLOW
BLUE
HAMILTON-STANDARD GROUND ADJUSTABLE PROPELLER

TX ANTENNA
RX ANTENNA

TRUE BLUE

STEP PLATE
RELEASE T-HANDLE
COMPASS WINDOW
HAND HOLD

8'-5"
13³⁄₁₆"

SILVER

4'-8"
28"
7½"

INSIGNIA BLUE 36" DIA.
TRUE BLUE WITH WHITE PIN STRIPE
AIRSHIP HANGAR TETHER RING

CHROME-YELLOW TOP SURFACE ONLY UPPER WING ONLY
Ⓦ FUEL FILL (60 GALS. MAX.)
Ⓧ CO 2 BOTTLE
Ⓨ AIRSHIP HOOK FITTINGS
Ⓩ ACCESS GUN LOADING
OIL FILL (4.8 GALS. MAX.)
ZIPPER, FLOAT & BAG HAND PUMP
GUN BLAST TUBES
25'-6"

Ⓩ Ⓨ Ⓧ Ⓦ

20'-5²⁷⁄₃₂"

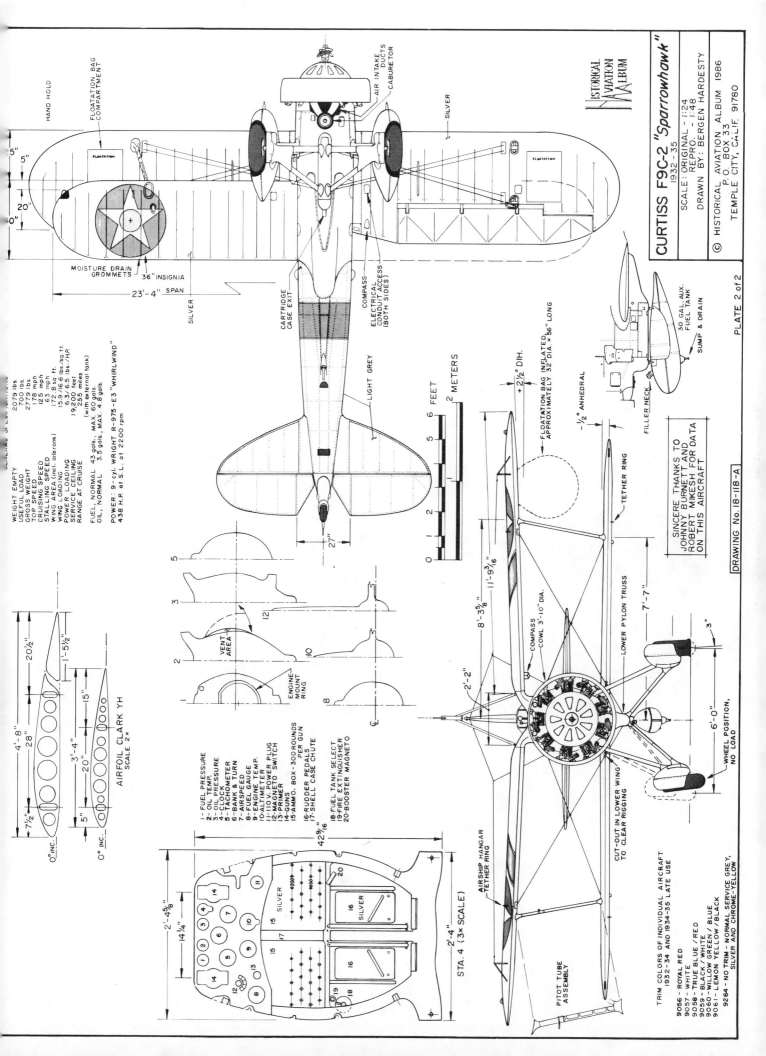

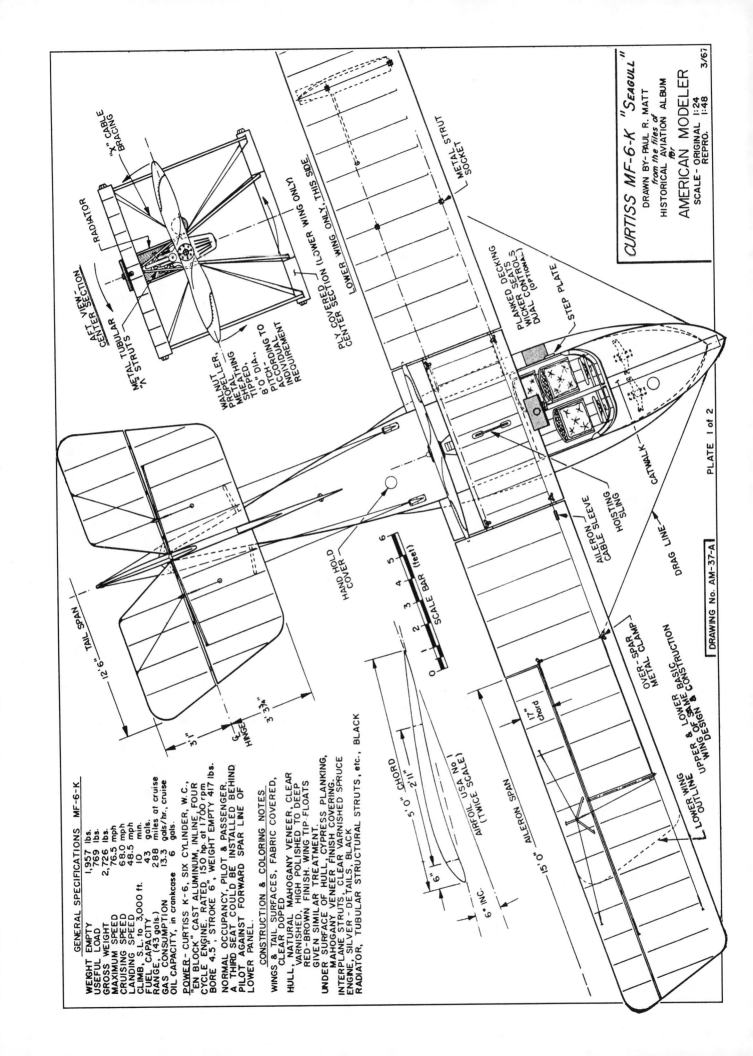

CURTISS MF-6-K "Seagull"

DRAWN BY- PAUL R. MATT
from the files of
HISTORICAL AVIATION ALBUM
for

AMERICAN MODELER

SCALE - ORIGINAL 1:24
REPRO. 1:48

3/67

PLATE 1 of 2

DRAWING No. AM-37-A

RADIATOR

"X" CABLE BRACING

AFT. VIEW —
CENTER SECTION

METAL TUBULAR
"A" STRUTS

WALNUT,
PROPELLER,
METAL HUB,
SHEATHING,
TIPPED,
8'0"DIA.—
PITCH ACCORDING TO
ACCORDUAL
INDIVIDUAL
REQUIREMENT

PLY COVERED (LOWER WING ONLY, THIS SIDE

LOWER WING SECTION ONLY)
CENTER WING

METAL STRUT
SOCKET

12'6" TAIL SPAN

3'1"

HINGE

3'3¾"

HAND HOLD
COVER

0 1 2 3 4 5 6
SCALE BAR (feet)

PLANKED DECKING
WICKER SEATS
DUAL CONTROLS
(OPTIONAL)

STEP PLATE

AILERON SLEEVE
CABLE
HOISTING
SLING

CATWALK

DRAG LINE

OVER-SPAR
METAL CLAMP

17" chord

LOWER WING
OUTLINE

UPPER & LOWER SAME BASIC CONSTRUCTION
WING DESIGN & CONSTRUCTION

5' 0" CHORD

6"

2'11"

6"

AIRFOIL USA No I
(TWICE SCALE)

AILERON SPAN

6" INC.

15'0"

GENERAL SPECIFICATIONS MF-6-K

WEIGHT EMPTY   1,957 lbs.
USEFUL LOAD   769 lbs.
GROSS WEIGHT   2,726 lbs.
MAXIMUM SPEED   76.5 mph
CRUISING SPEED   68.0 mph
LANDING SPEED   48.5 mph
CLIMB, S.L. to 3,000 ft.   10 min.
FUEL CAPACITY   43 gals.
RANGE, (43 gals.)   288 miles at cruise
GAS CONSUMPTION   13.3 gals/hr., cruise
OIL CAPACITY, in crankcase   6 gals.

POWER - CURTISS K-6, SIX CYLINDER, W.C.,
"EN BLOCK" CAST ALUMINUM, INLINE, FOUR
CYCLE ENGINE. RATED, 150 hp. at 1700 rpm
BORE 4.5, STROKE 6", WEIGHT EMPTY 417 lbs.

NORMAL OCCUPANCY, PILOT & PASSENGER.
A THIRD SEAT COULD BE INSTALLED BEHIND
PILOT AGAINST FORWARD SPAR LINE OF
LOWER PANEL.

CONSTRUCTION & COLORING NOTES

WINGS & TAIL SURFACES, FABRIC COVERED,
CLEAR DOPED.
HULL, NATURAL MAHOGANY VENEER, CLEAR
VARNISHED, HIGH POLISHED TO DEEP
RED-BROWN FINISH. WING TIP-FLOATS
GIVEN SIMILAR TREATMENT.
UNDER SURFACE OF HULL, CYPRESS PLANKING,
MAHOGANY VENEER FINISH COVERING.
INTERPLANE STRUTS, CLEAR VARNISHED SPRUCE
ENGINE, SILVER - DETAILS, BLACK
RADIATOR, TUBULAR STRUCTURAL STRUTS, etc., BLACK

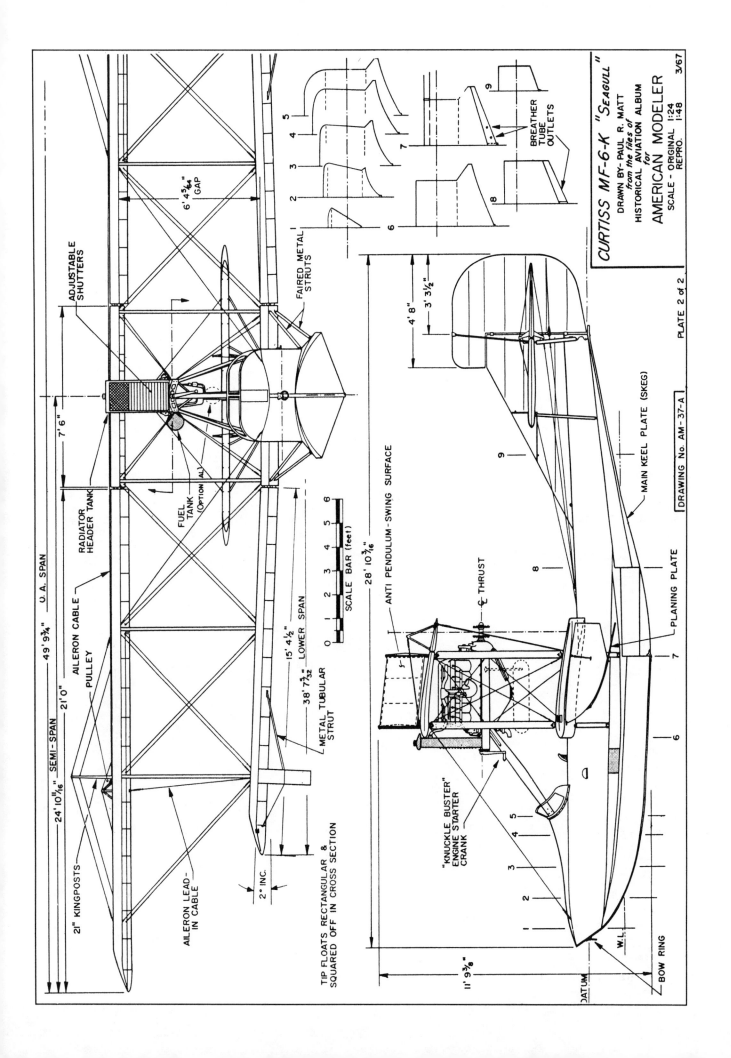

CURTISS MF-6-K "Seagull"

DRAWN BY- PAUL R. MATT
from the files of
HISTORICAL AVIATION ALBUM
for
AMERICAN MODELER

SCALE - ORIGINAL 1:24
REPRO. 1:48

3/67

PLATE 2 of 2

DRAWING No. AM-37-A

BREATHER TUBE OUTLETS

ADJUSTABLE SHUTTERS

FAIRED METAL STRUTS

6' 4⁵⁄₆₄" GAP

7' 6"

RADIATOR HEADER TANK

AILERON CABLE

PULLEY

FUEL TANK (OPTIONAL)

21' 0"

49' 9¾" O. A. SPAN

24' 10¹¹⁄₁₆" SEMI-SPAN

21" KINGPOSTS

AILERON LEAD-IN CABLE

2° INC.

15' 4½" LOWER SPAN

38' 7³⁄₃₂"

METAL TUBULAR STRUT

TIP FLOATS RECTANGULAR & SQUARED OFF IN CROSS SECTION

0 1 2 3 4 5 6
SCALE BAR (feet)

4' 8"

3' 3½"

ANTI PENDULUM-SWING SURFACE

28' 10³⁄₁₆"

9

8

7

6

MAIN KEEL PLATE (SKEG)

PLANING PLATE

Ȼ THRUST

"KNUCKLE BUSTER" ENGINE STARTER CRANK

5

4

3

2

11' 9³⁄₈"

W.L.

BOW RING

DATUM

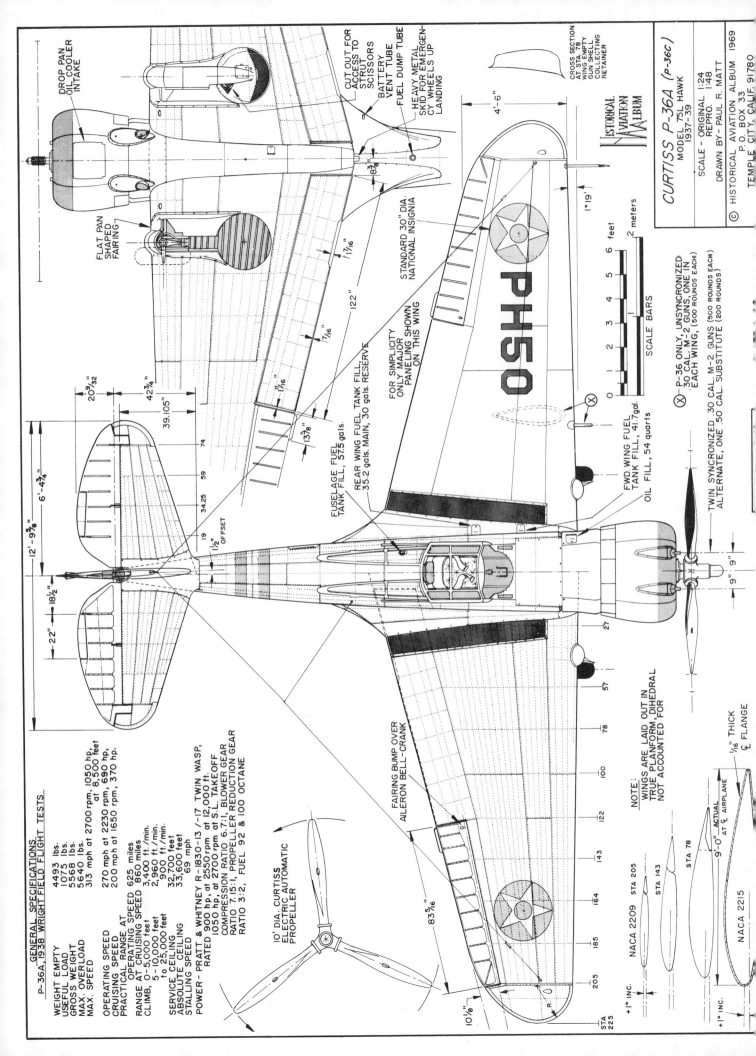

DROP PAN
OIL COOLER
INTAKE

FLAT PAN
SHAPED
FAIRING

CUT OUT FOR
ACCESS TO
STRUT
SCISSORS

BATTERY
VENT TUBE
FUEL DUMP TUBE

HEAVY METAL
SKID FOR EMERGEN-
CY WHEELS UP
LANDING

CROSS SECTION
AT STA. 78
WING EMPTY
GUN SHELL
COLLECTING
RETAINER

STANDARD 30" DIA.
NATIONAL INSIGNIA

FOR SIMPLICITY
ONLY MAJOR
PANELING SHOWN
ON THIS WING

PH50

FUSELAGE FUEL
TANK FILL, 57.5 gals.

REAR WING FUEL TANK FILL,
35.2 gals. MAIN, 30 gals. RESERVE

FWD. WING FUEL
TANK FILL, 41.7 gal.

OIL FILL, 54 quarts

⊗ P-36 ONLY, UNSYNCRONIZED
.30 CAL. M-2 GUNS, ONE IN
EACH WING, (500 ROUNDS EACH)

TWIN SYNCRONIZED .30 CAL. M-2 GUNS (500 ROUNDS EACH)
ALTERNATE, ONE .50 CAL. SUBSTITUTE (200 ROUNDS)

FAIRING BUMP OVER
AILERON BELL-CRANK

NOTE:
WINGS ARE LAID OUT IN
TRUE PLANFORM, DIHEDRAL
NOT ACCOUNTED FOR

10' DIA. CURTISS
ELECTRIC AUTOMATIC
PROPELLER

NACA 2209   STA 205

STA 143

STA 78

9'-0" ACTUAL
AT ℄ AIRPLANE

1/16" THICK
℄ FLANGE

NACA 2215

+1° INC.

+1° INC.

CURTISS P-36A (P-36C)
MODEL 75L HAWK
1937-39

SCALE - ORIGINAL 1:24
REPRO. 1:48
DRAWN BY - PAUL R. MATT

ℍISTORICAL
ℍVIATION
ℍLBUM

© HISTORICAL AVIATION ALBUM 1969
P.O. BOX 33
TEMPLE CITY, CALIF. 91780

SCALE BARS

2 meters

0 1 2 3 4 5 6 feet

GENERAL SPECIFICATIONS
P-36A, 1938 WRIGHT FIELD FLIGHT TESTS

WEIGHT EMPTY	4493 lbs.
USEFUL LOAD	1075 lbs.
GROSS WEIGHT	5568 lbs.
MAX. OVERLOAD	5640 lbs.
MAX. SPEED	313 mph at 2700 rpm, 1050 hp, at 8,500 feet

OPERATING SPEED	270 mph at 2230 rpm, 690 hp.
CRUISING SPEED	200 mph at 1650 rpm, 370 hp.
PRACTICAL RANGE AT OPERATING SPEED	625 miles
RANGE AT CRUISING SPEED	860 miles
CLIMB, 0-5,000 feet	3,400 ft./min.
5-10,000 feet	2,960 ft./min.
to 25,000 feet	900 ft./min.
SERVICE CEILING	32,700 feet
ABSOLUTE CEILING	33,600 feet
STALLING SPEED	69 mph

POWER - PRATT & WHITNEY R-1830-13/-17 TWIN WASP,
RATED 900 hp. at 2550 rpm at 12,000 ft.
1050 hp. at 2700 rpm at S.L. TAKEOFF
COMPRESSION RATIO 6.7:1, BLOWER GEAR
RATIO 7.15:1, PROPELLER REDUCTION GEAR
RATIO 3:2, FUEL 92 & 100 OCTANE

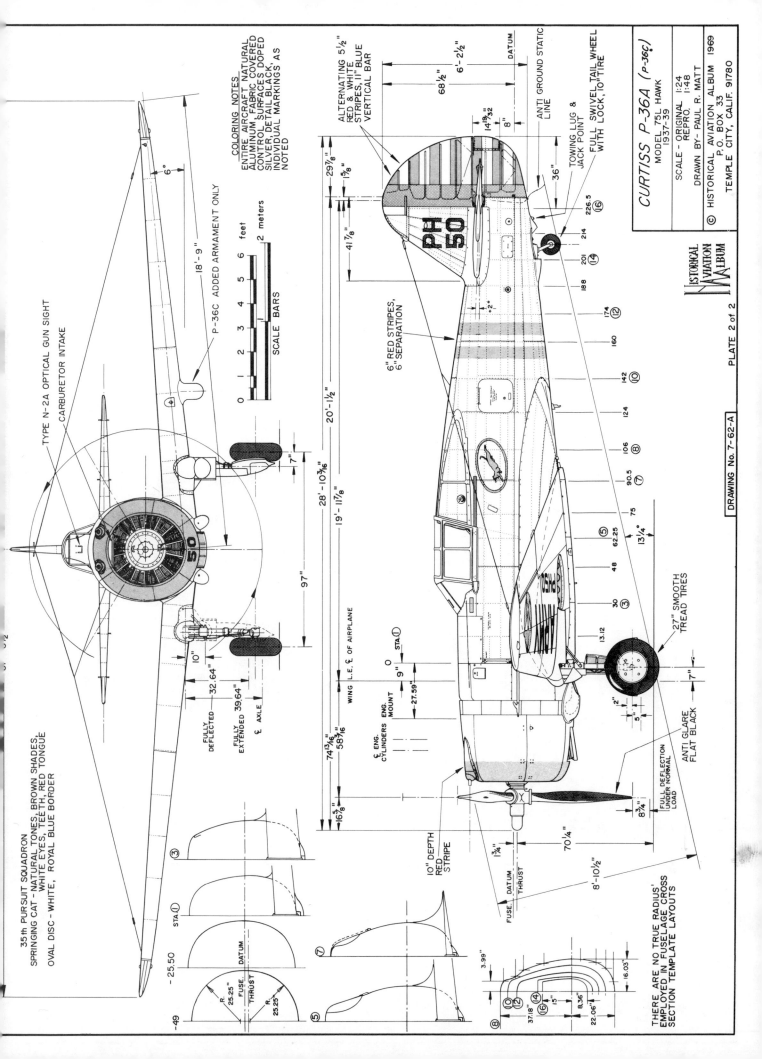

CURTISS P-36A (P-36C)

MODEL 75L HAWK
1937-39

SCALE - ORIGINAL   1:24
         REPRO.   1:48

DRAWN BY- PAUL R. MATT

© HISTORICAL AVIATION ALBUM 1969
P.O. BOX 33
TEMPLE CITY, CALIF. 91780

PLATE 2 of 2

DRAWING No. 7-62-A

THERE ARE NO TRUE RADIUS'
EMPLOYED IN FUSELAGE CROSS
SECTION TEMPLATE LAYOUTS

COLORING NOTES
ENTIRE AIRCRAFT NATURAL
ALUMINUM, FABRIC COVERED
CONTROL SURFACES DOPED
SILVER, DETAIL BLACK,
INDIVIDUAL MARKINGS AS
NOTED

35 th PURSUIT SQUADRON
SPRINGING CAT - NATURAL TONES, BROWN SHADES,
WHITE EYES, TEETH, RED TONGUE
OVAL DISC - WHITE, ROYAL BLUE BORDER

SCALE BARS

TYPE N-2A OPTICAL GUN SIGHT

CARBURETOR INTAKE

P-36C ADDED ARMAMENT ONLY

ALTERNATING 5½"
RED & WHITE
STRIPES, 11" BLUE
VERTICAL BAR

6" RED STRIPES,
6" SEPARATION

ANTI GROUND STATIC
LINE

TOWING LUG &
JACK POINT

FULL SWIVEL TAIL WHEEL
WITH LOCK, 10" TIRE

27" SMOOTH
TREAD TIRES

ANTI GLARE
FLAT BLACK

FULL DEFLECTION
UNDER NORMAL
LOAD

10" DEPTH
RED STRIPE

FUSE. DATUM
THRUST

WING L.E. ₵ OF AIRPLANE

₵ ENG.
CYLINDERS

ENG.
MOUNT

STA ①

FUSE.
THRUST
DATUM

R.
25.25"

R.
25.25"

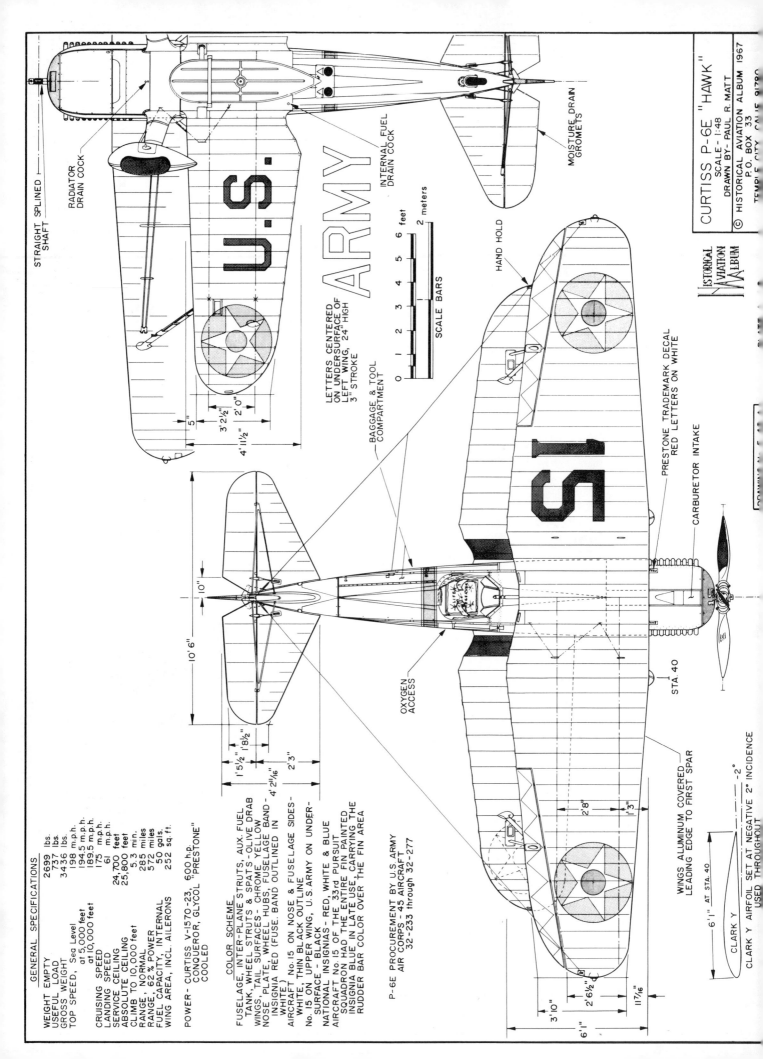

STRAIGHT SPLINED SHAFT

RADIATOR DRAIN COCK

U.S.

ARMY

INTERNAL FUEL DRAIN COCK

MOISTURE DRAIN GROMETS

LETTERS CENTERED ON UNDERSURFACE OF LEFT WING, 24" HIGH 3" STROKE

BAGGAGE & TOOL COMPARTMENT

| | | | | | | | feet |
|0|1|2|3|4|5|6| |

2 meters

SCALE BARS

HAND HOLD

15

PRESTONE TRADEMARK DECAL RED LETTERS ON WHITE

CARBURETOR INTAKE

OXYGEN ACCESS

STA. 40

WINGS ALUMINUM COVERED LEADING EDGE TO FIRST SPAR

6'1" AT STA. 40

CLARK Y   -2°

CLARK Y AIRFOIL SET AT NEGATIVE 2° INCIDENCE USED THROUGHOUT

5"
3' 2½"
2' 0"
4' 11½"

10"

10' 6"

1' 5½"
1' 8½"
2' 3"
4' 2¹¹⁄₁₆"

2' 8"
1' 3"

3' 10"
2' 6½"
6' 1"
11⁷⁄₁₆"

GENERAL SPECIFICATIONS

WEIGHT EMPTY	2699	lbs.
USEFUL LOAD	737	lbs.
GROSS WEIGHT	3436	lbs.
TOP SPEED, Sea Level	198	m.p.h.
at 5,000 feet	194.5	m.p.h.
at 10,000 feet	189.5	m.p.h.
CRUISING SPEED	175	m.p.h.
LANDING SPEED	61	m.p.h.
SERVICE CEILING	24,700	feet
ABSOLUTE CEILING	25,800	feet
CLIMB TO 10,000 feet	5.3	min.
RANGE, NORMAL	285	miles
RANGE, 62% POWER	572	miles
FUEL CAPACITY, INTERNAL	50	gals.
WING AREA, INCL. AILERONS	252	sq. ft.

POWER- CURTISS V-1570-23, 600 h.p. CONQUEROR, GLYCOL "PRESTONE" COOLED

COLOR SCHEME

FUSELAGE, INTER-PLANE STRUTS, AUX. FUEL TANK, WHEEL STRUTS & SPATS- OLIVE DRAB WINGS, TAIL SURFACES- CHROME YELLOW NOSE PLATE, WHEEL HUBS, FUSELAGE BAND- INSIGNIA RED (FUSE. BAND OUTLINED IN WHITE)
AIRCRAFT No. 15 ON NOSE & FUSELAGE SIDES- WHITE, THIN BLACK OUTLINE
No. 15 ON UPPER WING, U.S. ARMY ON UNDER- SURFACE - BLACK
NATIONAL INSIGNIAS - RED, WHITE & BLUE
AIRCRAFT No. 15 OF THE 33rd PURSUIT SQUADRON HAD THE ENTIRE FIN PAINTED INSIGNIA BLUE IN LATE USE, CARRYING THE RUDDER BAR COLOR OVER THE FIN AREA

P-6E PROCUREMENT BY U.S. ARMY AIR CORPS - 45 AIRCRAFT 32-233 through 32-277

CURTISS P-6E "HAWK"
SCALE- 1:48
DRAWN BY- PAUL R. MATT
© HISTORICAL AVIATION ALBUM 1967
P.O. BOX 33
TEMPLE CITY, CALIF. 91780

Historical Aviation Album

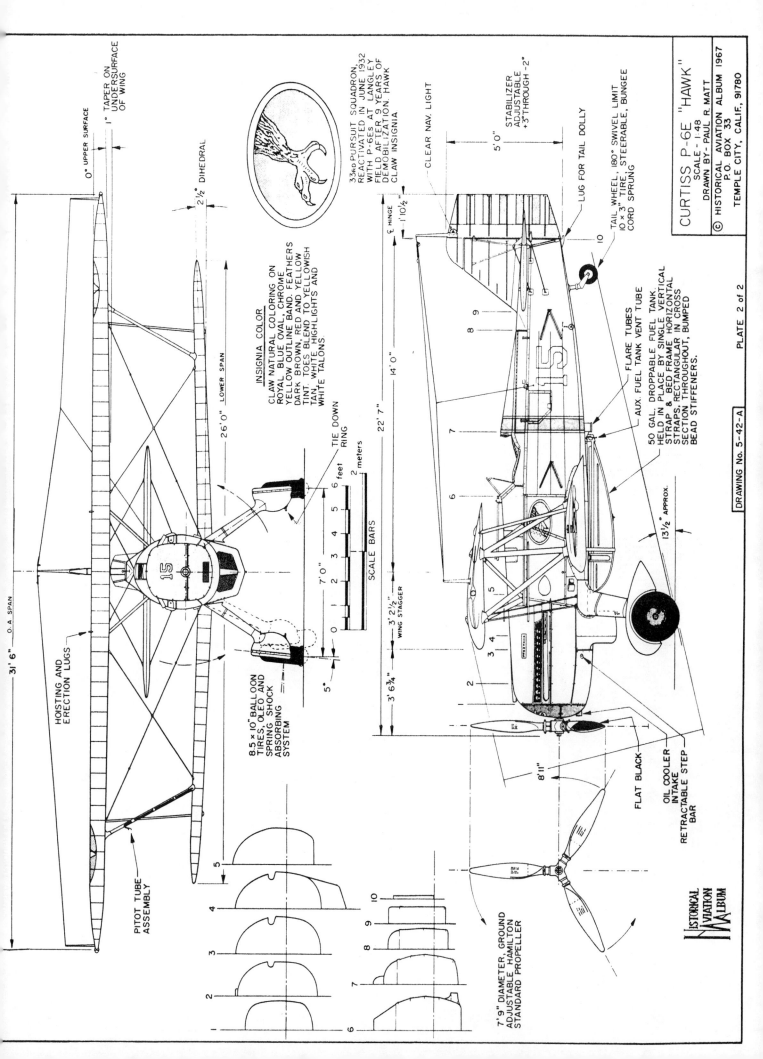

O° UPPER SURFACE

1° TAPER ON UNDERSURFACE OF WING

2½° DIHEDRAL

31' 6" O.A. SPAN

26' 0" LOWER SPAN

HOISTING AND ERECTION LUGS

PITOT TUBE ASSEMBLY

8.5 × 10" BALLOON TIRES, OLEO AND SPRING SHOCK ABSORBING SYSTEM

INSIGNIA COLOR
CLAW NATURAL COLORING ON ROYAL BLUE OVAL, CHROME YELLOW OUTLINE BAND. FEATHERS DARK BROWN, RED AND YELLOW TINT. TOES BLEND TO YELLOWISH TAN, WHITE HIGHLIGHTS AND WHITE TALONS.

33rd PURSUIT SQUADRON, REACTIVATED IN JUNE 1932 WITH P-6Es AT LANGLEY FIELD AFTER 9 YEARS OF DEMOBILIZATION. HAWK CLAW INSIGNIA.

TIE DOWN RING

SCALE BARS

feet
6 5 4 3 2 1 0

2 meters

7' 0"

5°

3' 6¾"

3' 2½" WING STAGGER

22' 7"

14' 0"

CLEAR NAV. LIGHT

STABILIZER ADJUSTABLE +3° THROUGH −2°

5' 0"

1' 10½"

€ HINGE

LUG FOR TAIL DOLLY

TAIL WHEEL, 180° SWIVEL LIMIT 10 × 3" TIRE, STEERABLE, BUNGEE CORD SPRUNG

FLARE TUBES

AUX. FUEL TANK VENT TUBE

50 GAL. DROPPABLE FUEL TANK. HELD IN PLACE BY SINGLE VERTICAL STRAP & BED FRAME HORIZONTAL STRAPS, RECTANGULAR IN CROSS SECTION THROUGHOUT, BUMPED BEAD STIFFENERS.

13½" APPROX.

8' 11"

FLAT BLACK

OIL COOLER INTAKE

RETRACTABLE STEP BAR

7' 9" DIAMETER, GROUND ADJUSTABLE HAMILTON STANDARD PROPELLER

10 9 8 7 6 5 4 3 2

CURTISS P-6E "HAWK"
SCALE - 1:48
DRAWN BY- PAUL R. MATT
© HISTORICAL AVIATION ALBUM 1967
P.O. BOX 33
TEMPLE CITY, CALIF., 91780

PLATE 2 of 2

DRAWING No. 5-42-A

Historical Aviation Album

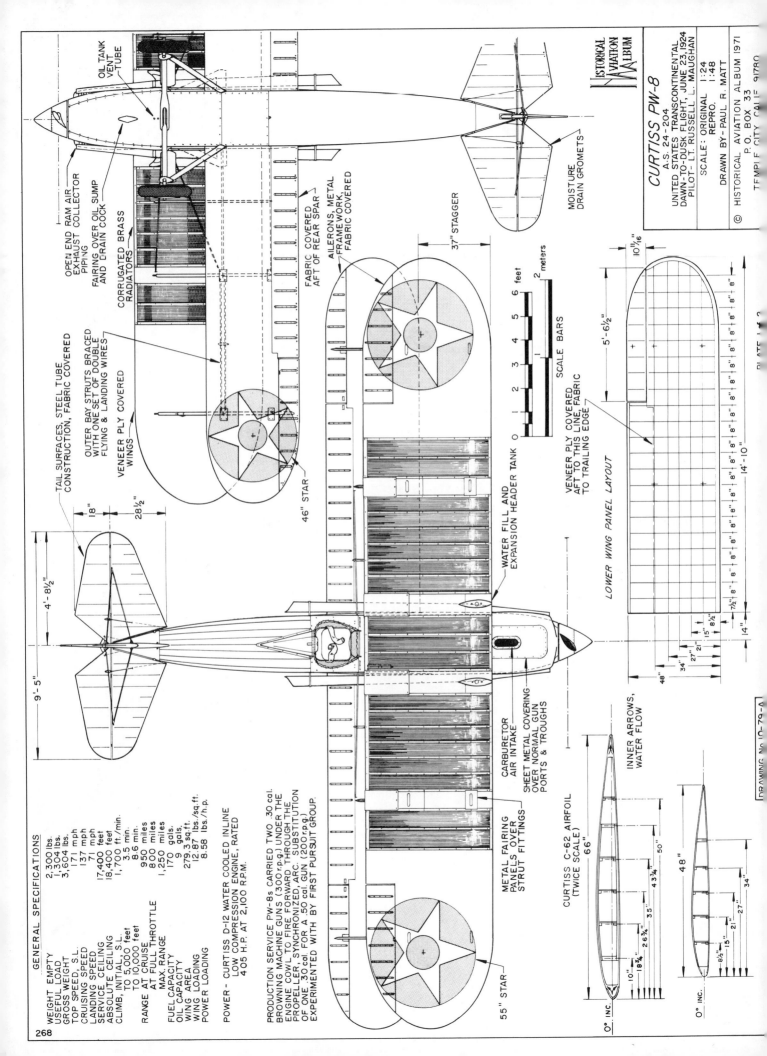

OIL TANK VENT TUBE

OPEN END RAM AIR EXHAUST COLLECTOR

FAIRING OVER OIL SUMP AND DRAIN COCK

CORRUGATED BRASS RADIATORS

OUTER BAY STRUTS BRACED WITH ONE SET OF DOUBLE FLYING & LANDING WIRES

VENEER PLY COVERED WINGS

TAIL SURFACES, STEEL TUBE CONSTRUCTION, FABRIC COVERED

FABRIC COVERED AFT OF REAR SPAR

AILERONS, METAL FRAMEWORK, FABRIC COVERED

37" STAGGER

MOISTURE DRAIN GROMETS

46" STAR

WATER FILL AND EXPANSION HEADER TANK

VENEER PLY COVERED AFT TO THIS LINE, FABRIC TO TRAILING EDGE

LOWER WING PANEL LAYOUT

SCALE BARS

0 1 2 3 4 5 6 feet

2 meters

10¹/₁₆"

5'-6½"

14'-10"

7½" 8" 8" 8" 8" 8" 8" 8" 8" 8" 8" 8" 8" 8" 8" 8" 8"

8½"
15"
27"
34"
48"
14"
2"
2"

18"

28½"

4'-8½"

9'-5"

CARBURETOR AIR INTAKE

SHEET METAL COVERING OVER NORMAL GUN PORTS & TROUGHS

METAL FAIRING PANELS OVER STRUT FITTINGS

55" STAR

INNER ARROWS, WATER FLOW

CURTISS C-62 AIRFOIL (TWICE SCALE)

66"

48"

10"
18¾"
2 6¾"
3 5"
4 3¾"
50"

0° INC.

8½"
15"
2"
27"
34"

0° INC.

GENERAL SPECIFICATIONS

WEIGHT EMPTY	2,300 lbs.
USEFUL LOAD	1,304 lbs.
GROSS WEIGHT	3,604 lbs.
TOP SPEED, S.L.	171 mph
CRUISING SPEED	137 mph
LANDING SPEED	71 mph
SERVICE CEILING	17,400 feet
ABSOLUTE CEILING	18,400 feet
CLIMB, INITIAL, S.L.	1,700 ft./min.
TO 5,000 feet	3.5 min.
TO 10,000 feet	8.6 min.
RANGE AT CRUISE	950 miles
AT FULL THROTTLE	800 miles
MAX. RANGE	1,250 miles
FUEL CAPACITY	170 gals.
OIL CAPACITY	9 gals.
WING AREA	279.3 sq.ft.
WING LOADING	12.87 lbs./sq.ft.
POWER LOADING	8.58 lbs./h.p.

POWER - CURTISS D-12 WATER COOLED INLINE LOW COMPRESSION ENGINE, RATED 405 H.P. AT 2,100 R.P.M.

PRODUCTION SERVICE PW-8s CARRIED TWO .30 cal. BROWNING MACHINE GUNS (300 r.p.g.) UNDER THE ENGINE COWL TO FIRE FORWARD THROUGH THE PROPELLER, SYNCHRONIZED, ARC. SUBSTITUTION OF ONE .30 cal. GUN (200 r.p.g.) FOR A .50 cal. GUN (200 r.p.g.) EXPERIMENTED WITH BY FIRST PURSUIT GROUP.

CURTISS PW-8
A.S. 24-204
UNITED STATES TRANSCONTINENTAL DAWN-TO-DUSK FLIGHT, JUNE 23, 1924
PILOT- LT. RUSSELL L. MAUGHAN

SCALE: ORIGINAL 1:24
REPRO. 1:48

DRAWN BY- PAUL R. MATT

© HISTORICAL AVIATION ALBUM 1971
P.O. BOX 33
TEMPLE CITY, CALIF. 91780

HISTORICAL AVIATION ALBUM

DRAWING No. IO-79-A

268

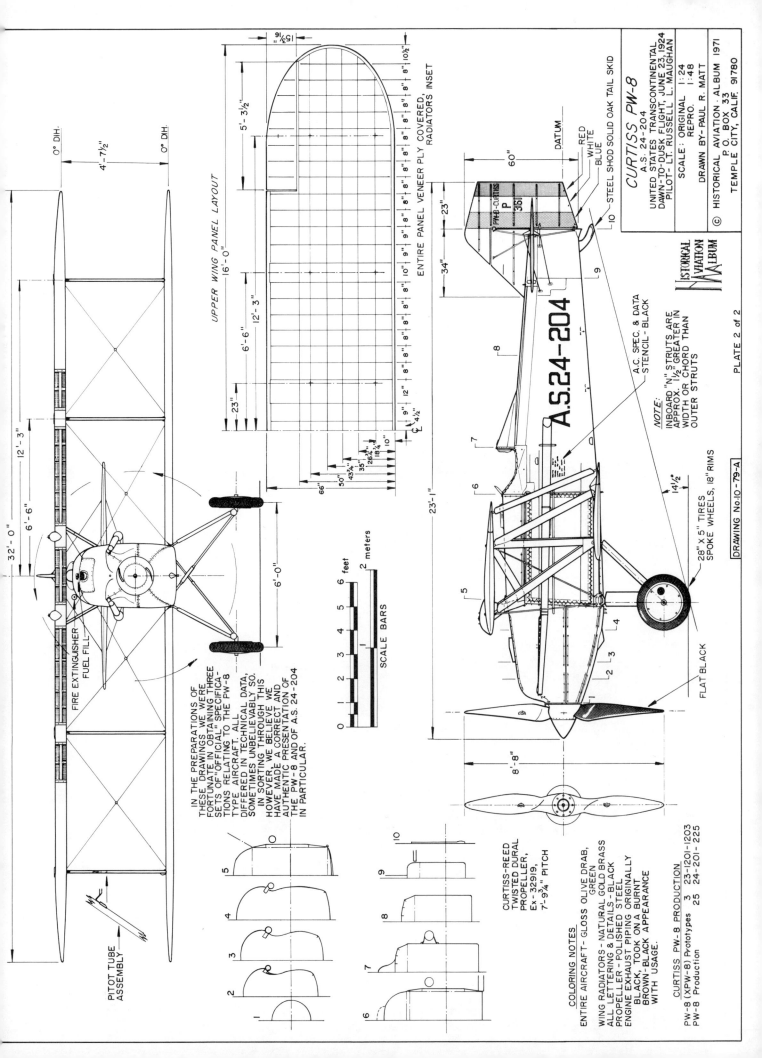

UPPER WING PANEL LAYOUT

ENTIRE PANEL VENEER PLY COVERED, RADIATORS INSET

CURTISS PW-8
A.S. 24-204
UNITED STATES TRANSCONTINENTAL
DAWN-TO-DUSK FLIGHT, JUNE 23, 1924
PILOT- LT. RUSSELL L. MAUGHAN

SCALE : ORIGINAL 1:24
REPRO.   1:48
DRAWN BY-PAUL R. MATT

© HISTORICAL AVIATION · ALBUM 1971
P. O. BOX 33
TEMPLE CITY, CALIF. 91780

Historical Aviation Album

PLATE 2 of 2

RED
WHITE
BLUE

10 - STEEL SHOD SOLID OAK TAIL SKID

DATUM

A.C. SPEC. & DATA
STENCIL- BLACK

NOTE:
INBOARD "N" STRUTS ARE
APPROX. 1½" GREATER IN
WIDTH OR CHORD THAN
OUTER STRUTS

28" X 5" TIRES
SPOKE WHEELS, 18" RIMS

FLAT BLACK

DRAWING No.10-79-A

FIRE EXTINGUISHER
FUEL FILL

PITOT TUBE
ASSEMBLY

IN THE PREPARATIONS OF
THESE DRAWINGS WE WERE
FORTUNATE IN OBTAINING THREE
SETS OF "OFFICIAL" SPECIFICA-
TIONS RELATING TO THE PW-8
TYPE AIRCRAFT. ALL
DIFFERED IN TECHNICAL DATA,
SOMETIMES UNBELIEVABLY SO.
IN SORTING THROUGH THIS
HOWEVER, WE BELIEVE WE
HAVE MADE A CORRECT AND
AUTHENTIC PRESENTATION OF
THE PW-8 AND OF A.S. 24-204
IN PARTICULAR.

6 feet
2 meters

SCALE BARS

CURTISS-REED
TWISTED DURAL
PROPELLER,
E x - 32919,
7'-9¾" PITCH

COLORING NOTES

ENTIRE AIRCRAFT- GLOSS OLIVE DRAB,
GREEN
WING RADIATORS- NATURAL GOLD BRASS
ALL LETTERING & DETAILS - BLACK
PROPELLER - POLISHED STEEL
ENGINE EXHAUST PIPING ORIGINALLY
BLACK, TOOK ON A BURNT
BROWN- BLACK APPEARANCE
WITH USAGE.

CURTISS PW-8 PRODUCTION

PW-8 (XPW-8) Prototypes 3 23-1201-1203
PW-8 Production   25 24-201-225

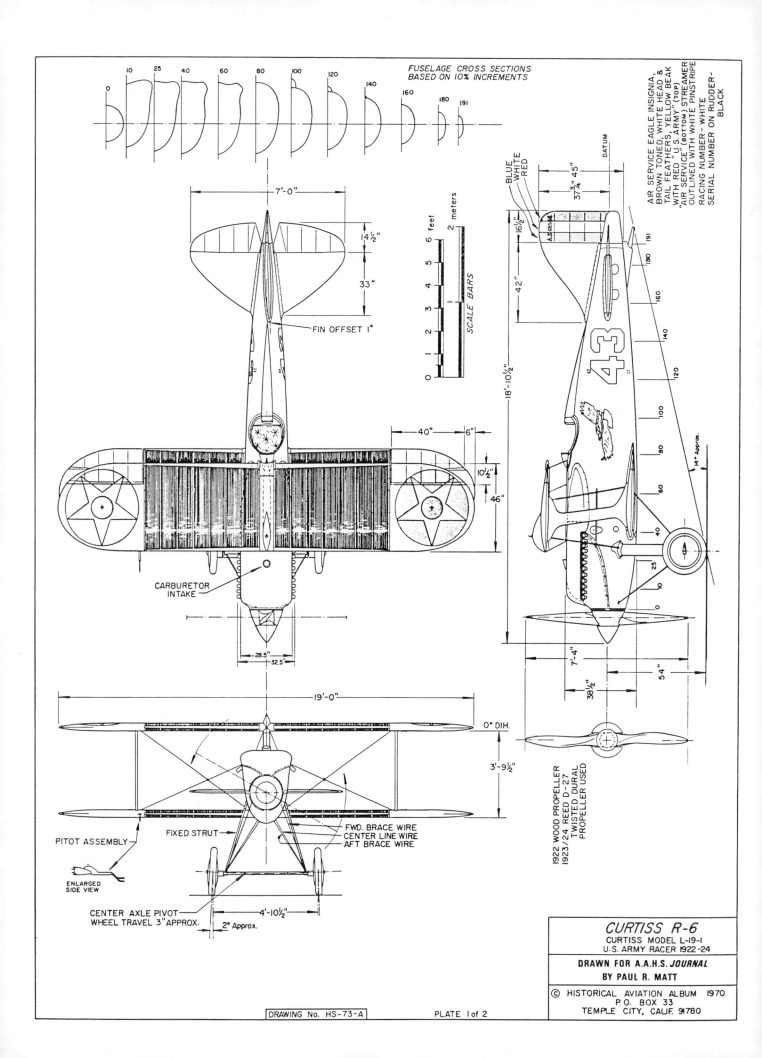

FUSELAGE CROSS SECTIONS
BASED ON 10% INCREMENTS

10 25 40 60 80 100 120 140 160 180 191

7'-0"

14½"

33"

FIN OFFSET 1°

feet
meters
SCALE BARS

40" 6"

10½"

46"

CARBURETOR
INTAKE

28.5"
32.5"

AIR SERVICE EAGLE INSIGNIA,
BROWN TONED, WHITE HEAD &
TAIL FEATHERS, YELLOW BEAK
WITH RED "U.S. ARMY" (TOP)
"AIR SERVICE" (BOTTOM) STREAMER
OUTLINED WITH WHITE PINSTRIPE
RACING NUMBER - WHITE
SERIAL NUMBER ON RUDDER-
BLACK

BLUE
WHITE
RED

37¾" 45"
16½"
42"
18'-10½"
A.S.68564
43
14° Approx.
191 180 160 140 120 100 80 60 40 25 10

DATUM

7'-4"
38½"
54"

1922 WOOD PROPELLER
1923/24 REED D-27
TWISTED DURAL
PROPELLER USED

19'-0"

0° DIH.

3'-9½"

PITOT ASSEMBLY

ENLARGED
SIDE VIEW

FIXED STRUT

FWD. BRACE WIRE
CENTER LINE WIRE
AFT BRACE WIRE

CENTER AXLE PIVOT
WHEEL TRAVEL 3" APPROX.

2° Approx.

4'-10½"

CURTISS R-6
CURTISS MODEL L-19-1
U.S. ARMY RACER 1922-24

DRAWN FOR A.A.H.S. *JOURNAL*
BY PAUL R. MATT

© HISTORICAL AVIATION ALBUM 1970
P.O. BOX 33
TEMPLE CITY, CALIF. 91780

DRAWING No. HS-73-A   PLATE 1 of 2

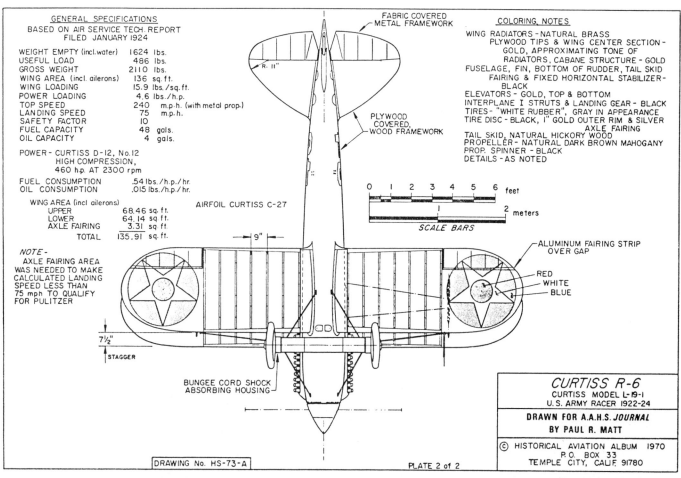

GENERAL SPECIFICATIONS
BASED ON AIR SERVICE TECH. REPORT
FILED JANUARY 1924

WEIGHT EMPTY (incl.water)   1624 lbs.
USEFUL LOAD   486 lbs.
GROSS WEIGHT   2110 lbs.
WING AREA (incl. ailerons)   136 sq.ft.
WING LOADING   15.9 lbs./sq.ft.
POWER LOADING   4.6 lbs./h.p.
TOP SPEED   240 m.p.h. (with metal prop.)
LANDING SPEED   75 m.p.h.
SAFETY FACTOR   10
FUEL CAPACITY   48 gals.
OIL CAPACITY   4 gals.

POWER - CURTISS D-12, No.12
HIGH COMPRESSION,
460 h.p. AT 2300 rpm
FUEL CONSUMPTION   .54 lbs./h.p./hr.
OIL CONSUMPTION   .015 lbs./h.p./hr.

WING AREA (incl ailerons)
UPPER   68.46 sq.ft.
LOWER   64.14 sq.ft.
AXLE FAIRING   3.31 sq.ft.
TOTAL   135.91 sq.ft.

NOTE -
AXLE FAIRING AREA
WAS NEEDED TO MAKE
CALCULATED LANDING
SPEED LESS THAN
75 mph TO QUALIFY
FOR PULITZER

AIRFOIL CURTISS C-27

FABRIC COVERED METAL FRAMEWORK

PLYWOOD COVERED, WOOD FRAMEWORK

R. 11"

9"

7½"
STAGGER

BUNGEE CORD SHOCK ABSORBING HOUSING

SCALE BARS
0 1 2 3 4 5 6 feet
1 2 meters

ALUMINUM FAIRING STRIP OVER GAP

RED
WHITE
BLUE

COLORING, NOTES
WING RADIATORS - NATURAL BRASS
PLYWOOD TIPS & WING CENTER SECTION -
GOLD, APPROXIMATING TONE OF
RADIATORS, CABANE STRUCTURE - GOLD
FUSELAGE, FIN, BOTTOM OF RUDDER, TAIL SKID
FAIRING & FIXED HORIZONTAL STABILIZER-
BLACK
ELEVATORS - GOLD, TOP & BOTTOM
INTERPLANE I STRUTS & LANDING GEAR - BLACK
TIRES - "WHITE RUBBER", GRAY IN APPEARANCE
TIRE DISC - BLACK, 1" GOLD OUTER RIM & SILVER
AXLE FAIRING
TAIL SKID, NATURAL HICKORY WOOD
PROPELLER - NATURAL DARK BROWN MAHOGANY
PROP. SPINNER - BLACK
DETAILS - AS NOTED

DRAWING No. HS-73-A

PLATE 2 of 2

CURTISS R-6
CURTISS MODEL L-19-1
U.S. ARMY RACER 1922-24
DRAWN FOR A.A.H.S. JOURNAL
BY PAUL R. MATT

© HISTORICAL AVIATION ALBUM 1970
P.O. BOX 33
TEMPLE CITY, CALIF. 91780

Curtiss 1922 Army Racer at Selfridge Field. Winner of Pulitzer Trophy, October 14, 1922.

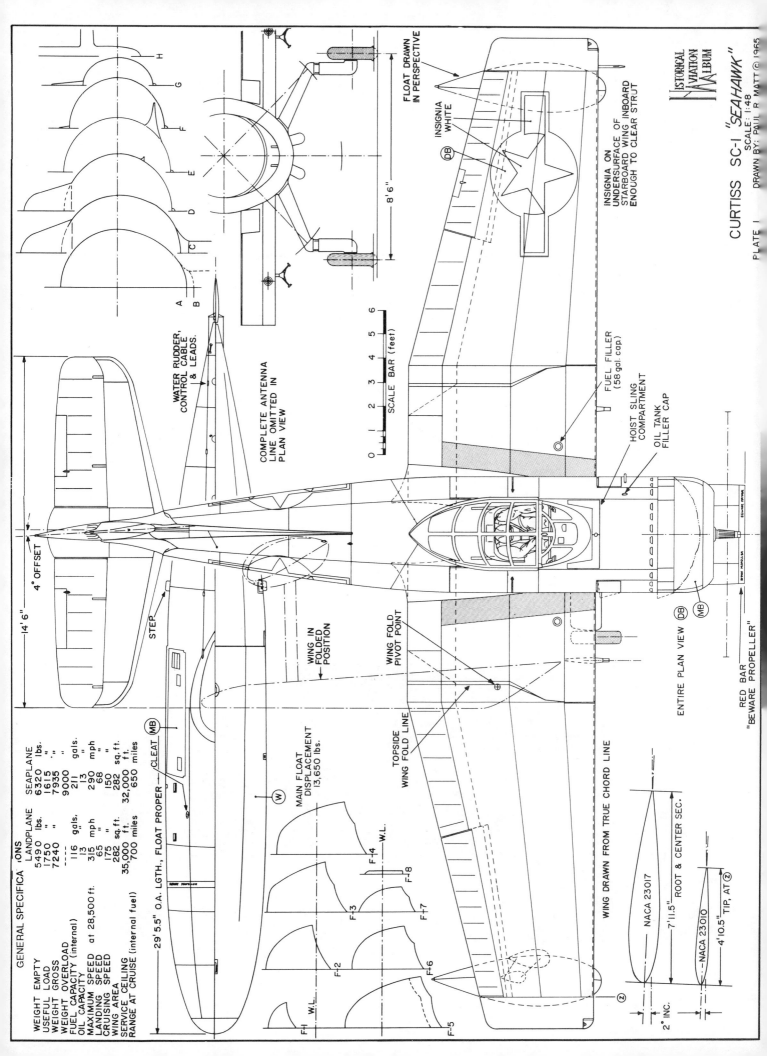

CURTISS SC-1 *"SEAHAWK"*
SCALE 1:48
DRAWN BY: PAUL R MATT © 1965

PLATE I

FLOAT DRAWN
IN PERSPECTIVE

8' 6"

INSIGNIA
WHITE

INSIGNIA ON
UNDERSURFACE OF
STARBOARD WING INBOARD
ENOUGH TO CLEAR STRUT

WATER RUDDER,
CONTROL CABLE
& LEADS.

COMPLETE ANTENNA
LINE OMITTED IN
PLAN VIEW

0 1 2 3 4 5 6
SCALE BAR (feet)

FUEL FILLER
(58 gal. cap.)

HOIST SLING
COMPARTMENT

OIL TANK
FILLER CAP

4° OFFSET

14' 6"

STEP

WING IN
FOLDED
POSITION

WING FOLD
PIVOT POINT

TOPSIDE
WING FOLD LINE

ENTIRE PLAN VIEW

RED BAR
"BEWARE PROPELLER"

WING DRAWN FROM TRUE CHORD LINE

NACA 23017

7' 11.5"
ROOT & CENTER SEC.

2° INC.

NACA 23010

4'10.5"
TIP, AT ②

29' 5.5" O.A. LGTH., FLOAT PROPER — CLEAT

MAIN FLOAT
DISPLACEMENT
13,650 lbs.

W.L.

F-4

F-8

F-3

F-7

F-2

F-6

F-1 W.L.

F-5

GENERAL SPECIFICATIONS

	LANDPLANE	SEAPLANE	
WEIGHT EMPTY	5490	6320	lbs.
USEFUL LOAD	1750	1615	"
WEIGHT GROSS	7240	7935	"
WEIGHT OVERLOAD	—	9000	"
FUEL CAPACITY (internal)	116	211	gals.
OIL CAPACITY	13	13	gals.
MAXIMUM SPEED at 28,500 ft.	315	290	mph
LANDING SPEED	65	68	"
CRUISING SPEED	175	150	"
WING AREA	282	282	sq. ft.
SERVICE CEILING	35,000	32,000	ft.
RANGE AT CRUISE (internal fuel)	700	650	miles

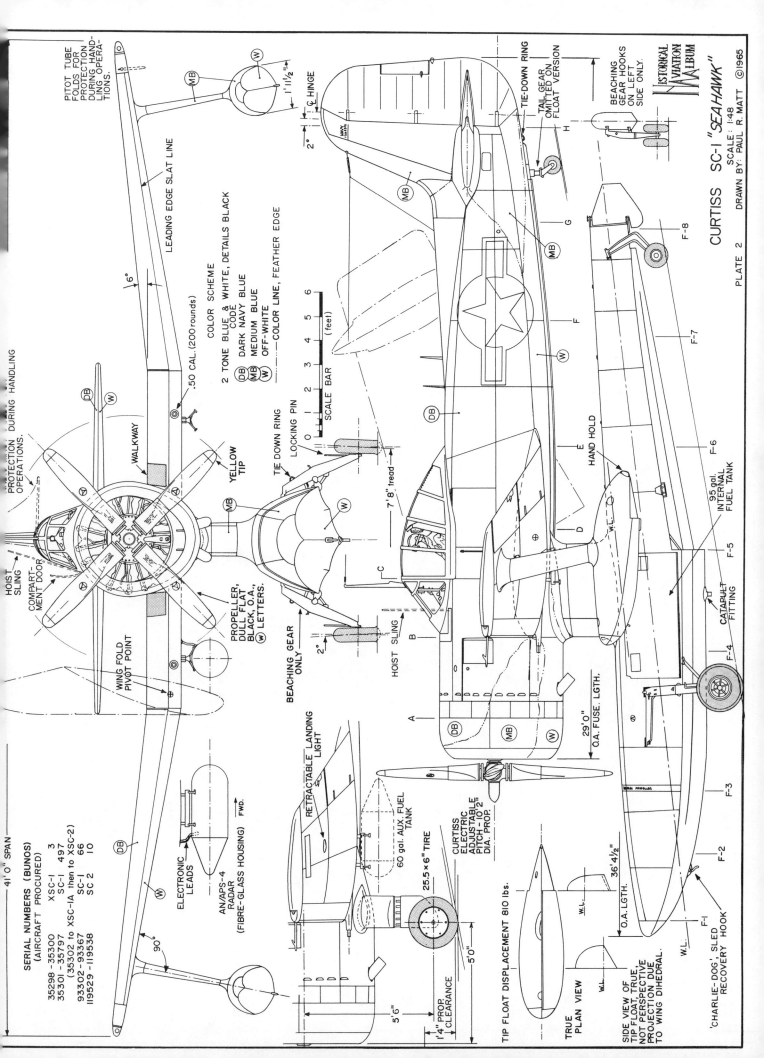

CURTISS SC-1 *"SEAHAWK"*

SCALE: 1:48   DRAWN BY: PAUL R. MATT

PLATE 2

Historical Aviation Album ©1965

PITOT TUBE FOLDS FOR PROTECTION DURING HANDLING OPERATIONS.

LEADING EDGE SLAT LINE

6°

.50 CAL. (200 rounds)

COLOR SCHEME
2 TONE BLUE & WHITE, DETAILS BLACK

CODE
(DB) DARK NAVY BLUE
(MB) MEDIUM BLUE
(W) OFF-WHITE

——— COLOR LINE, FEATHER EDGE

SCALE BAR (feet)
0 1 2 3 4 5 6

TIE DOWN RING

LOCKING PIN

7'8" tread

2°

HOIST SLING

B

A

DB MB W

29'0"
O.A. FUSE. LGTH.

BEACHING GEAR ONLY

2°

MB

W

C

PROTECTION DURING HANDLING OPERATIONS.

WALKWAY

YELLOW TIP

DB W

PROPELLER, DULL FLAT BLACK, O.A., (W) LETTERS.

WING FOLD PIVOT POINT

HOIST SLING

COMPARTMENT DOOR

41' 0" SPAN

SERIAL NUMBERS (BUNOS)
(AIRCRAFT PROCURED)

35298 - 35300   XSC-1   3
35301 - 35797   SC-1   497
(35302 to XSC-1A then to XSC-2)
93302 - 93367   SC-1   66
119529 - 119538   SC 2   10

ELECTRONIC LEADS

AN/APS-4 RADAR (FIBRE-GLASS HOUSING)

DB

90°

W

RETRACTABLE LANDING LIGHT

FWD.

60 gal. AUX. FUEL TANK

25.5×6" TIRE

5'0"

1'4" PROP. CLEARANCE

5'6"

TIP FLOAT DISPLACEMENT 810 lbs.

CURTISS ELECTRIC ADJUSTABLE PITCH - 10'2" DIA. PROP.

TRUE PLAN VIEW

W.L.

36'4½"
O.A. LGTH.

W.L.

SIDE VIEW OF TIP FLOAT, TRUE, NOT PERSPECTIVE PROJECTION DUE TO WING DIHEDRAL.

'CHARLIE-DOG', SLED RECOVERY HOOK

F-1

F-2

F-3

F-4

CATAPULT FITTING

F-5

F-6

F-7

95 gal. INTERNAL FUEL TANK

F-8

HAND HOLD

E

D

W.L.

F

G

MB

W

DB

H

TIE-DOWN RING

TAIL GEAR OMITTED ON FLOAT VERSION

BEACHING GEAR HOOKS ON LEFT SIDE ONLY.

1' 11½"

(C) HINGE

2°

MB

W

HOIST SLING

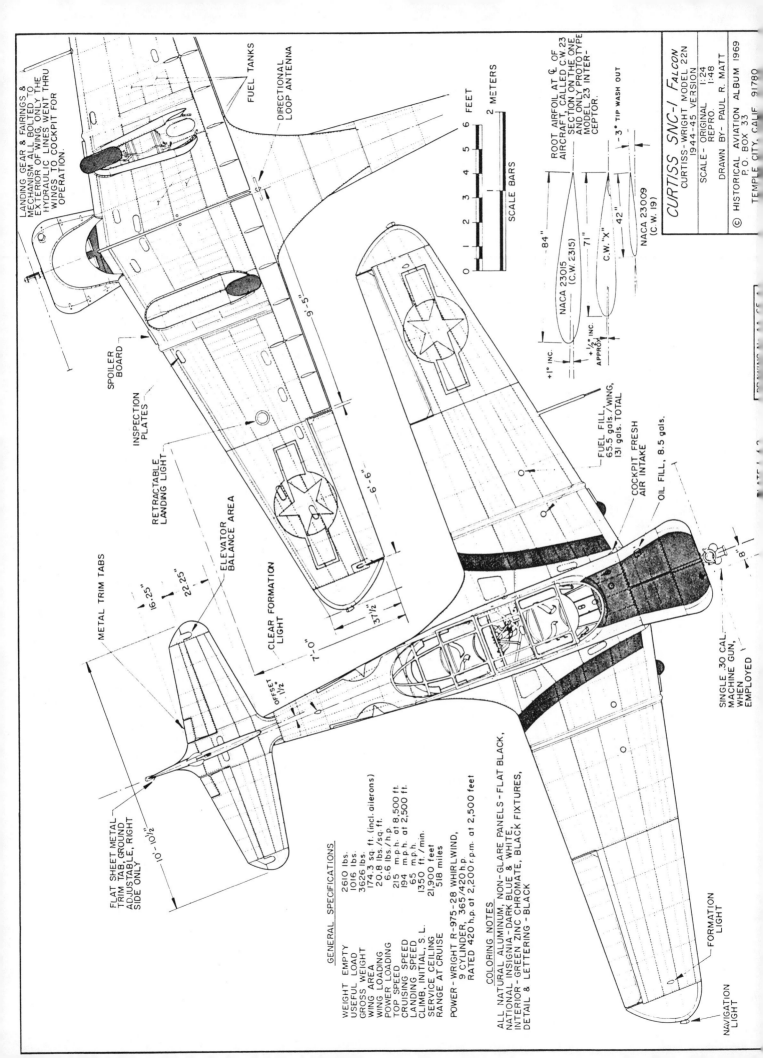

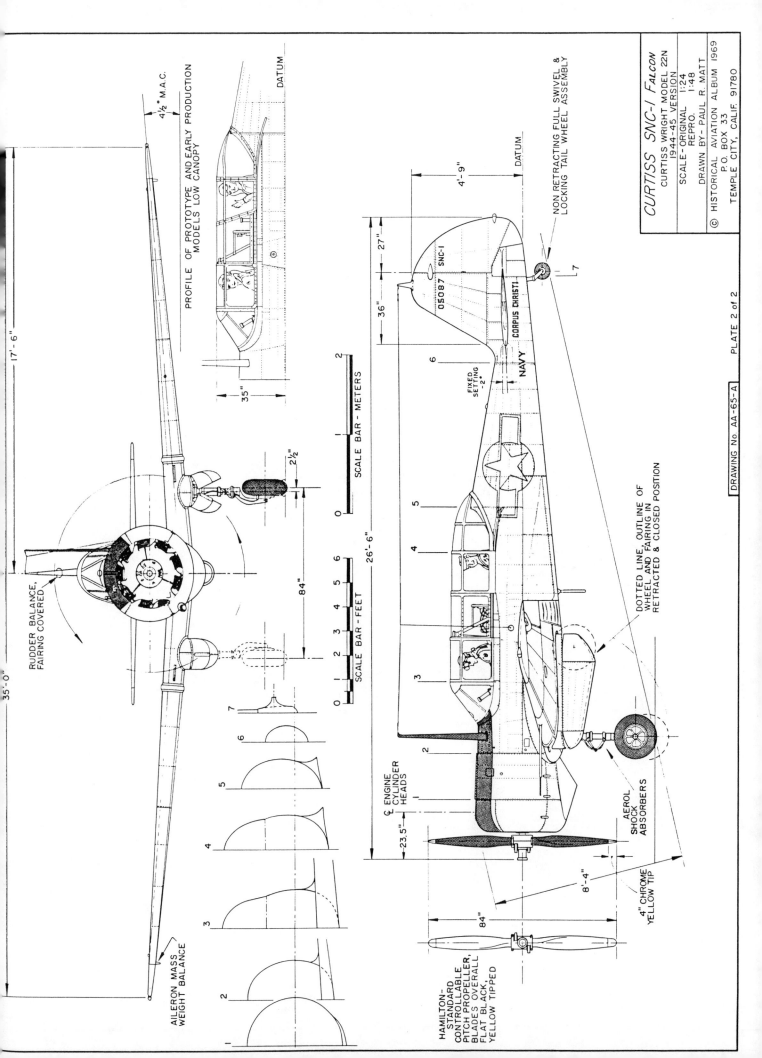

4½" M.A.C.

DATUM

PROFILE OF PROTOTYPE AND EARLY PRODUCTION MODELS LOW CANOPY

17'-6"

35"

RUDDER BALANCE, FAIRING COVERED

AILERON MASS WEIGHT BALANCE

35'-0"

2½"

SCALE BAR - METERS

84"

26'-6"

SCALE BAR - FEET

HAMILTON-STANDARD CONTROLLABLE PITCH PROPELLER, BLADES OVERALL FLAT BLACK, YELLOW TIPPED

84"

4" CHROME YELLOW TIP

AEROL SHOCK ABSORBERS

8-4"

23.5"

₵ ENGINE CYLINDER HEADS

DOTTED LINE, OUTLINE OF WHEEL AND FAIRING IN RETRACTED & CLOSED POSITION

NON RETRACTING FULL SWIVEL & LOCKING TAIL WHEEL ASSEMBLY

DATUM

4'-9"

27"

36"

05087 SNC-1

CORPUS CHRISTI.

NAVY

FIXED SETTING -2°

CURTISS SNC-1 FALCON
CURTISS WRIGHT MODEL 22N
1944-45 VERSION
SCALE-ORIGINAL   1:24
REPRO.   1:48
DRAWN BY- PAUL R. MATT
© HISTORICAL AVIATION ALBUM 1969
P.O. BOX 33
TEMPLE CITY, CALIF. 91780

DRAWING No AA-65-A   PLATE 2 of 2

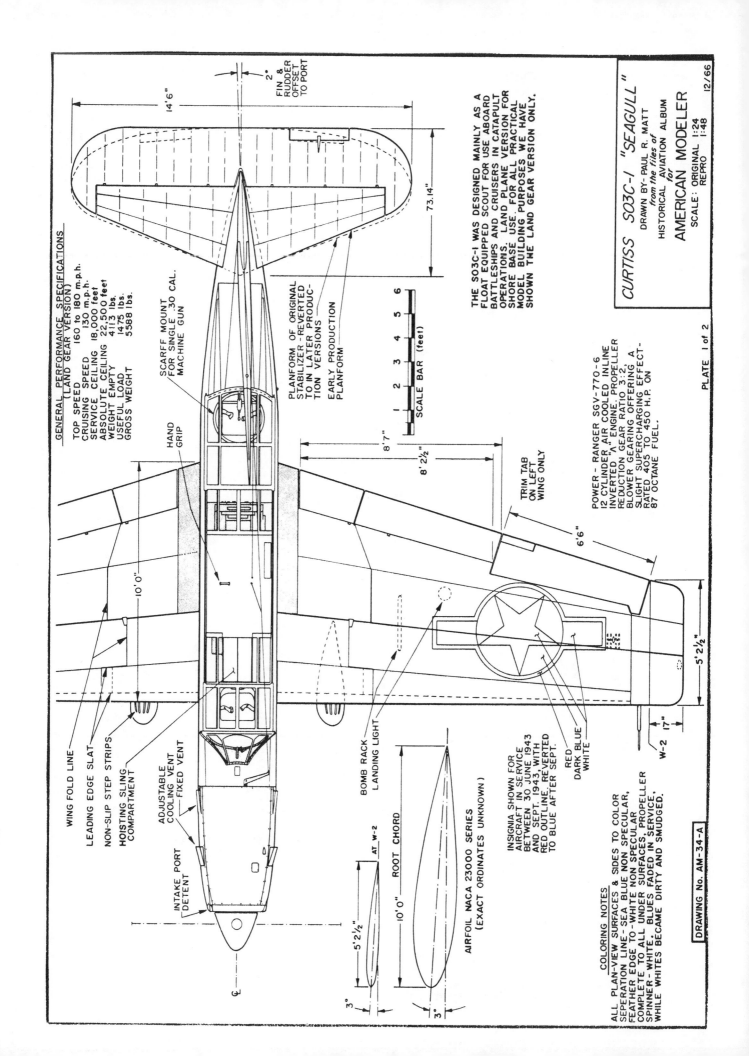

FIN & RUDDER OFFSET TO PORT

2°

14'6"

73.14"

GENERAL PERFORMANCE SPECIFICATIONS
(LAND GEAR VERSION)

TOP SPEED .... 160 to 180 m.p.h.
CRUISING SPEED .... 130 m.p.h.
SERVICE CEILING ..... 18,000 feet
ABSOLUTE CEILING ... 22,500 feet
WEIGHT EMPTY .... 4113 lbs.
USEFUL LOAD .... 1475 lbs.
GROSS WEIGHT .... 5588 lbs.

SCARFF MOUNT
FOR SINGLE .30 CAL.
MACHINE GUN

PLANFORM OF ORIGINAL
STABILIZER - REVERTED
TO IN LATER PRODUC-
TION VERSIONS

EARLY PRODUCTION
PLANFORM

1 2 3 4 5 6
SCALE BAR (feet)

THE SO3C-1 WAS DESIGNED MAINLY AS A
FLOAT EQUIPPED SCOUT FOR USE ABOARD
BATTLESHIPS AND CRUISERS IN CATAPULT
OPERATIONS. LAND PLANE VERSION FOR
SHORE BASE USE. FOR ALL PRACTICAL
MODEL BUILDING PURPOSES WE HAVE
SHOWN THE LAND GEAR VERSION ONLY.

CURTISS SO3C-1 "SEAGULL"
DRAWN BY- PAUL R. MATT
from the files of
HISTORICAL AVIATION ALBUM
for
AMERICAN MODELER
SCALE: ORIGINAL 1:24
REPRO 1:48

12/66

HAND
GRIP

8'7"

8'2½"

TRIM TAB
ON LEFT
WING ONLY

6'6"

POWER - RANGER SGV-770-6
12 CYLINDER AIR COOLED INLINE
INVERTED "A" ENGINE. PROPELLER
REDUCTION GEAR RATIO 3:2,
BLOWER GEARING OFFERING A
SLIGHT SUPERCHARGING EFFECT-
RATED 405 TO 450 H.P. ON
87 OCTANE FUEL.

10'0"

5'2½"

W-2   17"

WING FOLD LINE

LEADING EDGE SLAT

NON-SLIP STEP STRIPS

HOISTING SLING
COMPARTMENT

ADJUSTABLE
COOLING VENT
FIXED VENT

INTAKE PORT
DETENT

BOMB RACK
LANDING LIGHT

INSIGNIA SHOWN FOR
AIRCRAFT IN SERVICE
BETWEEN 30 JUNE 1943
AND SEPT. 1943, WITH
RED OUTLINE, REVERTED
TO BLUE AFTER SEPT.

RED
DARK BLUE
WHITE

5'2½"   AT W-2

10'0"   ROOT CHORD

AIRFOIL NACA 23000 SERIES
(EXACT ORDINATES UNKNOWN)

3°

3°

COLORING NOTES
ALL PLAN-VIEW SURFACES & SIDES TO COLOR
SEPERATION LINE - SEA BLUE NON SPECULAR,
FEATHER EDGE TO - WHITE NON SPECULAR
COMPLETE TO ALL UNDER SURFACES, PROPELLER
SPINNER - WHITE, BLUES FADED IN SERVICE,
WHILE WHITES BECAME DIRTY AND SMUDGED.

PLATE 1 of 2

DRAWING No. AM-34-A

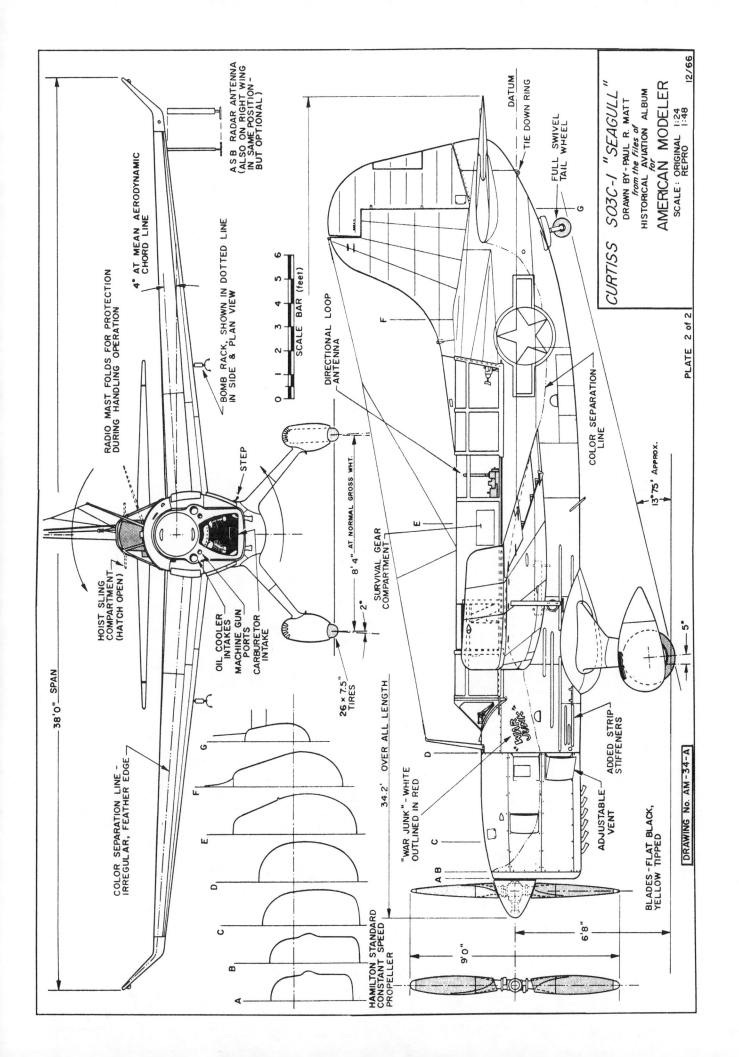

CURTISS SO3C-I "SEAGULL"

DRAWN BY - PAUL R. MATT

from the files of
HISTORICAL AVIATION ALBUM
for
AMERICAN MODELER

SCALE : ORIGINAL 1:24
REPRO 1:48

12/66

PLATE 2 of 2

DRAWING No. AM-34-A

A S B RADAR ANTENNA
(ALSO ON RIGHT WING
IN SAME POSITION -
BUT OPTIONAL)

4° AT MEAN AERODYNAMIC
CHORD LINE

RADIO MAST FOLDS FOR PROTECTION
DURING HANDLING OPERATION

BOMB RACK, SHOWN IN DOTTED LINE
IN SIDE & PLAN VIEW

COLOR SEPARATION LINE -
IRREGULAR, FEATHER EDGE

38'0" SPAN

HOIST SLING
COMPARTMENT
(HATCH OPEN)

STEP

OIL COOLER INTAKES
MACHINE GUN PORTS
CARBURETOR INTAKE

26 × 7.5"
TIRES

2°

8' 4" AT NORMAL GROSS WHT.

SCALE BAR (feet)
0 1 2 3 4 5 6

DIRECTIONAL LOOP
ANTENNA

SURVIVAL GEAR
COMPARTMENT

E

F

DATUM

TIE DOWN RING

FULL SWIVEL
TAIL WHEEL

G

COLOR SEPARATION
LINE

13'75' Approx.

5°

D

C

A B

"WAR JUNK" - WHITE
OUTLINED IN RED

34.2' OVER ALL LENGTH

ADJUSTABLE
VENT

ADDED STRIP
STIFFENERS

BLADES - FLAT BLACK,
YELLOW TIPPED

HAMILTON STANDARD
CONSTANT SPEED
PROPELLER

9'0"

6'8"

A B C D E F G

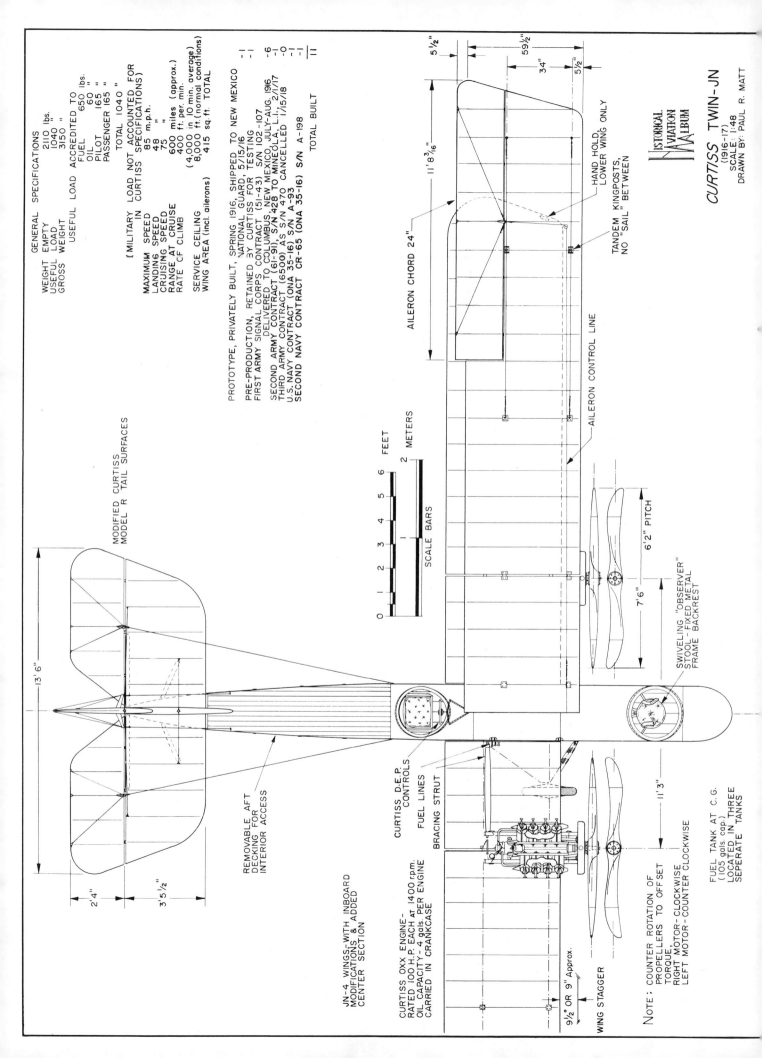

GENERAL SPECIFICATIONS

WEIGHT EMPTY   2110 lbs.
USEFUL LOAD   1040 "
GROSS WEIGHT   3150 "

USEFUL LOAD ACCREDITED TO
FUEL   650 lbs.
OIL   60 "
PILOT   165 "
PASSENGER   165 "
                TOTAL 1040

(MILITARY LOAD NOT ACCOUNTED FOR
IN CURTISS SPECIFICATIONS)

MAXIMUM SPEED   85 m.p.h.
LANDING SPEED   48 "
CRUISING SPEED   75 "
RANGE AT CRUISE   600 miles (approx.)
RATE OF CLIMB   400 ft. per. min.
                     (4,000 in 10 min. average)
SERVICE CEILING   8,000 ft. (normal conditions)
WING AREA (incl. ailerons) 415 sq. ft. TOTAL

PROTOTYPE, PRIVATELY BUILT, SPRING 1916, SHIPPED TO NEW MEXICO
    NATIONAL GUARD, 5/15/16
PRE-PRODUCTION, RETAINED BY CURTISS FOR TESTING
FIRST ARMY SIGNAL CORPS CONTRACT (51-43) S/N 102-107
SECOND ARMY CONTRACT DELIVERED TO COLUMBUS, NEW MEXICO, JULY-AUG. 1916
    (61-91), S/N 428 TO MINEOLA, L.I., 2/1/17
THIRD ARMY CONTRACT (6500) A'S S/N 470 CANCELLED 1/15/18
U.S. NAVY CONTRACT (ONA 35-16) S/N A-93
SECOND NAVY CONTRACT CR-65 (ONA 35-16) S/N A-198
                                    TOTAL BUILT

                    -1
                    -1
                    -6
                    -0
                    -1
                    -1
                    ——
                    11

5 1/2"   59 1/2"
                    34"   5 1/2"
                                 5 1/2"

11' 8 3/16"

AILERON CHORD 24"

HAND HOLD,
LOWER WING ONLY

TANDEM KINGPOSTS,
NO "SAIL" BETWEEN

AILERON CONTROL LINE

FEET
6 5 4 3 2 1 0

METERS
2 1

SCALE BARS

SWIVELING "OBSERVER"
STOOL - FIXED METAL
FRAME BACKREST

6' 2" PITCH

7' 6"

FUEL TANK AT C.G.
(105 gals. cap.)
LOCATED IN THREE
SEPERATE TANKS

NOTE: COUNTER ROTATION OF
PROPELLERS TO OFFSET
TORQUE,
RIGHT MOTOR-CLOCKWISE
LEFT MOTOR-COUNTER CLOCKWISE

CURTISS OXX ENGINE -
RATED 100 H.P. EACH at 1400 r.p.m.
OIL CAPACITY - 4 gals. PER ENGINE
CARRIED IN CRANKCASE

CURTISS D.E.P.
CONTROLS
FUEL LINES
BRACING STRUT

REMOVABLE AFT
DECKING FOR
INTERIOR ACCESS

MODIFIED CURTISS
MODEL R TAIL SURFACES

JN-4 WINGS - WITH INBOARD
MODIFICATIONS & ADDED
CENTER SECTION

13' 6"

2' 4"

3' 5 1/2"

11' 3"

9 1/2" OR 9" Approx.

WING STAGGER

HISTORICAL AVIATION ALBUM

CURTISS TWIN-JN
(1916-17)
SCALE: 1:48
DRAWN BY: PAUL R. MATT

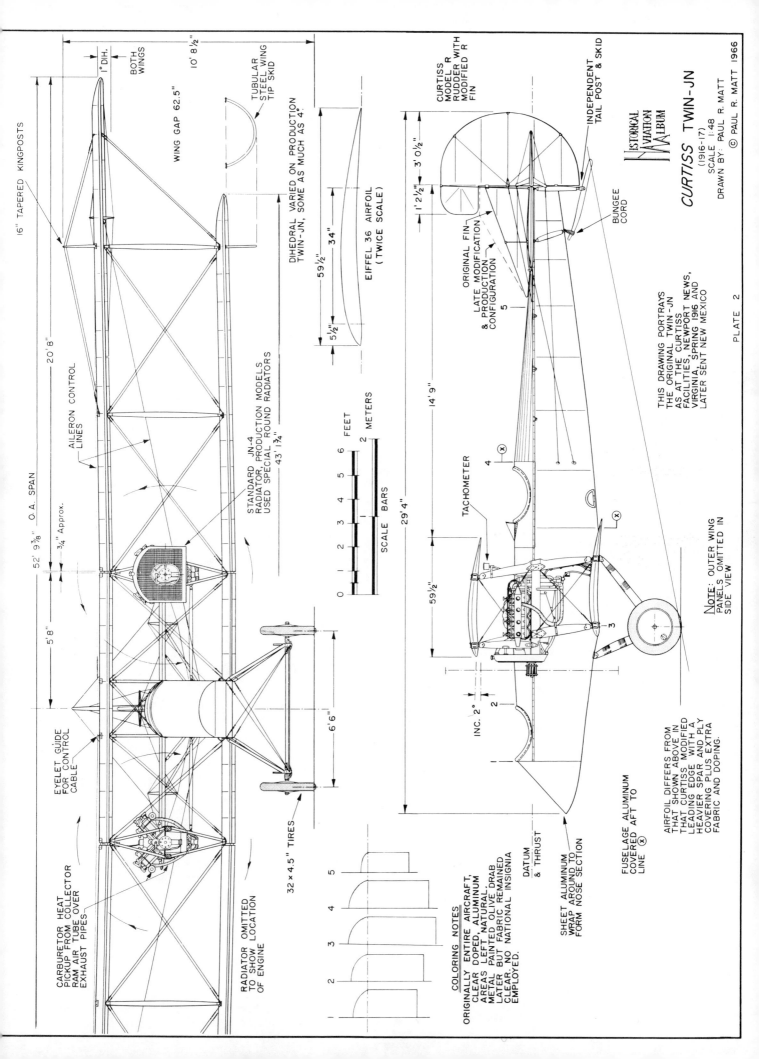

16" TAPERED KINGPOSTS

1° DIH.

BOTH WINGS

WING GAP 62.5"

10' 8½"

TUBULAR STEEL WING TIP SKID

DIHEDRAL VARIED ON PRODUCTION TWIN-JN, SOME AS MUCH AS 4°.

34"

59½"

5½"

EIFFEL 36 AIRFOIL (TWICE SCALE)

20' 8"

AILERON CONTROL LINES

STANDARD JN-4 RADIATOR, PRODUCTION MODELS USED SPECIAL ROUND RADIATORS

43' 1¾"

O. A. SPAN

52' 9⅜"

¾" Approx.

5' 8"

6' 6"

EYELET GUIDE FOR CONTROL CABLE

32 × 4.5" TIRES

CARBURETOR HEAT PICKUP FROM COLLECTOR RAM AIR TUBE OVER EXHAUST PIPES

RADIATOR OMITTED TO SHOW LOCATION OF ENGINE

FEET

METERS

0 1 2 3 4 5 6

SCALE BARS

2 3 4 5

CURTISS MODEL R RUDDER WITH MODIFIED R FIN

INDEPENDENT TAIL POST & SKID

BUNGEE CORD

ORIGINAL FIN

LATE MODIFICATION & PRODUCTION CONFIGURATION

5

3' 0½"

1' 2½"

14' 9"

TACHOMETER

4

59½"

INC. 2°

2

3

DATUM & THRUST

SHEET ALUMINUM WRAP AROUND TO FORM NOSE SECTION

FUSELAGE ALUMINUM COVERED AFT TO LINE ⊗

NOTE: OUTER WING PANELS OMITTED IN SIDE VIEW

AIRFOIL DIFFERS FROM THAT SHOWN ABOVE IN THAT CURTISS MODIFIED LEADING EDGE WITH A HEAVIER SPAR AND PLY COVERING PLUS EXTRA FABRIC AND DOPING.

THIS DRAWING PORTRAYS THE ORIGINAL TWIN-JN AS AT THE CURTISS FACILITIES, NEWPORT NEWS, VIRGINIA, SPRING 1916 AND LATER SENT NEW MEXICO

COLORING NOTES
ORIGINALLY ENTIRE AIRCRAFT, CLEAR DOPED, ALUMINUM AREAS LEFT NATURAL. METAL PAINTED OLIVE DRAB LATER BUT FABRIC REMAINED CLEAR. NO NATIONAL INSIGNIA EMPLOYED.

CURTISS TWIN-JN
(1916-17)
SCALE 1:48
DRAWN BY: PAUL R. MATT

Historical Aviation Album

© PAUL R. MATT 1966

PLATE 2

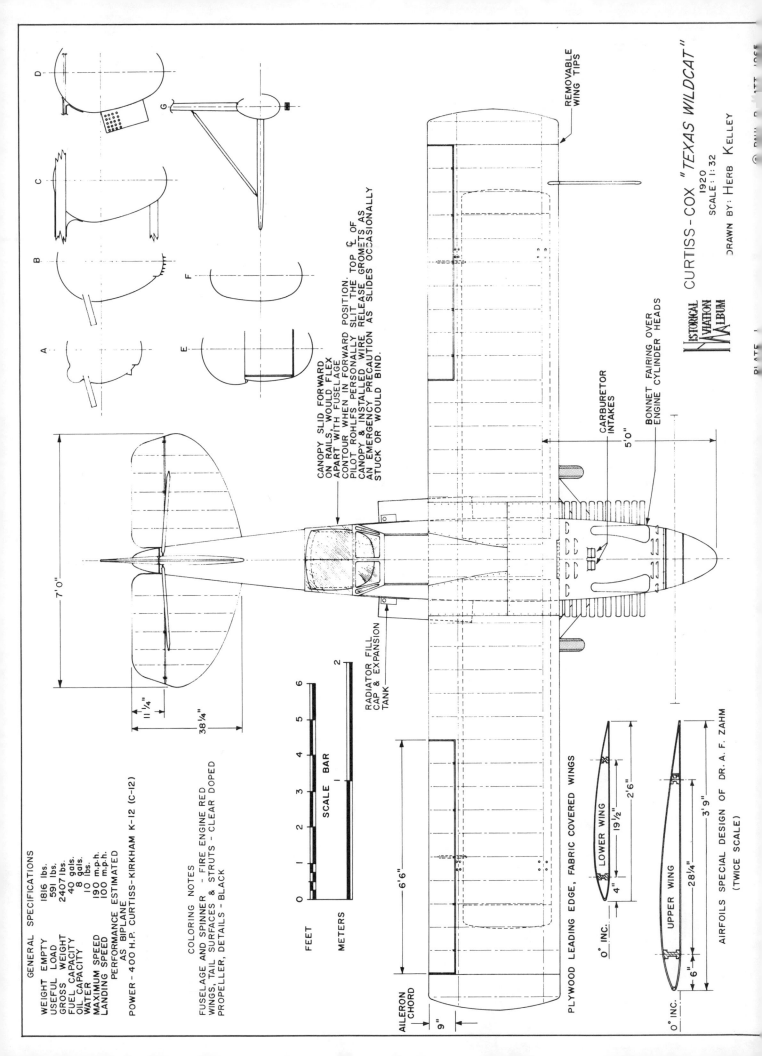

GENERAL SPECIFICATIONS

WEIGHT EMPTY .... 1816 lbs.
USEFUL LOAD .... 591 lbs.
GROSS WEIGHT .... 2407 lbs.
FUEL CAPACITY .... 40 gals.
OIL CAPACITY .... 8 gals.
WATER .... 10 lbs.
MAXIMUM SPEED .... 190 m.p.h.
LANDING SPEED .... 100 m.p.h.
PERFORMANCE ESTIMATED
AS BIPLANE
POWER - 400 H.P. CURTISS-KIRKHAM K-12 (C-12)

COLORING NOTES

FUSELAGE AND SPINNER - FIRE ENGINE RED
WINGS, TAIL SURFACES & STRUTS - CLEAR DOPED
PROPELLER, DETAILS - BLACK

SCALE BAR

FEET
METERS

CANOPY SLID FORWARD
ON RAILS, WOULD FLEX
APART WITH FUSELAGE
CONTOUR WHEN IN FORWARD POSITION. TOP C̵L OF
PILOT ROHLFS PERSONALLY SLIT THE
CANOPY & INSTALLED WIRE RELEASE GROMETS AS
AN EMERGENCY PRECAUTION AS SLIDES OCCASIONALLY
STUCK OR WOULD BIND.

RADIATOR FILL
CAP & EXPANSION
TANK

REMOVABLE
WING TIPS

CARBURETOR
INTAKES

BONNET FAIRING OVER
ENGINE CYLINDER HEADS

5'0"

7'0"

11 1/4"

38 1/4"

6'6"

PLYWOOD LEADING EDGE, FABRIC COVERED WINGS

AILERON
CHORD

9"

LOWER WING

0° INC.

4"

19 1/2"

2'6"

UPPER WING

0° INC.

6"

2 8/4"

3'9"

0° INC.

AIRFOILS SPECIAL DESIGN OF DR. A. F. ZAHM
(TWICE SCALE)

CURTISS-COX "TEXAS WILDCAT"
1920
SCALE: 1:32

DRAWN BY: HERB KELLEY

HISTORICAL AVIATION ALBUM

© PAUL R. MATT 1965

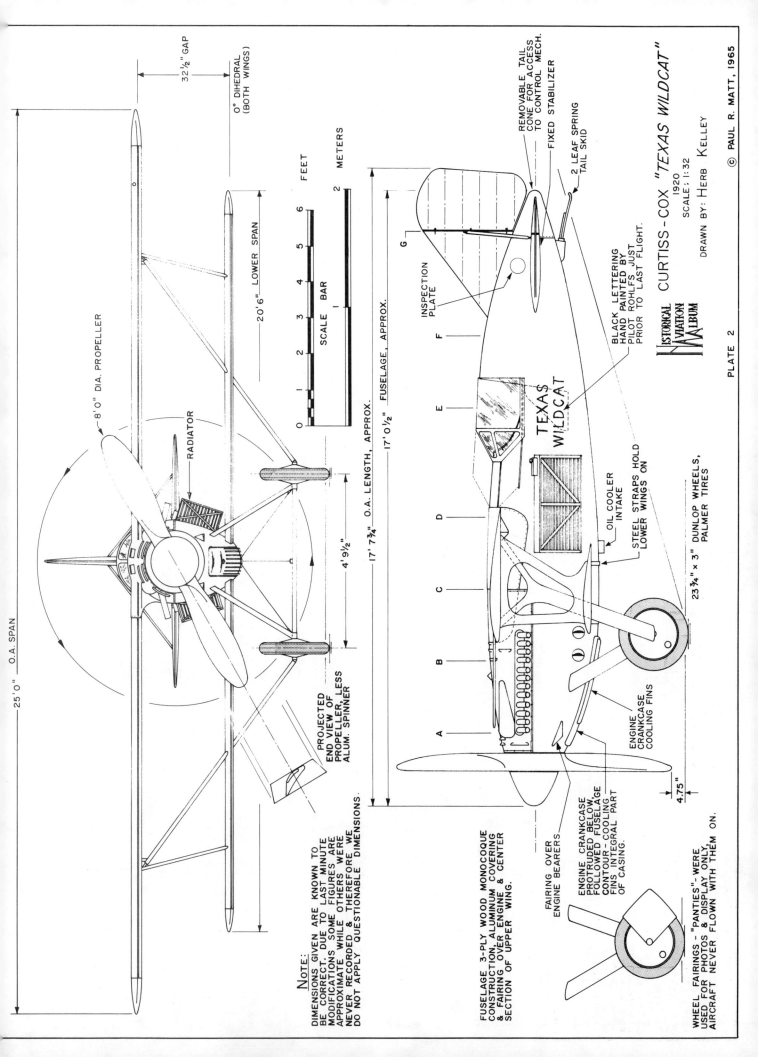

32½" GAP

0° DIHEDRAL
(BOTH WINGS)

25'0" O.A. SPAN

8'0" DIA. PROPELLER

RADIATOR

20'6" LOWER SPAN

FEET

METERS

SCALE BAR

PROJECTED
END VIEW OF
PROPELLER, LESS
ALUM. SPINNER

4'9½"

17'7¾" O.A. LENGTH, APPROX.

17'0½" FUSELAGE, APPROX.

FUSELAGE, APPROX.

NOTE:
DIMENSIONS GIVEN ARE KNOWN TO
BE CORRECT. DUE TO LAST MINUTE
MODIFICATIONS SOME FIGURES ARE
APPROXIMATE WHILE OTHERS WERE
NEVER RECORDED & THEREFORE WE
DO NOT APPLY QUESTIONABLE DIMENSIONS.

FUSELAGE 3-PLY WOOD MONOCOQUE
CONSTRUCTION, ALUMINUM COVERING
& FAIRING OVER ENGINE & CENTER
SECTION OF UPPER WING.

FAIRING OVER
ENGINE BEARERS

ENGINE CRANKCASE
PROTRUDED BELOW,
FOLLOWED FUSELAGE
CONTOUR — COOLING
FINS INTEGRAL PART
OF CASING.

WHEEL FAIRINGS — "PANTIES" — WERE
USED FOR PHOTOS & DISPLAY ONLY,
AIRCRAFT NEVER FLOWN WITH THEM ON.

ENGINE
CRANKCASE
COOLING FINS

4.75"

23¾" × 3" DUNLOP WHEELS,
PALMER TIRES

STEEL STRAPS HOLD
LOWER WINGS ON

OIL COOLER
INTAKE

TEXAS
WILDCAT

BLACK LETTERING
HAND PAINTED BY
PILOT ROHLFS JUST
PRIOR TO LAST FLIGHT.

INSPECTION
PLATE

A   B   C   D   E   F   G

REMOVABLE TAIL
CONE FOR ACCESS
TO CONTROL MECH.

FIXED STABILIZER

2 LEAF SPRING
TAIL SKID

CURTISS-COX "TEXAS WILDCAT"
1920
SCALE: 1:32

DRAWN BY: HERB KELLEY

Historical Aviation Album

PLATE 2

© PAUL R. MATT, 1965

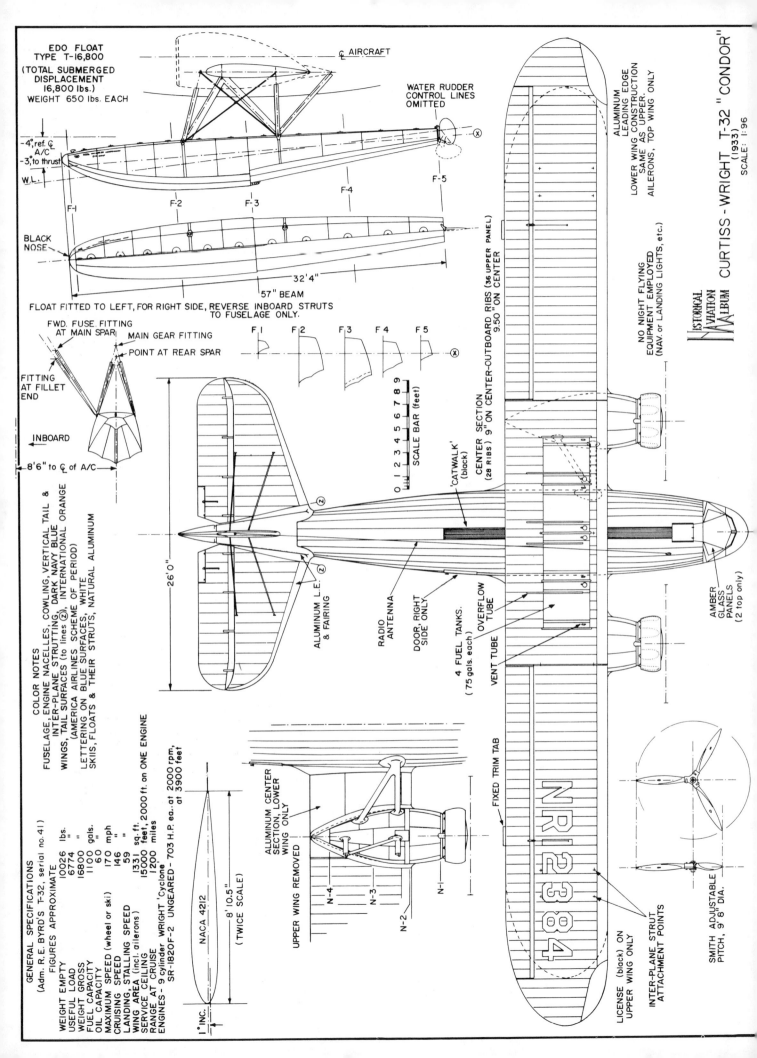

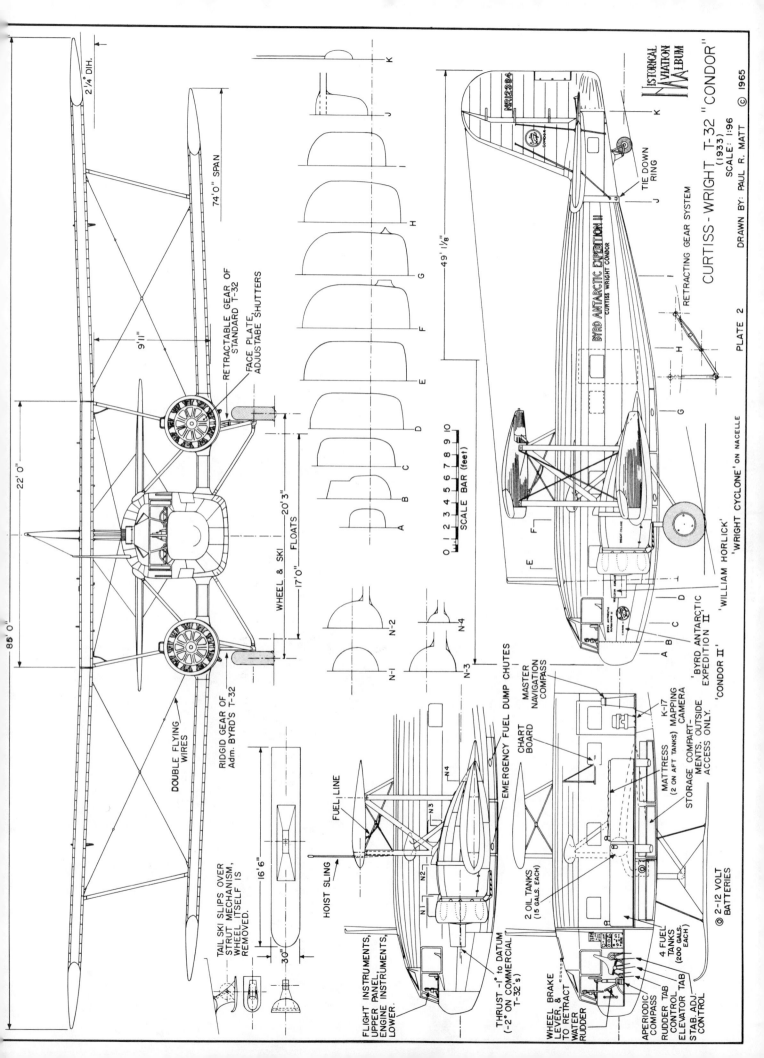

CURTISS - WRIGHT T-32 "CONDOR"
(1933)
SCALE: 1:96

DRAWN BY: PAUL R. MATT

PLATE 2

© 1965

HISTORICAL AVIATION ALBUM

2 1/4" DIH.

74'0" SPAN

85'0"

22'0"

9'11"

RETRACTABLE GEAR OF STANDARD T-32

FACE PLATE, ADJUSTABE SHUTTERS

20'3" FLOATS

17'0" WHEEL & SKI

DOUBLE FLYING WIRES

RIDGID GEAR OF Adm. BYRD'S T-32

TAIL SKI SLIPS OVER STRUT MECHANISM, WHEEL ITSELF IS REMOVED.

16'6"

30"

HOIST SLING

FUEL LINE

FLIGHT INSTRUMENTS, UPPER PANEL ENGINE INSTRUMENTS, LOWER.

THRUST -1° to DATUM (-2° ON COMMERCIAL T-32's)

WHEEL BRAKE LEVER, & TO RETRACT WATER RUDDER

APERIODIC COMPASS

RUDDER TAB CONTROL

ELEVATOR TAB

STAB. ADJ. CONTROL

4 FUEL TANKS (200 GALS. EACH)

2 OIL TANKS (15 GALS. EACH)

EMERGENCY FUEL DUMP CHUTES

MASTER NAVIGATION COMPASS

CHART BOARD

K-17 MAPPING CAMERA

MATTRESS (2 ON AFT TANKS)

STORAGE COMPARTMENTS, OUTSIDE ACCESS ONLY.

2-12 VOLT BATTERIES

'CONDOR II'

'BYRD ANTARCTIC EXPEDITION II'

'WILLIAM HORLICK'

'WRIGHT CYCLONE' ON NACELLE

N-1   N-2

N-3   N-4

A   B   C   D   E   F   G   H   J   K

SCALE BAR (feet)
0 1 2 3 4 5 6 7 8 9 10

NR12384

BYRD ANTARCTIC EXPEDITION II
CURTISS WRIGHT CONDOR

TIE DOWN RING

RETRACTING GEAR SYSTEM

49' 1 1/8"

N 623V, CW-1 "Junior", s/n 1011, in 1931 at St. Louis plant.

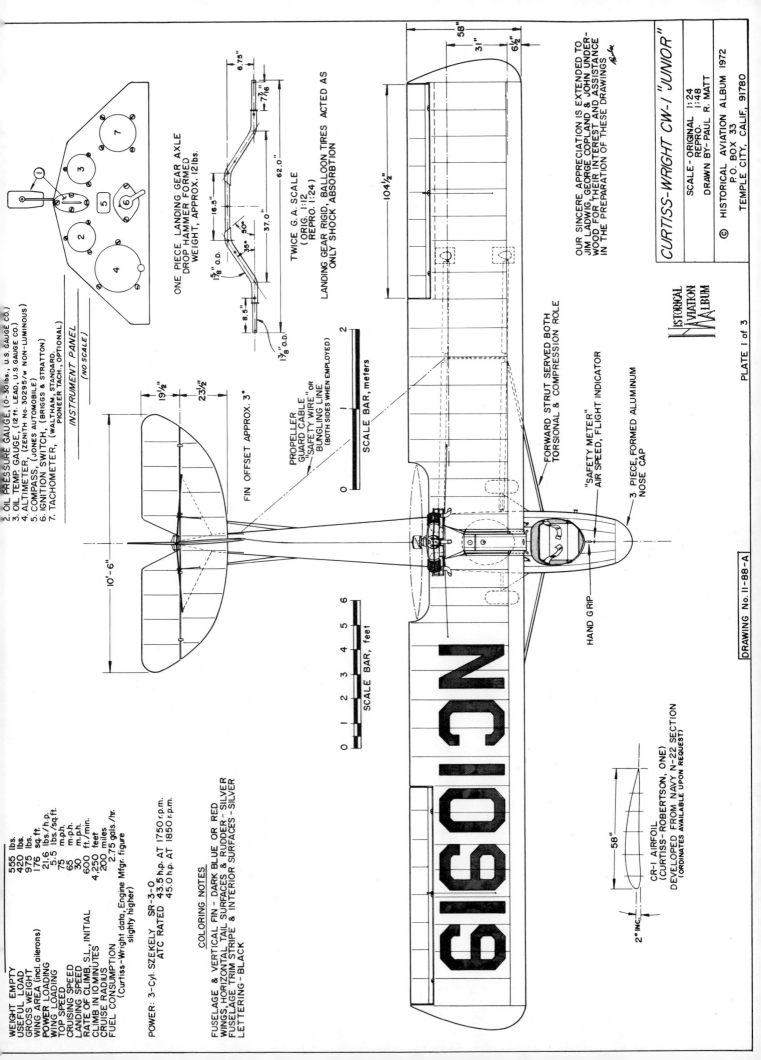

INSTRUMENT PANEL
(NO SCALE)

2. OIL PRESSURE GAUGE, (0-30 lbs., U.S. GAUGE CO.)
3. OIL TEMP. GAUGE, (12 ft. LEAD, U.S. GAUGE CO.)
4. ALTIMETER, (ZENITH No. 30295/w NON-LUMINOUS)
5. COMPASS, (JONES AUTOMOBILE)
6. IGNITION SWITCH, (BRIGGS & STRATTON)
7. TACHOMETER, (WALTHAM, STANDARD.
   PIONEER TACH., OPTIONAL)

ONE PIECE LANDING GEAR AXLE
DROP HAMMER FORMED
WEIGHT, APPROX. 12 lbs.

6.75"
7 7/16"
16.5"
62.0"
37.0"
50°
35°
1 5/8" O.D.
8.5"
1 3/8" O.D.

TWICE G.A. SCALE
(ORIG. 1:12
REPRO. 1:24)

LANDING GEAR RIGID, BALLOON TIRES ACTED AS
ONLY SHOCK ABSORBTION

19 1/2"
23 1/2"

FIN OFFSET APPROX. 3°

10' - 6"

PROPELLER
GUARD CABLE
"SAFETY WIRE" or
"BUNGLING LINE"
(BOTH SIDES WHEN EMPLOYED)

2
1
0
SCALE BAR, meters

6
5
4
3
2
1
0
SCALE BAR, feet

58"
31"
6 1/2"

104 1/2"

FORWARD STRUT SERVED BOTH
TORSIONAL & COMPRESSION ROLE

"SAFETY METER"
AIR SPEED, FLIGHT INDICATOR

3 PIECE, FORMED ALUMINUM
NOSE CAP

HAND GRIP

NC10919

CR-1 AIRFOIL
(CURTISS-ROBERTSON, ONE)
DEVELOPED FROM NAVY N-22 SECTION
(ORDINATES AVAILABLE UPON REQUEST)

58"
2° INC.

WEIGHT EMPTY   555 lbs.
USEFUL LOAD   420 lbs.
GROSS WEIGHT   975 lbs.
WING AREA (incl. ailerons) 176 sq. ft.
POWER LOADING   21.6 lbs./h.p.
WING LOADING   5.5 lbs./sq. ft.
TOP SPEED   75   m.p.h.
CRUISING SPEED   65   m.p.h.
LANDING SPEED   30   m.p.h.
RATE OF CLIMB, S.L., INITIAL   600 ft./min.
CLIMB IN 10 MINUTES   4,250 feet
CRUISE RADIUS   200 miles
FUEL CONSUMPTION   2.75 gals./hr.
(Curtiss-Wright data, Engine Mfgr. figure
slightly higher)

POWER: 3-Cyl. SZEKELY SR-3-0
       ATC RATED 43.5 h.p. AT 1750 r.p.m.
                  45.0 h.p. AT 1850 r.p.m.

COLORING NOTES

FUSELAGE & VERTICAL FIN - DARK BLUE OR RED
WINGS, HORIZONTAL TAIL SURFACES & RUDDER - SILVER
FUSELAGE TRIM STRIPE & INTERIOR SURFACES - SILVER
LETTERING - BLACK

CURTISS-WRIGHT CW-1 "JUNIOR"

SCALE - ORIGINAL 1:24
       REPRO.   1:48
DRAWN BY - PAUL R. MATT

© HISTORICAL AVIATION ALBUM 1972
P.O. BOX 33
TEMPLE CITY, CALIF., 91780

OUR SINCERE APPRECIATION IS EXTENDED TO
JIM LADWIG, GEORGE COPLAND & JOHN UNDER-
WOOD FOR THEIR INTEREST AND ASSISTANCE
IN THE PREPARATION OF THESE DRAWINGS

HISTORICAL
AVIATION
ALBUM

DRAWING No. II-88-A   PLATE I of 3

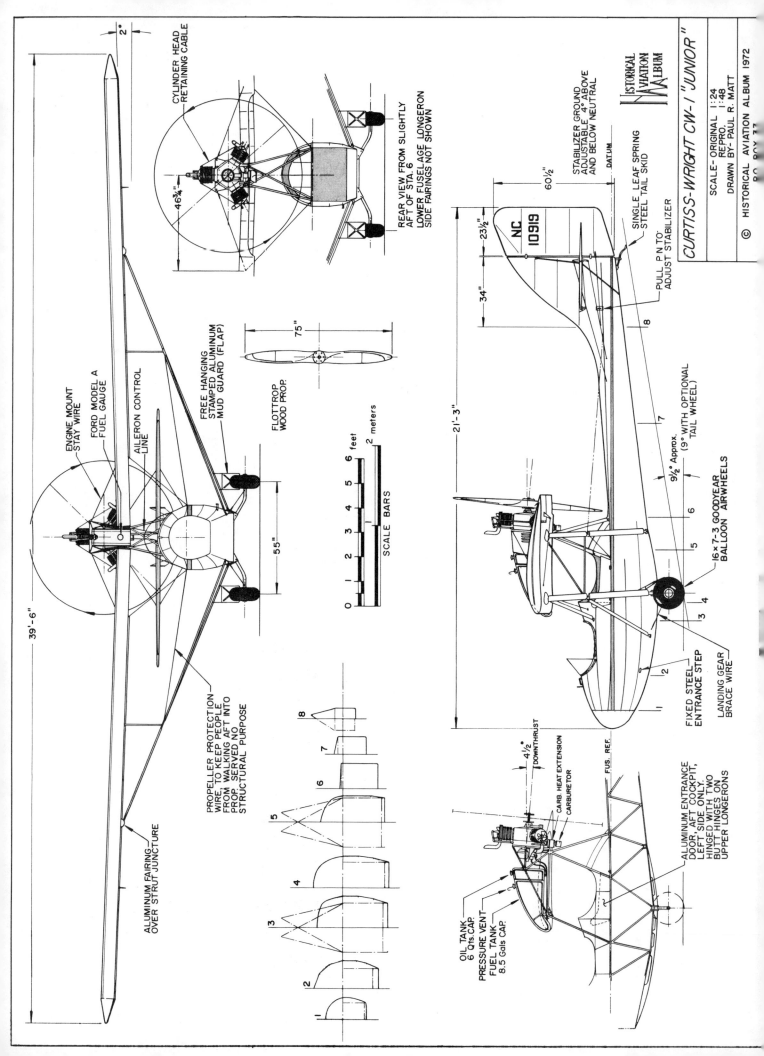

CYLINDER HEAD
RETAINING CABLE

2°

REAR VIEW FROM SLIGHTLY
AFT OF STA. 6
LOWER FUSELAGE LONGERON
SIDE FAIRINGS NOT SHOWN

46¾"

ENGINE MOUNT
STAY WIRE

FORD MODEL A
FUEL GAUGE

AILERON CONTROL
LINE

FREE HANGING
STAMPED ALUMINUM
MUD GUARD (FLAP)

75"

55"

FLOTTROP
WOOD PROP.

39'-6"

PROPELLER PROTECTION
WIRE, TO KEEP PEOPLE
FROM WALKING AFT INTO
PROP. SERVED NO
STRUCTURAL PURPOSE

ALUMINUM FAIRING
OVER STRUT JUNCTURE

6 feet
2 meters

SCALE BARS

0 1 2 3 4 5 6

8
7
6
5
4
3
2
1

NC
10919

23½"
34"
60½"

21'-3"

STABILIZER GROUND
ADJUSTABLE 4° ABOVE
AND BELOW NEUTRAL

DATUM

SINGLE LEAF SPRING
STEEL TAIL SKID

PULL PN TO.
ADJUST STABILIZER

9½° Approx.
(9° WITH OPTIONAL
TAIL WHEEL)

16 x 7-3 GOODYEAR
BALLOON AIRWHEELS

FIXED STEEL
ENTRANCE STEP

LANDING GEAR
BRACE WIRE

8
7
6
5
4
3
2
1

4½°
DOWNTHRUST

CARB. HEAT EXTENSION

CARBURETOR

FUS. REF.

OIL TANK
6 Qts. CAP.

PRESSURE VENT

FUEL TANK
8.5 Gals CAP.

ALUMINUM ENTRANCE
DOOR, AFT COCKPIT,
LEFT SIDE ONLY,
HINGED WITH TWO
BUTT HINGES ON
UPPER LONGERONS

CURTISS-WRIGHT CW-1 "JUNIOR"

SCALE- ORIGINAL 1:24
REPRO. 1:48
DRAWN BY- PAUL R. MATT

HISTORICAL
AVIATION
ALBUM

© HISTORICAL AVIATION ALBUM 1972

Curtiss-Wright CW-1 "Junior"

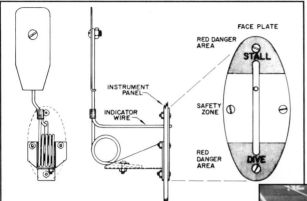

FACE PLATE

RED DANGER AREA

STALL

SAFETY ZONE

RED DANGER AREA

DIVE

INSTRUMENT PANEL

INDICATOR WIRE

Operation of simple airspeed "safety" indicator. Air pressure due to motion forced paddle backwards against force of an oil spring. Pointer, through instrument panel, moved lower as speed increased.

Excellent structured details of Jim Ludwig's rebuilt Junior, N 643V, in 1969.

PLEASE DO NOT TOUCH!

Photo by Jim Ludwig

AIRCRAFT S/N LOCATED ON INSIDE OF UPPER LONGERON

VEE BRACE BEHIND FRONT SEAT

ENGINE MOUNT BRACE STRUCTURE

CENTER LINE TUBULAR STRUCTURE DRAWINGS OF MAJOR COMPONENTS

TUBE DIAMETER VARIED ACCORDING TO STRUCTURAL DEMANDS
ALL TUBING CHROME-MOLYBDENUM
ALL FIGURES ARE INCHES

16   24   10   12   24   11   9

FIN OFFSET POINT

(18'-7") 223

HISTORICAL AVIATION ALBUM

ENGINE MOUNT

16.5

19

BOLT

37.5
25
16
16
31

35

26   24   33   30

BOLT

WOOD FAIRING STRIP ON ℄ FWD. OF THIS POINT

SINGLE TUBE ON FIN ℄

ENGINE MOUNTING PLATE

7.5   21   13.5
14   23.5
7   12
7   23.5
12
12   23.5
3   12
10   DATUM

OUR SINCERE APPRECIATION IS EXTENDED TO JIM LADWIG FOR HIS TIME AND EFFORTS IN SUPPLYING TECHNICAL DATA AND DIRECT CW-1 MEASUREMENTS THUS MAKING THESE DRAWINGS AS COMPREHENSIVE AS POSSIBLE

INSTRUMENT PANEL

FUS. REF.   20   42   52   20   69.5   24   36

11   14   20   19.5   22

20   27   22.5   19   22

26

39   18   20   31

FAIRING STRIPS (WOOD) ON ALL MODELS FASTENED TO LOWER LONGERONS

GUSSET PLATE

HORIZONTAL TAIL SURFACES WELDED CHROME-MOLYBDENUM CONSTRUCTION

23.25   40   21.25   17.25   9.25
23   10   12   12   12
33   19.25

AIRCRAFT ℄

1/32" 3-PLY BIRCH L.E.

WOOD COMPRESSION MEMBERS INBOARD OF RIBS

JURY STRUTS ATTACH POINTS

STRUT ATTACH POINT

DRAG WIRES ARE DOUBLE OUTBOARD OF JURY STRUTS

0   12   24   36
SCALE BAR, INCHES

8.5   8.5   8.5   8.5   11   12.5   14   14   14   14   13   15.5   12   13   13   13

31

11.5

1/2" O.D. ALUM. TUBE

1/2" O.D. alum. tube

11   14   13   13   13   13   14   13

END RIB BRACES, TOP AND BOTTOM

1×1" SPAR REINFORCEMENT (SIMILAR ON FRONT SPAR)

CRIMPED ALUMINUM T.E.

WING OF WOOD CONSTRUCTION SPRUCE SPARS, BIRCH RIBS

FALSE SPAR FRIZE AILERON

CURTISS-WRIGHT CW-1 "JUNIOR"

SCALE - ORIGINAL 1:24
REPRO. 1:48
DRAWN BY - PAUL R. MATT

© HISTORICAL AVIATION ALBUM 1972
P.O. BOX 33
TEMPLE CITY, CALIF. 91780

DRAWING No. II-88-A   PLATE 3 of 3

Douglas O-2

A line up of Douglas O-2s in 1926.

Douglas O-2 Observation plane with Curtiss D-12, 435hp, engine.

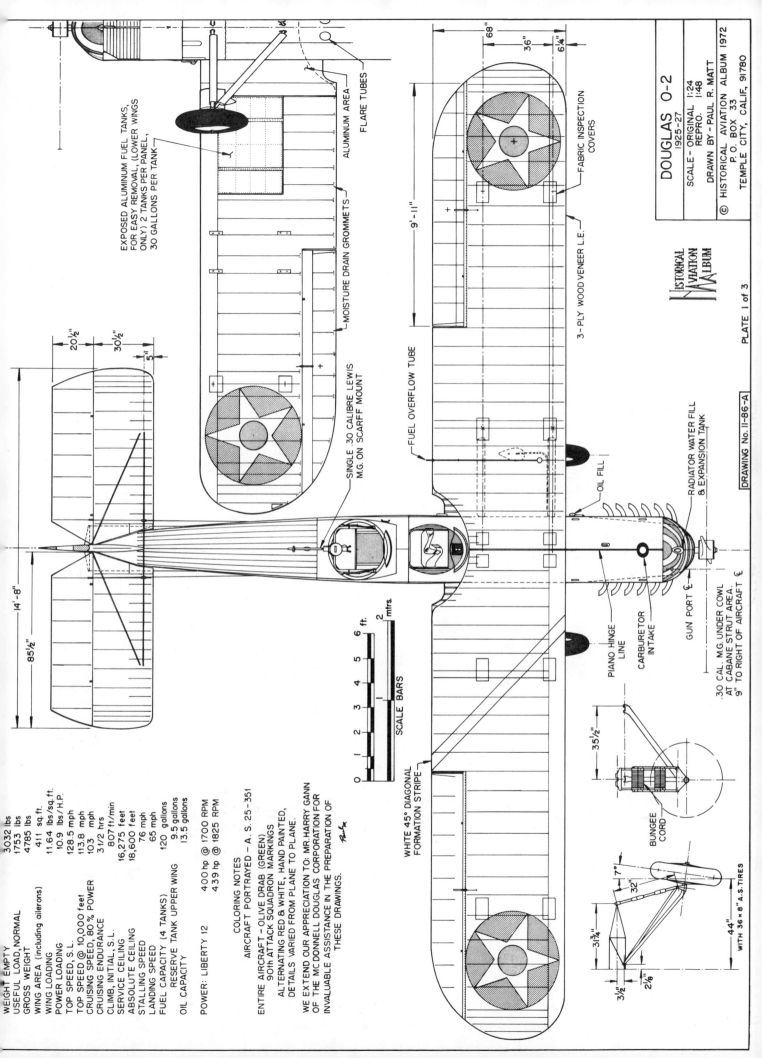

EXPOSED ALUMINUM FUEL TANKS,
FOR EASY REMOVAL, (LOWER WINGS
ONLY) 2 TANKS PER PANEL,
30 GALLONS PER TANK

FLARE TUBES

ALUMINUM AREA

MOISTURE DRAIN GROMMETS

SINGLE .30 CALIBRE LEWIS
M.G. ON SCARFF MOUNT

FABRIC INSPECTION
COVERS

3 - PLY WOOD VENEER L.E.

FUEL OVERFLOW TUBE

OIL FILL

RADIATOR WATER FILL
& EXPANSION TANK

PIANO HINGE
LINE

CARBURETOR
INTAKE

GUN PORT ℄

.30 CAL. M.G. UNDER COWL
AT CABANE STRUT AREA.
9" TO RIGHT OF AIRCRAFT ℄

68"
36"
6¼"
9'- 11"

20½"
30½"
5"
14'- 8"
85½"

WHITE 45° DIAGONAL
FORMATION STRIPE

BUNGEE
CORD

35½"
7°
32"
31¾"
44"
3½"
2⅛"

WITH 36 × 8" A.S. TIRES

SCALE BARS

6 5 4 3 2 1 0 ft.
2 1 mtrs.

WEIGHT EMPTY .... 3032 lbs
USEFUL LOAD, NORMAL .... 1753 lbs
GROSS WEIGHT .... 4785 lbs
WING AREA (including ailerons) ..... 411 sq.ft.
WING LOADING .... 11.64 lbs/sq.ft.
POWER LOADING .... 10.9 lbs/H.P.
TOP SPEED, S.L. .... 128.5 mph
TOP SPEED @ 10,000 feet .... 113.8 mph
CRUISING SPEED, 80 % POWER .... 103 mph
CRUISING ENDURANCE .... 3½ hrs
CLIMB, INITIAL, S.L. .... 807 ft/min
SERVICE CEILING .... 16,275 feet
ABSOLUTE CEILING .... 18,600 feet
STALLING SPEED .... 76 mph
LANDING SPEED .... 65 mph
FUEL CAPACITY (4 TANKS) .... 120 gallons
RESERVE TANK UPPER WING .... 9.5 gallons
OIL CAPACITY .... 13.5 gallons

POWER: LIBERTY 12   400 hp @ 1700 RPM
                         439 hp @ 1825 RPM

COLORING NOTES
AIRCRAFT PORTRAYED – A. S. 25 – 351
ENTIRE AIRCRAFT – OLIVE DRAB (GREEN).
90th ATTACK SQUADRON MARKINGS
ALTERNATING RED & WHITE, HAND PAINTED,
DETAILS VARIED FROM PLANE TO PLANE.

WE EXTEND OUR APPRECIATION TO: MR HARRY GANN
OF THE McDONNELL DOUGLAS CORPORATION FOR
INVALUABLE ASSISTANCE IN THE PREPARATION OF
THESE DRAWINGS.

DOUGLAS O-2
1925-27
SCALE - ORIGINAL   1:24
        REPRO.   1:48
DRAWN BY - PAUL R. MATT
P.O. BOX 33
TEMPLE CITY, CALIF, 91780
© HISTORICAL AVIATION ALBUM 1972

HISTORICAL AVIATION ALBUM

PLATE 1 of 3

DRAWING No. II-86-A

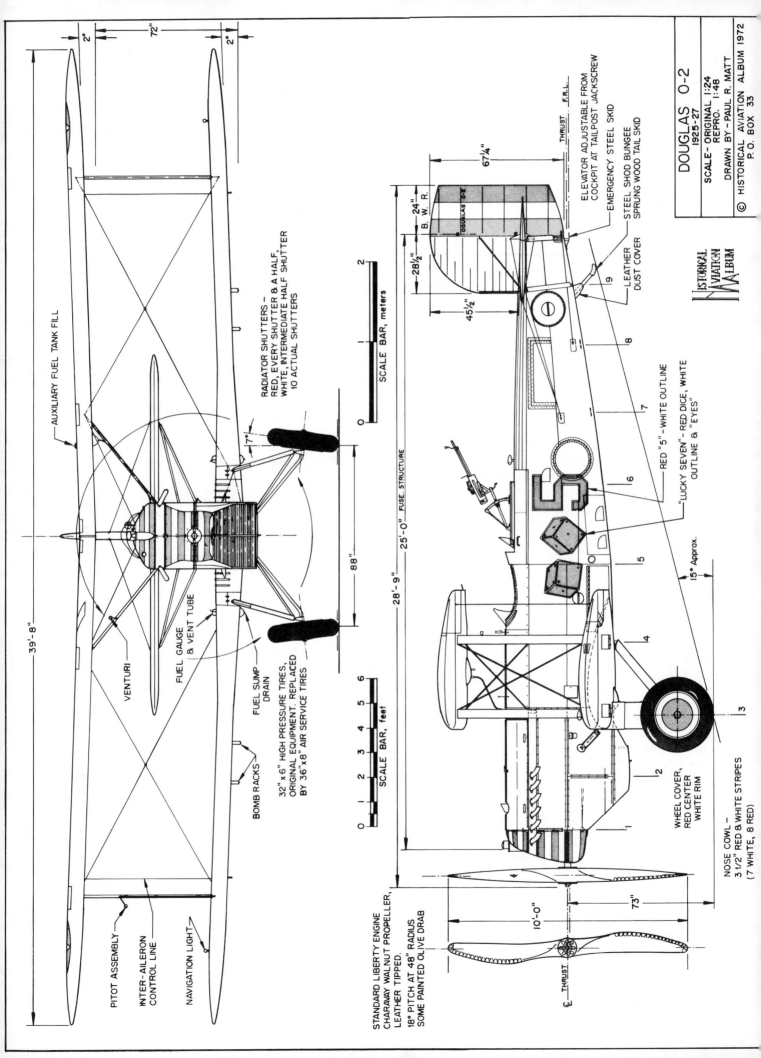

AUXILIARY FUEL TANK FILL

72"

2" 2"

39'-8"

RADIATOR SHUTTERS –
RED, EVERY SHUTTER & A HALF,
WHITE, INTERMEDIATE HALF SHUTTER
10 ACTUAL SHUTTERS

7°

88"

VENTURI

FUEL GAUGE
& VENT TUBE

FUEL SUMP
DRAIN

BOMB RACKS

32" x 6" HIGH PRESSURE TIRES,
ORIGINAL EQUIPMENT. REPLACED
BY 36" x 8" AIR SERVICE TIRES

PITOT ASSEMBLY

INTER-AILERON
CONTROL LINE

NAVIGATION LIGHT

STANDARD LIBERTY ENGINE
CHARAWAY WALNUT PROPELLER,
LEATHER TIPPED.
18° PITCH AT 48" RADIUS
SOME PAINTED OLIVE DRAB

SCALE BAR, meters

0   1   2

SCALE BAR, feet

0   1   2   3   4   5   6

25'-0" FUSE. STRUCTURE

28'-9"

67¼"

24"

B. W. R.

28½"

45½"

DOUGLAS O-2

THRUST   F.R.L.

ELEVATOR ADJUSTABLE FROM
COCKPIT AT TAILPOST JACKSCREW

EMERGENCY STEEL SKID

STEEL SHOD BUNGEE
SPRUNG WOOD TAIL SKID

LEATHER
DUST COVER

9

8

7

6

5

4

3

2

1

RED "5" – WHITE OUTLINE

"LUCKY SEVEN" – RED DICE, WHITE
OUTLINE & "EYES"

15° Approx.

WHEEL COVER,
RED CENTER
WHITE RIM

NOSE COWL –
3 1/2" RED & WHITE STRIPES
(7 WHITE, 8 RED)

10'-0"

73"

THRUST

DOUGLAS O-2
1925-27
SCALE- ORIGINAL 1:24
REPRO. 1:48
DRAWN BY-PAUL R. MATT

© HISTORICAL AVIATION ALBUM 1972
P.O. BOX 33

HISTORICAL AVIATION ALBUM

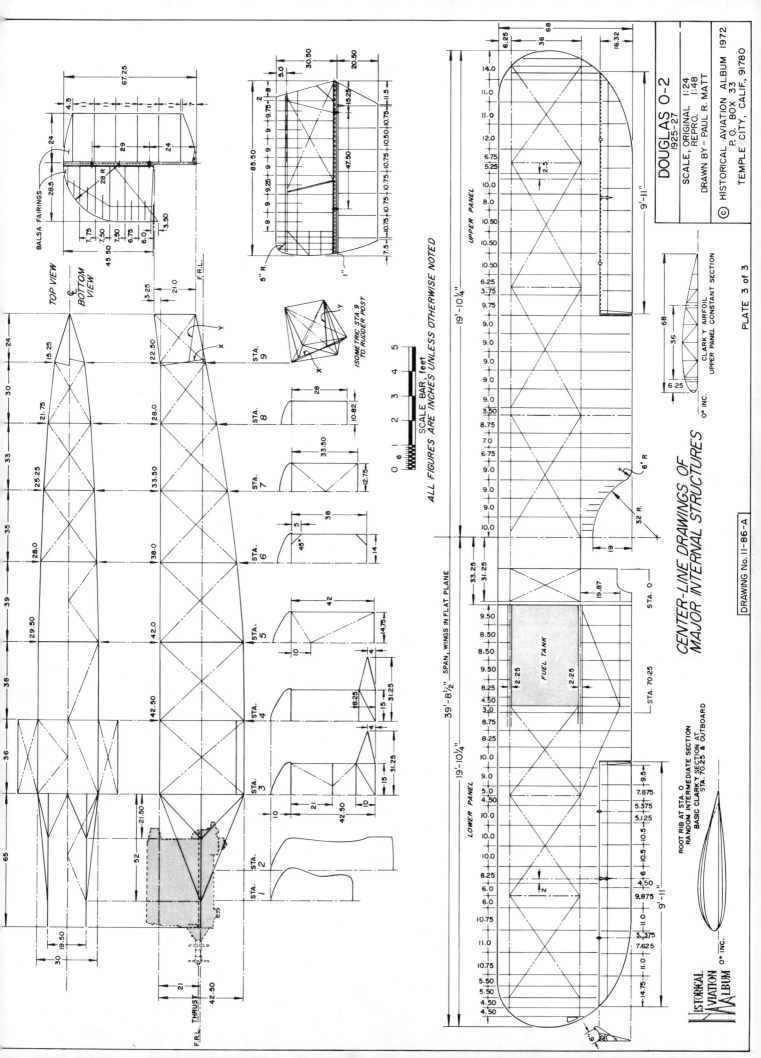

DOUGLAS O-2
1925-27

SCALE, ORIGINAL 1:24
REPRO. 1:48

DRAWN BY - PAUL R. MATT

© HISTORICAL AVIATION ALBUM 1972
P.O. BOX 33
TEMPLE CITY, CALIF. 91780

CENTER-LINE DRAWINGS OF
MAJOR INTERNAL STRUCTURES

PLATE 3 of 3

DRAWING No. II-86-A

ALL FIGURES ARE INCHES UNLESS OTHERWISE NOTED

SCALE BAR, feet

CLARK Y AIRFOIL
UPPER PANEL CONSTANT SECTION

ROOT RIB AT STA. 0
RANDOM INTERMEDIATE SECTION
BASIC CLARK Y SECTION AT
STA. 70.25 & OUTBOARD

FUEL TANK

UPPER PANEL

LOWER PANEL

TOP VIEW

BOTTOM VIEW

BALSA FAIRINGS

F.R.L. THRUST

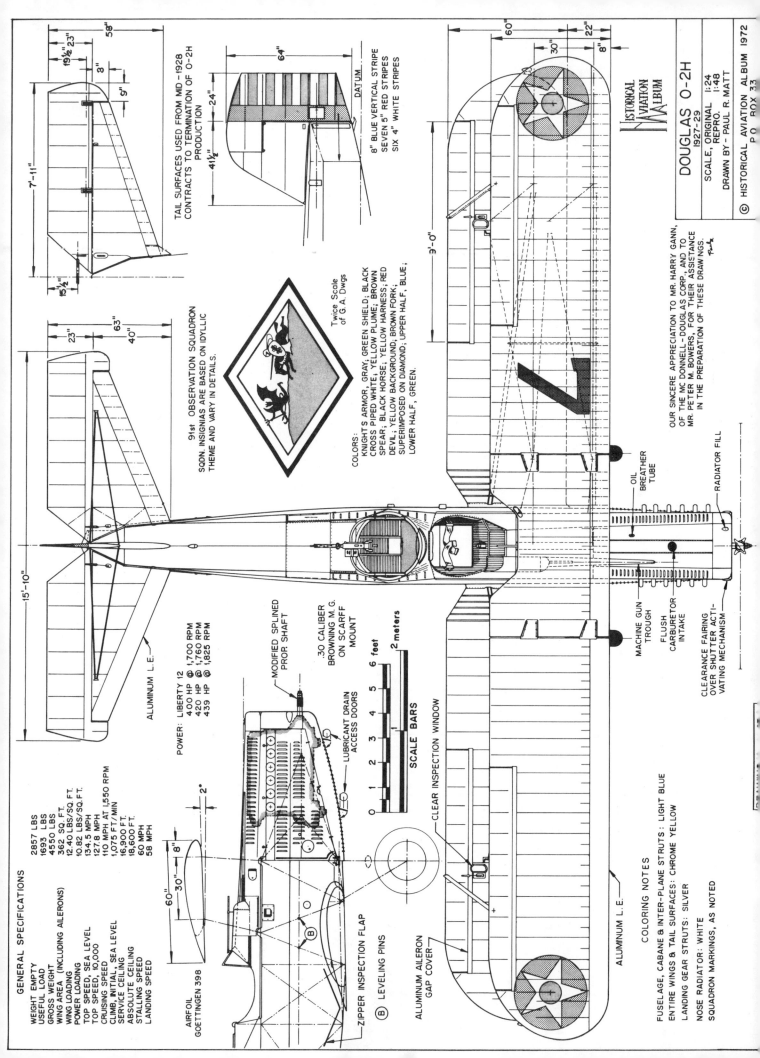

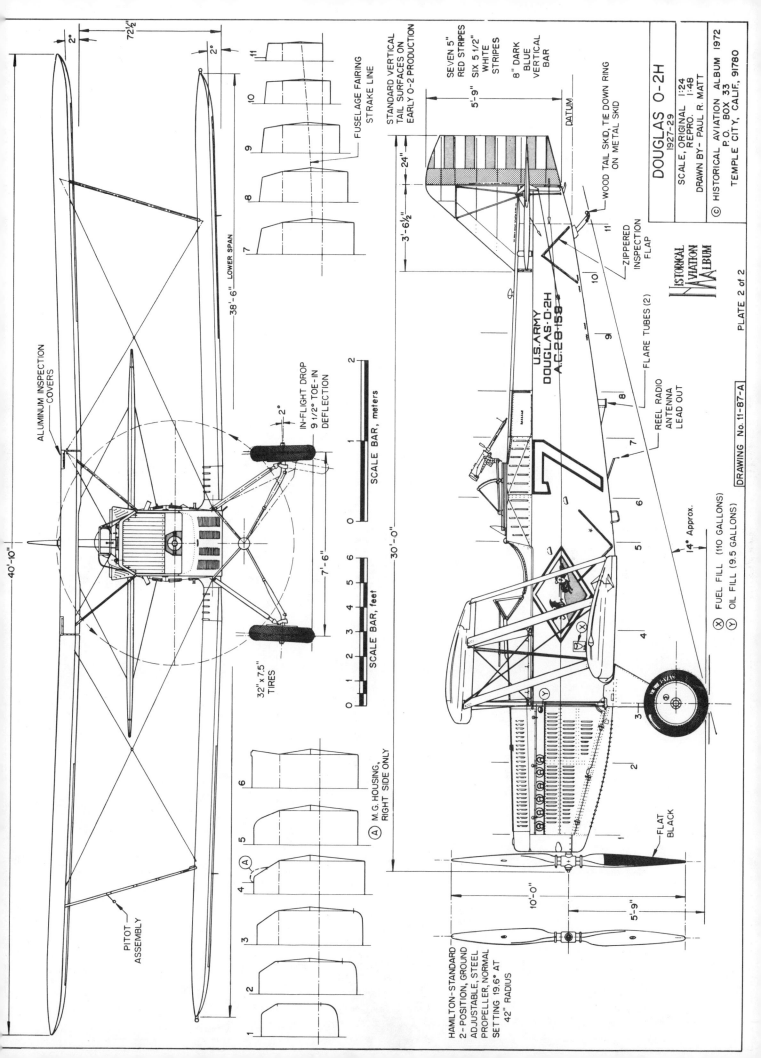

DOUGLAS O-2H
1927-29

SCALE, ORIGINAL 1:24
REPRO. 1:48
DRAWN BY- PAUL R. MATT

© HISTORICAL AVIATION ALBUM 1972
P.O. BOX 33
TEMPLE CITY, CALIF., 91780

PLATE 2 of 2

DRAWING No. 11-87-A

U.S. ARMY
DOUGLAS O-2H
A.C.28-158

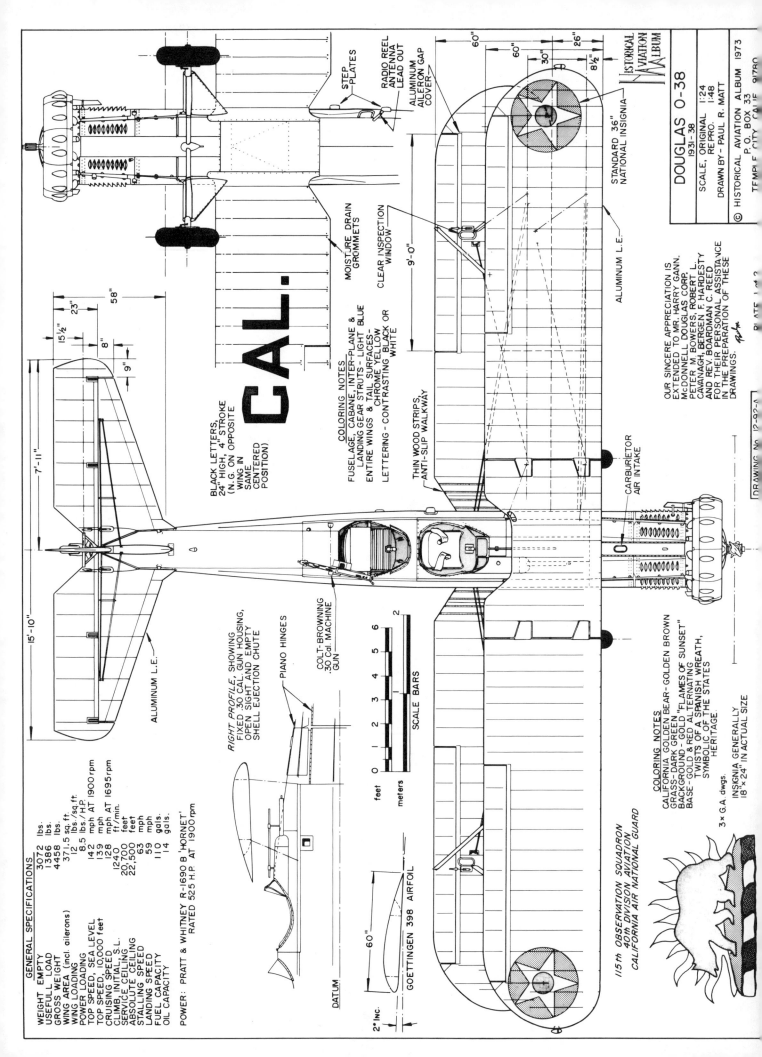

DOUGLAS O-38
1931-38

SCALE, ORIGINAL 1:24
RE PRO. 1:48
DRAWN BY - PAUL R. MATT

© HISTORICAL AVIATION ALBUM 1973
P.O. BOX 33
TEMPLE CITY, CALIF. 91780

OUR SINCERE APPRECIATION IS
EXTENDED TO MR. HARRY GANN,
McDONNELL DOUGLAS CORP.
PETER M. BOWERS, ROBERT L.
CAVANAGH, BERGEN F. HARDESTY
AND REV. BOARDMAN C. REED
FOR THEIR PERSONAL ASSISTANCE
IN THE PREPARATION OF THESE
DRAWINGS.

DRAWING No. 12-92-A

STEP PLATES

RADIO REEL ANTENNA LEAD OUT

ALUMINUM AILERON GAP COVER

MOISTURE DRAIN GROMMETS

CLEAR INSPECTION WINDOW

STANDARD 36" NATIONAL INSIGNIA

ALUMINUM L.E.

THIN WOOD STRIPS, ANTI-SLIP WALKWAY

CARBURETOR AIR INTAKE

CAL.

BLACK LETTERS,
24" HIGH, 4" STROKE
(N.G. ON OPPOSITE
WING IN
SAME
CENTERED
POSITION)

COLORING NOTES
FUSELAGE, CABANE, INTER-PLANE &
LANDING GEAR STRUTS - LIGHT BLUE
ENTIRE WINGS & TAIL SURFACES-
CHROME YELLOW
LETTERING - CONTRASTING BLACK OR
WHITE

ALUMINUM L.E.

GENERAL SPECIFICATIONS
WEIGHT EMPTY	3072	lbs.
USEFULL LOAD	1386	lbs.
GROSS WEIGHT	4458	lbs.
WING AREA (incl. ailerons)	371.5	sq. ft.
WING LOADING	12	lbs./sq.ft.
POWER LOADING	8.5	lbs./H.P.
TOP SPEED, SEA LEVEL	142	mph AT 1900 rpm
TOP SPEED, 10,000 feet	139	mph
CRUISING SPEED	128	mph AT 1695 rpm
CLIMB, INITAL, S.L.	1240	ft/min.
SERVICE CEILING	20,700	feet
ABSOLUTE CEILING	22,500	feet
STALLING SPEED	63	mph
LANDING SPEED	59	mph
FUEL CAPACITY	110	gals.
OIL CAPACITY	14	gals.

POWER: PRATT & WHITNEY R-1690 B 'HORNET'
RATED 525 H.P. AT 1900 rpm

DATUM

RIGHT PROFILE, SHOWING
FIXED .30 CAL. GUN HOUSING,
OPEN SIGHT AND EMPTY
SHELL EJECTION CHUTE

PIANO HINGES

COLT-BROWNING
.30 CAL. MACHINE
GUN

GOETTINGEN 398 AIRFOIL

2° Inc.

60"

SCALE BARS

feet
0 1 2 3 4 5 6

meters
0 1 2

3 × G.A. dwgs.

COLORING NOTES
CALIFORNIA GOLDEN BEAR- GOLDEN BROWN
GRASS - DARK GREEN
BACKGROUND - GOLD "FLAMES OF SUNSET"
BASE-GOLD & RED ALTERNATING
TWISTS OF A SPANISH WREATH,
SYMBOLIC OF THE STATES
HERITAGE.

INSIGNIA GENERALLY
18'×24" IN ACTUAL SIZE

115 th OBSERVATION SQUADRON
40th DIVISION AVIATION
CALIFORNIA AIR NATIONAL GUARD

60" 60" 30" 26" 8½"

9'-0"

15'-10"

7'-11"

58"

23"

15½"

8"

9"

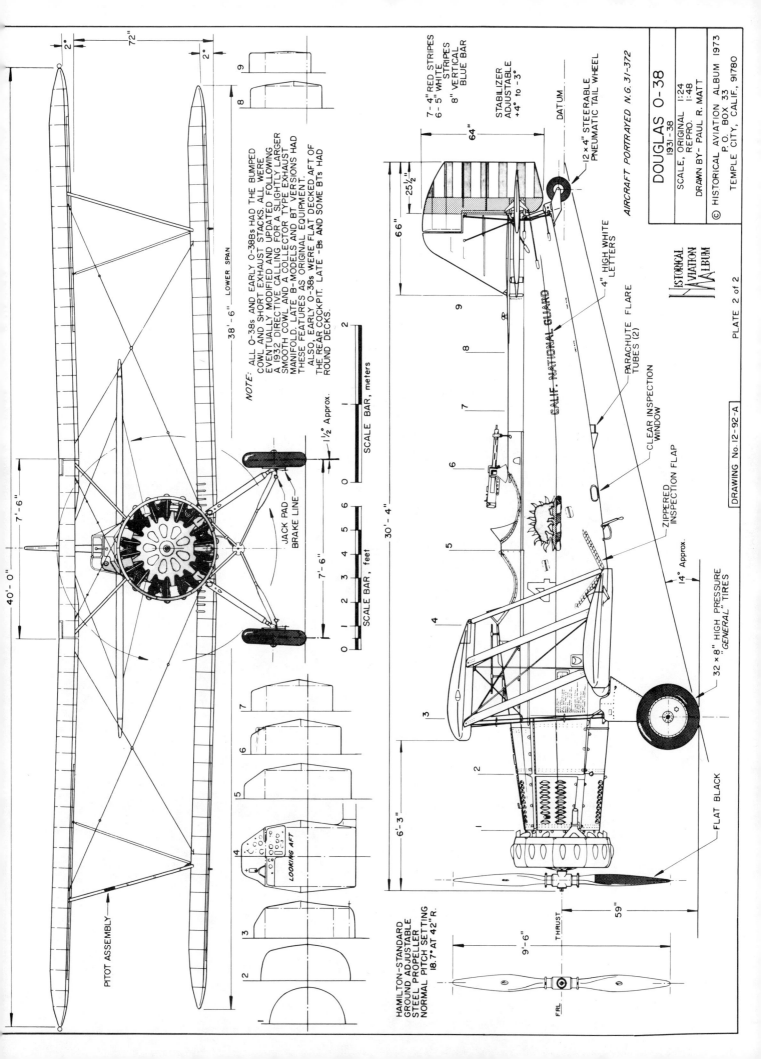

NOTE: ALL O-38s AND EARLY O-38Bs HAD THE BUMPED COWL AND SHORT EXHAUST STACKS. ALL WERE EVENTUALLY MODIFIED AND UPDATED FOLLOWING A 1932 DIRECTIVE CALLING FOR A SLIGHTLY LARGER SMOOTH COWL AND A COLLECTOR TYPE EXHAUST MANIFOLD. LATE B-MODELS AND BT VERSIONS HAD THESE FEATURES AS ORIGINAL EQUIPMENT.
ALSO, EARLY O-38s WERE FLAT DECKED AFT OF THE REAR COCKPIT. LATE -Bs AND SOME BTs HAD ROUND DECKS.

SCALE BAR, meters

SCALE BAR, feet

38'-6" LOWER SPAN

40'-0"

7'-6"

7'-6"

30'-4"

6'-3"

1½° Approx.

72"

2°

2°

PITOT ASSEMBLY

JACK PAD
BRAKE LINE

LOOKING AFT

HAMILTON-STANDARD
GROUND ADJUSTABLE
STEEL PROPELLER
NORMAL PITCH SETTING
18.7° AT 42" R.

9'-6"

FRL

THRUST

59"

FLAT BLACK

32 × 8" HIGH PRESSURE
"GENERAL" TIRES

14° Approx.

ZIPPERED
INSPECTION FLAP

CLEAR INSPECTION
WINDOW

PARACHUTE FLARE
TUBES (2)

CALIF · NATIONAL GUARD

4" HIGH WHITE
LETTERS

12 × 4" STEERABLE
PNEUMATIC TAIL WHEEL

DATUM

STABILIZER
ADJUSTABLE
+4° to -3°

7 - 4" RED STRIPES
6 - 5" WHITE
STRIPES
8" VERTICAL
BLUE BAR

64"

66"

25½"

DOUGLAS O-38
1931-38

SCALE, ORIGINAL   1:24
REPRO.   1:48
DRAWN BY- PAUL R. MATT

AIRCRAFT PORTRAYED N.G. 31-372

© HISTORICAL AVIATION ALBUM 1973
P.O. BOX 33
TEMPLE CITY, CALIF. 91780

Historical
Aviation
Album

DRAWING No. 12-92-A

PLATE 2 of 2

Douglas O-38

New York National Guard – Flexible Machine Gun (Browning) on Douglas O-38 airplane.

Sqdn. No.	Serial No.	Model	Factory c/n	Date Completed	Engine
	Aircraft Composition - 115th Observation Squadron and 115th Photo Section, 40th Division Aviation California National Guard Griffith Park, Los Angeles 1937-39 (Typical of all pre-WW II Air National Guard Units)				
1	NG 33-4	O-38E	1149	5-23-'33	P&W R-1690-9
2	NG 33-6	"	1151	5-25-'33	Hornet, 625hp
3	NG 33-7	"	1152	5-26-'33	
4	NG 31-372	O-38	905	12-19-'30	P&W R-1690-5
5	NG 31-373	"	906	12- -'30	Hornet, 525hp
6	NG 31-374	"	907	12- -'30	
7	NG 31-376	"	909	12-24-'30	
8	NG 31-356	"	889	12-12-'30	
9	NG 31-429	"	989	4-21-'31	
1	NG 37-334	O-47A	NA 25-277	10- 3-'38	Wright Cyclone
2	NG 37-347	"	NA 25-290	11-11-'38	R-1820-49,975hp
6	NG 32-331	O-38B	1096	1-21-'32	R-1690-5 Hornet
7	NG 32-326	"	1091	12- 5-'31	R-1690-7 Hornet

NOTES:
O-38 No. 7 crashed Feb. 1, 1934, No. 6 in mid-1935.
 The first O-38 to be disposed of occured Sept. 29, 1938, when No. 5 was flown to Rockwell Field, San Diego where it was surveyed. During the winter months of 1938-39 the remaining "high time" O-38s were flown to Rockwell Air Depot for disposal.

Complied by the Rev. Boardman C. Reed.

Douglas O-38 pilot's cockpit.

Douglas O-38E

Skeleton framework of first production O-38E, May 26, 1933. Note slanted aft horshoe gun mount.

Douglas O-38E.

*Douglas O-38E
Indiana National Guard
tests by Edo Float Corporation.*

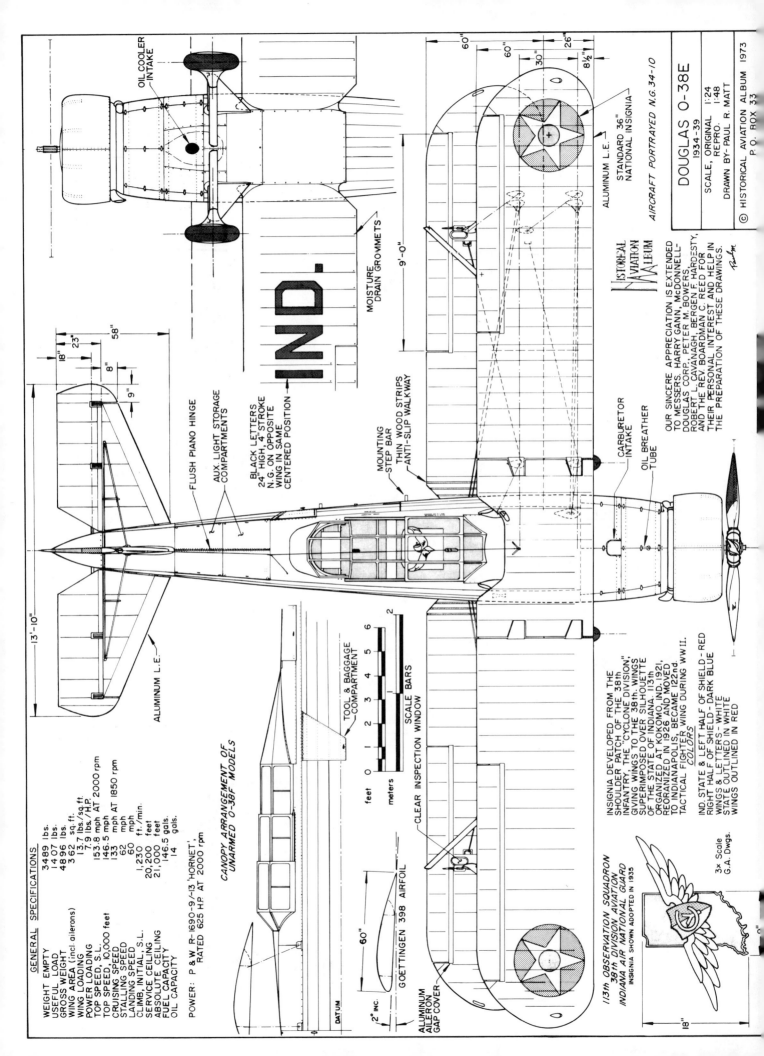

GENERAL SPECIFICATIONS

WEIGHT EMPTY	3489	lbs.
USEFUL LOAD	1407	lbs.
GROSS WEIGHT	4896	lbs.
WING AREA (incl. ailerons)	362	sq. ft.
WING LOADING	13.7	lbs./sq. ft.
POWER LOADING	7.9	lbs./H.P.
TOP SPEED, S.L.	153.8	mph AT 2000 rpm
TOP SPEED, 10,000 feet	146.5	mph AT 1850 rpm
CRUISING SPEED	133	mph
STALLING SPEED	62	mph
LANDING SPEED	60	mph
CLIMB, INITIAL, S.L.	1,230	ft./min.
SERVICE CEILING	20,200	feet
ABSOLUTE CEILING	21,000	feet
FUEL CAPACITY	146.5	gals.
OIL CAPACITY	14	gals.

POWER: P & W R-1690-9/-13 'HORNET',
RATED 625 H.P. AT 2000 rpm

CANOPY ARRANGEMENT OF UNARMED O-38F MODELS

GOETTINGEN 398 AIRFOIL

DATUM

2" INC.

TOOL & BAGGAGE COMPARTMENT

SCALE BARS

CLEAR INSPECTION WINDOW

feet

meters

ALUMINUM AILERON GAP COVER

60"

13'-10"

18"
23"
58"
8"
9"

FLUSH PIANO HINGE

AUX. LIGHT STORAGE COMPARTMENTS

BLACK LETTERS 24" HIGH, 4" STROKE N.G. ON OPPOSITE WING IN SAME CENTERED POSITION

ALUMINUM L.E.

OIL COOLER INTAKE

MOISTURE DRAIN GROMMETS

MOUNTING STEP BAR

THIN WOOD STRIPS ANTI-SLIP WALKWAY

CARBURETOR INTAKE

OIL BREATHER TUBE

9'-0"

60"
60"
30"
26"
8½"

ALUMINUM L.E.

STANDARD 36" NATIONAL INSIGNIA

AIRCRAFT PORTRAYED N.G. 34-10

DOUGLAS O-38E
1934-39

SCALE, ORIGINAL 1:24
REPRO. 1:48
DRAWN BY- PAUL R. MATT

HISTORICAL AVIATION MUSEUM

OUR SINCERE APPRECIATION IS EXTENDED TO MESSERS. HARRY GANN, McDONNELL-DOUGLAS CORP., PETER M. BOWERS, ROBERT L. CAVANAGH, BERGEN F. HARDESTY, AND THE REV. BOARDMAN C. REED FOR THEIR PERSONAL INTEREST AND HELP IN THE PREPARATION OF THESE DRAWINGS.

INSIGNIA DEVELOPED FROM THE SHOULDER PATCH OF THE 38th INFANTRY, THE "CYCLONE DIVISION," GIVING WINGS TO THE 38th. WINGS SUPERIMPOSED OVER SILHOUETTE OF THE STATE OF INDIANA. 113th ORGANIZED AT KOKOMO, IND. 1921, REORGANIZED IN 1926 AND MOVED TO INDIANAPOLIS, BECAME 122nd. TACTICAL FIGHTER WING DURING WW.II.

COLORS
IND. STATE & LEFT HALF OF SHIELD - RED
RIGHT HALF OF SHIELD- DARK BLUE
WINGS & LETTERS- WHITE
STATE OUTLINED IN WHITE
WINGS OUTLINED IN RED

113th OBSERVATION SQUADRON
38th DIVISION AVIATION
INDIANA AIR NATIONAL GUARD
INSIGNIA SHOWN ADOPTED IN 1935

3× Scale
G.A. Dwgs.

18"

IND·

© HISTORICAL AVIATION ALBUM 1973
P.O. BOX 33

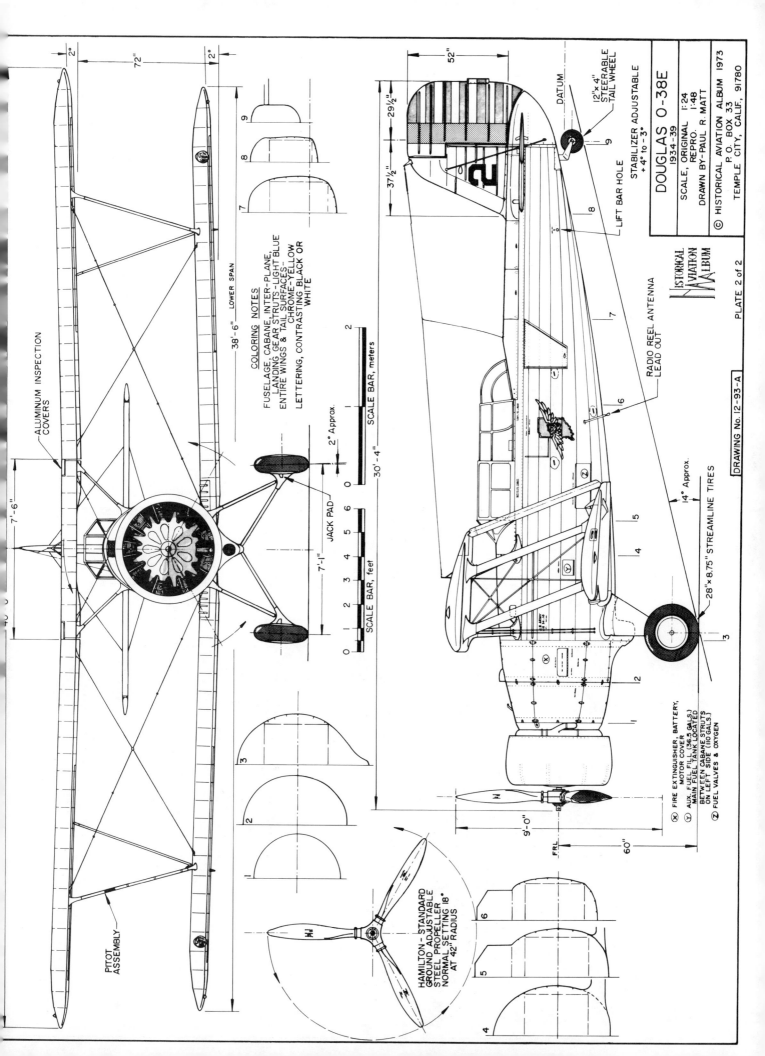

DOUGLAS O-38E
1934-39
SCALE, ORIGINAL 1:24 REPRO. 1:48
DRAWN BY—PAUL R. MATT
© HISTORICAL AVIATION ALBUM 1973
P.O. BOX 33
TEMPLE CITY, CALIF., 91780

DRAWING No. 12-93-A

PLATE 2 of 2

COLORING NOTES
FUSELAGE, CABANE, INTER-PLANE,
LANDING GEAR STRUTS—LIGHT BLUE
ENTIRE WINGS & TAIL SURFACES—
CHROME-YELLOW
LETTERING, CONTRASTING BLACK OR
WHITE

Ⓧ FIRE EXTINGUISHER, BATTERY,
MOTOR COVER
Ⓨ AUX. FUEL FILL (36.5 GALS.)
MAIN FUEL TANK LOCATED
BETWEEN CABANE STRUTS
ON LEFT SIDE (110 GALS.)
Ⓩ FUEL VALVES & OXYGEN

ALUMINUM INSPECTION
COVERS

PITOT
ASSEMBLY

JACK PAD

HAMILTON-STANDARD
GROUND ADJUSTABLE
STEEL PROPELLER
NORMAL SETTING 18°
AT 42" RADIUS

STABILIZER ADJUSTABLE
+4° to -3°

12"x 4" STEERABLE
TAIL WHEEL

DATUM

LIFT BAR HOLE

RADIO REEL ANTENNA
LEAD OUT

28" x 8.75" STREAMLINE TIRES

14° Approx.

2° Approx.

SCALE BAR, meters

SCALE BAR, feet

72"

2°

2°

38'-6" LOWER SPAN

7'-6"

7'-1"

30'-4"

52"

37½"

29½"

9'-0"

60"

FRL

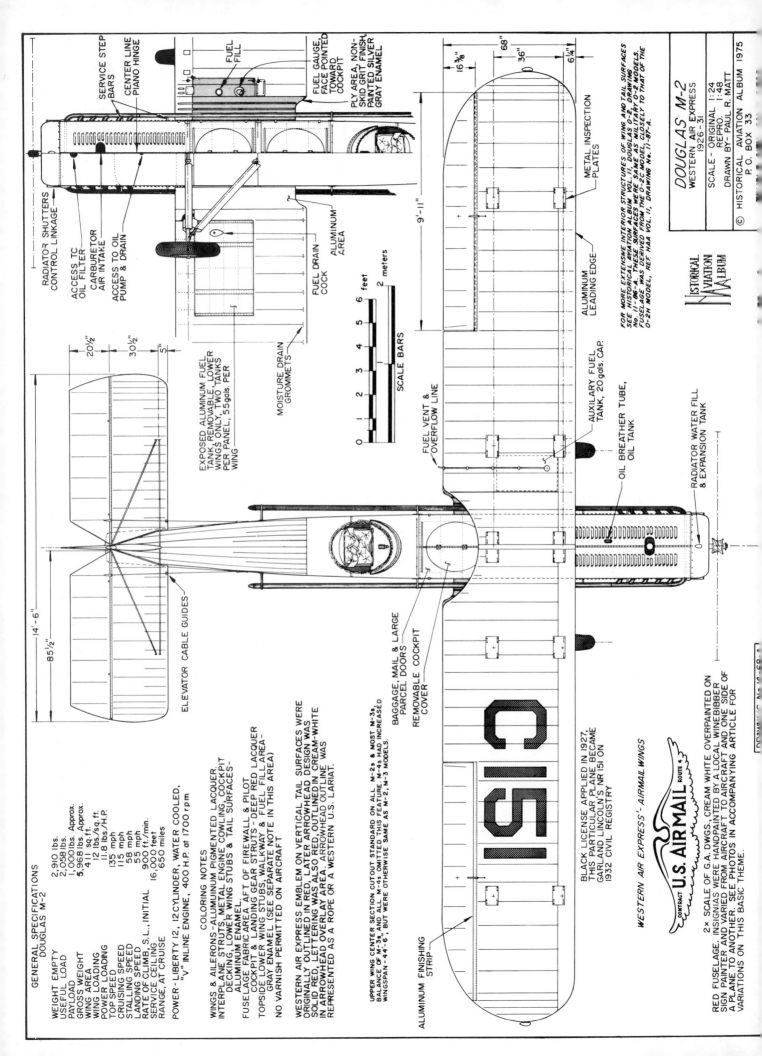

SERVICE STEP BARS
CENTER LINE
PIANO HINGE
FUEL FILL

FUEL GAUGE, FACE POINTED TOWARD COCKPIT

PLY AREA, NON-SKID GRIT FINISH, PAINTED SILVER GRAY ENAMEL

RADIATOR SHUTTERS CONTROL LINKAGE
ACCESS TO OIL FILTER
CARBURETOR AIR INTAKE
ACCESS TO OIL PUMP & DRAIN

FUEL DRAIN COCK
ALUMINUM AREA

MOISTURE DRAIN GROMMETS

EXPOSED ALUMINUM FUEL TANK, REMOVABLE, LOWER WINGS ONLY, TWO TANKS PER PANEL, 55 gals. PER WING

ELEVATOR CABLE GUIDES

ALUMINUM FINISHING STRIP

METAL INSPECTION PLATES

ALUMINUM LEADING EDGE

FUEL VENT & OVERFLOW LINE

AUXILARY FUEL TANK, 20 gals. CAP.

OIL BREATHER TUBE, OIL TANK

RADIATOR WATER FILL & EXPANSION TANK

BAGGAGE, MAIL & LARGE PARCEL DOORS

REMOVABLE COCKPIT COVER

68"
36"
6¼"
16⅜"
9'-11"

SCALE BARS
feet 0 1 2 3 4 5 6
meters 0 1 2

14'-6"
85½"
20½"
30½"
5"

GENERAL SPECIFICATIONS
DOUGLAS M-2

WEIGHT EMPTY	2,910 lbs.
USEFUL LOAD	2,058 lbs. Approx.
PAYLOAD	1,000 lbs. Approx.
GROSS WEIGHT	5,968 lbs.
WING AREA	411 sq. ft.
WING LOADING	12 lbs./sq.ft.
POWER LOADING	11.8 lbs./H.P.
TOP SPEED	135 mph
CRUISING SPEED	115 mph
STALLING SPEED	58 mph
LANDING SPEED	55 mph
RATE OF CLIMB, S.L., INITIAL	900 ft./min.
SERVICE CEILING	16,000 feet
RANGE, AT CRUISE	650 miles

POWER – LIBERTY 12, 12 CYLINDER, WATER COOLED, "V" INLINE ENGINE, 400 H.P. at 1700 rpm

COLORING NOTES

WINGS & AILERONS–ALUMINUM PIGMENTED LACQUER. INTERPLANE STRUTS, METAL ENGINE COWLING, COCKPIT DECKING, LOWER WING STUBS & TAIL SURFACES–ALUMINUM ENAMEL.

FUSELAGE FABRIC AREA AFT OF FIREWALL & PILOT COCKPIT & LANDING GEAR STRUTS – DEEP RED LACQUER. TOPSIDE LOWER WING STUBS, WALKWAY & FUEL FILL AREA–GRAY ENAMEL. (SEE SEPARATE NOTE IN THIS AREA)

NO VARNISH PERMITTED ON AIRCRAFT

WESTERN AIR EXPRESS EMBLEM ON VERTICAL TAIL SURFACES WERE ORIGINALLY OUTLINED IN RED. LATER ARROWHEAD DESIGN WAS SOLID RED, LETTERING WAS ALSO RED, OUTLINED IN CREAM-WHITE IN ARROWHEAD OVERLAY AREA. ARROWHEAD OUTLINE WAS REPRESENTED AS A ROPE OR A WESTERN U.S. LARIAT.

UPPER WING CENTER SECTION CUTOUT STANDARD ON ALL M-2s & MOST M-3s, BALANCE OF M-3s, AND ALL M-4s OMITTED THIS FEATURE. M-4s HAD INCREASED WINGSPAN—44'-6", BUT WERE OTHERWISE SAME AS M-2, M-3 MODELS.

BLACK LICENSE APPLIED IN 1927, THIS PARTICULAR PLANE BECAME GARLAND LINCOLN'S NR 151 ON 1932 CIVIL REGISTRY.

RED FUSELAGE. INSIGNIAS WERE HANDPAINTED BY A LOCAL WINEBIBBER SIGN PAINTER AND VARIED FROM AIRCRAFT TO AIRCRAFT AND ONE SIDE OF A PLANE TO ANOTHER. SEE PHOTOS IN ACCOMPANYING ARTICLE FOR VARIATIONS ON THIS BASIC THEME.

WESTERN AIR EXPRESS' · AIRMAIL WINGS

CONTRACT U.S. AIRMAIL ROUTE 4

2× SCALE OF G.A. DWGS., CREAM WHITE OVERPAINTED ON

C 151

DOUGLAS M-2
WESTERN AIR EXPRESS
1926-31

SCALE – ORIGINAL 1:24
REPRO. 1:48
DRAWN BY– PAUL R. MATT

© HISTORICAL AVIATION ALBUM 1975
P.O. BOX 33

FOR MORE EXTENSIVE INTERIOR STRUCTURES OF WING AND TAIL SURFACES SEE HISTORICAL AVIATION ALBUM VOL. II, DOUGLAS O-2 DRAWING No. 11-86-A. THESE SURFACES WERE SAME AS MILITARY O-2 MODELS. FUSELAGE WAS DERIVED FROM THE O-2C MODEL, CLOSELY TO THAT OF THE O-2H MODEL, REF. HAA VOL. II, DRAWING No. 11-87-A.

Historical Aviation Album

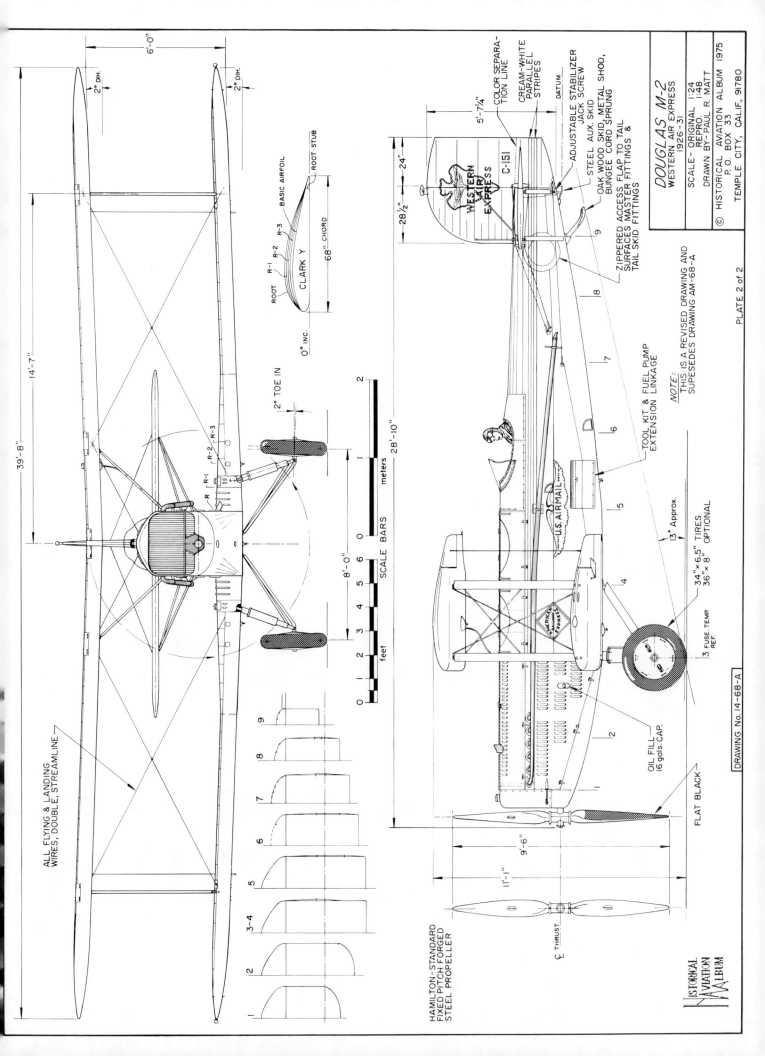

DOUGLAS M-2
WESTERN AIR EXPRESS
1926-31

SCALE- ORIGINAL 1:24
REPRO. 1:48
DRAWN BY- PAUL R. MATT
© HISTORICAL AVIATION ALBUM 1975
P.O. BOX 33
TEMPLE CITY, CALIF. 91780

PLATE 2 of 2

DRAWING No. 14-68-A

NOTE:
THIS IS A REVISED DRAWING AND
SUPESEDES DRAWING AM-68-A

COLOR SEPARA-
TION LINE

CREAM-WHITE
PARALLEL
STRIPES

DATUM

WESTERN
AIR
EXPRESS

C-151

ADJUSTABLE STABILIZER
JACK SCREW

STEEL AUX. SKID

OAK WOOD SKID, METAL SHOD,
BUNGEE CORD SPRUNG

ZIPPERED ACCESS FLAP TO TAIL
SURFACES MASTER FITTINGS &
TAIL SKID FITTINGS

5'-7 1/4"

28 1/2"

24"

9

8

7

6

5

4

2

TOOL KIT & FUEL PUMP
EXTENSION LINKAGE

13° Approx.

34" × 6.5" TIRES
36" × 8" OPTIONAL

3 FUSE. TEMP.
REF.

OIL FILL
16 gals. CAP.

FLAT BLACK

U.S. AIRMAIL

AMERICAN
RAILWAY
EXPRESS

C THRUST

9'-6"

11'-1"

HAMILTON-STANDARD
FIXED PITCH FORGED
STEEL PROPELLER

6'-0"

2° DIH.

2° DIH.

14'-7"

39'-8"

ALL FLYING & LANDING
WIRES, DOUBLE, STREAMLINE

R-1
R-2
R-3
R

2° TOE IN

28'-10"

meters

2

1

0

SCALE BARS

8'-0"

feet

6
5
4
3
2
1
0

9
8
7
6
5
3-4
2
1

ROOT STUB

BASIC AIRFOIL

R-1
R-2
R-3
ROOT

CLARK Y

68" CHORD

0° INC.

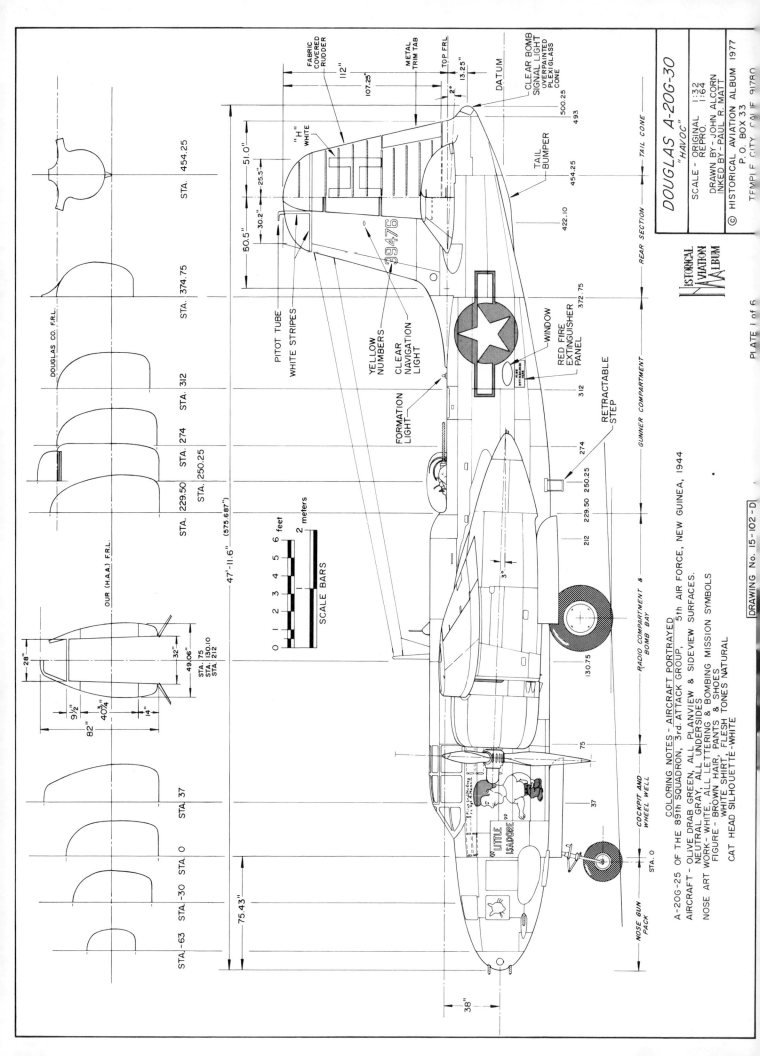

DOUGLAS A-20G-30
"HAVOC"

SCALE - ORIGINAL   1:32
        REPRO.   1:64

DRAWN BY - JOHN ALCORN
INKED BY - PAUL R. MATT

© HISTORICAL AVIATION ALBUM 1977
P.O. BOX 33
TEMPLE CITY, CALIF. 91780

PLATE 1 of 6

DRAWING No. 15-102-D

FABRIC COVERED RUDDER

METAL TRIM TAB

TOP FRL

DATUM

CLEAR BOMB SIGNAL LIGHT OVERPAINTED PLEXIGLASS CONE

"H" WHITE

PITOT TUBE

WHITE STRIPES

YELLOW NUMBERS

CLEAR NAVIGATION LIGHT

FORMATION LIGHT

WINDOW

RED FIRE EXTINGUISHER PANEL

RETRACTABLE STEP

TAIL BUMPER

REAR SECTION

TAIL CONE

GUNNER COMPARTMENT

RADIO COMPARTMENT & BOMB BAY

COCKPIT AND WHEEL WELL

NOSE GUN PACK

SCALE BARS

2 meters

6 feet

DOUGLAS CO. F.R.L.

OUR (H.A.A.) F.R.L.

COLORING NOTES - AIRCRAFT PORTRAYED
A-20G-25 OF THE 89th SQUADRON, 3rd. ATTACK GROUP, 5th AIR FORCE, NEW GUINEA, 1944
AIRCRAFT - OLIVE DRAB GREEN, ALL PLANVIEW & SIDEVIEW SURFACES.
           NEUTRAL GRAY, ALL UNDERSIDES
NOSE ART WORK - WHITE, ALL LETTERING & BOMBING MISSION SYMBOLS
           FIGURE - BROWN HAIR, PANTS & SHOES
           WHITE SHIRT, FLESH TONES NATURAL
           CAT HEAD SILHOUETTE-WHITE

"LITTLE ISADORE"

39476

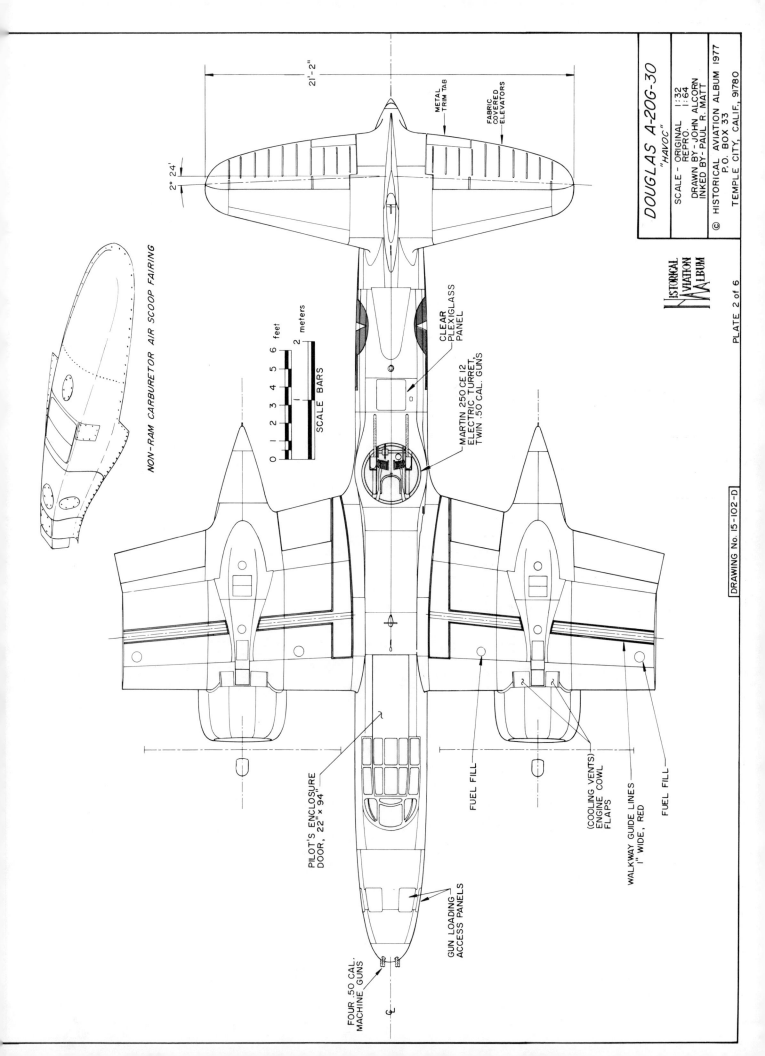

DOUGLAS A-20G-30
"HAVOC"

SCALE - ORIGINAL 1:32
REPRO. 1:64
DRAWN BY- JOHN ALCORN
INKED BY- PAUL R. MATT

© HISTORICAL AVIATION ALBUM 1977
P.O. BOX 33
TEMPLE CITY, CALIF., 91780

PLATE 2 of 6

DRAWING No. 15-102-D

21'-2"

2° 24'

METAL TRIM TAB

FABRIC COVERED ELEVATORS

NON-RAM CARBURETOR AIR SCOOP FAIRING

6 feet
5
4
3
2
2 meters
1
0
SCALE BARS

CLEAR PLEXIGLASS PANEL

MARTIN 250 CE 12 ELECTRIC TURRET, TWIN .50 CAL. GUNS

PILOT'S ENCLOSURE DOOR, 22" x 94"

GUN LOADING ACCESS PANELS

FOUR .50 CAL. MACHINE GUNS

FUEL FILL

(COOLING VENTS) ENGINE COWL FLAPS

WALKWAY GUIDE LINES 1" WIDE, RED

FUEL FILL

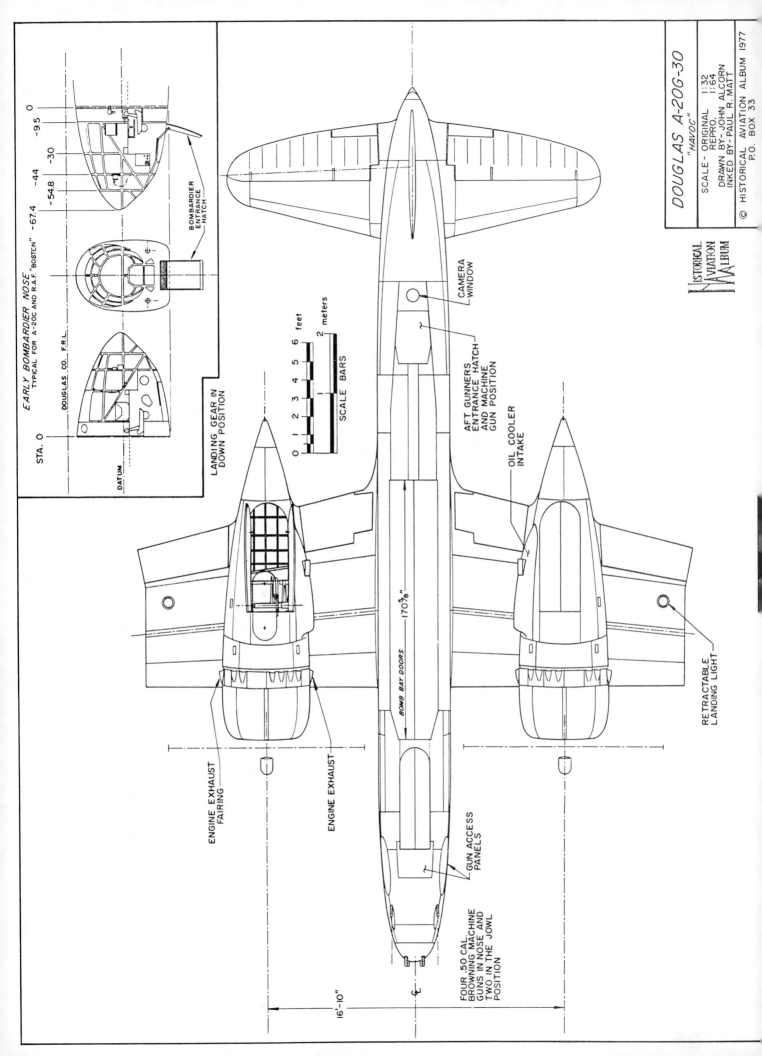

EARLY BOMBARDIER NOSE
TYPICAL FOR A-20C AND R.A.F. "BOSTON"

STA. O

DOUGLAS CO. F.R.L.

DATUM

BOMBARDIER ENTRANCE HATCH

0
-9.5
-30
-44
-54.8
-67.4

LANDING GEAR IN DOWN POSITION

SCALE BARS

0 1 2 3 4 5 6 feet

2 meters

CAMERA WINDOW

AFT GUNNERS ENTRANCE HATCH AND MACHINE GUN POSITION

OIL COOLER INTAKE

RETRACTABLE LANDING LIGHT

ENGINE EXHAUST FAIRING

ENGINE EXHAUST

170⅝"

BOMB BAY DOORS

GUN ACCESS PANELS

FOUR .50 CAL. BROWNING MACHINE GUNS IN NOSE AND TWO IN THE JOWL POSITION

16'-10"

DOUGLAS A-20G-30
"HAVOC"

SCALE - ORIGINAL   1:32
        REPRO.   1:64
DRAWN BY- JOHN J. ALCORN
INKED BY- PAUL R. MATT

© HISTORICAL AVIATION ALBUM 1977
P.O. BOX 33

Historical Aviation Album

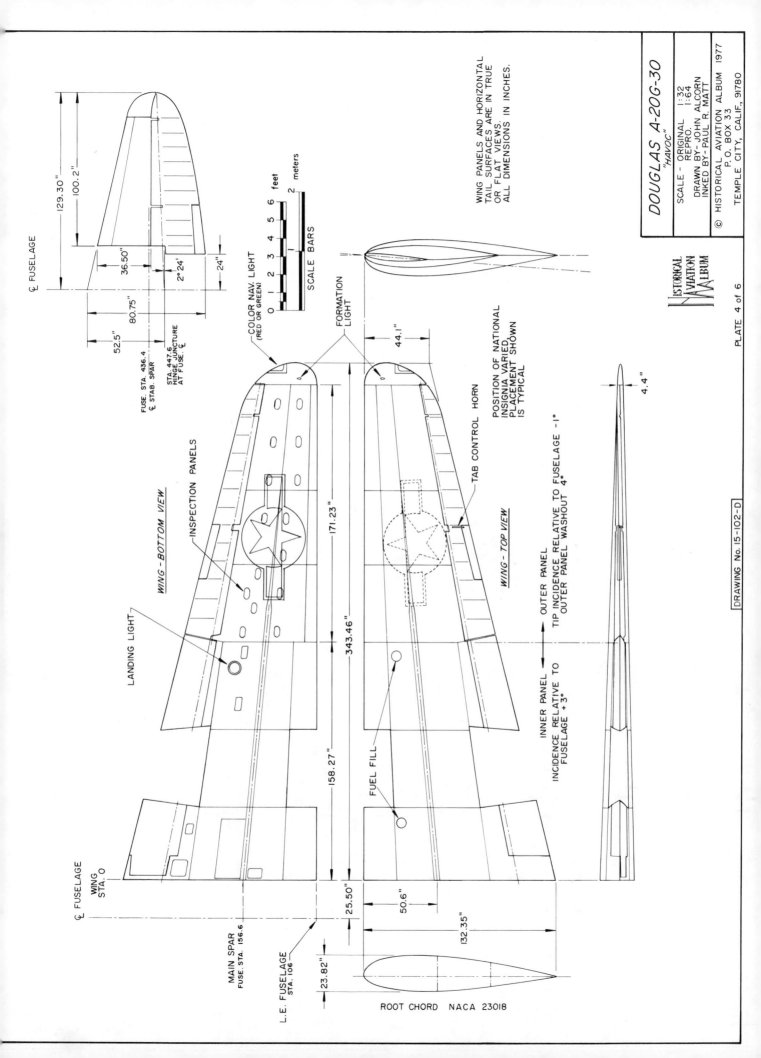

DOUGLAS A-20G-30
"HAVOC"

SCALE - ORIGINAL   1:32
        REPRO.   1:64
DRAWN BY- JOHN ALCORN
INKED BY- PAUL R. MATT

© HISTORICAL AVIATION ALBUM 1977
        P.O. BOX 33
TEMPLE CITY, CALIF., 91780

HISTORICAL AVIATION ALBUM

PLATE 4 of 6

DRAWING No.15-102-D

WING PANELS AND HORIZONTAL
TAIL SURFACES ARE IN TRUE
OR FLAT VIEWS.
ALL DIMENSIONS IN INCHES.

¢ FUSELAGE

129.30"
100.2"
36.50"
2° 24'
24"
80.75"
52.5"

FUSE. STA. 436.4
¢ STAB. SPAR

STA. 447.6
HINGE JUNCTURE
AT FUSE. ¢

COLOR NAV. LIGHT
(RED OR GREEN)

FORMATION
LIGHT

SCALE BARS

feet
meters

44.1"

POSITION OF NATIONAL
INSIGNIA VARIED,
PLACEMENT SHOWN
IS TYPICAL

TAB CONTROL HORN

INSPECTION PANELS

WING - BOTTOM VIEW

WING - TOP VIEW

LANDING LIGHT

171.23"

343.46"

158.27"

4.4"

OUTER PANEL

TIP INCIDENCE RELATIVE TO FUSELAGE -1°
OUTER PANEL WASHOUT 4°

INNER PANEL

INCIDENCE RELATIVE TO
FUSELAGE +3°

FUEL FILL

¢ FUSELAGE

¢ FUSELAGE
WING
STA. 0

MAIN SPAR
FUSE. STA. 156.6

L.E. FUSELAGE
STA. 106

25.50"

50.6"

132.35"

23.82"

ROOT CHORD NACA 23018

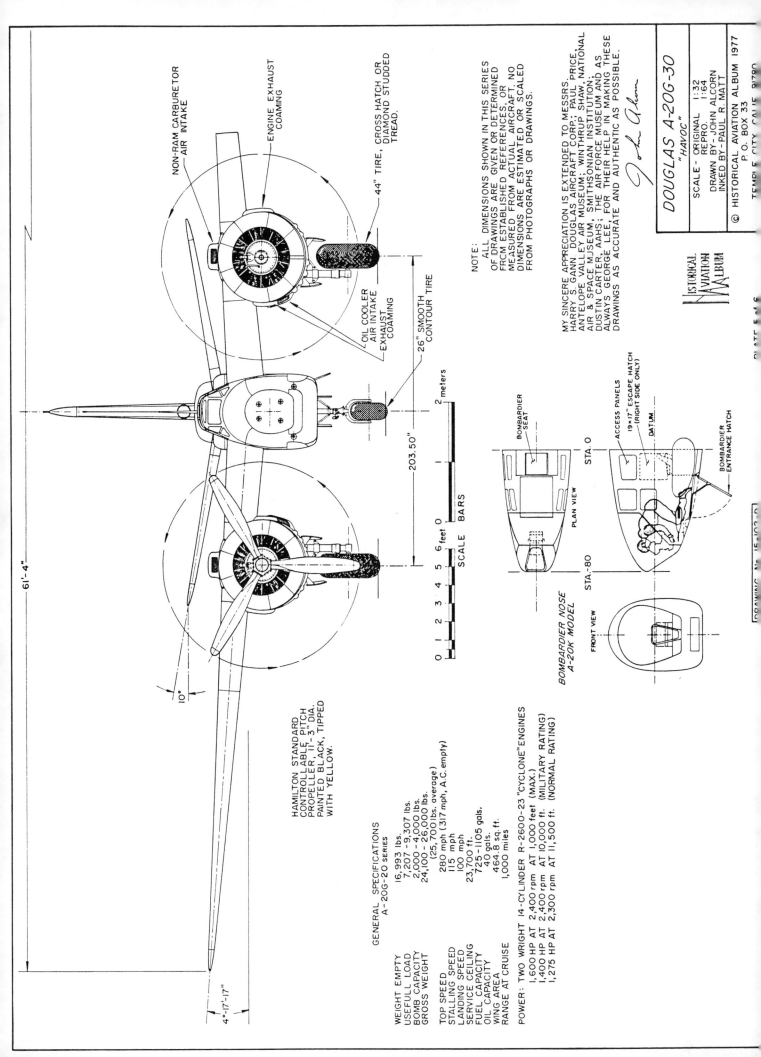

NON-RAM CARBURETOR
AIR INTAKE

ENGINE EXHAUST
COAMING

44" TIRE, CROSS HATCH OR
DIAMOND STUDDED
TREAD.

OIL COOLER
AIR INTAKE
EXHAUST
COAMING

26" SMOOTH
CONTOUR TIRE

203.50"

61'-4"

10°

4°-17'-17"

HAMILTON STANDARD
CONTROLLABLE PITCH
PROPELLER, 11'-3" DIA.
PAINTED BLACK, TIPPED
WITH YELLOW.

GENERAL SPECIFICATIONS
A-20G-20 SERIES

WEIGHT EMPTY .... 16,993 lbs.
USEFULL LOAD .... 7,207 - 9,307 lbs.
BOMB CAPACITY .... 2,000 - 4,000 lbs.
GROSS WEIGHT .... 24,100 - 26,000 lbs.
(25,700 lbs. average)
TOP SPEED .... 280 mph (317 mph, A.C. empty)
STALLING SPEED .... 115 mph
LANDING SPEED .... 100 mph
SERVICE CEILING .... 23,700 ft.
FUEL CAPACITY .... 725-1105 gals.
OIL CAPACITY .... 40 gals.
WING AREA .... 464.8 sq. ft.
RANGE AT CRUISE .... 1,000 miles
POWER: TWO WRIGHT 14-CYLINDER R-2600-23 "CYCLONE" ENGINES
1,600 HP AT 2,400 rpm AT 1,000 feet (MAX.)
1,400 HP AT 2,400 rpm AT 10,000 ft. (MILITARY RATING)
1,275 HP AT 2,300 rpm AT 11,500 ft. (NORMAL RATING)

2 meters

SCALE BARS

6 feet 0

0 1 2 3 4 5

0 1 2

BOMBARDIER
SEAT

PLAN VIEW

STA. 0

ACCESS PANELS

19x17" ESCAPE HATCH
(RIGHT SIDE ONLY)

DATUM

BOMBARDIER
ENTRANCE HATCH

STA. 80

BOMBARDIER NOSE
A-20K MODEL

FRONT VIEW

NOTE:
ALL DIMENSIONS SHOWN IN THIS SERIES
OF DRAWINGS ARE GIVEN OR DETERMINED
FROM ESTABLISHED REFERENCES, OR
MEASURED FROM ACTUAL AIRCRAFT. NO
DIMENSIONS ARE ESTIMATED OR SCALED
FROM PHOTOGRAPHS OR DRAWINGS.

MY SINCERE APPRECIATION IS EXTENDED TO MESSRS.
HARRY S. GANN DOUGLAS AIRCRAFT CORP.; PAUL PRICE,
ANTELOPE VALLEY AIR MUSEUM; WINTHRUP SHAW, NATIONAL
AIR & SPACE MUSEUM, SMITHSONIAN INSTITUTION;
DUSTIN CARTER, AAHS; THE AIR FORCE MUSEUM AND AS
ALWAYS GEORGE LEE, FOR THEIR HELP IN MAKING THESE
DRAWINGS AS ACCURATE AND AUTHENTIC AS POSSIBLE.

DOUGLAS A-20G-30
"HAVOC"

SCALE - ORIGINAL   1:32
REPRO.   1:64
DRAWN BY - JOHN ALCORN
INKED BY - PAUL R. MATT

© HISTORICAL AVIATION ALBUM 1977
P.O. BOX 33
TEMPLE CITY, CALIF. 91780

Historical Aviation Album

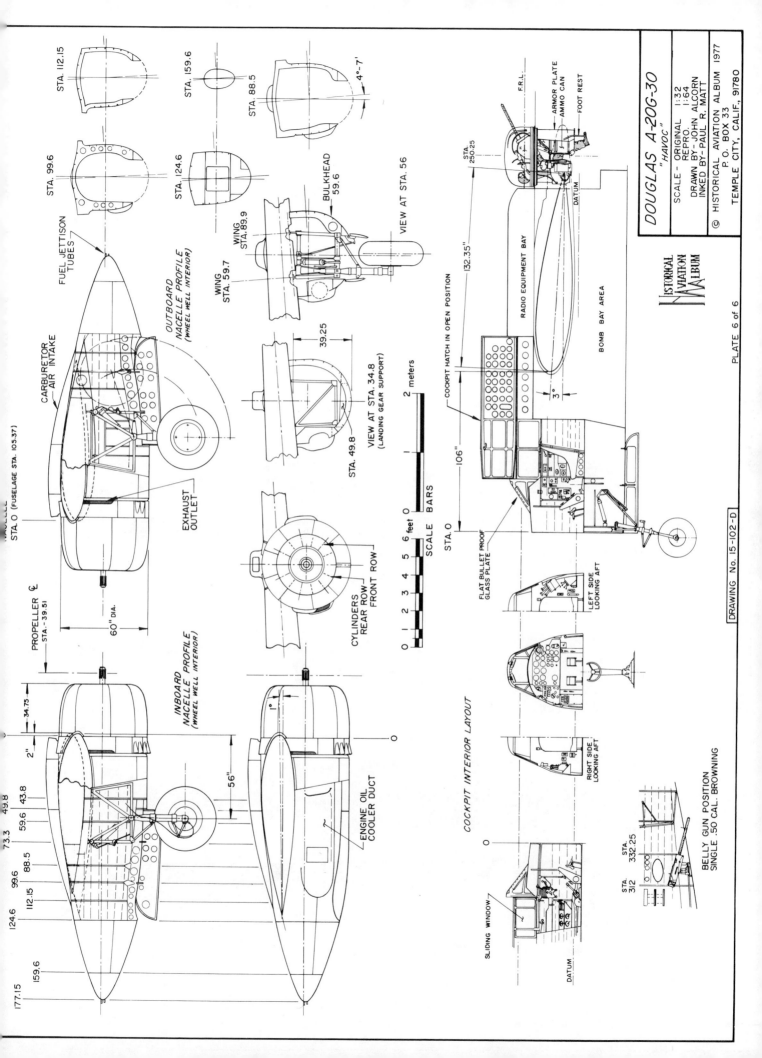

STA. 112.15

STA. 99.6

STA. 159.6

STA. 124.6

STA. 88.5

4°-7'

VIEW AT STA. 56

BULKHEAD
59.6

WING
STA. 89.9

WING
STA. 59.7

FUEL JETTISON
TUBES

*OUTBOARD
NACELLE PROFILE*
(WHEEL WELL INTERIOR)

CARBURETOR
AIR INTAKE

STA. 0 (FUSELAGE STA. 105.37)

EXHAUST
OUTLET

39.25

VIEW AT STA. 34.8
(LANDING GEAR SUPPORT)

STA. 49.8

CYLINDERS
REAR ROW
FRONT ROW

2 meters

SCALE
BARS

feet

6 5 4 3 2 1 0

PROPELLER ℄
STA. -39.51

60" DIA.

*INBOARD
NACELLE PROFILE*
(WHEEL WELL INTERIOR)

34.75

2"

56"

1°

ENGINE OIL
COOLER DUCT

49.8

43.8

73.3

59.6

88.5

99.6

112.15

124.6

159.6

177.15

COCKPIT INTERIOR LAYOUT

STA.
250.25

F.R.L.

ARMOR PLATE

AMMO CAN

FOOT REST

RADIO EQUIPMENT BAY

COCKPIT HATCH IN OPEN POSITION

132.35"

3°

DATUM

106"

STA. 0

FLAT BULLET PROOF
GLASS PLATE

LEFT SIDE
LOOKING AFT

RIGHT SIDE
LOOKING AFT

BOMB BAY AREA

SLIDING WINDOW

DATUM

STA.
312

STA.
332.25

BELLY GUN POSITION
SINGLE .50 CAL. BROWNING

DOUGLAS A-20G-30
"HAVOC"

SCALE - ORIGINAL   1:32
REPRO.   1:64
DRAWN BY - JOHN ALCORN
INKED BY - PAUL R. MATT

© HISTORICAL AVIATION ALBUM 1977
P.O. BOX 33
TEMPLE CITY, CALIF., 91780

*Historical
Aviation
Album*

PLATE 6 of 6

DRAWING No. 15-102-D

Fokker type M-4 monoplane.

Jeannine (Taube) of 1914 100 hp Argus engine.

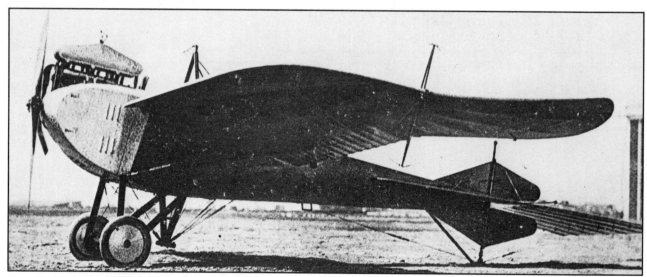

Rumpler "Taube" 100hp 3C Daimler engine.

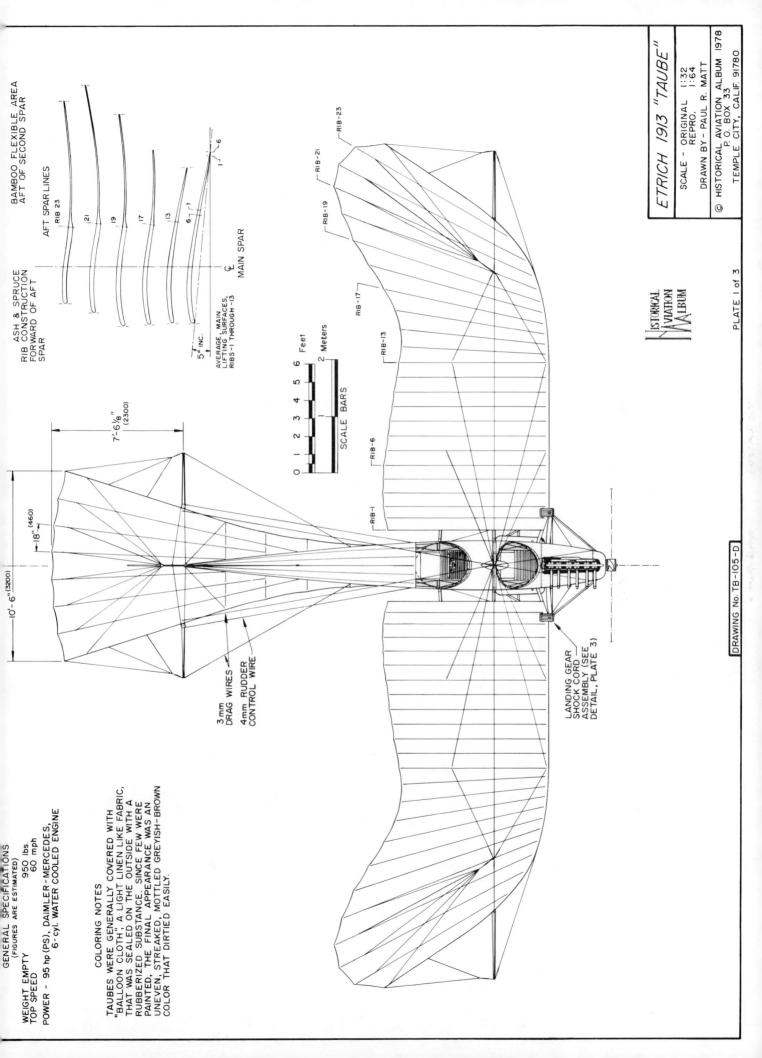

BAMBOO FLEXIBLE AREA
AFT OF SECOND SPAR

AFT SPAR LINES

RIB 23

21

19

17

13

6

ASH & SPRUCE
RIB CONSTRUCTION
FORWARD OF AFT
SPAR

MAIN SPAR

5° INC.

AVERAGE MAIN
LIFTING SURFACES,
RIBS-1 THROUGH-13

RIB-23

RIB-21

RIB-19

RIB-17

RIB-13

RIB-6

RIB-1

7'-6⅛"
(2300)

18" (460)

10'-6" (3200)

3mm
DRAG WIRES

4mm RUDDER
CONTROL WIRE

LANDING GEAR
SHOCK CORD
ASSEMBLY (SEE
DETAIL, PLATE 3)

Feet

0 1 2 3 4 5 6

Meters

2

SCALE BARS

GENERAL SPECIFICATIONS
(FIGURES ARE ESTIMATED)

WEIGHT EMPTY   950 lbs.
TOP SPEED   60 mph

POWER - 95 hp (PS), DAIMLER-MERCEDES,
6-cyl. WATER COOLED ENGINE

COLORING NOTES

TAUBES WERE GENERALLY COVERED WITH
"BALLOON CLOTH", A LIGHT LINEN LIKE FABRIC,
THAT WAS SEALED ON THE OUTSIDE WITH A
RUBBERIZED SUBSTANCE. SINCE FEW WERE
PAINTED, THE FINAL APPEARANCE WAS AN
UNEVEN, STREAKED, MOTTLED GREYISH-BROWN
COLOR THAT DIRTIED EASILY.

ETRICH 1913 "TAUBE"

SCALE - ORIGINAL 1:32
        REPRO.   1:64

DRAWN BY - PAUL R. MATT

© HISTORICAL AVIATION ALBUM 1978
P.O. BOX 33
TEMPLE CITY, CALIF. 91780

Historical Aviation Album

PLATE 1 of 3

DRAWING No. TB-105-D

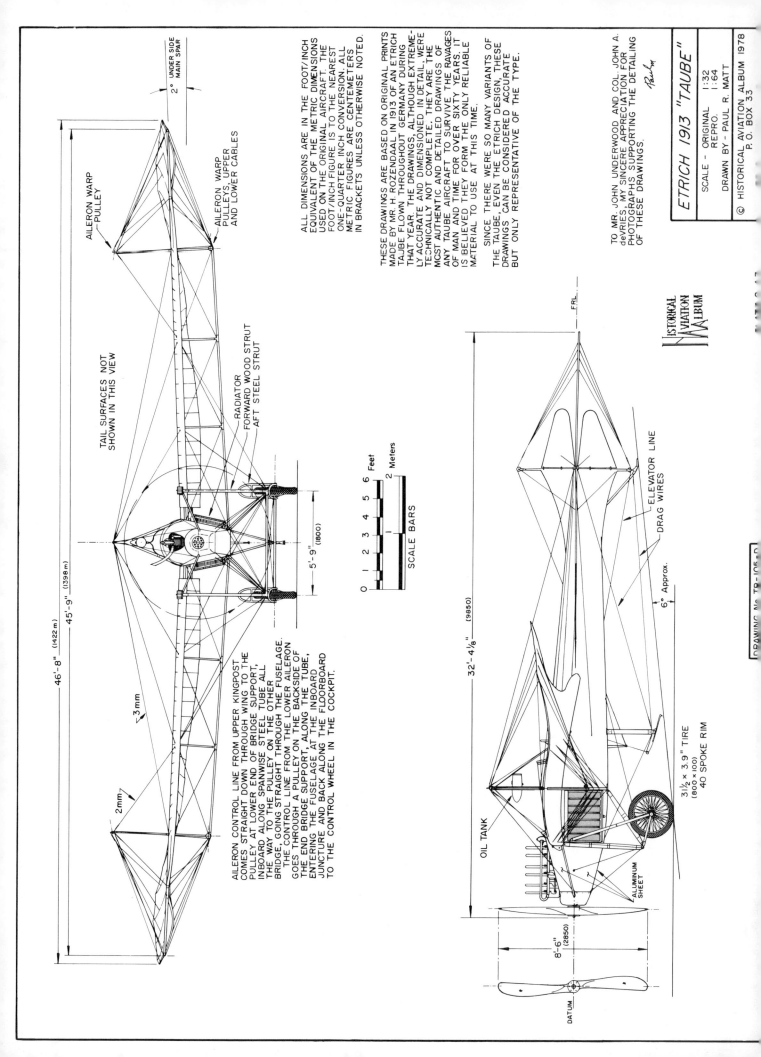

2° UNDER SIDE
MAIN SPAR

AILERON WARP
PULLEY

AILERON WARP
PULLEYS, UPPER
AND LOWER CABLES

TAIL SURFACES NOT
SHOWN IN THIS VIEW

RADIATOR
FORWARD WOOD STRUT
AFT STEEL STRUT

46'-8" (1422 m)

45'-9" (1398 m)

3mm

2mm

5'-9" (1800)

AILERON CONTROL LINE FROM UPPER KINGPOST
COMES STRAIGHT DOWN THROUGH WING TO THE
PULLEY AT LOWER END OF BRIDGE SUPPORT,
INBOARD ALONG SPANWISE STEEL TUBE ALL
THE WAY TO THE PULLEY ON THE OTHER
BRIDGE, GOING STRAIGHT THROUGH THE FUSELAGE.
THE CONTROL LINE FROM THE LOWER AILERON
GOES THROUGH A PULLEY ON THE BACKSIDE OF
THE END BRIDGE SUPPORT, ALONG THE TUBE,
ENTERING THE FUSELAGE AT THE INBOARD
JUNCTURE AND BACK ALONG THE FLOORBOARD
TO THE CONTROL WHEEL IN THE COCKPIT.

0 1 2 3 4 5 6 Feet

2 Meters

SCALE BARS

ALL DIMENSIONS ARE IN THE FOOT/INCH
EQUIVALENT OF THE METRIC DIMENSIONS
USED ON THE ORIGINAL AIRCRAFT. THE
FOOT/INCH FIGURE IS TO THE NEAREST
ONE-QUARTER INCH CONVERSION. ALL
METRIC FIGURES ARE CENTEMETERS
IN BRACKETS UNLESS OTHERWISE NOTED.

THESE DRAWINGS ARE BASED ON ORIGINAL PRINTS
MADE BY MR. H. ROZENDAAL IN 1913 OF AN ETRICH
TAJBE FLOWN THROUGHOUT GERMANY DURING
THAT YEAR. THE DRAWINGS, ALTHOUGH EXTREME-
LY ACCURATE AND DIMENSIONED IN DETAIL, WERE
TECHNICALLY NOT COMPLETE. THEY ARE THE
MOST AUTHENTIC AND DETAILED DRAWINGS OF
ANY TAUBE AIRCRAFT TO SURVIVE THE RAVAGES
OF MAN AND TIME FOR OVER SIXTY YEARS. IT
IS BELIEVED THEY FORM THE ONLY RELIABLE
MATERIAL TO USE AT THIS TIME.

SINCE THERE WERE SO MANY VARIANTS OF
THE TAUBE, EVEN THE ETRICH DESIGN, THESE
DRAWINGS CAN BE CONSIDERED ACCURATE
BUT ONLY REPRESENTATIVE OF THE TYPE.

TO MR. JOHN UNDERWOOD AND COL. JOHN A.
deVRIES, MY SINCERE APPRECIATION FOR
PHOTOGRAPHS SUPPORTING THE DETAILING
OF THESE DRAWINGS.

Paul M

ETRICH 1913 "TAUBE"

SCALE - ORIGINAL   1:32
         REPRO.   1:64

DRAWN BY - PAUL R. MATT

© HISTORICAL AVIATION ALBUM 1978
P. O. BOX 33

Historical Aviation Album

FRL

ELEVATOR LINE

DRAG WIRES

6° Approx.

32'-4⅛" (9850)

OIL TANK

3½ × 3.9" TIRE
(800 × 100)
40 SPOKE RIM

ALUMINUM
SHEET

8'-6" (2850)

DATUM

DRAWING No. TB-105-D

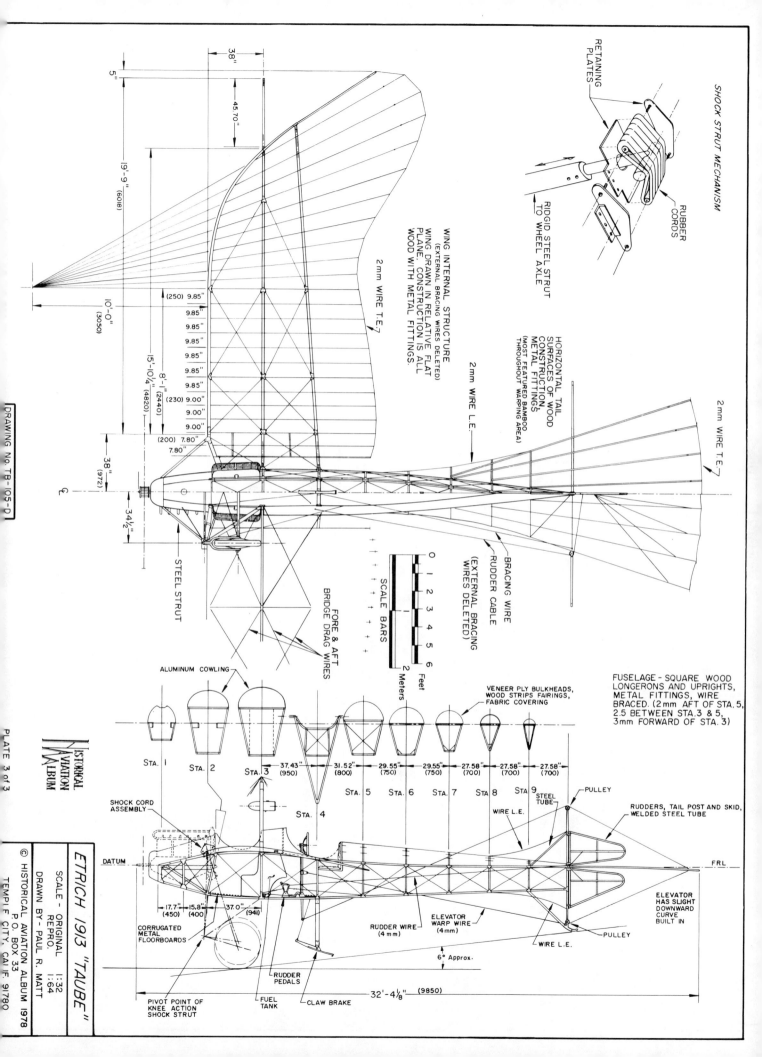

PLATE 3 of 3

SHOCK STRUT MECHANISM

RETAINING PLATES

RUBBER CORDS

RIGID STEEL STRUT TO WHEEL AXLE

WING INTERNAL STRUCTURE
(EXTERNAL BRACING WIRES DELETED)
WING DRAWN IN RELATIVE FLAT
PLANE. CONSTRUCTION IS ALL
WOOD WITH METAL FITTINGS.

2mm WIRE T.E.

2mm WIRE L.E.

HORIZONTAL TAIL
SURFACES OF WOOD
CONSTRUCTION,
METAL FITTINGS
(MOST FEATURED BAMBOO
THROUGHOUT WARPING AREA)

2mm WIRE T.E.

BRACING WIRE
(EXTERNAL BRACING
WIRES DELETED)

RUDDER CABLE

38"

5"

45.70"

19'-9" (6018)

(250) 9.85"
9.85"
9.85"
9.85"
9.85"
9.85"
9.85"
(230) 9.00"
9.00"
9.00"
(200) 7.80"
7.80"

10'-0" (3050)

15'-10¼" (4820)

8'-1" (2440)

38" (972)

34½"

₡

STEEL STRUT

FORE & AFT
BRIDGE DRAG WIRES

SCALE BARS

0 1 2 3 4 5 6 Feet
0 1 2 Meters

FUSELAGE - SQUARE WOOD
LONGERONS AND UPRIGHTS,
METAL FITTINGS, WIRE
BRACED. (2mm AFT OF STA. 5,
2.5 BETWEEN STA.3 & 5,
3mm FORWARD OF STA. 3)

ALUMINUM COWLING

VENEER PLY BULKHEADS,
WOOD STRIPS FAIRINGS,
FABRIC COVERING

STA. 1

STA. 2

STA. 3

STA. 4

37.43" (950)

31.52" (800)

29.55" (750)

29.55" (750)

27.58" (700)

27.58" (700)

27.58" (700)

STA. 5   STA. 6   STA. 7   STA 8   STA 9

STEEL TUBE

PULLEY

WIRE L.E.

RUDDERS, TAIL POST AND SKID,
WELDED STEEL TUBE

SHOCK CORD
ASSEMBLY

DATUM

CORRUGATED
METAL
FLOORBOARDS

17.7" (450)

15.8" (400)

37.0" (941)

RUDDER
PEDALS

FUEL
TANK

CLAW BRAKE

PIVOT POINT OF
KNEE ACTION
SHOCK STRUT

RUDDER WIRE
(4 mm)

ELEVATOR
WARP WIRE
(4mm)

WIRE L.E.

6° Approx.

32'-4⅛" (9850)

FRL

ELEVATOR
HAS SLIGHT
DOWNWARD
CURVE
BUILT IN

PULLEY

ETRICH 1913 "TAUBE"

SCALE - ORIGINAL
REPRO.
DRAWN BY- PAUL R. MATT

1:32
1:64

© HISTORICAL AVIATION ALBUM 1978
P.O. BOX 33
TEMPLE CITY, CALIF. 91780

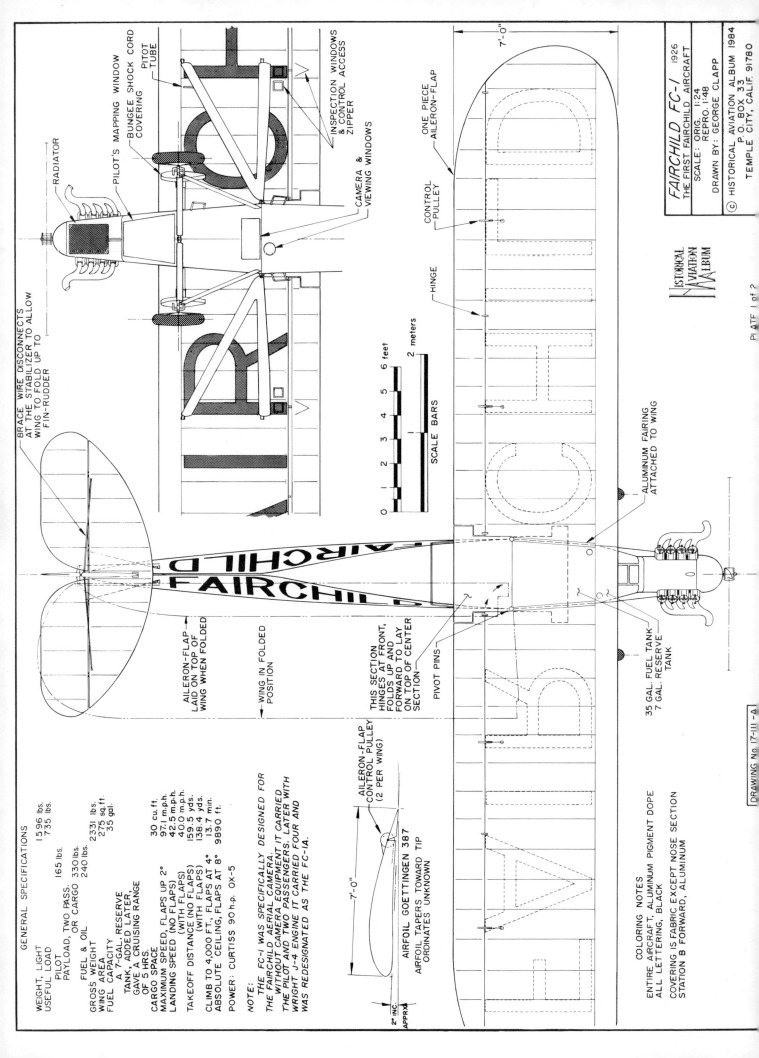

FAIRCHILD FC-1 1926
THE FIRST FAIRCHILD AIRCRAFT
SCALE: ORIG. 1:24
REPRO. 1:48
DRAWN BY: GEORGE CLAPP
© HISTORICAL AVIATION ALBUM 1984
P. O. BOX 33
TEMPLE CITY, CALIF. 91780

Historical Aviation Album

PLATE 1 of 2

DRAWING No. 17-III-A

SCALE BARS
6 feet
2 meters

RADIATOR
PILOT'S MAPPING WINDOW
BUNGEE SHOCK CORD COVERING
PITOT TUBE
INSPECTION WINDOWS & CONTROL ACCESS
CAMERA & VIEWING WINDOWS
ZIPPER

BRACE WIRE DISCONNECTS AT THE STABILIZER TO ALLOW WING TO FOLD UP TO FIN-RUDDER

ONE PIECE AILERON-FLAP
CONTROL PULLEY
HINGE
ALUMINUM FAIRING ATTACHED TO WING

AILERON-FLAP LAID ON TOP OF WING WHEN FOLDED
WING IN FOLDED POSITION

THIS SECTION HINGES AT FRONT, FOLDS UP AND FORWARD TO LAY ON TOP OF CENTER SECTION
PIVOT PINS
35 GAL. FUEL TANK
7 GAL. RESERVE TANK

AILERON-FLAP CONTROL PULLEY (2 PER WING)

7'-0"

AIRFOIL GOETTINGEN 387
AIRFOIL TAPERS TOWARD TIP
ORDINATES UNKNOWN

2" INC.
APPRX

GENERAL SPECIFICATIONS

WEIGHT, LIGHT   1596 lbs.
USEFUL LOAD   735 lbs.
   PILOT   165 lbs.
   PAYLOAD, TWO PASS.
   OR CARGO   330 lbs.
   FUEL & OIL   240 lbs.
GROSS WEIGHT   2331 lbs.
WING AREA   275 sq. ft.
FUEL CAPACITY   35 gal.
   A 7-GAL. RESERVE
   TANK, ADDED LATER,
   GAVE A CRUISING RANGE
   OF 5 HRS.
CARGO SPACE   30 cu. ft.
MAXIMUM SPEED, FLAPS UP 2°   97.1 m.p.h.
LANDING SPEED (NO FLAPS)   42.5 m.p.h.
            (WITH FLAPS)   40.0 m.p.h.
TAKEOFF DISTANCE (NO FLAPS) 159.5 yds.
            (WITH FLAPS)   138.4 yds.
CLIMB TO 4,000 FT., FLAPS AT 4°   13.7 min.
ABSOLUTE CEILING, FLAPS AT 8°   9890 ft.

POWER: CURTISS 90 h.p. OX-5

NOTE:
THE FC-1 WAS SPECIFICALLY DESIGNED FOR THE FAIRCHILD AERIAL CAMERA. WITHOUT CAMERA EQUIPMENT IT CARRIED THE PILOT AND TWO PASSENGERS. LATER WITH WRIGHT J-4 ENGINE IT CARRIED FOUR AND WAS REDESIGNATED AS THE FC-IA.

COLORING NOTES
ENTIRE AIRCRAFT, ALUMINUM PIGMENT DOPE
COVERING IS FABRIC EXCEPT NOSE SECTION
STATION B FORWARD, ALUMINUM
ALL LETTERING, BLACK

7'-0"

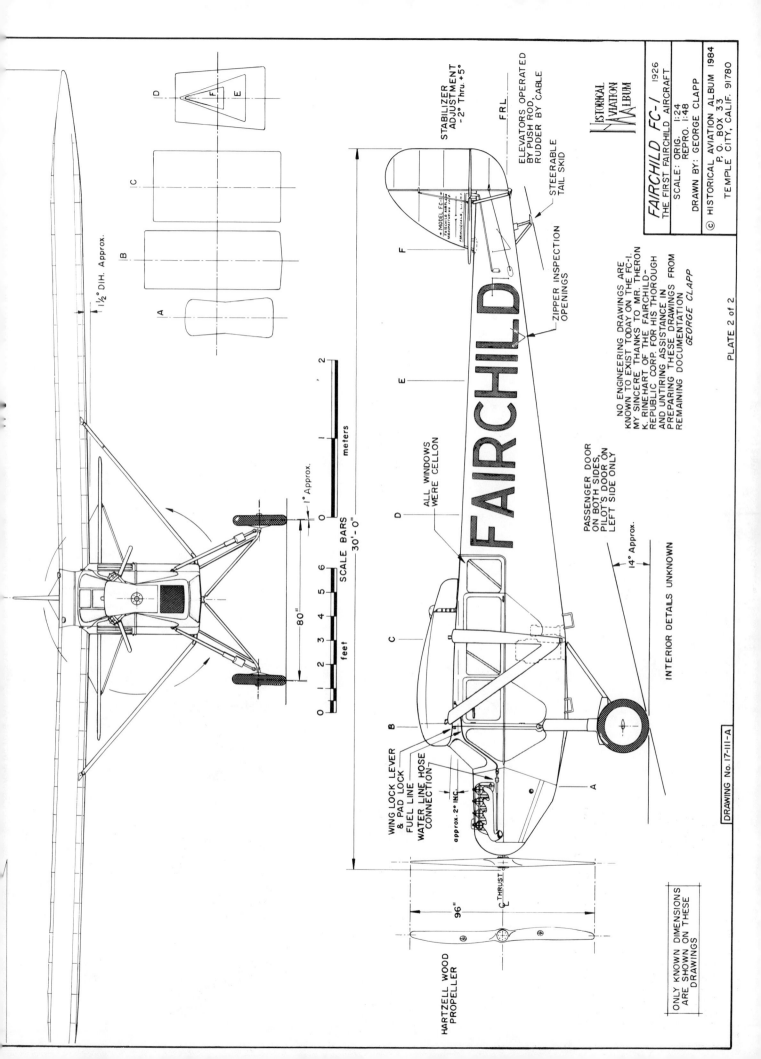

1½ DIH. Approx.

1° Approx.

80"

meters

SCALE BARS
30'-0"

feet

STABILIZER
ADJUSTMENT
-2° Thru +5°

FRL

ELEVATORS OPERATED
BY PUSH ROD,
RUDDER BY CABLE

STEERABLE
TAIL SKID

• MODEL FC-1•
FAIRCHILD AIRPLANE
MANUFACTURING CO.
FARMINGDALE N.Y.

ZIPPER INSPECTION
OPENINGS

FAIRCHILD

ALL WINDOWS
WERE CELLON

PASSENGER DOOR
ON BOTH SIDES,
PILOT'S DOOR ON
LEFT SIDE ONLY

14° Approx.

INTERIOR DETAILS UNKNOWN

WING LOCK LEVER
& PAD LOCK

FUEL LINE

WATER LINE HOSE
CONNECTION

approx. 2° INC.

96"

THRUST

HARTZELL WOOD
PROPELLER

ONLY KNOWN DIMENSIONS
ARE SHOWN ON THESE
DRAWINGS

FAIRCHILD FC-1 1926
THE FIRST FAIRCHILD AIRCRAFT

SCALE: ORIG. 1:24
       REPRO. 1:48

DRAWN BY: GEORGE CLAPP

HISTORICAL AVIATION ALBUM

© HISTORICAL AVIATION ALBUM 1984
P. O. BOX 33
TEMPLE CITY, CALIF. 91780

NO ENGINEERING DRAWINGS ARE
KNOWN TO EXIST TODAY ON THE FC-1.
MY SINCERE THANKS TO MR. THERON
K. RINEHART OF THE FAIRCHILD-
REPUBLIC CORP. FOR HIS THOROUGH
AND UNTIRING ASSISTANCE IN
PREPARING THESE DRAWINGS FROM
REMAINING DOCUMENTATION
                    GEORGE CLAPP

PLATE 2 of 2

DRAWING No. 17-III-A

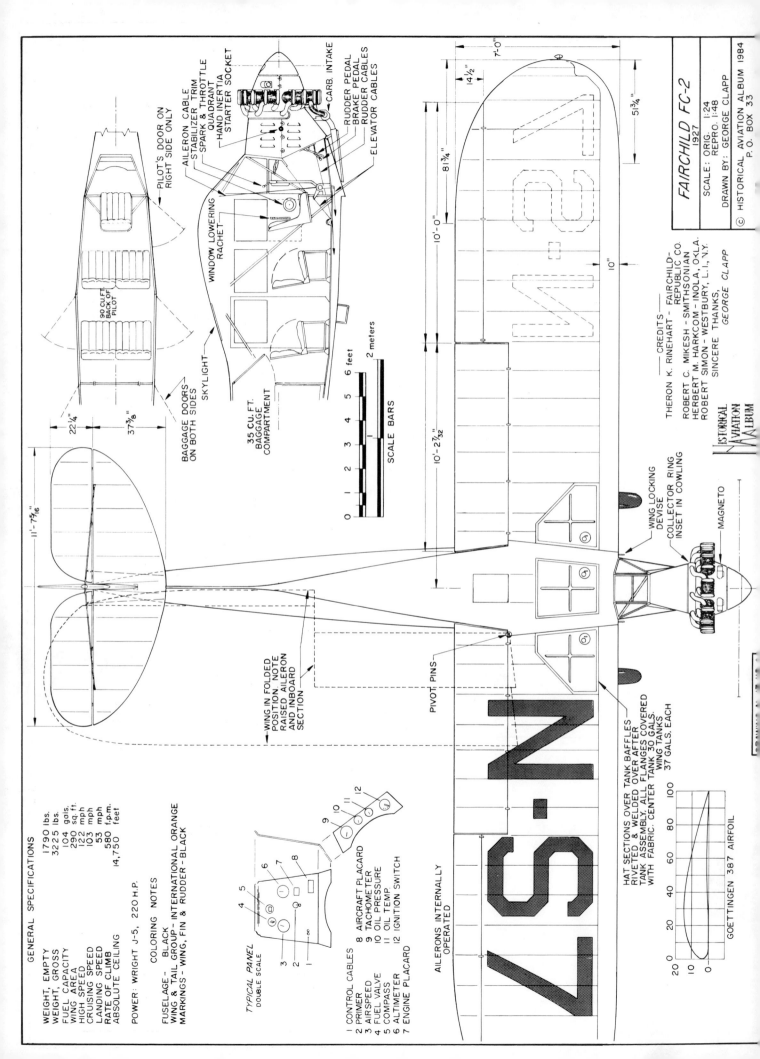

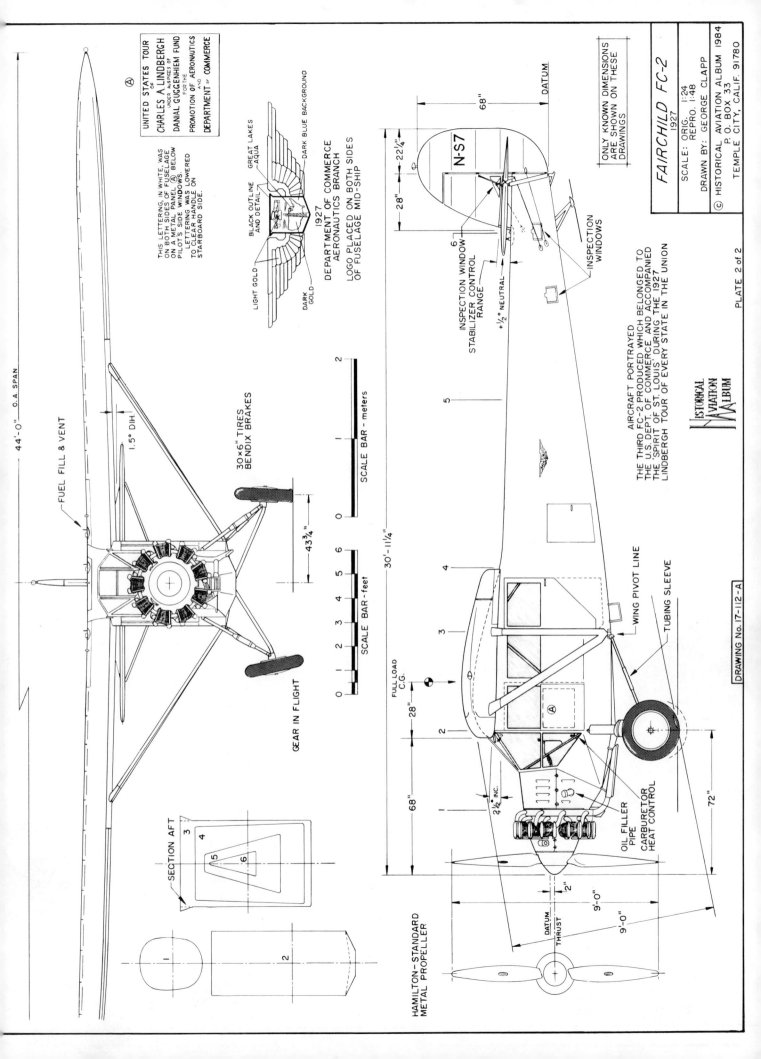

44'-0" O.A. SPAN

FUEL FILL & VENT

1.5° DIH.

30x6" TIRES
BENDIX BRAKES

43¾"

GEAR IN FLIGHT

SECTION AFT

HAMILTON-STANDARD
METAL PROPELLER

UNITED STATES TOUR
of
CHARLES A. LINDBERGH
under auspices of
DANIAL GUGGENHIEM FUND
FOR THE
PROMOTION OF AERONAUTICS
AND
DEPARTMENT OF COMMERCE

THIS LETTERING, IN WHITE, WAS
ON BOTH SIDES OF FUSELAGE
ON A METAL PANEL Ⓐ BELOW
PILOT'S SIDE WINDOWS.
LETTERING WAS LOWERED
TO CLEAR HANDLE ON
STARBOARD SIDE.

Ⓐ

GREAT LAKES
— AQUA

DARK BLUE BACKGROUND

LIGHT GOLD

BLACK OUTLINE
AND DETAIL

DARK
GOLD

1927
DEPARTMENT OF COMMERCE
AERONAUTICS BRANCH

LOGO PLACED ON BOTH SIDES
OF FUSELAGE MID-SHIP

SCALE BAR - meters

0   1   2

SCALE BAR - feet

0 1 2 3 4 5 6

FAIRCHILD FC-2
1927

SCALE: ORIG. 1:24
REPRO. 1:48

DRAWN BY: GEORGE CLAPP

© HISTORICAL AVIATION ALBUM 1984
P. O. BOX 33
TEMPLE CITY, CALIF. 91780

ONLY KNOWN DIMENSIONS
ARE SHOWN ON THESE
DRAWINGS

68"

28"

22¼"

N-S7

DATUM

INSPECTION WINDOW

STABILIZER CONTROL
RANGE

+ ½° NEUTRAL

INSPECTION
WINDOWS

AIRCRAFT PORTRAYED
THE THIRD FC-2 PRODUCED WHICH BELONGED TO
THE U.S. DEPT. OF COMMERCE AND ACCOMPANIED
THE 'SPIRIT OF ST. LOUIS' DURING THE 1927
LINDBERGH TOUR OF EVERY STATE IN THE UNION

30'-11¼"

FULL LOAD
C.G.

28"

68"

2½" INC.

WING PIVOT LINE

TUBING SLEEVE

OIL FILLER
PIPE

CARBURETOR
HEAT CONTROL

72"

9'-0"

9'-0"

DATUM

THRUST

2"

PLATE 2 of 2

HISTORICAL AVIATION ALBUM

DRAWING No. 17-112-A

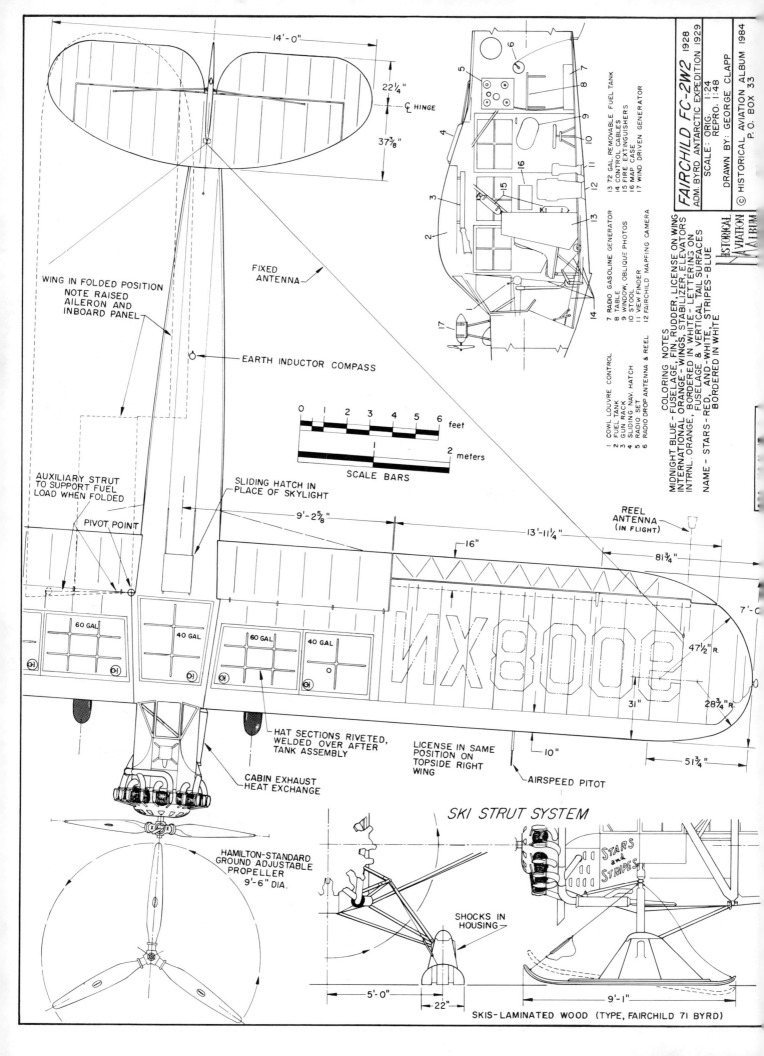

14'-0"

22¼"
℄ HINGE
37⅜"

WING IN FOLDED POSITION
NOTE RAISED AILERON AND INBOARD PANEL

FIXED ANTENNA

EARTH INDUCTOR COMPASS

AUXILIARY STRUT TO SUPPORT FUEL LOAD WHEN FOLDED

PIVOT POINT

SLIDING HATCH IN PLACE OF SKYLIGHT

SCALE BARS
0 1 2 3 4 5 6 feet
1 2 meters

9'-2⅝"

13'-11¼"

16"

REEL ANTENNA (IN FLIGHT)

81¾"

7'-0

NX8006

47½" R.

60 GAL   40 GAL   60 GAL   40 GAL

31"

28¾" R.

HAT SECTIONS RIVETED, WELDED OVER AFTER TANK ASSEMBLY

CABIN EXHAUST HEAT EXCHANGE

LICENSE IN SAME POSITION ON TOPSIDE RIGHT WING

10"

51¾"

AIRSPEED PITOT

HAMILTON-STANDARD GROUND ADJUSTABLE PROPELLER 9'-6" DIA.

SKI STRUT SYSTEM

SHOCKS IN HOUSING

STARS and STRIPES

5'-0"
22"
9'-1"

SKIS-LAMINATED WOOD (TYPE, FAIRCHILD 71 BYRD)

FAIRCHILD FC-2W2 1928
ADM. BYRD ANTARCTIC EXPEDITION 1929
SCALE: ORIG. 1:24
REPRO. 1:48
DRAWN BY: GEORGE CLAPP
© HISTORICAL AVIATION ALBUM 1984
P.O. BOX 33

HISTORICAL AVIATION ALBUM

1 COWL LOUVRE CONTROL
2 FUEL TANK
3 GUN RACK
4 SLIDING NAV. HATCH
5 RADIO SET
6 RADIO DROP ANTENNA & REEL
7 RADIO GASOLINE GENERATOR
8 TABLE
9 WINDOW, OBLIQUE PHOTOS
10 STOOL
11 VIEW FINDER
12 FAIRCHILD MAPPING CAMERA
13 72 GAL. REMOVABLE FUEL TANK
14 CONTROL CABLES
15 FIRE EXTINGUISHERS
16 MAP CASE
17 WIND DRIVEN GENERATOR

COLORING NOTES
MIDNIGHT BLUE - FUSELAGE, FIN, RUDDER, LICENSE ON WING
INTERNATIONAL ORANGE - WINGS, STABILIZER, ELEVATORS
INTRNL. ORANGE, BORDERED IN WHITE - LETTERING ON
FUSELAGE & VERTICAL TAIL SURFACES
NAME - STARS - RED AND WHITE, STRIPES - BLUE
BORDERED IN WHITE

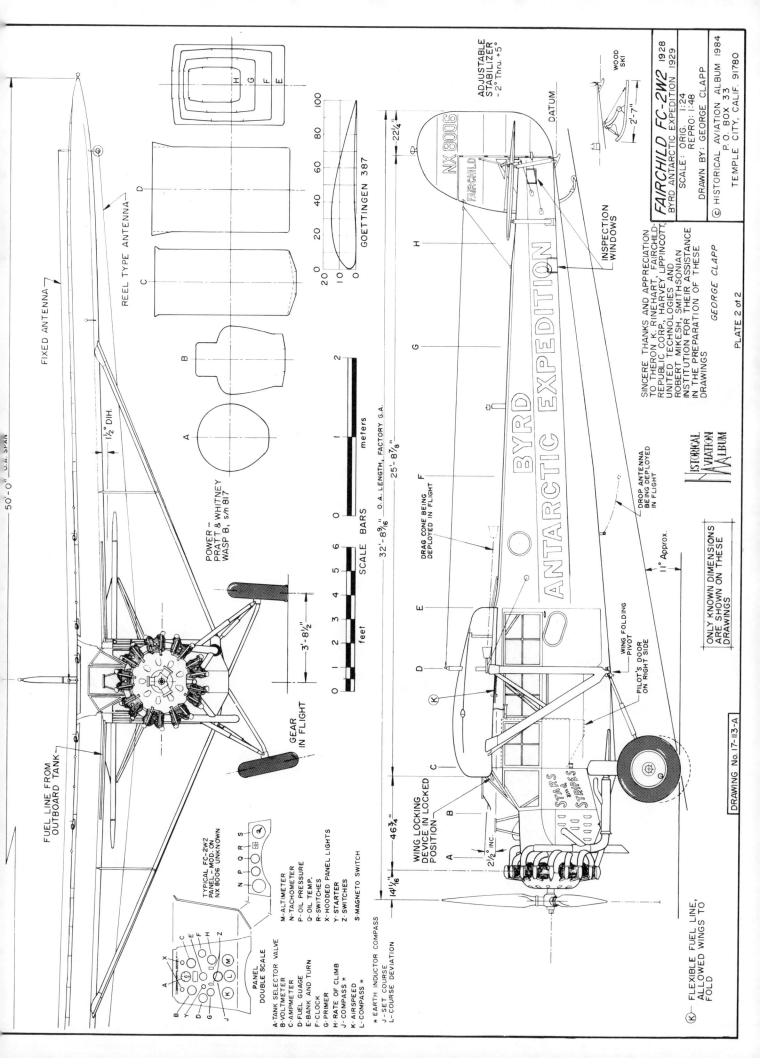

50'-0" O.A. SPAN

FIXED ANTENNA

REEL TYPE ANTENNA

1½" DIH.

POWER–
PRATT & WHITNEY
WASP B, s/n 817

GOETTINGEN 387

100 80 60 40 20 0

FUEL LINE FROM
OUTBOARD TANK

GEAR
IN FLIGHT

3'-8½"

SCALE BARS

meters
2 1 0

feet
0 1 2 3 4 5 6

**TYPICAL FC-2W2
PANEL– MOD. ON
NX 8006 UNKNOWN**

PANEL
DOUBLE SCALE

A-TANK SELECTOR VALVE
B-VOLTMETER
C-AMPMETER
D-FUEL GUAGE
E-BANK AND TURN
F-CLOCK
G-PRIMER
H-RATE OF CLIMB
J-COMPASS *
K-AIRSPEED
L-COMPASS *

M-ALTIMETER
N-TACHOMETER
P-OIL PRESSURE
Q-OIL TEMP.
R-SWITCHES
X-HOODED PANEL LIGHTS
Y-STARTER
Z-SWITCHES
S-MAGNETO SWITCH

* EARTH INDUCTOR COMPASS
J - SET COURSE
L - COURSE DEVIATION

Ⓚ — FLEXIBLE FUEL LINE,
ALLOWED WINGS TO
FOLD

ADJUSTABLE
STABILIZER
- 2° Thru. +5°

WOOD
SKI

2'-7"

DATUM

NX8006
FAIRCHILD

INSPECTION
WINDOWS

BYRD ANTARCTIC EXPEDITION

22¼"

32'-8⅞6" O.A. LENGTH, FACTORY G.A.

25'-8⅞"

DROP ANTENNA
BEING DEPLOYED
IN FLIGHT

DRAG CONE BEING
DEPLOYED IN FLIGHT

11° Approx.

WING FOLDING
PIVOT

PILOT'S DOOR
ON RIGHT SIDE

STARS &
STRIPES

WING LOCKING
DEVICE IN LOCKED
POSITION

46¾"

14½6"

2½° INC.

FAIRCHILD FC-2W2 1928
BYRD ANTARCTIC EXPEDITION 1929

SCALE: ORIG: 1:24
REPRO: 1:48

DRAWN BY: GEORGE CLAPP

Ⓒ HISTORICAL AVIATION ALBUM 1984
P.O. BOX 33
TEMPLE CITY, CALIF. 91780

SINCERE THANKS AND APPRECIATION
TO THERON K. RINEHART, FAIRCHILD-
REPUBLIC CORP, HARVEY LIPPINCOTT,
UNITED TECHNOLOGIES AND
ROBERT MIKESH, SMITHSONIAN
INSTITUTION FOR THEIR ASSISTANCE
IN THE PREPARATION OF THESE
DRAWINGS

GEORGE CLAPP

PLATE 2 of 2

Historical Aviation Album

ONLY KNOWN DIMENSIONS
ARE SHOWN ON THESE
DRAWINGS

DRAWING No. 17-113-A

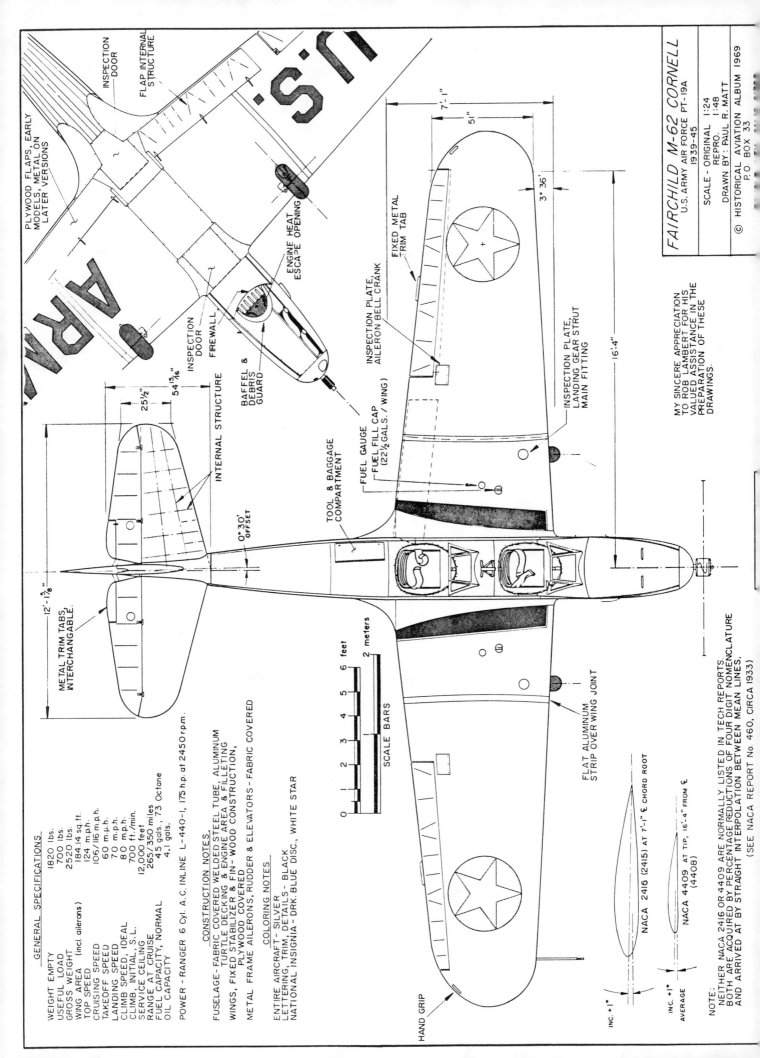

PLYWOOD FLAPS, EARLY MODELS, METAL ON LATER VERSIONS

INSPECTION DOOR

FLAP INTERNAL STRUCTURE

U.S.

ARM

INSPECTION DOOR

FIREWALL

INTERNAL STRUCTURE

BAFFEL & DEBRIS GUARD

ENGINE HEAT ESCAPE OPENING

FIXED METAL TRIM TAB

INSPECTION PLATE, AILERON BELL CRANK

FUEL FILL CAP (22½ GALS./WING)

FUEL GAUGE

TOOL & BAGGAGE COMPARTMENT

INSPECTION PLATE, LANDING GEAR STRUT MAIN FITTING

7'-1"

51"

3° 36'

16'-4"

25½"

54 ¹⁵⁄₁₆"

12'-1³⁄₈"

0° 30' OFFSET

METAL TRIM TABS, INTERCHANGEABLE.

FLAT ALUMINUM STRIP OVER WING JOINT

HAND GRIP

INC. +1°

INC. +1° AVERAGE

NACA 2416 (2415) AT 7'-1" ₵ CHORD ROOT

NACA 4409 AT TIP, 16'-4" FROM ₵ (4408)

6 feet

2 meters

5

6

4

3

2

1

0

SCALE BARS

GENERAL SPECIFICATIONS

WEIGHT EMPTY	1820 lbs.
USEFUL LOAD	700 lbs.
GROSS WEIGHT	2520 lbs.
WING AREA (incl. ailerons)	184.14 sq. ft.
TOP SPEED	124 m.p.h.
CRUISING SPEED	106/116 m.p.h.
TAKEOFF SPEED	60 m.p.h.
LANDING SPEED	70 m.p.h.
CLIMB SPEED, IDEAL	80 m.p.h.
CLIMB, INITIAL, S.L.	700 ft./min.
SERVICE CEILING	12,000 feet
RANGE AT CRUISE	265/350 miles
FUEL CAPACITY, NORMAL	45 gals., 73 Octane
OIL CAPACITY	4.1 gals.

POWER - RANGER 6 Cyl. A.C. INLINE L-440-I, 175 h.p. at 2450 r.p.m.

CONSTRUCTION NOTES,

FUSELAGE - FABRIC COVERED WELDED STEEL TUBE, ALUMINUM TURTLE DECKING & ENGINE AREA & FILLETING
WINGS, FIXED STABILIZER & FIN - WOOD CONSTRUCTION, PLYWOOD COVERED
METAL FRAME AILERONS, RUDDER & ELEVATORS - FABRIC COVERED

COLORING NOTES

ENTIRE AIRCRAFT - SILVER
LETTERING, TRIM, DETAILS - BLACK
NATIONAL INSIGNIA - DRK. BLUE DISC., WHITE STAR

NOTE:
NEITHER NACA 2416 OR 4409 ARE NORMALLY LISTED IN TECH REPORTS. BOTH ARE ACQUIRED BY PERCENTAGE REDUCTIONS OF FOUR DIGIT NOMENCLATURE AND ARRIVED AT BY STRAIGHT INTERPOLATION BETWEEN MEAN LINES.
(SEE NACA REPORT No. 460, CIRCA 1933)

FAIRCHILD M-62 CORNELL

U.S. ARMY AIR FORCE PT-19A
1939-45

SCALE - ORIGINAL 1:24
REPRO. 1:48
DRAWN BY: PAUL R. MATT

© HISTORICAL AVIATION ALBUM 1969
P.O. BOX 33

MY SINCERE APPRECIATION TO ROB LAMBERT FOR HIS VALUED ASSISTANCE IN THE PREPARATION OF THESE DRAWINGS.

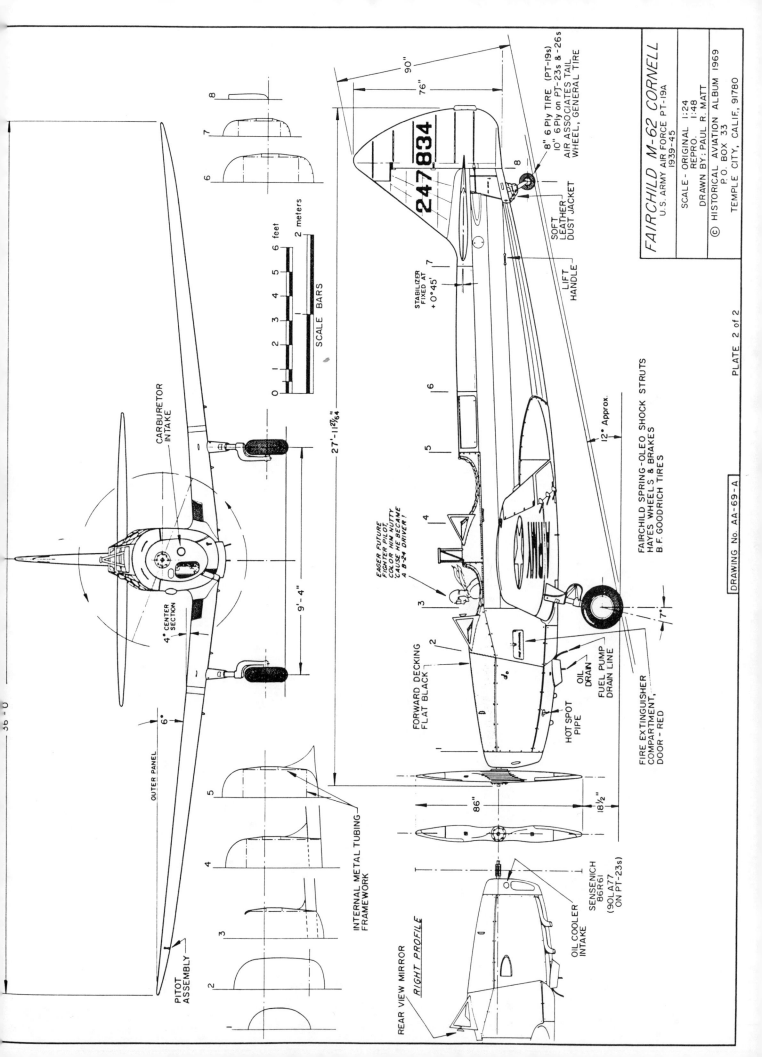

FAIRCHILD M-62 CORNELL

U.S. ARMY AIR FORCE PT-19A
1939-45

SCALE - ORIGINAL 1:24
REPRO. 1:48
DRAWN BY: PAUL R. MATT

© HISTORICAL AVIATION ALBUM 1969
P.O. BOX 33
TEMPLE CITY, CALIF., 91780

PLATE 2 of 2

DRAWING No. AA-69-A

8" 6 Ply TIRE (PT-19s)
10" 6 Ply on PT-23s & -26s
AIR ASSOCIATES TAIL
WHEEL, GENERAL TIRE

247834

SOFT
LEATHER
DUST JACKET

LIFT
HANDLE

STABILIZER
FIXED AT
+ 0°45'

EAGER FUTURE
FIGHTER PILOT
COLOR HIM NUTTY
'CAUSE HE BECAME
A B-24 DRIVER!

12° Approx.

FAIRCHILD SPRING-OLEO SHOCK STRUTS
HAYES WHEELS & BRAKES
B.F. GOODRICH TIRES

7°

FORWARD DECKING
FLAT BLACK

HOT SPOT
PIPE

OIL
DRAIN

FUEL PUMP
DRAIN LINE

FIRE EXTINGUISHER
COMPARTMENT,
DOOR - RED

86"

18½"

SENSENICH
86R61
(90LA77
ON PT-23s)

OIL COOLER
INTAKE

REAR VIEW MIRROR
RIGHT PROFILE

INTERNAL METAL TUBING
FRAMEWORK

27'-11 27/64"

9'-4"

CARBURETOR
INTAKE

4° CENTER
SECTION

4° CENTER
SECTION

6°

OUTER PANEL

PITOT
ASSEMBLY

36'-0"

SCALE BARS

0 1 2 3 4 5 6 feet

2 meters

90"

76"

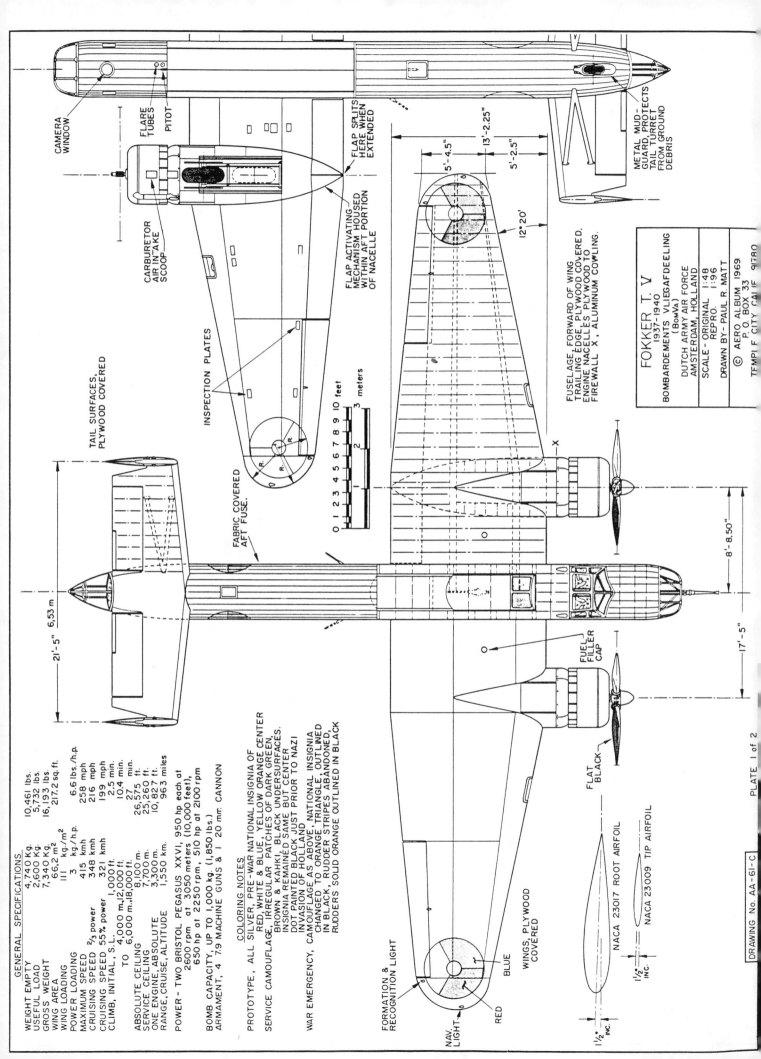

CAMERA WINDOW

FLARE TUBES

PITOT

CARBURETOR AIR INTAKE SCOOP

FLAP SPLITS HERE WHEN EXTENDED

FLAP ACTIVATING MECHANISM HOUSED WITHIN AFT PORTION OF NACELLE

INSPECTION PLATES

TAIL SURFACES, PLYWOOD COVERED

FABRIC COVERED AFT FUSE.

METAL MUD-GUARD, PROTECTS TAIL TURRET FROM GROUND DEBRIS

FUSELAGE, FORWARD OF WING TRAILING EDGE, PLYWOOD COVERED. ENGINE NACELLES PLYWOOD TO FIREWALL X, ALUMINUM COWLING.

5'-4.5"

13'-2.25"

5'-2.5"

12° 20'

8'-8.50"

17'-5"

21'-5"   6,53 m

0 1 2 3 4 5 6 7 8 9 10 feet

1 2 3 meters

FUEL FILLER CAP

FLAT BLACK

WINGS, PLYWOOD COVERED

NACA 23017 ROOT AIRFOIL

NACA 23009 TIP AIRFOIL

1½ INC.

1½ INC.

1½ INC.

FORMATION & RECOGNITION LIGHT

NAV. LIGHT

RED

BLUE

FOKKER T. V
1937-1940
BOMBARDEMENTS VLIEGAFDEELING
(BomVa)
DUTCH ARMY AIR FORCE
AMSTERDAM, HOLLAND
SCALE - ORIGINAL   1:48
REPRO.   1:96
DRAWN BY - PAUL R. MATT

© AERO ALBUM 1969
P.O. BOX 33
TEMPLE CITY, CALIF. 9780

GENERAL SPECIFICATIONS

WEIGHT EMPTY	4,740 Kg.	10,461 lbs.
USEFUL LOAD	2,600 Kg.	5,732 lbs.
GROSS WEIGHT	7,340 Kg.	16,193 lbs.
WING AREA	66,2 m²	217.2 sq. ft.
POWER LOADING	III	6.6 lbs./h.p.
WING LOADING	3	kg./m²
MAXIMUM SPEED	415 kmh	258 mph
CRUISING SPEED ⅔ power	348 kmh	216 mph
CRUISING SPEED 55% power	321 kmh	199 mph
CLIMB, INITIAL, S.L.		1,000 ft. 2.5 min.
TO 4,000 m.,12,000 ft.		10.4 min.
TO 6,000 m.,18,000 ft.		27 min.
ABSOLUTE CEILING	8,100 m.	26,575 ft.
SERVICE CEILING	7,700 m.	25,260 ft.
ONE ENGINE,ABSOLUTE	3,300 m.	10,827 ft.
RANGE, CRUISE, ALTITUDE		1,550 km. 963 miles

POWER - TWO BRISTOL PEGASUS XXVI, 950 hp each at 2600 rpm at 3050 meters (10,000 feet), 650 hp at 2250 rpm, 510 hp at 2100 rpm

BOMB CAPACITY, UP TO 1,000 kg. (1,850 lbs.)
ARMAMENT, 4 7.9 MACHINE GUNS & 1 20 mm. CANNON

COLORING NOTES

PROTOTYPE, ALL SILVER, PRE-WAR NATIONAL INSIGNIA OF RED, WHITE & BLUE, YELLOW ORANGE CENTER

SERVICE CAMOUFLAGE, IRREGULAR PATCHES OF DARK GREEN, BROWN & KAHKI, BLACK UNDERSURFACES. INSIGNIA REMAINED SAME BUT CENTER DOT PAINTED BLACK JUST PRIOR TO NAZI INVASION OF HOLLAND

WAR EMERGENCY, CAMOUFLAGE AS ABOVE, NATIONAL INSIGNIA CHANGED TO ORANGE TRIANGLE, OUTLINED IN BLACK, RUDDER STRIPES ABANDONED, RUDDERS SOLID ORANGE OUTLINED IN BLACK

DRAWING No. AA-61-C

PLATE 1 of 2

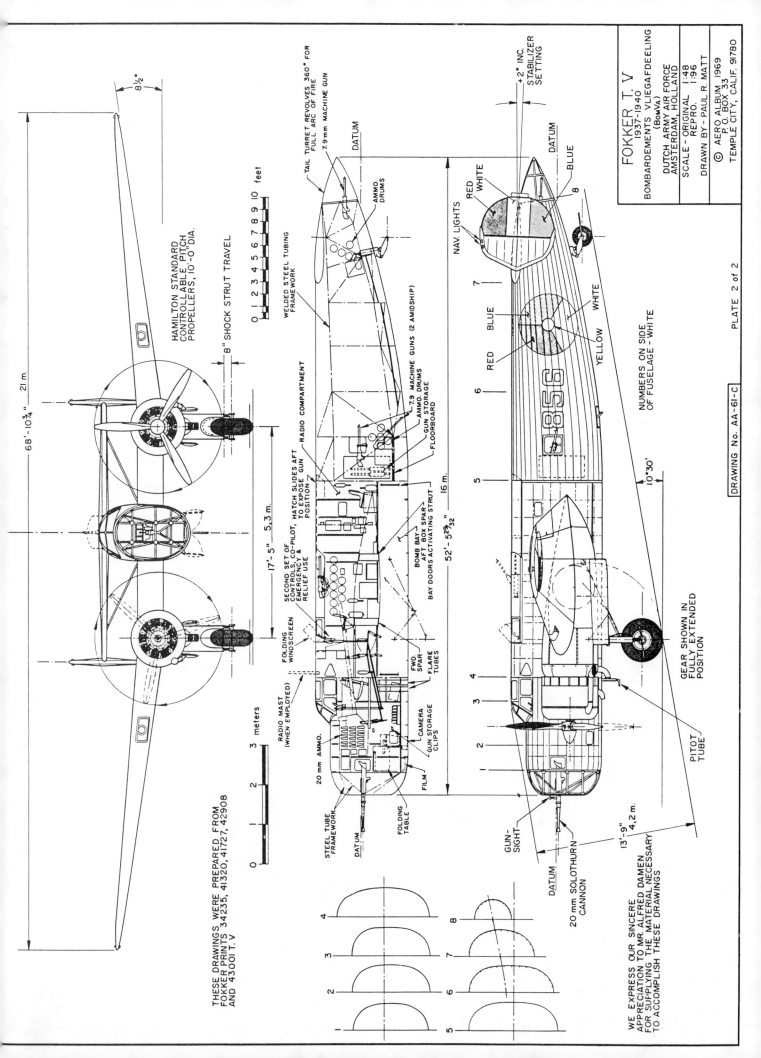

FOKKER T. V
1937-1940
BOMBARDEMENTS VLIEGAFDEELING
(BomVa)
DUTCH ARMY AIR FORCE
AMSTERDAM, HOLLAND

SCALE - ORIGINAL 1:48
REPRO. 1:96
DRAWN BY - PAUL R. MATT

© AERO ALBUM 1969
P. O. BOX 33
TEMPLE CITY, CALIF. 91780

PLATE 2 of 2

DRAWING No. AA-61-C

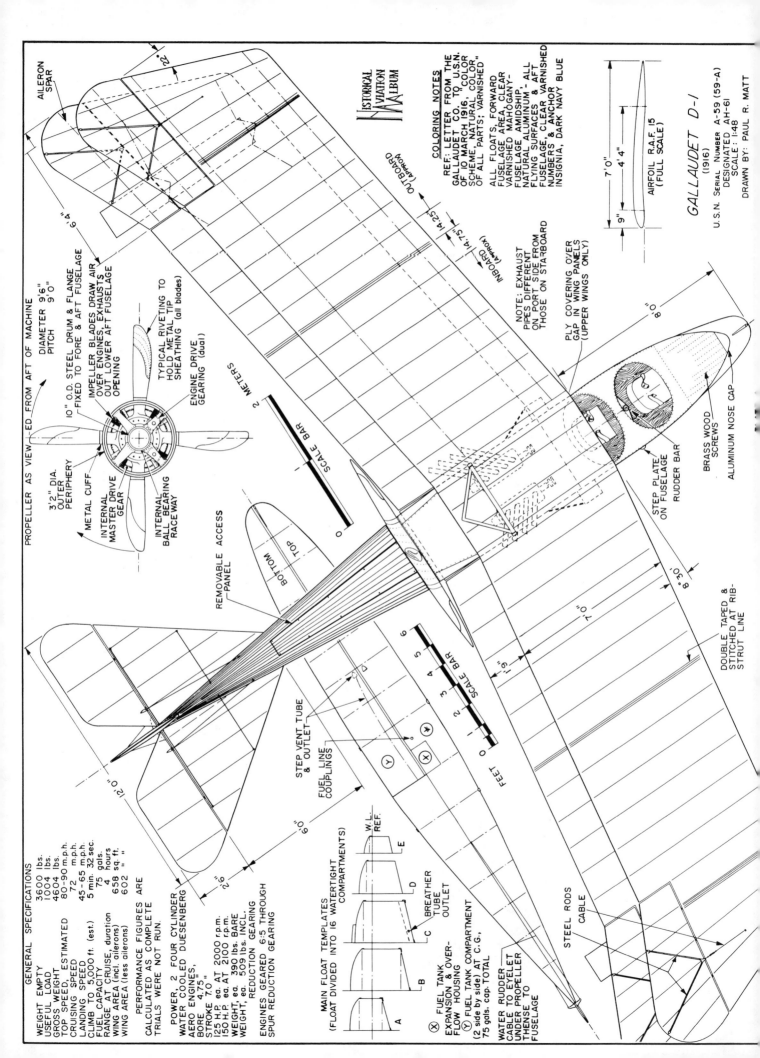

PROPELLER AS VIEWED FROM AFT OF MACHINE

DIAMETER 9'6"
PITCH 9'0"

AILERON SPAR

22°

10" O.D. STEEL DRUM & FLANGE
FIXED TO FORE & AFT FUSELAGE

IMPELLER BLADES DRAW AIR OVER ENGINES, EXHAUSTS OUT LOWER AFT FUSELAGE OPENING

TYPICAL RIVETING TO HOLD METAL TIP SHEATHING (all blades)

ENGINE DRIVE GEARING (dual)

3'2" DIA. OUTER PERIPHERY

METAL CUFF

INTERNAL MASTER DRIVE GEAR

INTERNAL BALL BEARING RACEWAY

HISTORICAL AVIATION ALBUM

COLORING NOTES
REF.: LETTER FROM THE GALLAUDET CO. TO U.S.N. OF 10 MARCH 1916, COLOR SCHEME, NATURAL, COLOR OF ALL PARTS; VARNISHED

ALL FLOATS, FORWARD FUSELAGE AREA, CLEAR VARNISHED MAHOGANY—FUSELAGE AMIDSHIP NATURAL ALUMINUM—ALL FLYING SURFACES & AFT FUSELAGE, CLEAR VARNISHED NUMBERS & ANCHOR INSIGNIA, DARK NAVY BLUE

METERS

SCALE BAR

2

1

0

OUTBOARD (APPROX)

4.25

4.75

4.75

INBOARD (APPROX)

NOTE: EXHAUST PIPES DIFFERENT ON PORT SIDE FROM THOSE ON STARBOARD

PLY COVERING OVER GAP IN WING PANELS (UPPER WINGS ONLY)

7'0"

4'4"

9"

AIRFOIL R.A.F. 15 (FULL SCALE)

GALLAUDET D-1
(1916)

U.S.N. SERIAL NUMBER A-59 (59-A)
DESIGNATED AH-61
SCALE: 1:48

DRAWN BY: PAUL R. MATT

8'0"

8'3.0"

7'0"

STEP PLATE ON FUSELAGE

RUDDER BAR

BRASS WOOD SCREWS

ALUMINUM NOSE CAP

DOUBLE TAPED & STITCHED AT RIB-STRUT LINE

REMOVABLE ACCESS PANEL

BOTTOM

TOP

SCALE BAR

0   1   2   3   4   5   6

FEET

STEEL RODS

CABLE

STEP VENT TUBE & OUTLET

FUEL LINE COUPLINGS

X

Y

6'0"

9'0"

12'0"

9'6"

2'6"

W.L. REF.

E

D

C

B

A

BREATHER TUBE OUTLET

MAIN FLOAT TEMPLATES
(FLOAT DIVIDED INTO 16 WATERTIGHT COMPARTMENTS)

X FUEL TANK EXPANSION & OVER-FLOW HOUSING
Y FUEL TANK COMPARTMENT (2 side by side) AT C.G., 75 gals. cap. TOTAL

WATER RUDDER CABLE TO EYELET UNDER PROPELLER THENCE TO FUSELAGE

GENERAL SPECIFICATIONS

WEIGHT EMPTY   3600 lbs.
USEFUL LOAD   1004 lbs.
GROSS WEIGHT   4604 lbs.
TOP SPEED, ESTIMATED 80-90 m.p.h.
CRUISING SPEED   72   m.p.h.
LANDING SPEED   45-65 m.p.h.
CLIMB TO 5,000 ft. (est.) 5 min. 32 sec.
FUEL CAPACITY   75 gals.
RANGE AT CRUISE, duration 4 hours
WING AREA (incl. ailerons) 658 sq. ft.
WING AREA (less ailerons)   602 "   "

PERFORMANCE FIGURES ARE CALCULATED AS COMPLETE TRIALS WERE NOT RUN.

POWER, 2 FOUR CYLINDER WATER COOLED DUESENBERG AERO ENGINES,
BORE   4.75"
STROKE 7.0"
125 H.P. ea. AT 2000 r.p.m.
150 H.P. ea. AT 2100 r.p.m.
WEIGHT, ea. 390 lbs. BARE
WEIGHT, ea. 509 lbs. INCL. REDUCTION GEARING

ENGINES GEARED 6:5 THROUGH SPUR REDUCTION GEARING

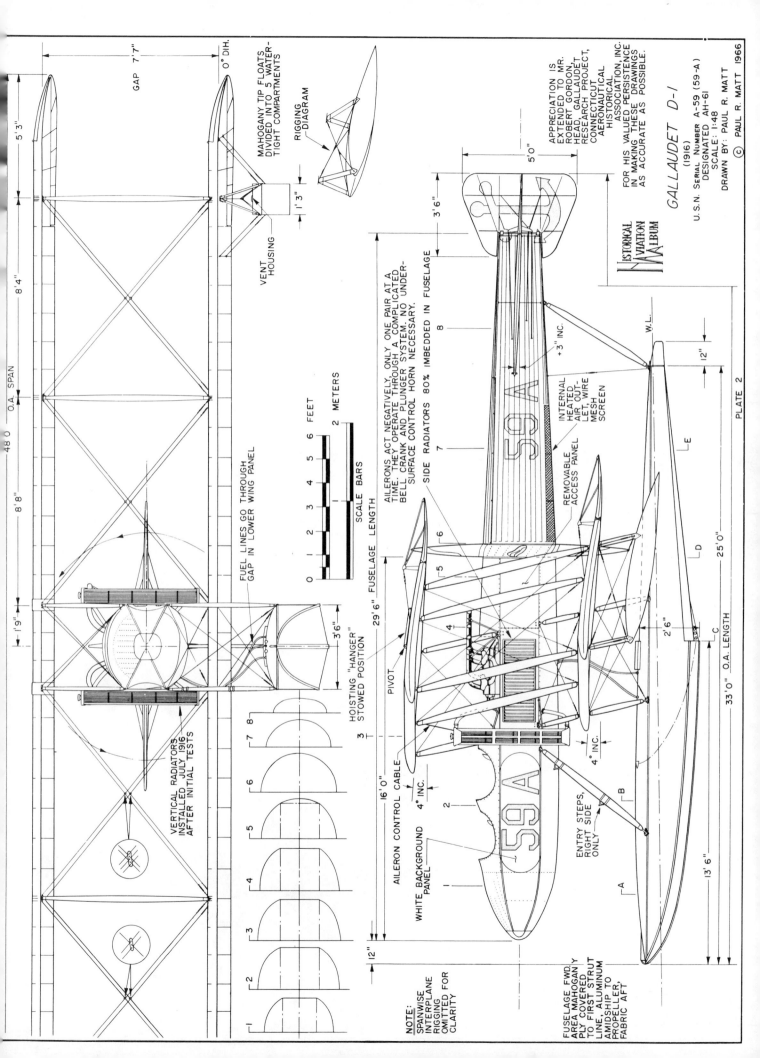

GALLAUDET D-1
(1916)
U.S.N. SERIAL NUMBER A-59 (59-A)
DESIGNATED AH-61
SCALE: 1:48
DRAWN BY: PAUL R. MATT

© PAUL R. MATT 1966

HISTORICAL AVIATION ALBUM

APPRECIATION IS EXTENDED TO MR. ROBERT GORDON, HEAD, GALLAUDET RESEARCH PROJECT, CONNECTICUT AERONAUTICAL HISTORICAL ASSOCIATION, INC. FOR HIS VALUED PERSISTENCE IN MAKING THESE DRAWINGS AS ACCURATE AS POSSIBLE.

PLATE 2

GAP 7'7"

0° DIH.

5'3"

8'4"

8'8"

1'9"

48' O.A. SPAN

MAHOGANY TIP FLOATS DIVIDED INTO 5 WATER-TIGHT COMPARTMENTS

RIGGING DIAGRAM

VENT HOUSING

1'3"

FUEL LINES GO THROUGH GAP IN LOWER WING PANEL

VERTICAL RADIATORS INSTALLED JULY 1916 AFTER INITIAL TESTS

3'6"

HOISTING "HANGER" STOWED POSITION

NOTE:
SPANWISE INTERPLANE RIGGING OMITTED FOR CLARITY

FEET
METERS
SCALE BARS

1 2 3 4 5 6 7 8

29'6" FUSELAGE LENGTH

AILERON CONTROL CABLE

WHITE BACKGROUND PANEL

AILERONS ACT NEGATIVELY, ONLY ONE PAIR AT A TIME. THEY OPERATE THROUGH A COMPLICATED BELL CRANK AND PLUNGER SYSTEM. NO UNDER-SURFACE CONTROL HORN NECESSARY.

SIDE RADIATORS 80% IMBEDDED IN FUSELAGE

INTERNAL HEATED AIR OUT-LET, WIRE MESH SCREEN

REMOVABLE ACCESS PANEL

5'0"

3'6"

+3" INC.

W.L.

12"

PIVOT

4° INC.

4° INC.

2'6"

+3" INC.

16'0"

12"

ENTRY STEPS, RIGHT SIDE ONLY

FUSELAGE FWD. AREA MAHOGANY PLY COVERED TO FIRST STRUT LINE, ALUMINUM AMIDSHIP TO PROPELLER, FABRIC AFT

13'6"

25'0"

33'0" O.A. LENGTH

A B C D E

59-A

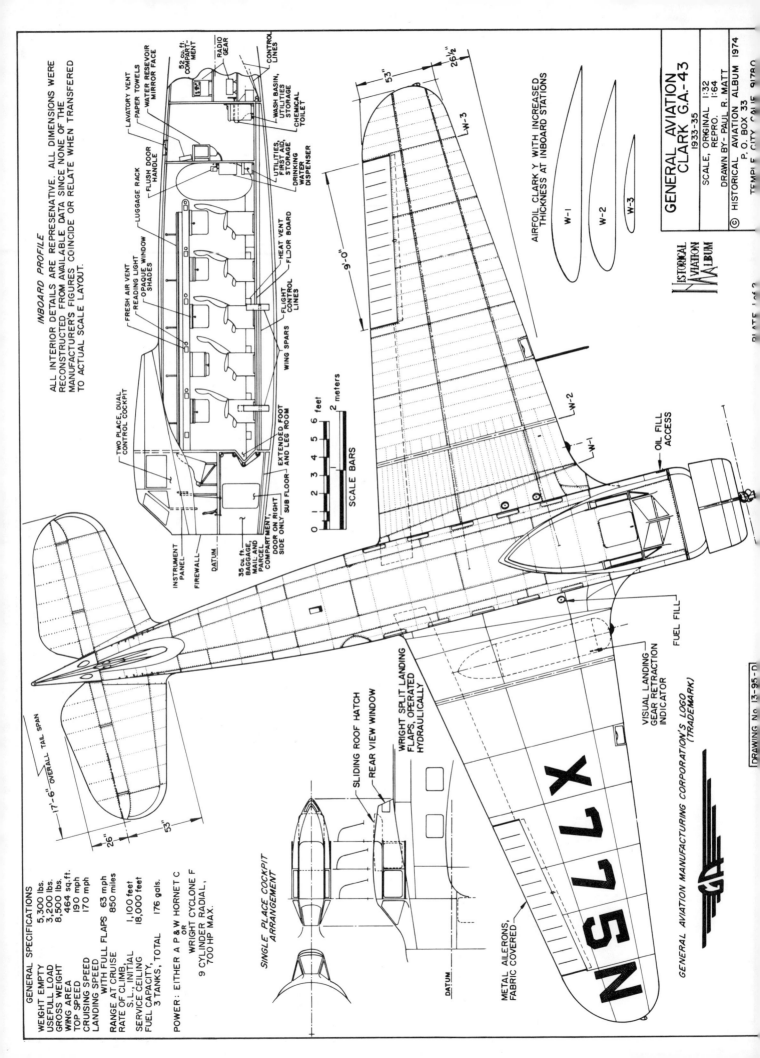

GENERAL SPECIFICATIONS

WEIGHT EMPTY   5,300 lbs.
USEFULL LOAD   3,200 lbs.
GROSS WEIGHT   8,500 lbs.
WING AREA   464 sq.ft.
TOP SPEED   190 mph
CRUISING SPEED   170 mph
LANDING SPEED
  WITH FULL FLAPS 63 mph
RANGE AT CRUISE 850 miles
RATE OF CLIMB,
  S.L. INITIAL 1,100 feet
SERVICE CEILING 18,000 feet
FUEL CAPACITY,
  3 TANKS, TOTAL 176 gals.

POWER: EITHER A P & W HORNET C
  OR
  WRIGHT CYCLONE F
  9 CYLINDER RADIAL,
  700 HP MAX.

17'-6" OVERALL TAIL SPAN

26"
53"

SINGLE PLACE COCKPIT ARRANGEMENT

SLIDING ROOF HATCH
REAR VIEW WINDOW

WRIGHT SPLIT LANDING FLAPS, OPERATED HYDRAULICALLY

DATUM

METAL AILERONS, FABRIC COVERED

X775N

GENERAL AVIATION MANUFACTURING CORPORATION'S LOGO
(TRADEMARK)

VISUAL LANDING GEAR RETRACTION INDICATOR
FUEL FILL

OIL FILL ACCESS

INBOARD PROFILE

ALL INTERIOR DETAILS ARE REPRESENATIVE. ALL DIMENSIONS WERE RECONSTRUCTED FROM AVAILABLE DATA SINCE NONE OF THE MANUFACTURERS FIGURES COINCIDE OR RELATE WHEN TRANSFERED TO ACTUAL SCALE LAYOUT.

52 cu.ft. COMPARTMENT
RADIO GEAR
CONTROL LINES
LAVATORY VENT
PAPER TOWELS
WATER RESERVOIR
MIRROR FACE
WASH BASIN, UTILITIES STORAGE
CHEMICAL TOILET
FLUSH DOOR HANDLE
LUGGAGE RACK
UTILITIES, FIRST AID, STORAGE
DRINKING WATER DISPENSER
FRESH AIR VENT
READING LIGHT
OPAQUE WINDOW SHADES
HEAT VENT
FLOOR BOARD
FLIGHT CONTROL LINES
WING SPARS
TWO PLACE, DUAL CONTROL COCKPIT
EXTENDED FOOT AND LEG ROOM
SUB FLOOR
35 cu. ft. BAGGAGE, MAIL AND PARCEL COMPARTMENT, DOOR ON RIGHT SIDE ONLY
INSTRUMENT PANEL
FIREWALL
DATUM

SCALE BARS
0 1 2 3 4 5 6 feet
2 meters

9'-0"

53"
26½"

W-3
W-2
W-1

AIRFOIL CLARK Y WITH INCREASED THICKNESS AT INBOARD STATIONS

W-1
W-2
W-3

GENERAL AVIATION
CLARK G.A.-43
1933-35

SCALE, ORIGINAL 1:32
  REPRO. 1:64
DRAWN BY - PAUL R. MATT

© HISTORICAL AVIATION ALBUM 1974
P. O. BOX 33
TEMPLE CITY CALIF 91780

HISTORICAL AVIATION ALBUM

DRAWING No 13-95-D

PLATE 1 of 2

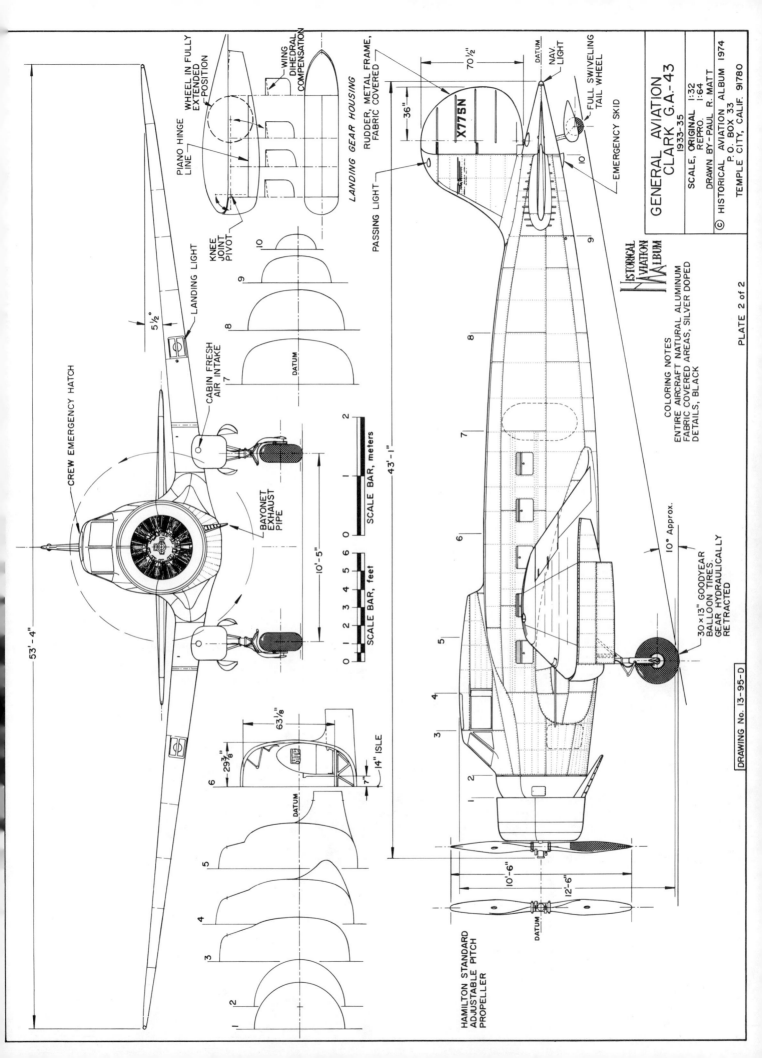

WING DIHEDRAL COMPENSATION

PIANO HINGE LINE

WHEEL IN FULLY EXTENDED POSITION

KNEE JOINT PIVOT

LANDING GEAR HOUSING

RUDDER, METAL FRAME, FABRIC COVERED

PASSING LIGHT

DATUM

NAV. LIGHT

FULL SWIVELING TAIL WHEEL

EMERGENCY SKID

X775N

36"

70½"

10

9

8

7

6

5

LANDING LIGHT

5½"

CREW EMERGENCY HATCH

CABIN FRESH AIR INTAKE

BAYONET EXHAUST PIPE

53' - 4"

DATUM

10

9

8

7

SCALE BAR, meters
2 1 0

SCALE BAR, feet
0 1 2 3 4 5 6

10'-5"

43'-1"

63½"

29⅜"

7"

14" ISLE

DATUM

6

5

4

3

2

1

HAMILTON STANDARD ADJUSTABLE PITCH PROPELLER

DATUM

10'-6"

12'-6"

9

8

7

6

5

4

3

2

DATUM

30 × 13" GOODYEAR BALLOON TIRES. GEAR HYDRAULICALLY RETRACTED

10° Approx.

GENERAL AVIATION CLARK G.A.-43
1933-35

SCALE, ORIGINAL 1:32
REPRO. 1:64

DRAWN BY-PAUL R. MATT

© HISTORICAL AVIATION ALBUM 1974
P.O. BOX 33
TEMPLE CITY, CALIF. 91780

COLORING NOTES
ENTIRE AIRCRAFT NATURAL ALUMINUM FABRIC COVERED AREAS, SILVER DOPED DETAILS, BLACK

Historical Aviation Album

PLATE 2 of 2

DRAWING No. 13-95-D

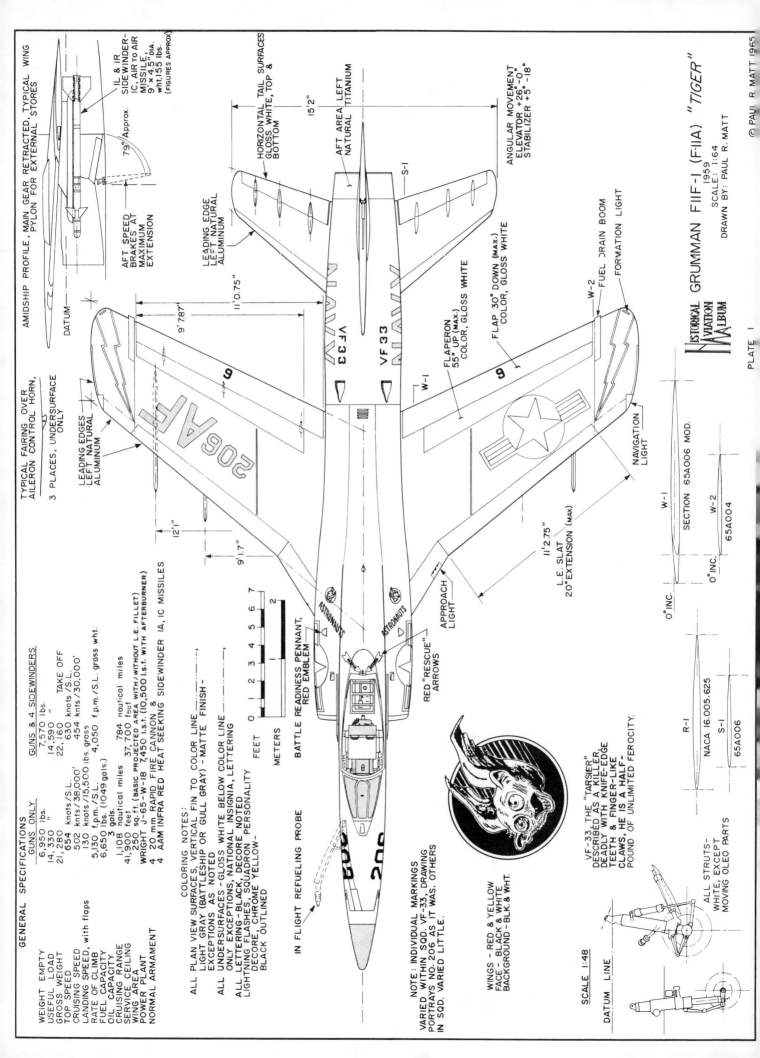

© PAUL R MATT 1965

AMIDSHIP PROFILE, MAIN GEAR RETRACTED, TYPICAL WING
PYLON FOR EXTERNAL STORES

TYPICAL WING

IL & IR SIDEWINDER-
IC, AIR TO AIR
MISSILE,
9' x 4.5" DIA.
wht.155 lbs.
(FIGURES APPROX)

79° Approx.

AFT SPEED
BRAKES AT
MAXIMUM
EXTENSION

DATUM

HORIZONTAL TAIL SURFACES
GLOSS WHITE, TOP &
BOTTOM

AFT AREA LEFT
NATURAL
TITANIUM

15'2"

ANGULAR MOVEMENT
ELEVATOR +26°-0°
STABILIZER +5°-18°

S-1

LEADING EDGE
LEFT NATURAL
ALUMINUM

TYPICAL FAIRING OVER
AILERON CONTROL HORN,

3 PLACES, UNDERSURFACE
ONLY

LEADING EDGES
LEFT NATURAL
ALUMINUM

11' 0.75"

9' 7.87"

NAVY

VF 33

VF 33

NAVY

6

9

FLAPERON
55° UP (MAX.)
COLOR, GLOSS WHITE

FLAP 30° DOWN (MAX.)
COLOR, GLOSS WHITE

W-1

W-2

FUEL DRAIN BOOM

FORMATION LIGHT

206AF

6

9

12'1"

9' 1.7"

NAVIGATION
LIGHT

APPROACH
LIGHT

L.E. SLAT
20° EXTENSION (MAX)

11' 2.75"

W-1

SECTION 65A006 MOD.

W-2

65A004

0° INC.

0° INC.

ASTRONAUTS

ASTRONAUTS

RED "RESCUE"
ARROWS

R-1

NACA 16.005.625

S-1

65A006

7
6
5
4
3
2
1
0

2

1

FEET

METERS

BATTLE READINESS PENNANT,
RED EMBLEM

IN FLIGHT REFUELING PROBE

GENERAL SPECIFICATIONS

	GUNS ONLY	GUNS & 4 SIDEWINDERS
WEIGHT EMPTY	6,950 lbs.	7,570 lbs.
USEFUL LOAD	14,330 "	14,590 "
GROSS WEIGHT	21,280 "	22,160 " TAKE OFF
TOP SPEED	654 knots/S.L.	630 knots/S.L.
CRUISING SPEED	502 knts/38,000'	454 knts/30,000'
LANDING SPEED, with flaps	130 knts/15,500 gross	
RATE OF CLIMB	5,130 f.p.m./S.L.	4,050 f.p.m./S.L. gross wht.
FUEL CAPACITY	6,650 lbs. (1049 gals.)	
OIL CAPACITY	3 gals.	
CRUISING RANGE	1,108 nautical miles	784 nautical miles
SERVICE CEILING	41,900 feet	37,700 feet
WING AREA	250 sq. ft. BASIC PROJECTED AREA WITH/WITHOUT L.E. FILLET)	
POWER PLANT	WRIGHT J-65-W-18 7,450 l.s.t. (10,500 l.s.t. WITH AFTERBURNER)	
NORMAL ARMAMENT	4 20 mm RAPID FIRE CANNON &	
	4 AAM INFRA RED HEAT SEEKING SIDEWINDER IA, IC MISSILES	

COLORING NOTES:

ALL PLAN VIEW SURFACES, VERTICAL FIN TO COLOR LINE
LIGHT GRAY (BATTLESHIP OR GULL GRAY) - MATTE FINISH -
EXCEPTIONS AS NOTED
ALL UNDERSURFACES - GLOSS WHITE BELOW COLOR LINE
ONLY EXCEPTIONS, NATIONAL INSIGNIA, LETTERING
ALL LETTERING - BLACK, DECORE NOTED
LIGHTNING FLASHES, SQUADRON PERSONALITY
DECORE, CHROME YELLOW-
BLACK OUTLINED

NOTE: INDIVIDUAL MARKINGS
VARIED WITHIN SQD. VF-33, DRAWING
PORTRAYS NO. 206 AS IT WAS. OTHERS
IN SQD. VARIED LITTLE.

WINGS - RED & YELLOW
FACE - BLACK & WHITE
BACKGROUND - BLK.& WHT.

VF-33, THE "TARSIER"
DESCRIBED AS A KILLER
DEADLY WITH KNIFE-EDGE
TEETH & FINGER-LIKE
CLAWS, HE IS A HALF-
POUND OF UNLIMITED FEROCITY.

SCALE 1:48

DATUM LINE

ALL STRUTS-
WHITE, EXCEPT
MOVING OLEO PARTS

HISTORICAL GRUMMAN F11F-1 (F-11A) "TIGER"
AVIATION 1959
ALBUM SCALE: 1:64
DRAWN BY: PAUL R. MATT

PLATE 1

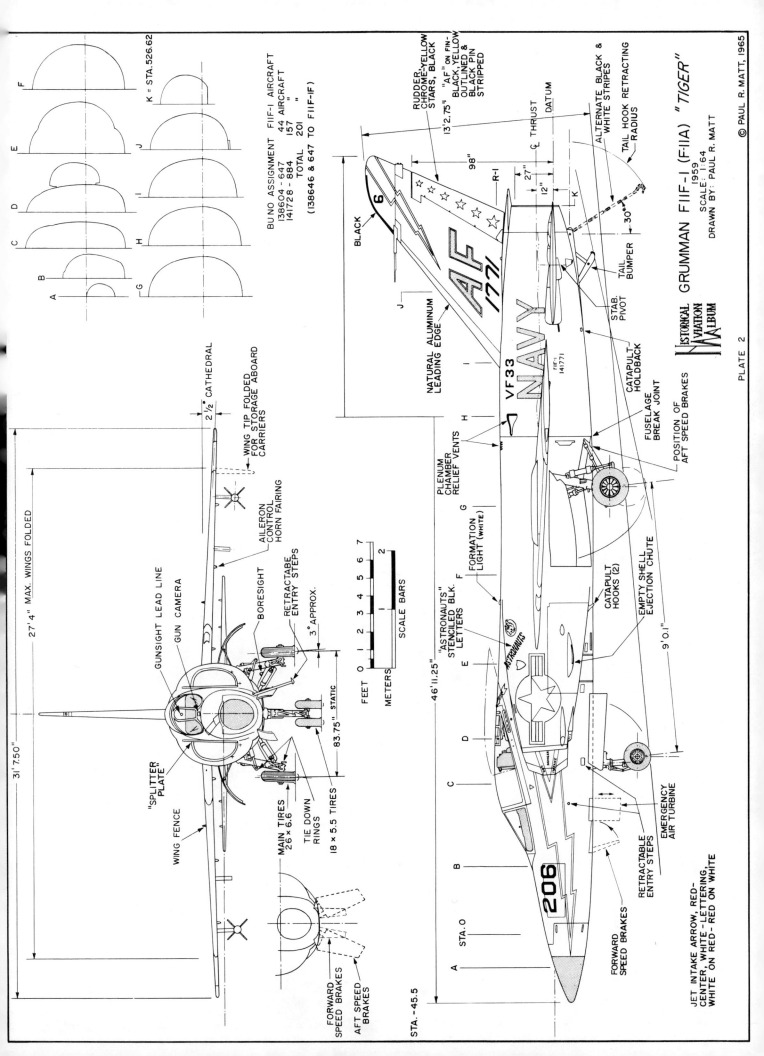

GRUMMAN F11F-1 (F-11A) "TIGER"
1959
SCALE: 1:64
DRAWN BY: PAUL R. MATT

© PAUL R. MATT, 1965

Historical Aviation Album

PLATE 2

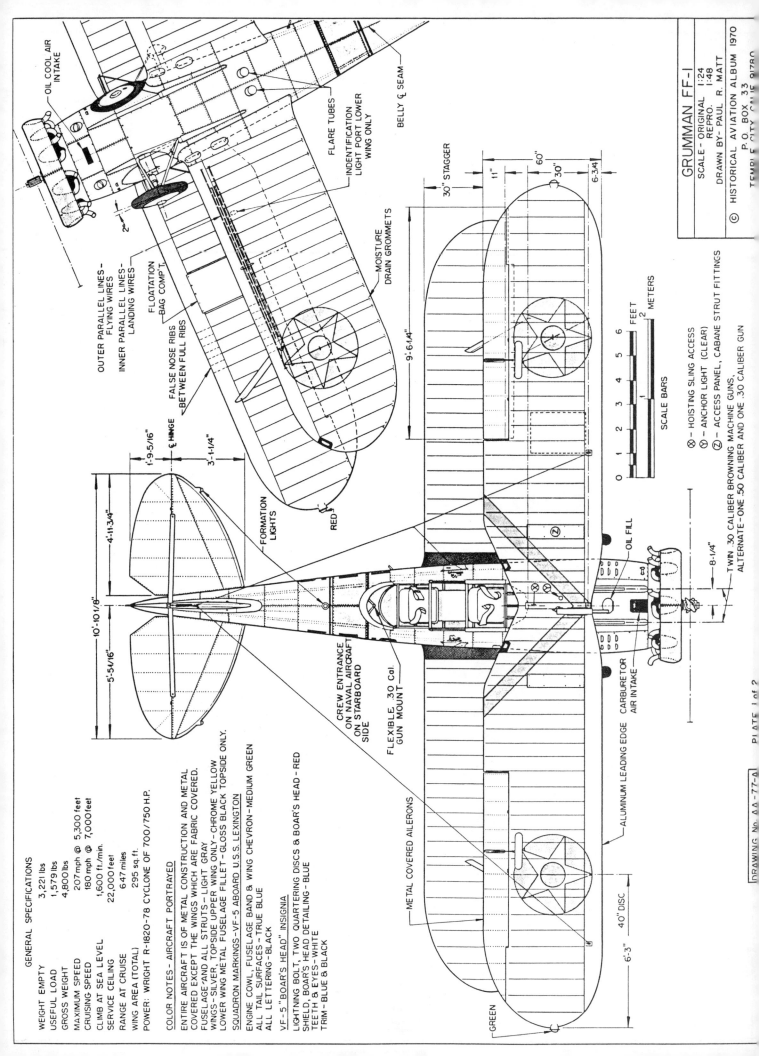

OIL COOL AIR INTAKE

BELLY ℄ SEAM

30" STAGGER

11"

60"

30"

6-3·4

9'-6·1/4"

MOISTURE DRAIN GROMMETS

IDENTIFICATION LIGHT PORT LOWER WING ONLY

FLARE TUBES

OUTER PARALLEL LINES – FLYING WIRES

INNER PARALLEL LINES – LANDING WIRES

FLOATATION BAG COMP'T.

FALSE NOSE RIBS BETWEEN FULL RIBS

RED

1'-9-5/16"

℄ HINGE

3-1/4"

4'-11·3/4"

FORMATION LIGHTS

10'-10·1/8"

5'-5·1/16"

SCALE BARS

FEET

METERS

0   1   2   3   4   5   6

⊗ – HOISTING SLING ACCESS

Ⓥ – ANCHOR LIGHT (CLEAR)

Ⓩ – ACCESS PANEL, CABANE STRUT FITTINGS

Ⓩ

OIL FILL

8-1/4"

TWIN .30 CALIBER BROWNING MACHINE GUNS,
ALTERNATE–ONE .50 CALIBER AND ONE .30 CALIBER GUN

CREW ENTRANCE ON NAVAL AIRCRAFT ON STARBOARD SIDE

FLEXIBLE .30 Cal. GUN MOUNT

CARBURETOR AIR INTAKE

ALUMINUM LEADING EDGE

METAL COVERED AILERONS

40" DISC

6-3"

GREEN

GENERAL SPECIFICATIONS

WEIGHT EMPTY — 3,221 lbs
USEFUL LOAD — 1,579 lbs
GROSS WEIGHT — 4,800 lbs
MAXIMUM SPEED — 207 mph @ 5,300 feet
CRUISING SPEED — 180 mph @ 7,000 feet
CLIMB AT SEA LEVEL — 1,600 ft./min.
SERVICE CEILING — 22,000 feet
RANGE AT CRUISE — 647 miles
WING AREA (TOTAL) — 295 sq. ft.
POWER: WRIGHT R-1820-78 CYCLONE OF 700/750 H.P.

COLOR NOTES – AIRCRAFT PORTRAYED

ENTIRE AIRCRAFT IS OF METAL CONSTRUCTION AND METAL
COVERED EXCEPT THE WINGS WHICH ARE FABRIC COVERED.
FUSELAGE AND ALL STRUTS– LIGHT GRAY
WINGS–SILVER, TOPSIDE UPPER WING ONLY–CHROME YELLOW
LOWER WING METAL FUSELAGE FILLET–GLOSS BLACK TOPSIDE ONLY.

SQUADRON MARKINGS–VF-5 ABOARD U.S.S. LEXINGTON

ENGINE COWL, FUSELAGE BAND & WING CHEVRON–MEDIUM GREEN
ALL TAIL SURFACES–TRUE BLUE
ALL LETTERING–BLACK

VF–5 "BOAR'S HEAD" INSIGNIA

LIGHTNING BOLT, TWO QUARTERING DISCS & BOAR'S HEAD–RED
SHIELD, BOAR'S HEAD DETAILING–BLUE
TEETH & EYES–WHITE
TRIM–BLUE & BLACK

GRUMMAN FF-I

SCALE – ORIGINAL   1:24
REPRO.   1:48
DRAWN BY– PAUL R. MATT

© HISTORICAL AVIATION ALBUM 1970

P.O. BOX 33
TEMPLE CITY, CALIF. 91780

DRAWING No. AA-77-A   PLATE 1 of 2

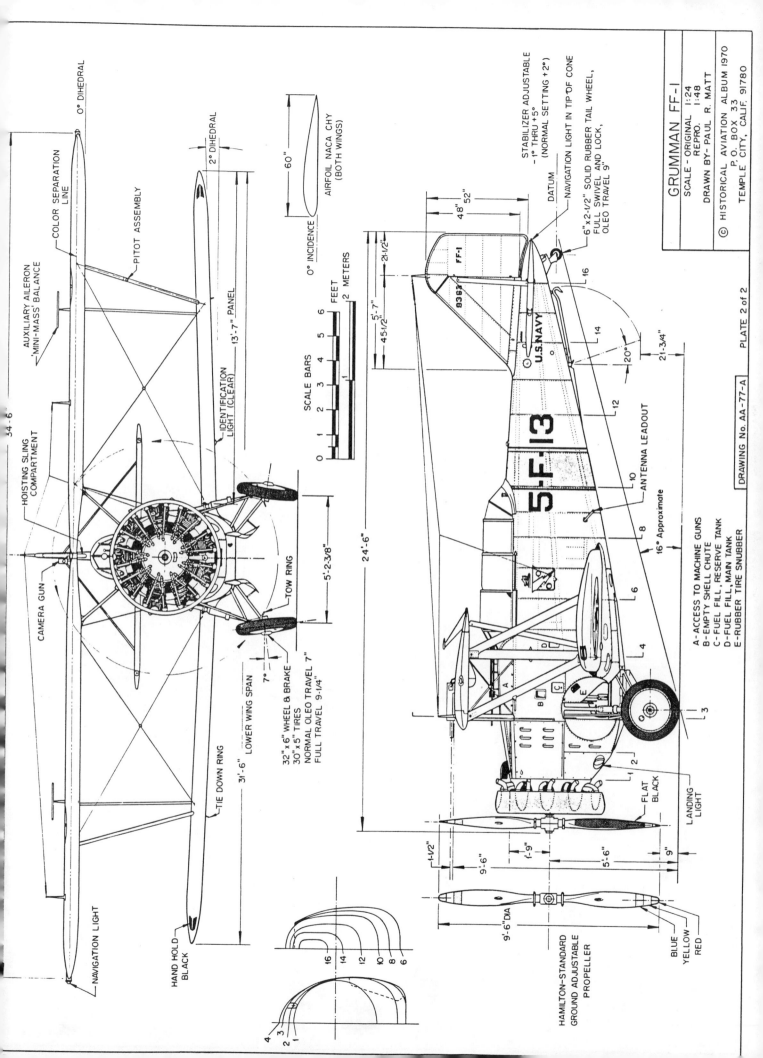

GRUMMAN FF-1

SCALE - ORIGINAL 1:24
REPRO. 1:48
DRAWN BY- PAUL R. MATT

© HISTORICAL AVIATION ALBUM 1970
P.O. BOX 33
TEMPLE CITY, CALIF. 91780

DRAWING No. AA-77-A

PLATE 2 of 2

0° DIHEDRAL

COLOR SEPARATION LINE

PITOT ASSEMBLY

AUXILIARY AILERON 'MINI-MASS' BALANCE

2° DIHEDRAL

13'-7" PANEL

IDENTIFICATION LIGHT (CLEAR)

60"

AIRFOIL NACA CHY (BOTH WINGS)

0° INCIDENCE

34-6

HOISTING SLING COMPARTMENT

CAMERA GUN

TIE DOWN RING

31'-6" LOWER WING SPAN

TOW RING

5'-2-3/8"

24'-6"

FEET
SCALE BARS
2 METERS

0 1 2 3 4 5 6

32" x 6" WHEEL & BRAKE
30" x 5" TIRES
NORMAL OLEO TRAVEL 7"
FULL TRAVEL 9-1/4"

7°

NAVIGATION LIGHT

HAND HOLD BLACK

16 14 12 10 8 6

4 3 2 1

STABILIZER ADJUSTABLE
- 1° THRU + 5°
(NORMAL SETTING + 2°)

52"
48"

5'-7"

45-1/2"

2'-1/2"

DATUM

NAVIGATION LIGHT IN TIP OF CONE

6" x 2-1/2" SOLID RUBBER TAIL WHEEL,
FULL SWIVEL AND LOCK,
OLEO TRAVEL 9"

FF-1

B363

16

U.S.NAVY

14

5-F-13

20°

2'-3/4"

12

10

ANTENNA LEADOUT

8

16° Approximate

6

A- ACCESS TO MACHINE GUNS
B- EMPTY SHELL CHUTE
C- FUEL FILL, RESERVE TANK
D- FUEL FILL, MAIN TANK
E- RUBBER TIRE SNUBBER

4

2

1

FLAT BLACK

LANDING LIGHT

3

1-1/2"

9'-6"

1'-9"

5'-6"

9"

9'-6" DIA

HAMILTON-STANDARD
GROUND ADJUSTABLE
PROPELLER

BLUE
YELLOW
RED

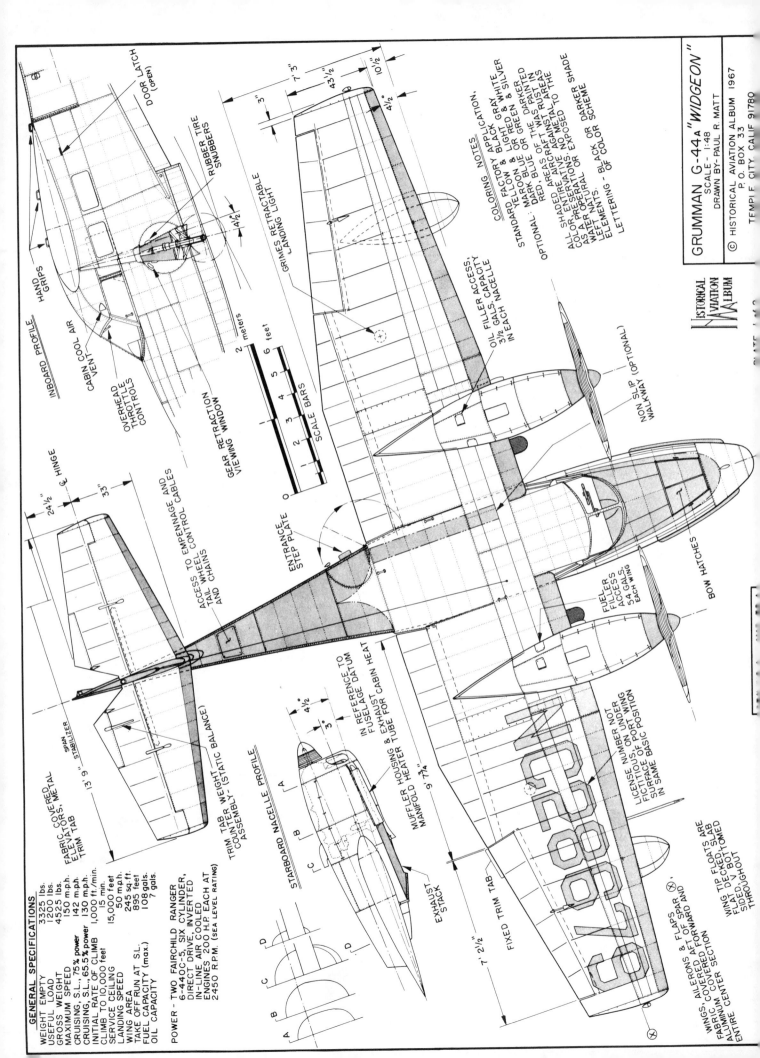

GENERAL SPECIFICATIONS

WEIGHT EMPTY	3325 lbs.
USEFUL LOAD	1200 lbs.
GROSS WEIGHT	4525 lbs.
MAXIMUM SPEED	150 m.p.h.
CRUISING, S.L., 75% power	142 m.p.h.
CRUISING, S.L., 65.5% power	130 m.p.h.
INITIAL RATE OF CLIMB	1,000 ft./min.
CLIMB TO 10,000 feet	15 min.
SERVICE CEILING	15,000 feet
LANDING SPEED	50 m.p.h.
TAKE OFF RUN AT S.L.	895 feet
WING AREA	245 sq.ft.
FUEL CAPACITY (max.)	108 gals.
OIL CAPACITY	7 gals.

POWER – TWO FAIRCHILD RANGER
6-440C-5, SIX CYLINDER,
DIRECT DRIVE, INVERTED
IN-LINE AIR COOLED
ENGINES 200 H.P. EACH AT
2450 R.P.M. (SEA LEVEL RATING)

INBOARD PROFILE

DOOR LATCH
(OPEN)
RUBBER TIRE
SNUBBERS
HAND GRIPS
CABIN COOL AIR VENT
OVERHEAD THROTTLE CONTROLS
GEAR RETRACTION VIEWING WINDOW

24½"   ₵ HINGE
33"
FABRIC COVERED, METAL
ELEVATORS, TRIM TAB

ACCESS TO EMPENNAGE AND
WHEEL CONTROL CABLES
TAIL AND CHAINS

SPAN
₵ STABILIZER
13' 9"
TRIM TAB WEIGHT (STATIC BALANCE)
COUNTER - (STATIC BALANCE)
ASSEMBLY)

ENTRANCE STEP PLATE

3"
7' 3"
43½"
10½"
4½"

GRIMES RETRACTABLE
LANDING LIGHT

meters
2   1
6 feet   5   4   3   2   1   0
SCALE BARS

OIL FILLER ACCESS,
3½ GALS. CAPACITY
IN EACH NACELLE

NON SLIP (OPTIONAL)
WALKWAY

BOW HATCHES

FUEL FILLER
ACCESS,
54 GALS.
EACH WING

LICENSE NUMBER NOT UNDER
SURFACE OF PORT WING
FICTITIOUS, ON WING
IN SAME BASIC POSITION

STARBOARD NACELLE PROFILE

4½"
3"

IN REFERENCE TO
FUSELAGE DATUM
EXHAUST FOR CABIN HEAT

MUFFLER HOUSING &
MANIFOLD HEATER TUBE FOR CABIN HEAT

9' 7¾"

EXHAUST
STACK

7' 2½"

FIXED TRIM TAB

WINGS, AILERONS & FLAPS ⊗
AILERONS & FLAPS AFT OF SPAR ⊗
FABRIC, COVERED SECTION
ALUMINUM CENTER SECTION
ENTIRE WING DECKED-TOPPED
WING TIP FLOATS ARE
FLAT V BOTTOMED
SIDED, V BOTTOM
THROUGHOUT

GRUMMAN G-44A "WIDGEON"
SCALE - 1:48
DRAWN BY- PAUL R. MATT

© HISTORICAL AVIATION ALBUM 1967
P. O. BOX 33
TEMPLE CITY, CALIF 91780

ᴴISTORICAL
ᴬVIATION
ᴬLBUM

COLORING NOTES
COLORING APPLICATION,
STANDARD FACTORY & BLACK GRAY
YELLOW & LIGHT & RED & SILVER
OPTIONAL: MAROBLUE OR GREEN OR DARKER
DARK BLUE OF THE PAINT IS
RED, BLUE OF TWAS RUST IN
ALL SHADED AREAS AIRCRAFT AGAINST THE
COLOR ENTIRE AIRE METAL IN
COLOR OPERATIONS EXPOSED TO THE
AS AR OPERAL OR DARKER SHADE
WATER NAT-
LEFT NATS. ELEMENTS – BLACK OR
LETTERING – OF COLOR SCHEME

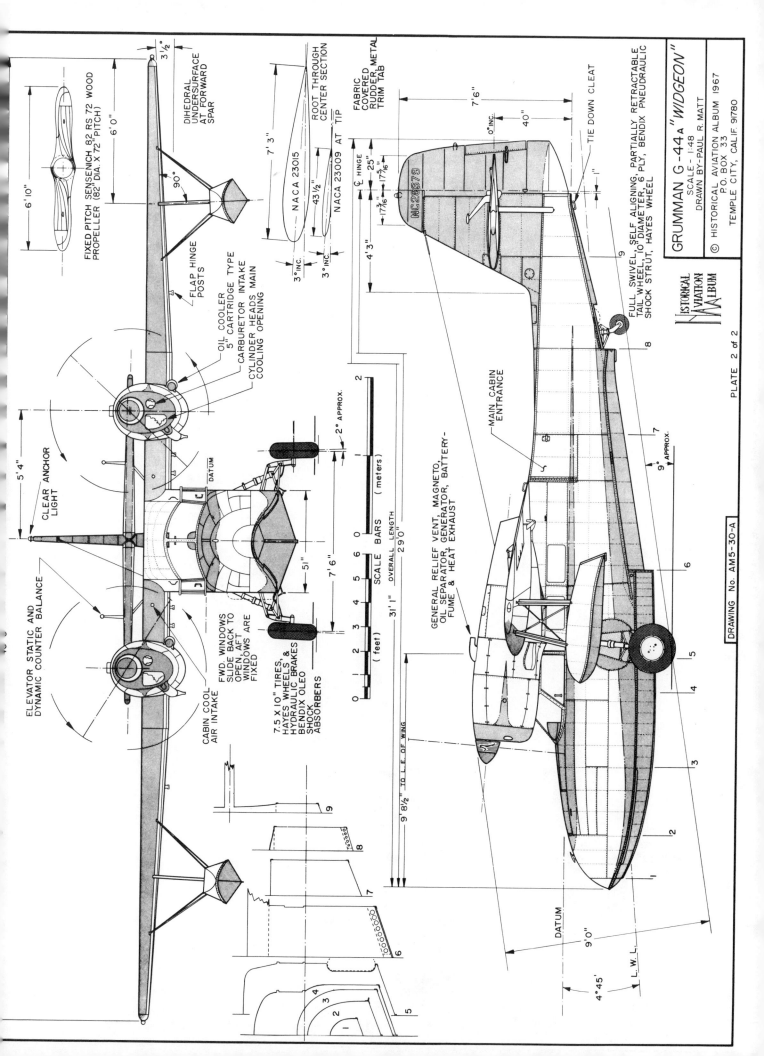

GRUMMAN G-44A "WIDGEON"
SCALE · 1:48
DRAWN BY · PAUL R. MATT

© HISTORICAL AVIATION ALBUM 1967
P.O. BOX 33
TEMPLE CITY, CALIF. 91780

PLATE 2 of 2

DRAWING No. AM5-30-A

Grumman J2F-5 "Duck"

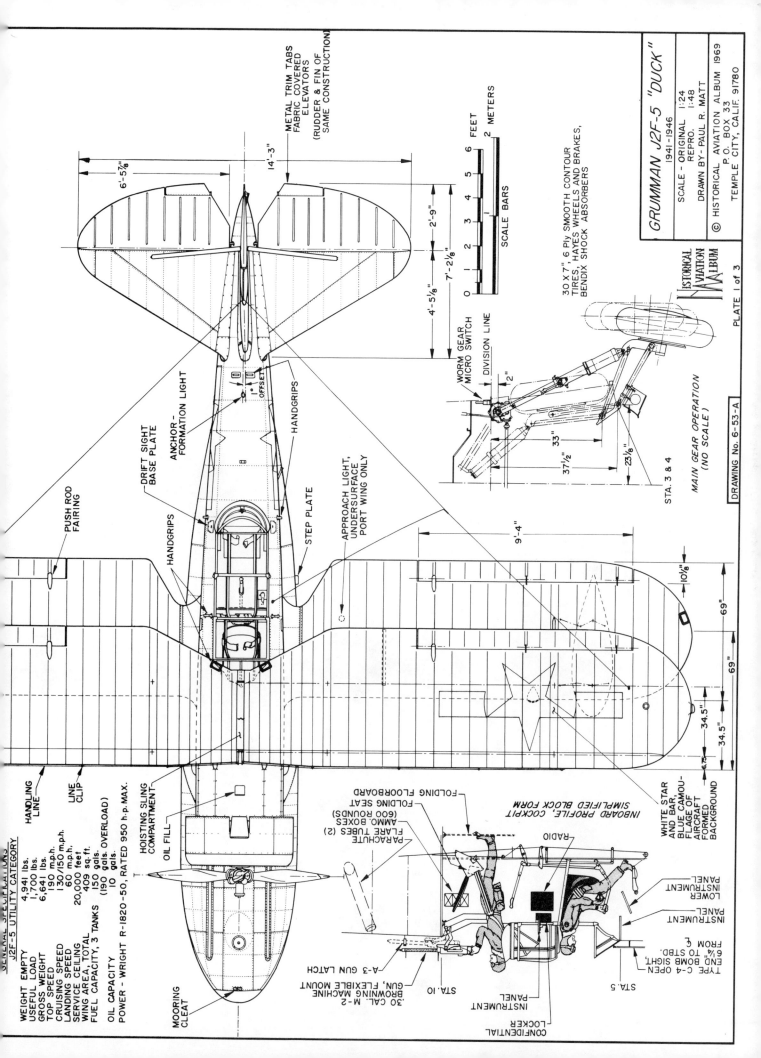

GENERAL SPECIFICATIONS
J2F-5 UTILITY CATEGORY

WEIGHT EMPTY	4,941 lbs.
USEFUL LOAD	1,700 lbs.
GROSS WEIGHT	6,641 lbs.
TOP SPEED	190 m.p.h.
CRUISING SPEED	130/150 m.p.h.
LANDING SPEED	60 m.p.h.
SERVICE CEILING	20,000 feet
WING AREA, TOTAL	409 sq. ft.
FUEL CAPACITY, 3 TANKS	150 gals.
	(190 gals. OVERLOAD)
OIL CAPACITY	10 gals.
POWER - WRIGHT R-1820-50, RATED 950 h.p. MAX.	

GRUMMAN J2F-5 "DUCK"
1941-1946

SCALE - ORIGINAL 1:24
REPRO. 1:48
DRAWN BY- PAUL R. MATT

© HISTORICAL AVIATION ALBUM 1969
P.O. BOX 33
TEMPLE CITY, CALIF. 91780

PLATE 1 of 3

DRAWING No. 6-53-A

30 x 7", 6 PLY SMOOTH CONTOUR
TIRES, HAYES WHEELS AND BRAKES,
BENDIX SHOCK ABSORBERS

MAIN GEAR OPERATION
(NO SCALE)

WORM GEAR
MICRO SWITCH

DIVISION LINE

STA. 3 & 4

SCALE BARS

FEET
METERS

METAL TRIM TABS
FABRIC COVERED
ELEVATORS
(RUDDER & FIN OF
SAME CONSTRUCTION)

14'-3"

6'-5⅝"

2'-9"

7'-2⅛"

4'-5⅝"

1° OFFSET

DRIFT SIGHT
BASE PLATE

ANCHOR -
FORMATION LIGHT

HANDGRIPS

PUSH ROD
FAIRING

HANDGRIPS

HANDGRIPS

STEP PLATE

APPROACH LIGHT,
UNDERSURFACE
PORT WING ONLY

9'-4"

10⅞"

69"

69"

34.5"

34.5"

6.75"

HANDLING
LINE

LINE
CLIP

HOISTING SLING
COMPARTMENT

OIL FILL

MOORING
CLEAT

WHITE STAR
AND BAR,
BLUE CAMOU-
FLAGE OF
AIRCRAFT
FORMED
BACKGROUND

33"

37½"

23⅛"

2"

FOLDING FLOORBOARD

FOLDING SEAT

AMMO. BOXES
(600 ROUNDS)

PARACHUTE
FLARE TUBES (2)

INBOARD PROFILE, COCKPIT
SIMPLIFIED BLOCK FORM

RADIO

LOWER INSTRUMENT
PANEL

INSTRUMENT
PANEL

TYPE C-4 OPEN
END BOMB SIGHT,
6½" TO STBD.
FROM ₵

STA. 5

INSTRUMENT
PANEL

STA. 10

.30 CAL. M-2
BROWNING MACHINE
GUN, FLEXIBLE MOUNT

A-3 GUN LATCH

CONFIDENTIAL
LOCKER

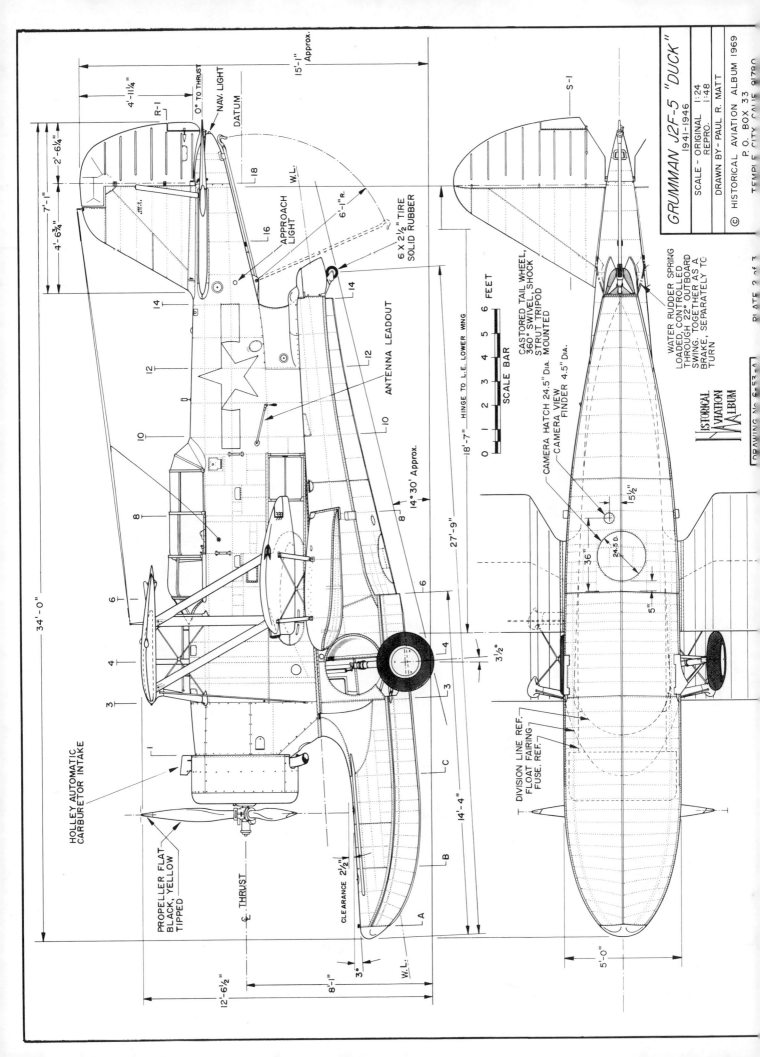

GRUMMAN J2F-5 "DUCK"
1941-1946
SCALE - ORIGINAL   1:24
REPRO.   1:48
DRAWN BY - PAUL R. MATT
© HISTORICAL AVIATION ALBUM 1969
P.O. BOX 33
TEMPLE CITY CALIF. 91780

NAV. LIGHT
0° TO THRUST
4'-11¼"
2'-6¼"
R-1
7'-1"
4'-6¾"
DATUM
APPROACH LIGHT
W.L.
15'-1" Approx.
18
16
14
14
12
10
8
6
4
3

34'-0"

HOLLEY AUTOMATIC CARBURETOR INTAKE

PROPELLER FLAT BLACK, YELLOW TIPPED

℄ THRUST

CLEARANCE 2½"

12'-6½"

8'-1"

3°

W.L.

ANTENNA LEADOUT

6 x 2½" TIRE SOLID RUBBER

6'-1" R.

14°30' Approx.

18'-7" HINGE TO L.E. LOWER WING

27'-9"

3½°

14'-4"

A
B
C

SCALE BAR
0 1 2 3 4 5 6 FEET

CASTORED TAIL WHEEL, 360° SWIVEL, SHOCK STRUT TRIPOD MOUNTED

CAMERA HATCH 24.5" Dia.
CAMERA VIEW FINDER 4.5" Dia.

5½"
36"
24.5 D.
5"

S-1

WATER RUDDER SPRING LOADED, CONTROLLED THROUGH 22° OUTBOARD SWING, TOGETHER AS A BRAKE, SEPARATELY TO TURN

DIVISION LINE REF.
FLOAT FAIRING
FUSE. REF.

5'-0"

Historical AVIATION ALBUM
DRAWING No. 6-53-A
PLATE 2 of 3

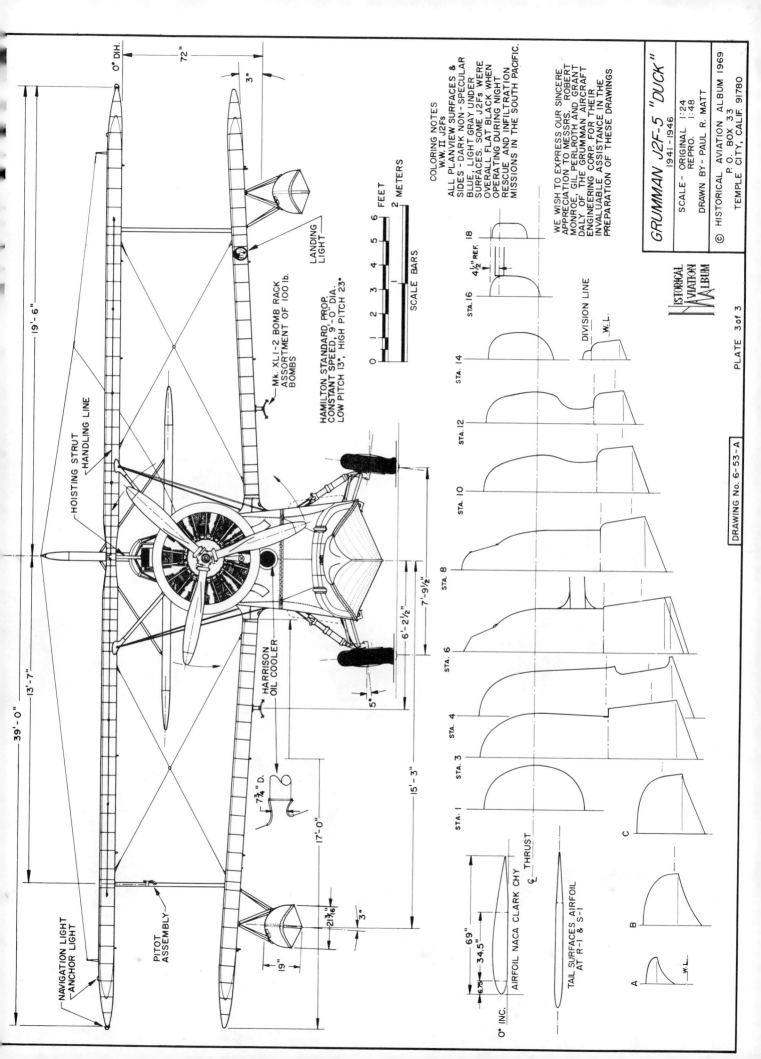

NAVIGATION LIGHT
ANCHOR LIGHT

PITOT ASSEMBLY

HOISTING STRUT
HANDLING LINE

Mk. XLI-2 BOMB RACK
ASSORTMENT OF 100 lb.
BOMBS

LANDING LIGHT

HARRISON OIL COOLER

HAMILTON STANDARD PROP.
CONSTANT SPEED, 9'-0" DIA.
LOW PITCH 13°, HIGH PITCH 23°

O° DIH.

72"

3°

39'- 0"

13'- 7"

19'- 6"

17'- 0"

15'- 3"

7'-9½"

6'-2½"

5°

3°

2 1 3/16"

19"

7¾" D.

69"

34.5"

6.75"

O° INC.

AIRFOIL NACA CLARK CHY

TAIL SURFACES AIRFOIL
AT R-1 & S-1

⅊ THRUST

FEET
6 5 4 3 2 1 0

METERS
2

SCALE BARS

COLORING NOTES
W.W. II J2Fs
ALL PLANVIEW SURFACES &
SIDES - DARK NON- SPECULAR
BLUE, LIGHT GRAY UNDER
SURFACES. SOME J2Fs WERE
OVERALL FLAT BLACK WHEN
OPERATING DURING NIGHT
RESCUE AND INFILTRATION
MISSIONS IN THE SOUTH PACIFIC.

WE WISH TO EXPRESS OUR SINCERE
APPRECIATION TO MESSRS. ROBERT
MONROE, GIL PERLROTH AND GRANT
DALY OF THE GRUMMAN AIRCRAFT
ENGINEERING CORP. FOR THEIR
INVALUABLE ASSISTANCE IN THE
PREPARATION OF THESE DRAWINGS

STA. 1
STA. 3
STA. 4
STA. 6
STA. 8
STA. 10
STA. 12
STA. 14
STA. 16
18
4½" REF.

DIVISION LINE

W.L.

A
B
C
W.L.

GRUMMAN J2F-5 "DUCK"
1941-1946

SCALE - ORIGINAL 1:24
REPRO. 1:48

DRAWN BY- PAUL R. MATT

HISTORICAL AVIATION ALBUM

© HISTORICAL AVIATION ALBUM 1969
P. O. BOX 33
TEMPLE CITY, CALIF. 91780

PLATE 3 of 3

DRAWING No. 6-53-A

3-View Scale Drawings by Paul Matt

Volume 1 contains all airplanes listed from A through G. Volume 2 contains all airplanes listed from H through W. If you would like individual, large sheets of any of the below listed scale drawings, send request, catalog #, appropriate fee, and shipping charge of $2.50. If you want your drawing rolled in a tube – add $4.00. Clear, concise, uncluttered 3- and 4-view engineering presentations, in large (17" x 22"), easy to work with standard scales. Drawing is highly detailed and is an accurate working print with all dimensions, specifications, airfoils, cross sections, templates, and color scheme included. These drawings are part of the collection of the internationally acclaimed and highly honored *Historical Aviation Album*. All orders are folded unless a tube is ordered. Each has 2 to 6 large sheets. **Rolled in tube– add $4.00.**

DRAWING SCALE:
CODE: Last letter of catalog numer indicates scale of drawing.
A = 1:24 .... 1/2" = 1'
B = 1:16 .... 3/4" = 1'
C = 1:48 .... 1/4" = 1'
D = 1:32 .... 3/8" = 1'
E = 1:8 ... 1 1/2" = 1'
F = 1:6 .... 2" = 1'

Volume 1 contents:

_Aeromarine 39B .... (#9-78A, 3 shts.) $9.50
_Aeronca 7AC "Champion" .... (#AM-41A, 2 shts.) 8.00
_Aeronca C-2 .... (#10-80A, 2 shts.) 8.00
_Aeronca C-3 "Collegian" .... (#10-01A, 2 shts.) 8.00
_Aeronca C-3 "Master" .... (#10-82A, 2 shts.) 8.00
_Aeronca K .... (#15-103A, 2 shts.) 8.00
_Aeronca LB "Low wing" .... (#AM-60A, 2 shts.) 8.00
_Alcor C.6.1 Jr. Transport .... (#4-33D, 2 shts.) 8.00
_Anderson-Greenwood AG-14 .... (#12-94A, 2 shts.) 8.00
_Beechcraft D-18S Twin .... (#6-59A, 3 shts.) 9.50
_Bell P-39Q "Airacobra" .... (#1-7A, 2 shts.) 8.00
_Berckmans "Speed Scout" .... (#2-12B, 2 shts.) 8.00
_Berliner-Joyce OJ-2 .... (#AM-48A, 2 shts.) 8.00
_Berliner-Joyce XF3J-1 .... (#15-104A, 2 shts.) 8.00
_Boeing 307 "Stratoliner" .... (#7-63C, 2 shts.) 8.00
_Boeing F3B-1 .... (#AM-56A, 2 shts.) 8.00
_Boeing XF7B-1 .... (#AM-38A, 2 shts.) 8.00
_Brewster F2A-3 "Buffalo" .... (#5-47A, 2 shts.) 8.00
_Cessna 120/140 .... (#1-9A, 2 shts.) 8.00
_Cessna C-37 "Airmaster" .... (#6-50A, 2 shts.) 8.00
_Cessna T-50 "Bobcat" .... (#17-115A, 2 shts.) 8.00
_Consolidated P2Y-2 .... (#9-71C,3 shts.) 9.50
_Consolidated PBY-5A "Catalina" .... (#17-114C, 4shts.) 11.00
_Curtiss "Carrier Pigeon I" .... (#2-15A, 2 shts.) 8.00
_Curtiss 1st Milit. Tract. S.C. No. 21/22 1913.(#6-55A, 2 shts.) 8.00
_Curtiss A-3B "Falcon" .... (#AM-39A, 2 shts.) 8.00
_Curtiss AT-9 "Jeep" .... (#2-18A, 2 shts.) 8.00
_Curtiss B-2 Condor Bomber .... (#18-116C, 2 shts.) 8.00
_Curtiss B-20 Condor Transport .... (#18-117C, 2 shts.) 8.00
_Curtiss F Boat .... (#1-1A, 2 shts.) 8.00
_Curtiss F92 "Sparrowhawk" .... (#18-118A, 2 shts.) 8.00
_Curtiss MF-K-6 "Seagull" .... (#AM-37A, 2 shts.) 8.00
_Curtiss P-36 "Hawk" .... (#7-62A, 2 shts.) 8.00
_Curtiss P-6E "Hawk" .... (#5-42A, 2 shts.) 8.00
_Curtiss PW-8 .... (#10-79A, 2 shts.) 8.00
_Curtiss R-6 Racer .... (#HS-73A, 2 shts.) 8.00
_Curtiss SC-1 "Seahawk" .... (#1-8A, 2 shts.) 8.00
_Curtiss SNC-1 "Falcon" .... (#AA-65A, 2 shts) 8.00
_Curtiss SO3C-1 "Seagull" .... (#AM-34A, 2 shts.) 8.00
_Curtiss Twin JN .... (#3-21A, 2 shts.) 8.00
_Curtiss-Cox "Texas Wildcat" .... (#2-14B, 2 shts.) 8.00
_Curtiss-Wright "Condor II" .... (#1-6C, 2 shts) 8.00
_Curtiss-Wright CW-1 "Jr." .... (#11-88A, 3 shts.) 9.50
_Douglas 0-2 .... (#11-86A, 3 shts.) 9.50
_Douglas 0-2H .... (#11-87A, 2 shts.) 8.00
_Douglas 0-38 .... (#12-92A, 2 shts.) 8.00
_Douglas 0-38E .... (#12-93A, 2 shts.) 8.00
_Douglas M-2 .... (#14-68A, 2 shts.) 8.00
_Douglas A-20G "Havoc" .... (#15-102D, 6 shts.) 13.00
_Etrich 1913 Taube .... (#TB-105D, 3 shts.) 9.50
_Fairchild FC-1 .... (#17-111A, 2 shts.) 8.00
_Fairchild FC-2 .... (#17-112A, 2 shts.) 8.00
_Fairchild FC-2W "Stars & Stripes" ..... (#17-113A, 2 shts.) 8.00
_Fairchild M-62, PT-19 "Cornell" .... (#AA-69A, 2 shts.) 8.00
_Fokker T.5 Netherlands Bomber .... (#AA-61C, 2 shts.) 8.00
_Gallaudet D-1 .... (#3-20A, 2 shts.) 8.00
_General Aviation Clark GA-43 .... (#13-95D, 2 shts.) 8.00
_Grumman F-11F-1 "Tiger" .... (#2-19D, 2 shts.) 8.00
_Grumman FF-1 .... (#AA-77A, 2 shts.) 8.00
_Grumman G-44 "Widgeon" .... (#AM5-30A, 2 shts.) 8.00
_Grumman J2F-5 "Duck" .... (#6-53A, 3 shts.) 9.50

Volume 2 contents:

_Heath LNB-4 Parasol .... (#4-35B, 2 shts.) $8.00
_Howard DGA-15P .... (#AM-52A, 2 shts.) 8.00
_Howard DGA-3 "Pete" .... (#12-89A, 2 shts.) 8.00
_Howard DGA-4 "Mike" .... (#13-90A, 2 shts.) 8.00
_Howard DGA-5 "Ike" .... (#13-91A, 2 shts.) 8.00
_Howard DGA-6 "Mr. Mulligan" .... (#14-99A, 3 shts.) 9.50
_Hughes 1B Longwing Racer .... (#16-108A, 3 shts.) 9.50
_Hughes 1B Shortwing Racer .... (#16-107A, 3 shts.) 9.50
_Laird LC-DW-300 "Solution" .... (#7-64A, 2 shts.) 8.00
_Laird LC-DW-500 "Super Solution" .... (#8-74A, 2 shts.) 8.00
_Laird-Turner LTR-14 .... (#10-83A, 2 shts.) 8.00
_Lavochkin LA-7 .... (#AA-46A, 4 shts.) 11.00
_Lockheed F-80 "Shooting Star" .... (#2-10A, 2 shts.) 8.00
_Lockheed Model 9 "Orion" .... (#3-22A, 2 shts.) 8.00
_Lockheed PV-1 "Ventura" .... (#E-101C, 3 shts.) 9.50
_LWF Cato Model L "Butterfly" .... (#10-84A, 2 shts.) 8.00
_LWF Model G-2 .... (#2-13A, 2 shts.) 8.00
_LWF Model H "Owl" .... (#11-85C, 2 shts.) 8.00
_Martin BM-1/2 .... (#1-5A, 2 shts.) 8.00
_Martin T4M-1, Great Lakes TG-1 .... (#4-29D, 2 shts.) 8.00
_Martin TT, 1913 Trainer .... (#5-40A, 2 shts.) 8.00
_Messerschmitt ME 109E-3 .... (#AA-75A, 2 shts.) 8.00
_Morehouse 2 Cyl. Aero Engine .... (#3-27E, 1 sht.) 8.00
_Navy-Wright NW-1 Mystery Racer ...... (#4-31A, 2 shts.) 8.00
_Navy-Wright NW-2 Mystery Racer ...... (#4-32A, 2 shts.) 8.00
_North American 0-47A .... (#13-98A, 3 shts.) 9.50
_North American AT-6D .... (#16-106A, 3 shts.) 9.50
_North American XB-70-1 "Valkyrie" ..... (#7-66G, 3 shts.) 9.50
_Packard-Lepere LUSAC-11 .... (#1-3A, 2 shts.) 8.00
_Pfitzner 1910 Monoplane .... (#2-11A, 2 shts.) 8.00
_Piper J-3 "Cub" .... (#18-121A, 2 shts.) 8.00
_Piper J-4 "Cub Coupe" .... (#18-122A, 2 shts.) 8.00
_Piper PA-12 "Super Cruiser" .... (#4-36A, 2 shts.) 8.00
_Republic RC-3 Seabee .... (#16-109A, 3 shts.) 9.50
_Rover Inverted Aero Engine .... (#5-45F, 1 sht.) 5.00
_Ryan B-5 "Brougham" .... (#RB-96A, 2 shts.) 8.00
_Ryan FR-1 "Fireball" .... (#3-26A, 2 shts.) 8.00
_Ryan SCW Low Wing .... (#AM9-49A, 2 shts.) 8.00
_Ryan ST-A .... (#9-76A, 2 shts.) 8.00
_Seversky BT-8 .... (#3-23A, 2 shts.) 8.00
_Seversky P-35 .... (#AA-57A, 2 shts.) 8.00
_Sikorsky S-39B .... (#14-100A, 5 shts.) 10.50
_Standard J-1 .... (#17-110A, 2 shts.) 8.00
_Taylor E-2 "Cub" .... (#18-119A, 2 shts.) 8.00
_Taylor J-2 "Cub" .... (#18-120A, 2 shts.) 8.00
_Thomas-Boeing MB-3A
_Thomas-Morse MB-3 .... (#4-28B, 2 shts.) 8.00
_Timm TC-170 "Collegiate" .... (#8-72A, s shts.) 8.00
_Verville R-3 Racer .... (#6-58A, 2 shts.) 8.00
_Vought F4U-1 "Corsair" .... (#AA-51A, 3 shts.) 9.50
_Vought SBU-1 .... (#3-24A, 2 shts.) 8.00
_Vought XF5U .... (#8-70A, 3 shts.) 9.50
_Vultee V-1A .... (#2-16A, 2 shts.) 8.00
_Waco UMF/YMF-5 .... (#13-97A, 3 shts.) 9.50
_Waco UPF-7 .... (#8-67A, 2 shts.) 8.00
_Waco YKS-6 Cabin .... (#2-17A, 2 shts.) 8.00
_Waterman "Arrowbile" .... (#3-25A, 2 shts.) 8.00
_Waterman "Gosling" Racer .... (#1-4B, 2 shts.) 8.00
_Wright F2W-1 Racer .... (#5-43A, 1 sht.) 4.50
_Wright F2W-2 Racer .... (#5-44A, 2 shts.) 8.00
_Wright Brothers 1903 Flyer .... (#0-123A, 2 shts.) 8.00
_Wright-Martin V .... (#1-2A, 2 shts.) 8.00

send to: **Aviation Heritage**
P.O. Box 2065
Terre Haute, IN 47802